PROGRAMMING WITH FORTRAN 77
A Structured Approach

PROGRAMMING WITH FORTRAN 77
A Structured Approach

R.S. Dhaliwal
Department of Mathematics and Statistics
The University of Calgary
Calgary, Alberta, Canada

S. Kumar
Power Math Associates, Inc.
Del Mar, California, U.S.A.

S.K. Gupta
National Thermal Power Corporation
New Delhi, India

JOHN WILEY & SONS
New York   Chichester   Brisbane   Toronto   Singapore

First Published in 1989 by
WILEY EASTERN LIMITED
4835/24, Ansari Road, Daryaganj
New Delhi 110 002, India

Distributors:

Australia and New Zealand:
JACARANDA WILEY LTD.
GPO Box 859, Brisbane, Queensland 4001, Australia

Canada:
JOHN WILEY & SONS CANADA LIMITED
22 Worcester Road, Rexdale, Ontario, Canada

Europe and Africa:
JOHN WILEY & SONS LIMITED
Baffins Lane, Chichester, West Sussex, England

South East Asia:
JOHN WILEY & SONS, (Pte) LIMITED
05-04, Block B, Union Industrial Building
37 Jalan Pemimpin, Singapore 2057

Africa and South Asia:
WILEY EASTERN LIMITED
4835/24, Ansari Road, Daryaganj
New Delhi 110 002, India

North and South America and rest of the world:
JOHN WILEY & SONS, INC.
605 Third Avenue, New York, NY 10158, USA

Library of Congress of Cataloging-in-Publication Data

Dhaliwal, Ranjit S.
    Programming with FORTRAN 77: a structured approach/
    Ranjit S. Dhaliwal, Sudhir Kumar, Subodh K. Gupta.
        p.   cm.
    Bibliography: p.
    Includes index.
    1. FORTRAN (Computer program language) I. Kumar, Sudhir, 1958.
    II. Gupta, Subodh K. III. Title. IV. Title: Programming with
    FORTRAN seventy-seven.
QA76.73.F25D49   1989   88-32718
005.13'3—dc19   CIP

ISBN 0-470-21356-6 John Wiley & Sons, Inc.
ISBN 81-224-0094-9 Wiley Eastern Limited

Printed in India at Gidson Printing Works, New Delhi.

To
our family members
for enduring our preoccupation with this work
for three years

Preface

FORTRAN (FORmula TRANslation) is the lingua franca of applications in engineering and science. It has traditionally been accepted as the most effective programming language for a variety of applications, particularly applications involving numerical calculations. This text introduces the concept of FORTRAN programming using an easy-to-understand explanation of various features available with the language. It concentrates on teaching how to develop and write a complete program for a given problem. The book presents:

—a practical, systematic and structured approach to program design,
—pragmatic, useful programs for solving problems,
—portable and tested programs for real problems,
—portable programs which may be run on a variety of FORTRAN systems with minimal changes.

A criticism of many FORTRAN textbooks is a lack of examples depicting how FORTRAN statements can be used to write a program that works. This text has included many programming examples involving business, mathematics, engineering, and scientific applications at a level consistent with the fact that a course of this type is often taught in the first year or second year of an undergraduate program. It is intended for persons who have had no exposure to computer programming but wish to learn FORTRAN 77 language quickly, easily and with a practical flavor. At the same time we have also attempted to include some advanced applications and new features available with FORTRAN 77 that will increase the knowledge of a person who knows FORTRAN programming.

A great emphasis is placed on good and structured programming style. At every step the advantages resulting from using a structured and modular design approach have been clearly pointed out. We have, however, included some of the less desirable non-structured features (such as the arithmetic IF, the GOTO's statements, etc.) for those programmers who may have to maintain and document FORTRAN programs containing these features. However, the use of these features in writing new programs must be highly discouraged.

The book is divided into nine chapters. Chapter 1 gives a brief history of the computer and an overview of computer systems. Chapter 2 provides a systematic approach to problem solving. Algorithm design tool, the flow chart and the pseudocode are introduced. Chapter 3 presents the fundamental

FORTRAN 77 instructions. This chapter introduces the basic FORTRAN statements and describes how to write and code a complete program. Chapter 4 teaches a student about the decision making construct and the repetition construct. Chapter 5 gives a brief description of the concepts associated with FORTRAN files. The Input/Output statements are also discussed. Chapter 6 introduces the concepts of arrays and the application of arrays to business and mathematical problems. Chapter 7 explains user-defined functions and subroutine subprograms. Character string data types and their FORTRAN 77 implementation are described in Chapter 8. The last chapter gives programming examples for scientific, engineering and business applications. This chapter also introduces concepts associated with some advanced data structures such as stacks, queues, linked lists, and trees.

Several special features have been included in the text to help the student to better grasp the material. Objective questions with answers at the end of a chapter are included as a means of self testing before proceeding to the next chapter. The general format of a chapter is as follows:

*Introduction of the chapter
*Description of subject matter under various sections
*Summary of the chapter
*Objective questions with answers
*Drill exercises to test the knowledge of a student about the material presented in the chapter.
*Programming exercises that involve writing a complete FORTRAN program.

We would like to thank Ms. Pat Dalgetty for typing the manuscript with amazing skill. It is a pleasure to express our gratitude to the fine people, specially Mr. Poplai, at Wiley Eastern Ltd. for doing an excellent job. We would also like to acknowledge the support of the Natural Sciences and Engineering Research Council of Canada, The University of Calgary, The Indian Institute of Technology, Kharagpur, and the Cement Corporation of India. Last of all, but not the least, we sincerely thank our respective wives, Gurdèv, Renu, and Sudha, whose sacrifices have made this work possible.

January, 1989
Calgary, Canada
San Diego, USA   RANJIT S. DHALIWAL
New Delhi, India   SUDHIR KUMAR
                                                            SUBODH K. GUPTA

Contents

Some Computer Systems and Peripherals

(Courtesy of International Business Machines Corporation, U.S.A.)

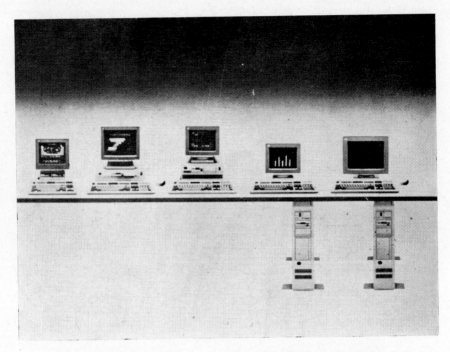

IBM Personal System/2 (PS/2) microcomputers, models 25, 30, 50, 60 and 80

IBM Personal System/2 (PS/2) model 60 microcomputer

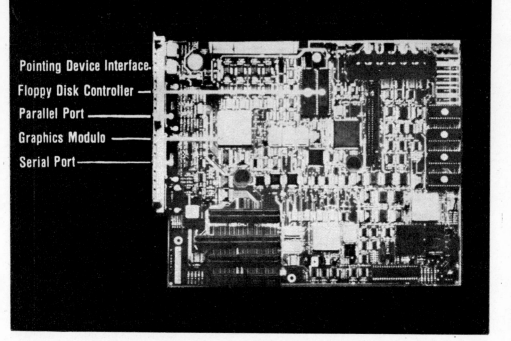

Pointing Device Interface
Floppy Disk Controller
Parallel Port
Graphics Modulo
Serial Port

IBM Personal System/2 (PS/2) Planar Board

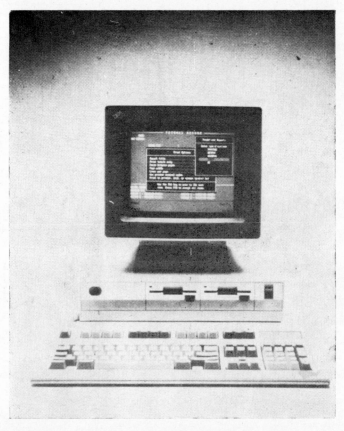

IBM Personal System/2 (PS/2) monochrome CRT Display, model 8503

IBM Personal System/2 (PS/2) Color CRT Display, model 8512

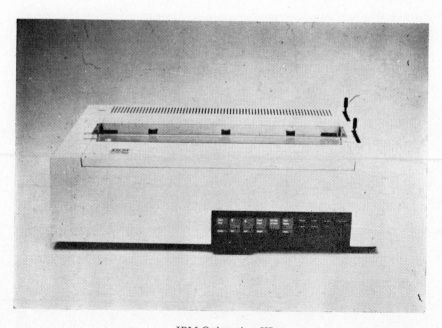

IBM Quietwriter III

IBM Color Plotter

IBM Computer System 38

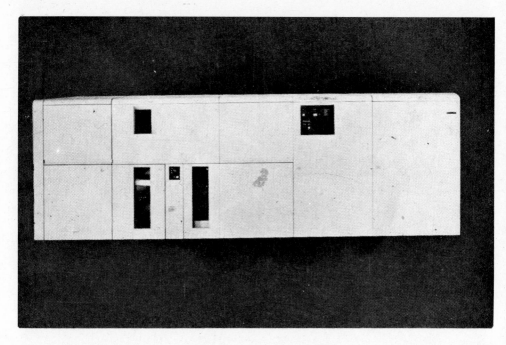

IBM Computer System 3800

IBM Computer System 3090, model 600E

Chapter 1

Computer Systems—History, Hardware and Software

1.1 INTRODUCTION

We encounter computers regularly in the everyday business of our lives. They keep track of our financial transactions and control games sophisticated enough to keep intelligent players engaged for hours or even days at a time. Computers also control manufacturing processes, keep track of airline reservations, predict weather, compute government economic forecasts, control space probes—the list goes on seemingly without end. But just what are these things called computers? Or to be precise, what does a computer really do? In this sense, computers are surprisingly simple. They are machines that perform very simple tasks according to specific instructions. Their ability to perform so many of these simple tasks with such great speed and accuracy is what makes computers so useful.

1.2 HISTORICAL DEVELOPMENT OF COMPUTERS

The development of computers is the story of man's search for better ways to write, count and communicate. The achievement of these goals has always been closely related to the technology and energy supplies of the day. The three distinct stages in the development of computers are briefly discussed in this chapter.

1.2.1 Early Computing Devices

In the early days, man was mainly interested in counting and processing numbers. Therefore, one of the earliest "computers" was the simple, muscle-powered device called the *abacus*. Although its exact origin is unknown, the abacus was used by the Chinese and the Egyptians perhaps three to four thousand years ago and is used to this day. This device consists of rows of beads strung on wires in a rectangular frame. The beads are used to keep track of powers of 10 in the course of a computation. In the hands of a skilled operator, the abacus can rival a pocket calculator in speed.

1

Although manual devices such as the abacus certainly speed up computations, machines provide an even more powerful means for extending human calculating capability. Stimulated by the industrial revolution in 1642, the young French scientist and philosopher Blaise Pascal (1623-1662) invented one of the first mathematical adding machines. This device, called the *Pascaline*, used a system of gears and wheels. The pascaline could both add and subtract, and it was invented to calculate taxes. In the 1670s, the German mathematician Gottfried Leibnitz (1646-1716) developed a similar mechanical calculator that could also multiply and divide.

The next major advances in computing technology came in the 1800s. An important breakthrough in the development of computing was the concept of a stored program to control calculations. In the early 19th century, a Frenchman, Joseph Jacquard (1752-1834), invented a loom that used punched cards to automatically control the manufacturing of patterned cloth. To this day, punched cards are used to transmit information to and from some computers. Jacquard's idea of storing a sequence of instructions on the cards is also conceptually similar to modern computer programs.

The two concepts of mechanized calculations and stored program control were combined by the English mathematician Charles Babbage (1792-1871), who began work in 1822 on a machine that he called the *difference engine*. Babbage was motivated by the large number of errors he found in mathematical tables. He developed the difference engine so that it could compute and print tables automatically. He also conceived, but never built, an analytical machine that incorporated many features of modern computers, including punched card instructions, internal memory and an arithmetic unit to perform calculations. Charles Babbage's engines were more closely related to modern computers than any of their predecessors.

A major breakthrough of the 19th century occurred when Herman Hollerith, a young mathematician employed by the Census Bureau of the United States, used punched cards to tabulate the US census of 1890. This innovation reduced the time of tabulation from one decade to three years. Hollerith went on to found the Tabulating Machine Company, which in 1911 merged with several other firms to form International Business Machines Corporation (IBM).

During the early part of the 20th century, IBM and other manufacturers produced a variety of computing devices for business use. These were all electromechanical; i. e., they were powered by electricity and had moving parts. The best of these devices was the *Mark I* developed in 1944 by Howard Aiken in collaboration with IBM. Although an awesome piece of technology, the slowness of the Mark I's electromechanical components made it quickly obsolete in the face of a more advanced technology—electronics. Nonetheless, this machine was the best known computer built before 1945 and it may be regarded as the first realisation of Babbage's analytical engine.

1.2.2 Early Electronic Computers

The first electronic computers employed vacuum tubes as their primary logic elements. These machines were one-of-a-kind devices built for experimental purposes. For example, the ABC (Atanasoff-Berry Computer) was developed at Iowa State University to solve simultaneous equations in the late 1930s.

A few years later, a more general purpose machine, the *ENIAC* (*Electronic Numerical Integrator and Calculator*), was developed by J. Presper Eckert, Jr. and John W. Mauchly in 1946. It contained over 18,000 vacuum tubes and 1,500 relays, nearly filled a room 20 ft × 40 ft in size, and consumed large quantities of electricity. Though slow and unreliable by present-day standards, it represented the first successful general purpose electronic computer.

Although the ENIAC represented a major advance, it had to be rewired every time a new task was performed. A new scheme to circumvent this problem was developed by the Hungarian mathematician John Von Neumann. He suggested that instructions for processing information could be stored in the computer's memory. Thus, when the operator needed to perform a new task, a set of instructions could be fed into the machine along with the data. Two such stored-program computers, the *EDSAC* (*Electronic Delay Storage Automatic Calculator*) and the *EDVAC* (*Electronic Discrete Variable Automatic Computer*), were developed at the end of the 1940s. With that, the stage was set for modern computers.

1.2.3 The Modern Computers

Early electronic computers were for the exclusive use of the military and experimental scientists and engineers. In the early 1950s, computers began to be sold commercially. It was this—the development of a commercial computer industry—that was really the beginning of the computer revolution.

The modern era can be conveniently broken down into four distinct generations, distinguished by the primary electronic component or circuit element within the computer. Each new logic unit has led to computers that are faster, smaller, more reliable and more economical than their precursors.

The ENIAC and the *UNIVAC* (*Universal Automatic Computer*) are examples of first-generation computers, which are characterized by their extensive use of vacuum tubes. Advances in electronics brought changes in computing systems, and in 1958, IBM introduced the first of the second-generation computers, the *IBM 7090*. These computers were built between 1959 and 1965 and used transistors in place of vacuum tubes. They were smaller, less expensive, required less power and were more reliable than their predecessors. The development of easy-to-use programming languages such as FORTRAN also made computers accessible to large numbers of practising engineers for the first time in history.

The next technological breakthrough, which ushered in the third generation, of the late 1960s, was the *integrated-circuit*. An integrated circuit, or

IC, consists of a tiny silicon chip on which thousands of transistors are fabricated. As with the previous advances, the IC resulted in the large-scale manufacture of computers that were faster, more efficient and more reliable. Meanwhile, other changes occurred that went beyond mere increases in computer power and heralded the beginning of the micro-electronic revolution.

We are now in the fourth generation of computers which use *large-scale integration chips* (*LSICs*) and *very large-scale integration chips* (VLSICs). Computer scientists and engineers are now talking about developing fifth-generation computers which can "think". The emphasis is now shifting from developing reliable, faster and smaller but "dumb" machines to more "intelligent" machines. An effective fifth-generation computer will be a highly complex knowledge-process system. We must realize that we could not have conceived this idea of intelligence (called *Artificial intelligence, AI*) without going through the various stages of technological development. Table 1.1 gives a summary of the four computer generations, their dates, the type of circuit elements used, the access time and a few examples of computers belonging to each generation. Access time refers to the speed at which a data item can be obtained from memory.

Table 1.1: The Four Generations of Computers

Generation	Period	Circuit Elements	Access Time	Examples
First	1940-1958	Vacuum Tubes	Milliseconds $(10^{-3}$ seconds)	IBM 650, UNIVAC, ENIAC
Second	1959-1964	Transistors	Microseconds $(10^{-6}$ seconds)	IBM 7090, IBM 704, NCR 304
Third	1965-1970	Integrated Circuits	Nanoseconds $(10^{-9}$ seconds)	IBM 360, RCA Spectra 70, ICL 1900
Fourth	1971-present	Large-scale integration chips and very large-scale integration	Nanoseconds $(10^{-9}$ seconds)	IBM 3081, Fujitsu M380, CDC 6800

1.2.3.1 *Super and Mainframe Computers, Mini-Computers and Microcomputers*

The tremendous progress in the field of computing has made computers a household commodity, at least in North America. Not only have super and mainframe computers been manufactured but a large number of mini-and microcomputers have also flooded the market. All of these computers belong to the fourth generation. According to the size of the memory and the speed (capability and throughput), computers are generally classified as:

(1) Super and Mainframe Computers
(2) Mini-computers
(3) Microcomputers

Table 1.2 gives a summary of some of the features for each classification. The world market for computers is dominated by American manufacturers. The largest of these include International Business Machines (IBM), Burroughs Machines, Control Data Corporation (CDC), Honeywell and Digital Equipment Corporation (DEC). Other componies that manufacture and market computers are in Japan and Western Europe. International Computers Limited (ICL) is formed by the joint interests of English Electric, International Computers and Tabulators, Ferranti and Elliots of England. Some of the main European companies are Philips of Netherlands and Siemens of West Germany, while, the Japanese companies include Hitachi and Fujitsu. In the USSR, considerable developments have been made in computers, but these are solely for internal use and not for worldwide distribution.

Table 1.2: Classification of Computers

Classification	Characteristics/Applications	Examples	Price (US$)
Super Computers	Fast, performs billions of operations per second; Large size and large internal memory; Used in scientific and engineering research to process huge quantities of information	CDC Cyber 205 family, Cray-2, Cray X-MP/216 Hitachi HAP-1, Fujitsu VP 100, VP 200	Over $1 million
Mainframe Computers	Slower than super computers, large size and large internal memory; Used in scientific, engineering and business applications that require millions upon millions of numeric calculations or maintain and process vast amount of data	IBM 360, IBM 370, CDC 6800, CDC 7600, Burroughs B7850, DEC 2065, DEC VAX 8800, UNIVAC 1108, UNIVAC 1110	$40,000 to $1 million
Mini-Computers	Relatively small size and lower cost compared to mainframe; Used in small businesses, small research centres where mainframe computers would be cost-prohibitive	IBM 17, DEC PDP-8, DEC PDP-11, HP 2000, HP 3000	$5000 to $40,000
Micro-computers (Home Computers or Personal Computers)	Relatively slow and less expensive as compared to mini computers; Wide acceptance due to significant computing power at low prices	IBM PCs, APPLE, TRS-80 (Radio Shack)	$100 to $5000

1.2.3.2 *The Stored Program Concept, Compilers and Operating Systems*

The stored program concept was a significant improvement over manual programming methods, but early computers were still difficult to use because of the complex coding schemes required for the representation of programs and data. Consequently, in addition to improved hardware, computer manufacturers began to develop collections of programs known as *system software* to provide easier access to their machines by the users. One of the more important advances in this area was the development of *high-level languages*, which allow users to write programs in languages similar to natural languages. A program written in a high-level language is usually called a *source program*. For most high-level languages, the instructions that make up a source program have to be translated into machine language, i.e., the language used by a particular computer. This machine language program is called an *object program*. The programs that translate source programs into object programs are called *compilers*. A compiler is thus a somewhat peculiar sort of program where its input or data is some other program and its output a different program altogether. Another part of the system software is the *operating system*, a set of control programs which are kept permanently in store. The operating system does many of the routine tasks needed to prepare and run a user's program, e.g., deciding which program to run next, making ready its input, bringing the program into store, allocating it some processor time and so on. There are many different operating systems, e.g., *OS/360, OS/MVS, VMS, CP/M, MULTICS* and *UNIX*. You should familiarize yourself with the main features of the one you will be using to help you with your own programs.

FORTRAN compilers and operating systems are called *system programs* because they are an integral part of the computer system being used. The FORTRAN programs given in this book, as well as the FORTRAN program that you will write, are called *application programs*. They are not an integral part of the computer system, so they are not called system programs. All computer programs, both system programs and application programs, are called *system software*.

1.3 PROGRAMMING LANGUAGES

The earlier computers were programmed in machine code; in other words, by giving them instructions directly in numerical form. However, the following drawbacks were soon realized:

(a) Because of the very primitive nature of machine instructions, machine-code programming is both tedious and error-prone;

(b) For the same reason, machine-code programs are difficult to understand and to modify;

(c) Programming is a time-consuming and expensive business; it would be a great saving to be able to use the same program on different computers, but a machine-code program is specific to one model of computer and may not work on any other.

For these reasons, scientists developed high-level languages, which resembled human languages in many ways. These were designed to make reading and writing programs much easier.

One of the first high-level languages to gain widespread acceptance was *FORTRAN* (*FORmula TRANslation*). It was developed for the IBM 704 computer by John Backus and a team of 13 other programmers at IBM over a three-year period (1954-1957). Since that time many other high-level languages have been developed, including *Ada, ALGOL, APL, BASIC, C, COBOL, LISP, PASCAL and PL/1*. In this book, we will discuss the FORTRAN programming language. We will, however, give a brief description of the other languages.

1.3.1 High-Level Languages—A Brief Description

Ada: A relatively new programming language sponsored by the Department of Defense, USA. The language is named after the world's first programmer, Augusta Ada Byron. At present, Ada is the only high-level language to combine real-time features with structured programming capabilities. It has great potential for commercial as well as military applications.

ALGOL: ALGOrithmic Language is a structured language that is well-suited for scientific and mathematical projects but has limited file-processing capabilities. It is popular in Europe and it is similar to FORTRAN.

APL: An acronym for A Programming Language, it is a highly compact, interactive language best suited for short, mathematically-oriented, problem-solving programs. A special APL keyboard is required for programming in this language. It is ideal for handling complex problems in a free-form style of coding.

BASIC: The Beginner's All-purpose Symbolic Instruction Code is the most widely used programming language for use in mini and microcomputers. It was developed as an interactive language designed to make it easy for beginners and users to learn, debug and correct syntax errors. It is ideal for people with no previous programming background.

C: A general purpose, portable programming language featuring concise expressions and a design that permits well-structured programs. Originally developed at Bell Labs, USA, as a language for writing operating system UNIX, it is now also used to write application programs for research and business.

COBOL: COmmon Business-Oriented Language, widely used for processing business information and file-oriented applications. It is considered a self-documenting language because it is English-like, making it easy for users to read and for programmers to debug.

LISP: LISt Programming language is the primary language for research on artificial intelligence. It is basically designed to process non-numerical data such as characters or words.

Pascal: A more recently developed and more promising programming language, it was named after the mathematician and inventor Blaise Pascal, who developed one of the earliest calculating machines. The language is considered to have a great deal of potential for computer users because it facilitates the use of structured programming techniques.

PL/1:   Programming Language/1 is a symbolic language that is designed to combine the major advantages and features of COBOL and FORTRAN in order to meet the needs of both scientists and businessmen with a single language.

1.3.2 More on Fortran

FORTRAN has undergone several revisions and improvements since its inception. Successive versions have been called *FORTRAN, FORTRAN II, FORTRAN IV* and *FORTRAN 77*. The increasing use of FORTRAN has prompted the evolution and adoption of various versions of the FORTRAN language. The main objective is to promote portability of FORTRAN programs for use on different computer systems and to add more powerful features to enhance the use of language in solving a variety of complex problems.

The development of student-oriented compilers with powerful error-diagnosing capabilities has played an instrumental role in the acceptance of FORTRAN as a teaching language. One of the most popular compilers, *WATFOR*, (*WATerloo FORtran*), developed at the University of Waterloo, Canada, is essentially equivalent to FORTRAN IV. An augmented version of WATFOR is *WATFIV*, which has certain non-numerical capabilities. Certain control structures which facilitate structured programming have subsequently been added to WATFIV. This new version is called *WATFIV-S* (*WATFIV-Structured*).

In 1978 a new *ANSI* (*American National Standard Institute*) standard called FORTRAN 77 was approved. Most of the features of FORTRAN 77 are available in WATFIV-S with some minor differences. The University of Minnesota, USA, developed *M77* for CDC 6000/7000/Cyber series computers to provide a highly powerful, efficient, and structured FORTRAN compiler that complies with the FORTRAN 77 standard. Other universities and computer companies have developed structured FORTRAN compilers. Some of them are: IBM FORTRAN IV, Honeywell 6000, Univac 1100, PDP-11 FORTRAN IV PLUS and VAX-11 FORTRAN. However, FORTRAN 77 is rapidly becoming a primary FORTRAN programming language taught by colleges and universities. In this book we have mostly followed FORTRAN 77 features. Any feature which is not available in FORTRAN 77 but available in other dialects of FORTRAN has been pointed out while discussing those features. At the end of the book, we have attempted to include a comparative list of statements and features that are available in various important FORTRAN compilers.

1.4 MODERN DIGITAL COMPUTING SYSTEMS

Figure 1.1 shows the various components in a computer system and the relationship among them.

The brain of any computing system is its *central processing unit (CPU)*. The CPU controls the operation of the entire system, performs the arithmetic and logic operations and stores instructions and data. The three functional components of a CPU are:

   (i) The Control Unit—for coordinating and directing the operations of the computer.

  (ii) The Arithmetic-Logic Unit (ALU)—for performing the calculations and decision-making operations.

 (iii) The Memory Unit—for storing computer instructions and data.

The instructions and data are encoded as sequences of 0's and 1's and are stored in a *high-speed memory-unit*. The control unit fetches these instructions from memory, decodes them, and directs the system to execute the operations indicated by the instructions. Those operations that are arithmetical or logical in nature are carried out using special registers of the ALU.

Instructions, input data and computed output results must be communicated between the user and the CPU. There are many input/output devices designed for this purpose, such as card readers, remote terminals, paper-tape readers, optical scanners and high-speed printers. The function of these input/output devices is to convert information from an external form understandable to the user to electrical pulses decodable by the CPU, and vice versa.

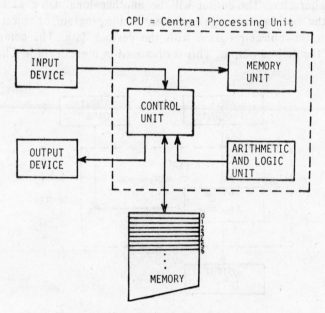

Figure 1.1: Main Components of a Computer.

The CPU memory unit is called the *internal memory* or *main memory* of the computing system. In the older machines, this memory usually consisted of magnetic cores, whereas new machines use complementary metal oxide semiconductors (CMOS). Although these devices allow for the rapid retrieval of information stored in them, they are rather expensive, and so most computing systems also contain components that serve as *external memory* or *secondary memory*. Common forms of this type of memory are *disks* and *magnetic tapes*. These provide relatively inexpensive storage for large collections of information, but the rate of transfer of information to and from the CPU is considerable slower than that for internal memory.

1.5 RUNNING OF A PROGRAM

A program is a set of instructions written in a language that can be fed into a computer. As shown in Figure 1.2, the input to a computer can be thought of as consisting of two parts: a program and some data. The data is the input to the program, and the program and the data combined are input to the computer. The word *input* is thus being used in two slightly different ways. This does require some care to keep from getting confused, but this is standard usage, so you may as well get used to it.

Now, suppose you want to *run* a program. In order to get the computer to follow your instructions, proceed as follows. First, run the compiler using your source program. Notice that in this case, the program is not being treated as a set of instructions. To the compiler, your program is just a long string of characters. The output will be another long string of characters, which is the machine-language equivalent of the program, or object program. Next, run this object program with the desired data. The computer then produces the desired output. This is discussed in more detail in Chapter 2.

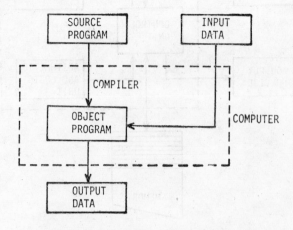

Figure 1.2: Compiling and Running a Program.

1.6 A GUIDE TO THIS BOOK

This book has two major goals. One is to introduce the FORTRAN 77 language and its new features that are not available in the older versions of FORTRAN. The other, more important goal is to introduce computer-assisted problem-solving methodology. The main reason for learning a programming language is to be able to use a computer for solving problems. Several solved examples and their FORTRAN implementation are therefore included at the end of most chapters.

We also feel that an intelligent user of the computer must have some elementary understanding of the manner in which a computer operates and how it stores and processes information. For this reason, this chapter has been devoted to a brief history of computers and a sketchy description of the main features of a computing system.

This book also emphasizes the importance of structured programming and discusses at length FORTRAN 77 tools that are quite helpful in writing structured programs. This aspect has been kept in mind throughout the text and has been amply demonstrated through programming examples in each chapter.

OBJECTIVE QUESTIONS

(1) Which of the following statements is false ?
    (a) Pascal invented an adding machine.
    (b) Babbage constructed an analytical engine.
    (c) Abacus was one of the earliest computers.
    (d) Punched cards are a gift of Jacquard's loom.
    (e) Hollerinth used punched cards to tabulate the U.S. census of 1890.
(2) Which of the following statements is false ?
    (a) Mark I was an electromechanical computing device.
    (b) ENIAC and UNIVAC were among the first electronic computers employing vacuum tubes.
    (c) IBM 7090 used Integrated Circuits.
    (d) Most of the computers now in use are third or fourth-generation computers.
    (e) ABC was developed to solve simultaneous equations in the late 1930s.
Study the following statements and answer questions 3 and 4:
    1. First-generation computers were cheaper than third-generation computers.
    2. Second-generation computers are smaller than third-generation computers.
    3. The reliability of a new-generation computer is greater than that of its predecessor generation.
(3) Which of the following choices is correct ?
    (a) Statement '1' is true.
    (b) Statement '2' is true.
    (c) Statement '3' is true.
    (d) Statements '1' and '2' are both true.
    (e) All statements are false.
(4) Which of the following choices is the most appropriate ?
    (a) Statement '1' is false and statement '2' is true.
    (b) Statement '2' is false and statement '3' is true.

(c) Statements '1' and '2' are false and statement '3' is true.

(d) Statements '1' and '3' are true and statement '2' is false.

(e) Statement '1' is false and statements '2' and '3' are true.

(5) Which of the following languages is not a high-level language ?

  (a) FORTRAN II

  (b) MACHINE

  (c) PL/1

  (d) Ada

  (e) BASIC

(6) Which of the following objects is not a system software ?

  (a) Source program

  (b) Compiler

  (c) Object program

  (d) Memory

  (e) Operating system

(7) CPU stands for ?

  (a) Central Processing Unit

  (b) Computer Processing Unit

  (c) Control Processing Unit

  (d) Control Primary Unit

  (e) Computer Programming Unit

(8) Which of the following units is not a part of CPU ?

  (a) Internal memory

  (b) Registers

  (c) Control unit

  (d) Arithmetic unit

  (e) Secondary memory

(9) Which of the following statements is true ?

  (a) Instructions to a computer are given in English.

  (b) Instructions to a computer must be in one of the high-level languages.

  (c) Instructions and data are encoded as sequences of 0's and 1's before they can be processed by a CPU.

  (d) Only instructions are encoded as sequences of 0's and 1's before these can be processed by a CPU.

  (e) Instructions to a computer are given in FORTRAN only.

(10) Which of the following statements is false ?

  (a) Each memory cell has a corresponding address.

  (b) Computer hardware includes all the physical components of a computer system.

  (c) Compiler and operating system both refer to the same thing.

  (d) The term software refers to things like compiler, assembler, loader and so on.

  (e) High-level languages are essentially machine-independent.

(11) Which of the following statements is false ?

  (a) Microcomputers are quite slow in speed but they are widely used due to their low cost.

  (b) Computers in the family of CDC Cyber 205 are classified as super computers.

  (c) IBM, CDC and DEC are among the top computer manufacturers in North America.

  (d) A fifth-generation computer has been conceived with a slight modification over a fourth-generation computer.

  (e) DEC PDP-8 computers are classified as mini computers.

(12) Fill in the blanks:

  (a) ....invented a more complex machine than Pascaline some 30 years later. The machine could also .... and .... Charles Babbage, who was born in................, developed a................and conceived the.................., which had all the essential parts of the modern computer such as................and............ ...., etc.

(b) The..............generation computer ENIAC had over..................vacuum tubes and nearly filled a room................sq. ft. in size. The second generation computer used................as circuit elements while the third generation computers used ....

(c) FORTRAN program is a................language program which can be translated into machine language by a................ This machine-language program is called an................program.

(d) The essential parts of any modern computer are................and.................., etc. The CPU is the................of any computing system.

ANSWERS TO OBJECTIVE QUESTIONS

(1) b; (2) c; (3) c; (4) c; (5) b; (6) d; (7) a; (8) e; (9) c; (10) c; (11) d.

(12) (a) Gottfried Leibnitz; multiply; devide; England; difference engine; analytic engine; CPU; input device [or output device].

(b) first; 18,000; 20 × 40; transistors; ICs.

(c) high-level; compiler; object.

(d) input device; output device; [CPU or external storage]; b ain.

Chapter 2

Programming and Algorithm

2.1 INTRODUCTION

The computer is capable of solving problems by accepting data, performing prescribed operations on the data and supplying the results of these operations. At least three steps can be identified in the computer-aided problem-solving process.

1. Problem analysis and algorithm development.
2. Transformation of the algorithm into a program.
3. Program execution and validation.

In this chapter, we will discuss these three phases of the problem-solving process.

2.2 PROBLEM ANALYSIS AND ALGORITHM DEVELOPMENT

We will first consider the most difficult part of the problem-solving process, namely, the analysis of the problem and the formulation of an algorithm for its solution. It is this phase that requires the greatest imagination, ingenuity and creativity on the part of the programmer. Depending on the nature and complexity of the problem (e.g. mathematical, business-oriented or scientific and engineering problems), a methodology of many steps is developed. For example, the solution of a mathematical problem generally proceeds through these three basic stages:

1. Precise formulation of the problem.
2. Development of a mathematical model and its analysis.
3. Computation of a solution.

The first stage is the precise formulation of the problem under consideration. This step requires an unambiguous statement of the problem and assumptions for the development of a mathematical model. To develop a model, we must establish a relationship among the variables under consideration. We then apply the appropriate methods and procedures for the mathematical analysis. The final stage is of calculations to obtain the desired results.

14

Let us now illustrate these basic steps by taking an example:

If we wish to calculate the time taken by a person to travel 100 km at a speed of 50 km per hour, we go through the following stages:

Stage 1: The problem is to calculate the time taken to travel 100 km at the specified speed, with neither delay nor destruction.

Stage 2: The distance (s), speed (u) and time (t) are related as follows:

$$s = u*t$$

In order to know the time, the above relation is expressed as:

$$t = s/u$$

Stage 3: By substituting the values of distance (s) and speed (u), the exact time can be calculated:

$$t = \frac{100 \text{ km}}{50 \text{ km/hr}} = 2 \text{ hours.}$$

Let us now re-state the three stages of problem-solving with the subsidiary steps noted:

1. Precise formulation of the problem:
   a. Study the problem.
   b. Identify the important variables.
   c. Formulate a precise problem statement.
2. Development of a mathematical model and its analysis:
   a. Make assumptions about the variables and their relationships.
   b. Formulate a mathematical model.
   c. Analyze the model.
3. Computation of a solution:
   a. Compute desired results.
   b. Check accuracy of results by comparing them with some known results.
   c. Check the precision of the results.

Besides solving the mathematical problems, the computer may also be used to solve problems that are not mathematical in nature provided a mathematical model of a problem can be developed.

Stage 3 of the solution is typically accomplished by a computer. In order for a computer to provide a solution to a problem, we must have a precise, unambiguous procedure for the solution of the problem. In the next section, we will examine how the procedure, also called an algorithm, is developed.

2.3 ALGORITHM

An algorithm is defined as:

"A complete, unambiguous, finite number of logical steps for solving a specified problem."

The word algorithm is derived from the name of a 9th century Arab mathematician, Al-Khowarizmi, who developed methods for solving problems which used specific step-by-step instructions.

Aside from accomplishing its objectives, an algorithm must have a number of specific properties:

1. Each step must be deterministic and the final results should be independent of the individual following the algorithm.
2. The algorithm cannot be open-ended and the process must always end after a finite number of steps.
3. The algorithm must be general enough to deal with any contingency. Figure 2.1(a) shows an algorithm for the solution of the simple problem of calculating the time taken by a person to travel a distance. Two programmers working independently from this algorithm might develop different programs, but, given the same data, their programs should yield identical results.

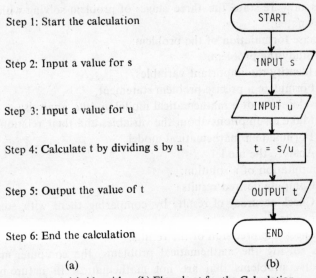

Step 1: Start the calculation	START
Step 2: Input a value for s	INPUT s
Step 3: Input a value for u	INPUT u
Step 4: Calculate t by dividing s by u	t = s/u
Step 5: Output the value of t	OUTPUT t
Step 6: End the calculation	END

(a)   (b)

Figure 2.1 (a) Algorithm (b) Flowchart for the Calculation.

Step-by-step English descriptions of the sort depicted in Figure 2.1(a) are one way of writing an algorithm. They are particularly useful for small problems, but for detailed representations of complicated programs, they prove inadequate. For this reason, more versatile visual alternatives, called *flowcharts*, have been developed.

2.4 FLOWCHARTING

A flowchart is a visual or graphic representation of an algorithm. The flowchart employs a series of blocks and arrows, each of which represents a particular operation or step in an algorithm. The arrows represent the sequence in which the operations are implemented. Figure 2.1(b) shows a flowchart for the calculation.

2.4.1 Flowchart Symbols

A flowchart is a blueprint of the logic of the solutions to any problem. A set of the symbols used in this text is shown in Figure 2.2. For example, a rectangle indicates the action of processing and a diamond indicates a decision or logical choice; it may have two or more branches exiting from it.

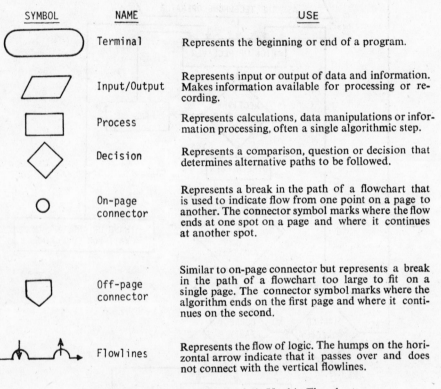

SYMBOL	NAME	USE
	Terminal	Represents the beginning or end of a program.
	Input/Output	Represents input or output of data and information. Makes information available for processing or recording.
	Process	Represents calculations, data manipulations or information processing, often a single algorithmic step.
	Decision	Represents a comparison, question or decision that determines alternative paths to be followed.
	On-page connector	Represents a break in the path of a flowchart that is used to indicate flow from one point on a page to another. The connector symbol marks where the flow ends at one spot on a page and where it continues at another spot.
	Off-page connector	Similar to on-page connector but represents a break in the path of a flowchart too large to fit on a single page. The connector symbol marks where the algorithm ends on the first page and where it continues on the second.
	Flowlines	Represents the flow of logic. The humps on the horizontal arrow indicate that it passes over and does not connect with the vertical flowlines.

Figure 2.2: Common ANSI Symbols Used in Flowcharts.

Not every computer programmer agrees that flowcharting is a productive endeavor. In fact, some experienced programmers do not even use flowcharts. However, we feel that there are four good reasons for studying them.

1. The flowchart shows the logic of a problem displayed in pictorial fashion which facilitates easier checking of an algorithm.
2. The flowchart is a good means of communication to other users. It is also a compact means of recording an algorithm solution to a problem.
3. The flowchart allows the problem-solver to break the problem into parts. The parts can be connected to make a master chart.
4. The flowchart is a permanent record of the solution which can be consulted at a later time.

Flowcharts can represent the algorithm solution to problems of all types. A detailed flowchart for placing a telephone call is shown in Figure 2.3. This

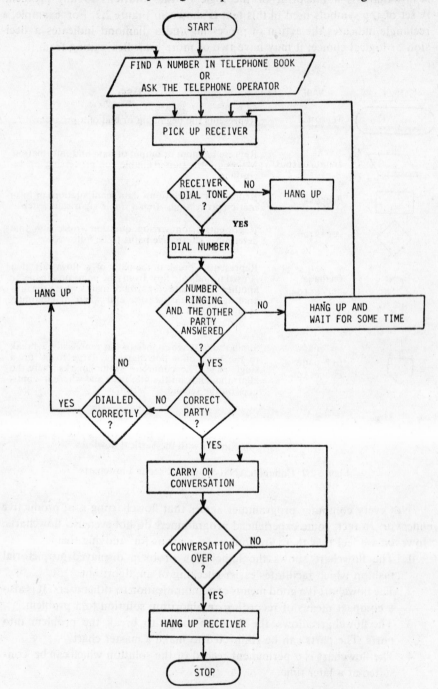

Figure 2.3: Flowchart for Making a Telephone Call.

flowchart contains enough details so that a person could, with the aid of the chart, make a phone call without any prior knowledge of the process.

2.4.2 Levels of Flowchart Complexity

There are no set standards for how detailed a flowchart should be. For a complex problem, developing a detailed flowchart involves a good deal of effort and it is often possible to make errors. A more realistic approach is to first draw a flowchart showing the major steps. Once this flowchart is drawn, it can be refined or modified by adding details necessary for these major tasks. As an example, Figure 2.4 depicts a hierarchy of three charts that might be used in the development of an algorithm to determine the grade-point average (GPA) of a student. The system flowchart, shown in Figure 2.4 (a),

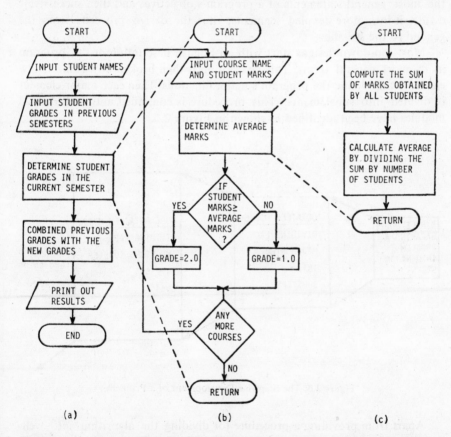

(a)   (b)   (c)

Figure 2.4: An Hierarchy of Flowchart Dealing with the Problem of Assigning Student's Grades. The Complete Flowchart in (a) Describes Major Steps for the Problem. A More Detailed Flowchart for a Major Module, "DETERMINE STUDENT GRADES IN THE CURRENT SEMESTER", is Shown (b). An Even More Detailed Flowchart to "DETERMINE AVERAGE MARKS" is Given in (c). This Technique of Solving a Problem is Called Top-down Design.

delineates the big picture and identifies the major tasks, or modules, and the sequence that is required to solve the entire problem.

A major module can be broken off and charted in greater detail, as shown in Figure 2.4 (b). It is sometimes advantageous to break down the major modules into even more manageable units, as in Figure 2.4 (c). The process of subdividing an algorithm into major segments and then breaking these down into successively refined modules is referred to as *top-down design*. The other two designs are: *bottom-up design* and *side-to-side design*. In this book we will restrict our discussion to top-down design.

2.4.3 Top-Down Design

Top-down design is a systematic development process that begins with the most general statements of a program's objectives and then successively divides it into more detailed segments; thus the design proceeds from the general to the specific.

Most top-down designs start with an English description of the program in its most general terms. This description is then broken down into a few elements that define the program's major functions. Then each major element is divided into subelements. This procedure is continued until well-defined modules have been identified as shown in Figure 2.5.

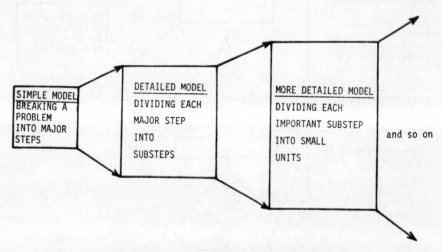

Figure 2.5: The Stepwise Development of a Problem.

Apart from providing a procedure for dividing the algorithm into well-defined units, top-down design has other benefits. One of the most important benefits is that a programmer is less likely to overlook important operations since one starts with a broad definition and progressively adds detail.

Returning to our discussion on flowcharts, the general form of a flowchart may represent the solution of a problem as shown in Figure 2.6.

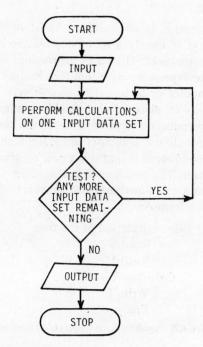

Figure 2.6: The General Form of a Flowchart for the Solution of a Problem.

The three fundamental operations that normally constitute a flowchart for solving a problem are:

(1) Sequence

(2) Selection

(3) Repetition

In a sequential flow, the operation follows from one action to the other. The flowchart shown in Figure 2.1 represents a sequential flow only. The flowchart shown in Figure 2.6 represents all three operations. Notice how the diamond-shaped decision symbol in figure 2.6 permits the branchings of the flow. Depending on the answer to the question contained in the box, the flow follows one of the two possible paths. If there is any test data set left to be processed, then the flow follows the right branch, else it follows the bottom branch. This type of operation is called selection.

The third operation, repetition, is also depicted in Figure 2.6. If the answer is yes, the flow branches to the right and the right branch allows the flow to return to the previous block and repeat the calculations for another data set. This repetition (or looping) is among the most important tools available to a computer programmer.

Readers will know more about selection and repetition operations in subsequent chapters.

2.5 PSEUDOCODE

The object of flowcharting is obviously to assist in developing computer programs. A program is merely a set of step-by-step instructions to direct the computer to perform tasks. The set of instructions is also called the *code*. An alternative way to express an algorithm that bridges the gap between the flowcharts and computer code is called *pseudocode*. This technique uses English-like statements in place of the graphic symbols of the flowchart. Figure 2.7 shows a pseudocode representation of the flowchart of Figure 2.1 which looks much more like a computer program than a flowchart. Thus, one advantage of pseudocode is that it is easier to develop a program with it than with a flowchart. The pseudocode is also easier to modify. However, because of their visual form, flowcharts sometimes are better suited for designing algorithms that are complex.

Start calculation of the time
Read S
Read U
Calculate T = S/U
Write T
End

Figure 2.7: Pseudocode to Compute Travelling Time.

2.6 FLOWCHART AND PSEUDOCODE EXAMPLES

Example (a)

Simple interest is calculated using the formula:

$$\text{Interest (I)} = \frac{\text{Principal amount (P)*Rate of interest (R)*Time (T)}}{100}$$

The flowchart and the pseudocode for calculating interest are given in Figure 2.8. You must input three values P, R and T.

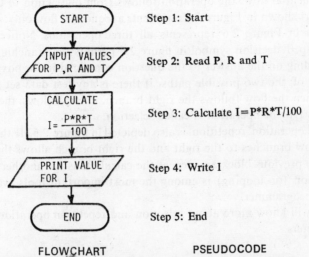

FLOWCHART   PSEUDOCODE

Figure 2.8: Flowchart and Pseudocode for Example (a).

Example (b)

Victor Construction Company plans to give a 5% year-end bonus to each of its employees earning Rs 5,000 or more per year, and a fixed Rs 250 bonus to the other employees. The flowchart and pseudocode for calculating the BONUS for an employee is shown in Figure 2.9.

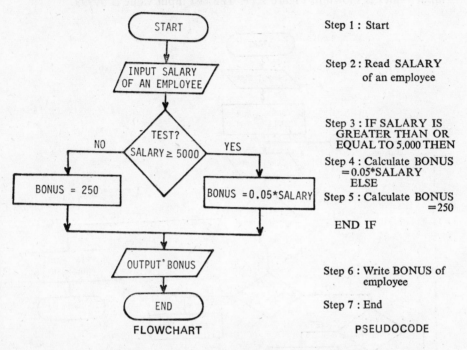

Step 1 : Start

Step 2 : Read SALARY of an employee

Step 3 : IF SALARY IS GREATER THAN OR EQUAL TO 5,000 THEN

Step 4 : Calculate BONUS =0.05*SALARY ELSE

Step 5 : Calculate BONUS =250

END IF

Step 6 : Write BONUS of employee

Step 7 : End

FLOWCHART   PSEUDOCODE

Figure 2.9: Flowchart and Pseudocode for Example (b).

Example (c)

The flowchart and pseudocode for adding the integers from 1 to 10 are shown in Figure 2.10.

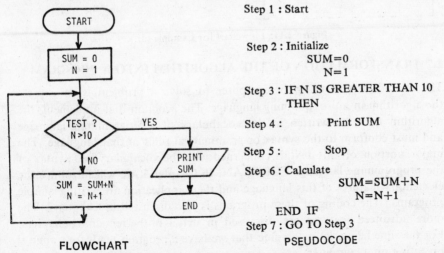

Step 1 : Start

Step 2 : Initialize
SUM=0
N=1

Step 3 : IF N IS GREATER THAN 10 THEN

Step 4 :   Print SUM

Step 5 :   Stop

Step 6 : Calculate
SUM=SUM+N
N=N+1

END IF

Step 7 : GO TO Step 3

FLOWCHART   PSEUDOCODE

Figure 2.10: Flowchart and Pseudocode for Example (c).

Example (d)

A flowchart to calculate the largest and the smallest numbers in a list of input values is shown in Figure 2.11. The last input value is 99999.

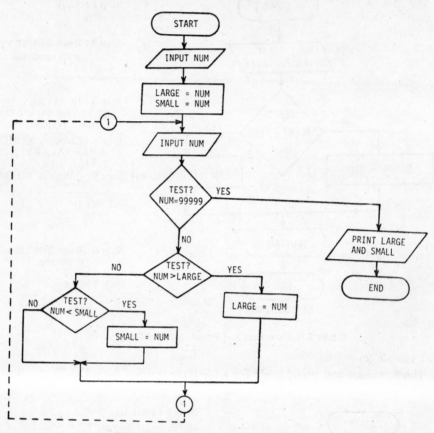

Figure 2.11: Flowchart for Example (d).

2.7 TRANSFORMATION OF THE ALGORITHM INTO A PROGRAM

The second step in using the computer to solve a problem is to express the algorithm in a programming language. The program that implements the algorithm must be written in the vocabulary of a programming language and must conform to the syntax or grammatical rules of that language. The major portion of this text is concerned with the vocabulary and syntax of the programming language FORTRAN. In Chapter 3, we will introduce the elementary features of this language and their application in writing simple programs. The coding of these programs is also discussed in Chapter 3. The more advanced features are discussed in detail in the remaining chapters. For the time being, let us assume that we have a program ready for running/ executing on a computer.

2.8 PROGRAM EXECUTION

The third step in using the computer to solve a problem is to submit the program to a computer for execution. This procedure varies according to the computer system and the language. The details regarding your specific computer system can be obtained from your instructor, computer center personnel, or user's manual supplied by the manufacturers.

In many computer systems, programs and data can be entered from a typewriter-like terminal. To establish a connection between the terminal and the computer system, some *log-in* procedure may be required. Once the *log-in* has been completed, the program must be entered from the terminal. Often, the system's software includes editing packages to help the user enter information and correct errors.

Once the entire program is typed in, it is ready for execution. If your computer has a FORTRAN run-time subsystem, you simply type the command

RUN

to execute your program. If the program is executed successfully, you may get a message "RUN COMPLETE", "READY" or "DONE", etc. after the run is complete. If there are some syntax errors in your program, a suitable message will be displayed on your terminal; you must correct the error(s) and give the RUN command again.

If your computer does not have a FORTRAN run-time subsystem, you have to usually go through three steps to obtain results. These steps involve compilation, linkage and execution of a program using appropriate system commands, and the results are returned to the user via the terminal and/or some other output device. A typical set of system commands used to execute a computer program stored in a file called 'ABC.FOR', is listed below:

(1) To compile the program
   FORTRAN ABC
(2) To link the program
   LINK ABC
(3) To run the program
   RUN ABC

2.9 PROGRAM DOCUMENTATION, STYLE, TESTING AND DEBUGGING

Since program development cost is a major element in the cost of using a computer to solve a problem, much effort is concentrated on developing techniques that assist in designing programs that can be easily read and understood. This is extremely important because many real-world applications involve complex programs that are written by more than one person. Each part of the program must be clearly written so that its function can be easily understood by all members of the programming team. Such programs are generally used for several years and may require modification as time passes. More often than not, these modifications are made by someone not involved in the original design, so the programs must be easy to understand and modify. In this section, we will discuss some of the programming practices used in designing such programs.

2.9.1 Documentation

Documentation refers to information that explains the working of a program. It includes diagrams such as flowcharts that display the logical structure of the program as well as any other documents that describe the input to and output from the program, variables used in the program, the processing carried out by the program, and so on. It is also possible to write the program in such a way that it is at least partially self-documenting. Here are some programming practices useful in this regard:

1. Each variable name should suggest the quantity it represents. For example, the statement

    TIME = DISTAN / SPEED

    means more than does the statement

    T = S/U

2. The program should include explanatory comments to make it easier to understand. These may include comments at the beginning of the program that briefly describe the variables and the purpose of the program. In addition, comments should be used throughout the program to explain the purpose of the main sections of the program.

2.9.2 Program Style

Other practices, that can improve a program's physical appearance are:

1. Blank spaces between items in a FORTRAN statement should be used as/and when required to improve its readability. For example, the statement

    TIME = DISTAN / SPEED

    is more readable and pleasing to the eye than either

    TIME = DISTAN / SPEED

    or   TIME = DISTAN / SPEED

2. Comment lines may be used to separate program sections.

3. Statements making up a block should be indented to emphasize the relationship.

2.9.3 Program Testing and Debugging

The output produced when a program is run (executed) may contain messages indicating errors in the program. These messages are generated by the computer system to help the user find and correct these errors, or *bugs*.

Errors can be detected at various stages of program processing and may cause the processing to be terminated or *aborted*. For example, errors in the program's syntax (construction of a program statement), such as incorrect punctuation or misspelled key words will be detected during compilation of the program. These are called *compile-time-errors*. Other errors, such as an attempt to divide a number by zero in an arithmetic expression, may not be detected until the execution of the program has begun. Such errors are called *run-time errors*. The error messages displayed by your particular system and their interpretations can be found in the user's manual supplied by the manufacturer. In any case, the errors must be corrected by replacing the erroneous statements with correct ones and the modified program must be rerun.

Errors that are detected by the computer system are relatively easy to identify and correct. Human errors in programming occur quite frequently and increase as program size and complexity increase. It is extremely difficult to develop an error-free program in the first attempt. In addition to syntax errors, there are other errors that are more subtle and difficult to identify. These are logical errors that arise in the design of the algorithm or in the coding of the program that implements the algorithm. For example, if the statement

TIME = DISTAN / SPEED

in the program of Figure 2.1 erroneously entered as

TIME = DISTAN + SPEED

with the division symbol (/) replaced by the symbol for addition (+), the program would still be syntactically correct. No error would occur during the compilation or execution of the program, but the results produced by the program would be incorrect because an incorrect formula would have been used to calculate the time. Thus, if the values 38.5 and 1.1 were entered for the variables DISTAN and SPEED respectively the output produced by the program would be

TIME = 39.6

instead of the correct output

TIME = 35.0

Since it may not be obvious that the results produced by a program are incorrect, it is important that the user runs a program several times with input data for which the correct results are known in advance. For the preceding example, it is easy to calculate by hand, the correct answer for values such as 10.0 and 2.0 for DISTAN and SPEED respectively, to check the output produced by the program. This process of program validation is extremely important, as a program cannot be considered correct until it has been validated with several sets of test data. The test data should be carefully selected so that each part of the program can be checked.

2.10 A BRIEF NOTE ON MODULAR DESIGN AND STRUCTURED PROGRAMMING

Computer scientists have systematically studied the factors and procedures needed to develop high-quality software of this kind. Although the resulting methods are oriented somewhat towards large-scale programming efforts, most of the general techniques are also extremely useful for the types of programs that engineers develop routinely in the course of their work. Collectively, we will call these techniques *structured design and programming*. We will now discuss two of these approaches—*modular design* and *structured programming*.

2.10.1 Modular Design

Imagine how difficult it would be to study a textbook that had no chapters, sections or paragraphs. Breaking complicated tasks or subjects into more manageable parts is one way of making them easier to handle. In the same spirit, computer programs can be divided into smaller subprograms, or modules, that can be developed and tested separately. This approach is called modular design.

A module is defined as an independent segment of logically-related statements that perform some necessary task(s). The most important attribute of modules is that they should be as independent and self-contained as possible. In addition, they are typically designed to perform a specific, well-defined function.

Two of the primary programming elements used to represent each module are the *subroutine subprogram* and the *function subprogram*. A subprogram is a series of computer instructions that perform a given task. A calling program invokes these modules as they are needed. Subprograms are discussed in detail in Chapter 7.

Modular design has a number of advantages. The use of small, self-contained units makes the underlying logic easier to devise and to understand for both the developer and the user. Development is facilitated because each module can be tested and corrected in isolation. In fact, for complex projects involving large amounts of software, different programmers can work on different parts. Modular design also increases the ease with which a program can be debugged and tested as errors are more easily isolated. Not only this, program maintenance, documentation and modification are also facilitated. This is primarily due to the fact that new modules can be developed to perform additional tasks and then easily incorporated into the already coherent and organized scheme.

2.10.2 Structured Programming

Structured programming deals with how the actual program code is developed so that it is easy to understand, correct and modify. What constitutes structured programming is a matter of individual opinion. In the present context, we define it as a set of rules that prescribe good style habits for the programmer. The following rules are the most commonly followed:

1. Programs should consist solely of the three fundamental control structures of sequence, selection and repetition (recall Figure 2.6). Computer scientists have proved that any program can be constructed from these basic structures.

2. Each of the structures should normally have only one entrance and one exit.

3. Unconditional transfers (GOTOs) should be avoided. These statements are discussed in Chapter 4.

4. The structures should be clearly identified with comments and visual devices such as indentation, blank lines and blank spaces.

Although these rules may appear deceptively simple, they are extremely powerful tools for increasing program clarity. Because of their benefits, these rules and other structured programming practices will be stressed continually in subsequent chapters of this book.

2.11 SUMMARY

Computer programs can be viewed as descriptions of actions on data. A computer program should be appropriate, friendly, simple, flexible, robust and verifiable. The most important factor is simplicity. Writing a simple and successful computer program is not easy. Any programmer can add complications to any given computer program and can complicate it beyond his or her own or anybody else's comprehension. This is something a good programmer must always avoid.

In the following chapters, we have described the FORTRAN language, its syntax rules, its features and how to write programs to perform a variety of tasks.

OBJECTIVE QUESTIONS

(1) Which of the following statements is true ?
    (a) Transformation of an algorithm into a computer program is done by the compiler.
    (b) A computer assists in the precise formulation of a problem.
    (c) A computer can solve mathematical problems only.
    (d) The terms algorithm and flowchart are synonymous.
    (e) A flowchart is a graphic representation of an algorithm.
(2) Which of the following conditions may not be satisfied by an algorithm ?
    (a) An algorithm must be complete.
    (b) An algorithm must have a finite number of steps.
    (c) Each step of an algorithm must be unambiguous.
    (d) An algorithm should produce different results on different computing machines.
    (e) An algorithm should be quite general.

(3) The diamond-shaped flowchart symbol represents ?
   (a) Decision.
   (b) Terminal.
   (c) Input/Output.
   (d) Process.
   (e) None of the above.
(4) Which of the following statements is false ?
   (a) The flowchart represents the logic of a problem pictorially.
   (b) The terms top-down design and bottom-up design are not synonymous.
   (c) It is easier to develop a program with a flowchart than with a pseudocode.
   (d) The selection operation permits the branching of the flow in a flowchart.
   (e) Top-down design involves dividing an algorithm into well-defined and manageable
       units (modules).
(5) Which of the following statements is true ?
   (a) Logical errors can be detected during the compilation of a program.
   (b) Syntax errors are generally detected during the execution of a program.
   (c) Syntax errors arise from the improper construction of a program statement.
   (d) Logical errors are generally detected during the linking of a program.
   (e) An error resulting from the division of a number by zero is detected during the
       compilation of a program.

ANSWERS TO OBJECTIVE QUESTIONS

   (1) e; (2) d; (3) a; (4) c; (5) c.

DRILL EXERCISES

(1) Give the shape of the flowchart symbol for (i) Input (ii) Decision (iii) Process
   (iv) On-page Connector.
(2) Study the flowchart in Figure 2.12 What will be printed if the values of the SCORE
   are: (a) 65 (b) 50 (c) 85 (d) 67 ?
(3) Study the flowchart in Figure 2.13. What will be printed if the values of A, B and C
   are: (a) A = 1, B = 2, C = 1 (b) A = 5, B = 10, C = 10 (c) A = 2, B = 10, C = 8 ?
(4) Convert the following pseudocodes into flowcharts:
   (a) Start
        Read I, J and K
        Initialize
          Calculate MAX = I
        IF MAX IS LESS THAN J THEN
          Calculate MAX = J
          IF MAX IS LESS THAN K THEN
            Calculate MAX = K
          END IF
        END IF
        End
   (b) Step 1: Start
        Step 2: Read MARKS of a student
        Step 3: IF MARKS ARE MORE THAN 60 THEN
        Step 4:   Calculate GRADE = 2
        Step 5:   IF MARKS ARE MORE THAN 80 THEN
        Step 6:   Calculate GRADE = 1
                   END IF
                ELSE
        Step 7:   IF MARKS ARE EQUAL TO -10 THEN

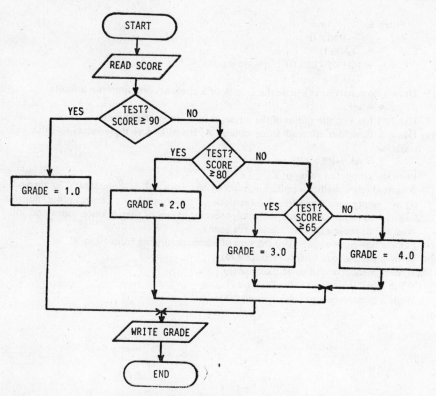

Figure 2.12: Flowchart for Exercise (2).

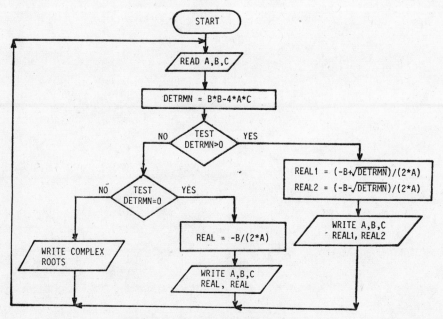

Figure 2.13: Flowchart for Exercise (3).

Step 8:   End
            END IF
            END IF
Step 9: PRINT GRADE
            GO TO Step 2

(5) Draw a flowchart to calculate the area A of a circle according to the formula:

$$A = \pi r^2$$

Use 22/7 for π. r, the radius of the circle, is input to your program.

(6) Draw a flowchart to read three values—A, B and C. Use these values to solve the equation

$$Z = A^2 + B^2 + C^2$$

Print the computed value of Z.

(7) A certain city classifies a pollution index of less than 30 as "pleasant", 30 through 60 as 'unpleasant" and 60 as "hazardous'. The city pollution control office desires you to draw a flowchart that will accept several values of the pollution index and will print the appropriate classification for each.

(8) Draw a flowchart to calculate the sum of numbers ranging from 10 to 30.

(9) Write a pseudocode to solve Exercise (5).

(10) Write a pseudocode to solve Exercise (6).

(11) Write a pseudocode to solve Exercise (7).

(12) Write a pseudocode to solve Exercise (8).

Chapter 3

Introduction to Fortran

3.1 INTRODUCTION

A simple definition of a computer program is that it is a sequence of specific instructions to be performed by a digital computing system. These instructions include the acceptance of data from input devices, the manipulation of numeric and/or alphanumeric data and the transmission of results to output devices. Generally, for "applications" programs, these sets of instructions are written in high-level languages, which allow users to write programs in a language similar to natural language.

One of the first high-level languages to gain widespread acceptance was FORTRAN (FORmula TRANslation). FORTRAN was developed for the IBM 704 computer by John Backus and a team of 13 other programmers at IBM over a period of three years (1954-1957). It has remained a "living" language in that it has undergone several revisions and improvements. Successive versions have been called FORTRAN, FORTRAN II, FORTRAN IV and FORTRAN 77. The latest version—FORTRAN 77—was approved in March 1978, but since the documentation had been done a year earlier, it was designated "FORTRAN 77".

In this chapter, some of the elementary programming concepts associated with FORTRAN 77 are discussed. The main thrust of all the material presented in this chapter will be aimed at the development of skills related to the writing of simple arithmetic-type statements in FORTRAN. All those basic features of FORTRAN 77 that are needed to implement simple sequence logical structures are treated in this chapter. The purpose of this chapter is to try to develop skills in writing simple but complete programs. In order to do this, it will be necessary to have a clear understanding of the use of FORTRAN constants, variables, expressions, functions, simple input/output statements, coding of source programs and entering these programs into the computer. Towards the end of the chapter, we have also included some important features that are available with FORTRAN 77 and are quite useful in writing computer programs.

While much of the material presented in this and subsequent chapters is applicable to the FORTRAN IV version, all of the material will be developed

33

in terms of its application in FORTRAN 77. This is implied throughout the book. Those additional special features of FORTRAN 77, that are not available in FORTRAN IV or vice versa are clearly pointed out. Depending on the availability of the FORTRAN compiler, users may write their programs either in FORTRAN IV or in FORTRAN 77, or for that matter, in any other FORTRAN dialect.

3.2 FORTRAN CONSTANTS

Constants are quantities whose valves do not vary during the execution of the program. There are two important types of constants:
   (1) Integer Constants
   (2) Real Constants.

3.2.1 Integer Constants

An integer constant is a string of decimal digits 0-9, prefixed by an optional plus or minus sign. No other character is permitted in the representation of an integer. Negative integer constants must be preceded by a minus sign, but a plus sign is optional for non-negative numbers.

The size and the accuracy of a FORTRAN constant are limited by the wordlength of a computer. For example, if a computer uses an eight-bit (one-byte) wordlength, it can handle any integer constant in the range of -2^7 to $+2^7-1$, i.e. -128 to $+127$. Wordlengths on different computers vary from eight bits to sixty bits. Table 3.1 gives typical wordlengths for specific computers.

Table 3.1: Wordlength and Maximum Value of an Integer Constant

Computer	Wordlength (Bits)	Range of Integer Value	Number of Decimal Digits
TRS-80 II, and DEC PDP-11	16	-2^{15} to $2^{15}-1$ -32768 to 32767	5
IBM 360 and 370 series, and DEC VAX-11 series	32	-2^{31} to $2^{31}-1$ -2147483648 to 2147483647	10
DEC 2060, and HONEYWELL 6000	36	-2^{35} to $2^{35}-1$ -68719476736 to 68719476735	11
CDC Cyber/6000	60	$-2^{59}+1$ to $2^{59}-1$ -576460752303423488 to 576460752303423487	18

In general, for an n-bit computer, the range of integer number representation is -2^{n-1} to $+2^{n-1}-1$. The user should consult the FORTRAN 77 reference manual to find the precise range of allowable integer numbers on the computer being used.

Examples of *valid* integer constants are:

   (i)   0
  (ii) 1234
 (iii) -8004
 (iv) 0531

whereas the following are *invalid* for the reasons indicated:

   (i) 1,23   (commas are not allowed in integer constants)
  (ii) 8.00   (integer constants may not contain decimal points)
 (iii) $--1$ (only one algebraic sign is allowed)
 (iv) $5-$ (the algebraic sign must precede the string of digits)
  (v) 999999999999 (too large integer number for most of the computers).

Integer constants are also referred to as *fixed-point constants*.

3.2.2 Real Constants

A real constant may be represented by the decimal digits 0-9 and a decimal point, prefixed by an optional $+$ or $-$ sign. The decimal point must always be used for a real constant. It is the only way for the compiler to distinguish between real and integer constants. A general form for real constants can be represented as

$$\pm n.m$$

where n is the integral whole part and m is the fractional part; n or m can be zero. One of them may be null (not present), but the decimal point is essential. The total number of digits in the fractional part that can be carried is dependent on the wordlength of the computer being used. In general, six to ten digits of precision are possible. TRS-80, IBM/360 and 370 series, DEC 2060 and VAX-11 family computers allow a precision of seven digits. Computer CDC Cyber/6000 allows 15 digit precision. A FORTRAN reference manual should, however, be consulted to determine the actual precision for the computer being used. For a seven-digits precision, the division of 1 by 3 (0.3333333....) will be rounded to an approximation, such as 0.3333333 while the division of 2 by 3(0.6666666....) will be rounded to an approximation, such as 0.6666667. Real constants, unlike integers, are therefore not necessarily stored exactly in the memory of a computer.

Examples of *valid* real constants are:

   (i) 1.234
  (ii) .0
 (iii) -0.56789
 (iv) $+98765.$

Examples of *invalid* real constants are:

   (i) 0   (real constants in decimal form must contain a decimal)
  (ii) 1,234   (commas are not allowed in real constants)

(iii)   5.6.7   (more than one decimal point is not permitted)
(iv)   3.14567891234   (too many significant digits for a 32-bit word
                            length).

Real constants are also called *floating-point constants*. A second form for
real constants used in FORTRAN is called the *scientific* or *exponential form*.
The general form of the scientific notation can be represented as

$$\overbrace{\pm \text{n.m}}^{\text{Mantissa}} \; E \; \overbrace{\pm \text{k}}^{\text{Exponent}}$$

where, mantissa $\pm$n.m is a standard real constant as previously defined,
except that the decimal point can be omitted if m is not present. The letter
E must be present and the exponent $\pm$k must be an integer constant. Exponent sign can be omitted if it is positive.

The magnitude and the number of significant digits in the mantissa and the
exponent depend on the computer being used. In the DEC-2060, for example,
the mantissa may have up to eight digits and the exponent may be between
−38 and 38 while in the IBM 360, the mantissa may have up to seven digits
and the exponent may be between −78 to +75. Once again, to determine
the precise range for the computer being used, one should refer to the reference manual.

Some *valid* real constants in the exponent (scientific) form are:
  (i) (a) +12.0E+08   (b) 12.0E+08   (c) 12.E+08   (d) 12.E08
    (e) 12.E8
  (ii) −123.E+01
  (iii) −4567.8E−20
  (iv) 0.250E−02

The following are *invalid* real constants for the reasons indicated:
  (i)   0.25E−440   (exponent too large for most of the computers)
  (ii)   E10   (no real number before exponent sign E)
  (iii) 1.23−E07   (minus sign in wrong place)
  (iv)   123,6.E−3   (use of comma not allowed)
  (v)   0.1E   (E must be followed by an integer exponent)
  (vi)   −153.4E+1.1 (exponent must be an integer).

3.3 FORTRAN VARIABLES

In computations, a symbolic name is often used to refer to a quantity that
may vary. For example, the formula

$$\text{area} = \text{length} \times \text{width}$$

is used to calculate the area of a rectangle. The symbolic names, "area",
"length" and "width", are called variables, If specific values are assigned to
the length and the width, the area can be calculated. Numerical values of
these variables may change throughout a program, which is why they are

called variables. Variables are referenced by way of identifiers or symbolic names. Variable names are governed by the following rule:

A variable name or indentifier is composed of a sequence of one to six alphabetic characters (A...Z or a...z) or decimal digits (0...9). It is essential that a variable name must start with an alphabetic character. The variable must not contain any special characters.

When a variable is used in a FORTRAN program, the compiler associates it with a particular memory location. The value of a variable at any time is the number or the value stored in the associated memory location. It logically follows that variables are also of two types, namely integer variables and real variables, to represent two types of numbers, integer and real. If the first character of a variable name happens to be one of the six alphabetic letters I, J, K, L, M, N, then it is considered as an integer variable name; otherwise it is treated as a real variable name.

Examples of a few *valid* variable names are shown below:

Integer variable	Real variable
I	A
ME	AREA
LENGTH	X15
NOA2	FORT77

The following are some *invalid* names for the reason indicated:

1ABCD5	(first character not alphabetic)
X,Z	(no special character "," allowed)
I+J2	(no special character "+" allowed)

The limitation of a maximum of six characters in a variable name can be quite restrictive when it comes to choosing meaningful ones. In the interest of writing clear and easily understood programs, it is a good practice to assign variable names to variable quantities with a high degree of mnemonic content. Thus, for example, if one wants to calculate the perimeter of a rectangle in terms of length and width, the corresponding variables may be named PERIME, ALENTH and WIDTH. Notice the A in front of ALENTH, which serves to make the variable real. Similarly, in an integer arithmetic if the name of the variable starts with a letter other than I, J, K, L, M or N, one should append one of these at the front of the variable name. For example, to represent the number of physical activities in which a group of athletes is being tabulated, one may use the variable name NPHACT. There is, however, another way of declaring LENTH as a real variable and PHACT as an integer variable. This is discussed in the following section.

3.4 TYPE DECLARATION

By now you must have realized that the first character of the name of a variable determines whether it is a real variable or an integer variable. This is an implicit declaration of a variable type. In some cases, it may be desirable for a real variable to begin with one of the letters I, J, K, L, M and N, and vice versa for an integer variable in other cases. Electrical engineers use L for inductance, chemical engineers and scientists use μ (MU) for viscosity, and there are similar conventions in other disciplines. In general, inductance (L) and viscosity (MU) have values that may not be integer constants, therefore L and MU should be treated as real variables. In FORTRAN, the implicit declaration can be overriden by an explicit declaration as illustrated by the following examples:

```
REAL            L, MU, LENGTH
INTEGER         PHACT
```

L, MU and LENGTH are treated as real variables while PHACT (abbreviation for PHysical ACTivities) is treated as an integer variable.

The general forms of these declaration statements are as follows:

```
INTEGER x₁, x₂,...
REAL      x₃, x₄,...
```

x_1, x_2, x_3,...indicate that the key word (INTEGER or REAL) is followed by the variable names (separated by commas), which are declared to be of the indicated type. Thus we may write.

```
INTEGER      BETA, THETA, MASS, PAY, COUNT
REAL         LENGTH, INTRST, ALPHA, LAMBDA
```

In the above declarations, the variable MASS is declared the INTEGER variable and ALPHA the REAL variable even though by definition they are integer and real variables, respectively. This explicit declaration in a program is grammatically allowed though it does not serve any useful purpose. A program can have any number of INTEGER and REAL declaration statements.

Note that type declarations are irrevocable, i.e., a variable name can appear in only one type statement, for example, in a program the following construction is invalid:

```
INTEGER      THETA, MASS
REAL         BETA, MASS
```

The variable name MASS appears in two separate type statements. The following are *invalid* declaration statements for the reasons indicated:

```
INTEGER,    A,B,C    (no comma allowed after INTEGER)
REAL        I,J,K,   (no comma allowed at the end of the statement)
REAL        L.M      (no special character, is allowed, only commas
                      are allowed).
```

3.5 INTEGER AND REAL ARITHMETIC

As noted in Section 3.2, the primary distinction between integer and real data is that real data contains a decimal point and that it can contain a fractional part while integer data cannot. When the arithmetic uses two integer constants and/or variables, no fractional part is retained; that is, the result is truncated to an integer value by removing the decimal part. For example, if the integer 9 is divided by the integer 5, the result is integer 1, and not 1.8 Note that the result is truncated, not rounded off. With two real constants and/or variables, the fractional part is retained.

Examples

  (a) The integer 3 divided by the integer 5 yields the integer 0.
  (b) The real 3.0 divided by the real 5.0 yields the real 0.6.
  (c) The real 3.0 divided by the integer 5 yields the real 0.6. In this case the integer is converted to real before performing the division.

3.6 ARITHMETIC OPERATIONS

FORTRAN provides five basic arithmetic operations. These are addition, subtraction, multiplication, division and exponentiation. All other arithmetic operations are built up from these five basic operations. The FORTRAN symbols used for designating basic operations are:

Operation	FORTRAN Symbol	Hierarchy
Addition	+	Lowest
Subtraction	−	Lowest
Multiplication	*	Intermediate
Division	/	Intermediate
Exponentiation	**	Highest

(Increases ↓)

The character "*" (asterisk) should not be confused with lowercase "x". The exponentiation combination "**" is considered as two characters but it represents a single symbol. It is not correct to write two mathematical operation symbols side by side in a FORTRAN statement.

These five basic arithmetic operations are used to combine FORTRAN constants, variables and functions into meaningful arithmetic expressions, which are discussed in the next section. The hierarchy of these operations is discussed in Section 3.8 (Rule 2).

3.7 THE ASSIGNMENT STATEMENT AND ARITHMETIC EXPRESSIONS

In FORTRAN, formulas are expressed primarily in terms of assignment statements. The general form of the FORTRAN assignment statement is:

$$result = expression$$

The interpretation of the above statement is that a particular value (indicated by the expression on R.H.S.) is assigned to the variable indicated by result (L.H.S.). The expression on the R.H.S. may involve numeric on non-numeric quantities (e.g. character constants, character variables, etc.) but not both. In this chapter, we will discuss only arithmetic expressions involving numeric quantities. Expressions involving character variables and character constants are discussed in Chapter 8. A simple example of the arithmetic expression is the calculation of the simple interest on a deposit in a savings account after a fixed number of years for a given annual interest rate. The formula for calculating interest is:

$$interest = \frac{deposit \times rate \times time}{100}$$

This formula is written and evaluated in FORTRAN as:

result   expression

INTRST = DEPOS * RATE * TIME/100.0

Note that in an assignment statement, the formulation of R.H.S. expression is quite important and certain rules must be followed to write these expressions. Before discussing these rules, consider an example of algebraic expressions and their FORTRAN equivalents.

Example

Assume that a, b, c, d and e are REAL variables and that i, j, k and 1 are INTEGER variables.

Algebraic Expressions	FORTRAN Equivalents
$a + \dfrac{b}{d} + c^e$	A + B/D + C ** E
$a^2 + b^3 - d$	A ** 2 + B ** 3 - D
$ij + kl$	I * J + K * L
$i^2 - k^2$	I ** 2 - K ** 2

In general, arithmetic expressions are formed by adding or subtracting terms. A term is formed from a sequence of arithmetic operations involving multiplication, division and/or exponentiation. Consider the first expression in the above example. There are three terms, A, B/D and C**E which form the expression.

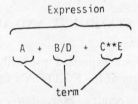

3.8 RULES FOR ARITHMETIC EXPRESSIONS

3.8.1 Rule 1: Type Conversion

For all arithmetic operations involving a real and an integer operand, the real equivalent of the integer operand must be obtained before the operation can be performed. The only exception to this rule is an exponentiation operation. Where exponentiation is involved (i.e. real ** integer or integer ** real). the rule is as follows:

- a. Real ** integer is evaluated by repeated multiplication (e.g. x^3 is evaluated as x * x * x). Thus no type conversion occurs.
- b. For integer ** real, the integer value is first converted to a real value. So type conversion occurs. Notice that the integer quantity must be a non-negative quantity, since real exponentiation of a negative quantity is not mathematically defined. This is explained in detail in Rule 4.

It can be inferred from the above rule that if both operands are either real or integer, no type conversion occurs and the result after performing the operation will be real if both operands are real, and integer if both operands are integer. Table 3.2 sumarizes the types of results for different types of operands.

Table 3.2: A Summary of Type Conversion

1st Operand (type)	2nd Operand (type)	Result (type)
Integer	Integer	Integer
Integer	Real	Real
Real	Integer	Real
Real	Real	Real

The following example illustrates type conversion:

Example (a)

Suppose that X, Y and Z are real and that I is an integer. Let X = 1.0, Y = 2.0, Z = 3.0 and I = 4. Shown below are some arithmetic expressions and the resulting quantities.

Expression	Result		Type	Remarks
X+Y+Z	1.0+2.0+3.0	= 6.0	Real	No type conversion
X+I	1.0+4	= 5.0	Real	Type conversion
I/Z	4/3.0	= 1.333	Real	Type conversion
Z/I	3.0/4	= 0.75	Real	Type conversion
Y**I	2.0**4	= 16.0	Real	No type conversion
I**3	4**3	= 64	Integer	No type conversion
I+2	4+2	= 6	Integer	No type conversion
I+2·0	4+2.0	= 6.0	Real	Type conversion

3.8.2 Rule 2: Hierarchy of Operations

The sequence of operations in an arithmetic expression is governed by what is called an hierarchy of operations. This is necessary to avoid any confusion while evaluating an expression, e.g. in the expression X+Y*X−Z what is the sequence of operations? Is it X + ((Y*X)−Z) or (X+Y)*(X−Z) or X+(Y*(X−Z)) or ((X+Y)*X)−Z? A set of rules, which is based upon the algebraic rules of operator precedence, is summarized as follows:

 (a) All parenthesized subexpressions must be evaluated first. Nested parenthesized subexpressions must be evaluated inside-out, with the innermost expression evaluated first.

If the above expression is written as (X+((Y*X)−Z)) then the innermost parenthesized subexpression (Y*X) is evaluated first. If subexpression (Y*X) is represented by A then the second innermost parenthesized expression (A−Z) is evaluated. If this is represented by B, then the outermost parenthesized expression (X+B) is evaluated.

 (b) Operators in the same subexpression are evaluated according to the following hierarchy:
   1. Exponentiations (**) are performed first.
   2. Multiplications (*) and divisions (/) are performed next.
   3. Additions (+) and subtractions (−) are performed the last.

 (c) Operators in the same subexpression and having the same precedence, i.e. at the same hierarchical level (such as * and /), are evaluated left to right. Thus, X+Y*X−Z would be computed as (X+(Y*X))−Z.

The only exception to the left-to-right rule is that successive exponentiations are performed from right to left. Thus A**B**C is evaluated as A** (B**C).

The following examples elaborate more on hierarchy of operations:

Example (b)

Consider the arithmetic expression X*Y**I−A+B/C−D. According to above rule, this would be computed by the following sequence:

1. (Y**I)	Exponentiation first
2. X*(Y**I)	Multiplication is left to the division
3. (B/C)	Division before addition and subtraction
4. (X*(Y**I))−A	− A is to the left of + (B/C)
5. ((X*(Y**I))−A)+(B/C)	+ (B/C) is to the left of − D
6. ((X*(Y**I))−A+(B/C))−D	Final result.

Example (c)

Suppose that the expression of the above example is written as

$$X*Y**I-((A+B)/(C-D))$$

then the sequence of operations would be:

1. (A+B)	Addition within the innermost parenthesis and it is left to the (C−D)
2. (C−D)	Subtraction within innermost parenthesis
3. ((A+B)/(C−D))	Division within the outermost parenthesis
4. Y**I	Exponentiation first after parenthesized operations
5. X*(Y**I)	Multiplication before subtraction of ((A+B)/(C−D))
6. X*Y**I −((A+B)/(C−D))	Final result.

3.8.3 Rule 3: Arithmetic Operators

Never write two arithmetic operators in succession; they must be separated by an operand or parenthesis.

Example (d)

Write a FORTRAN expression to calculate x^{-k}.

It is incorrect in FORTRAN 77 to write

$$X**-K$$

The correct way to write it is

$$X**(-K).$$

Likewise, $\dfrac{X}{-Y}$ must be written as $X/(-Y)$ and not as $X/-Y$.

3.8.4 Rule 4: Real Exponentiation

With real exponents, the number to be raised cannot be negative.

Consider evaluation of X**Y. Let X = − 2.5 and Y=1.5, then $(-2.5)^{1.5}$ is not defined mathematically. Similarly, consider I**Y and let I = − 2, then

$(-2)^{1.5}$ is also not permissible. However, if the exponent is an integer, the number to be raised can be negative. For example, $(-1.7)^2$ means $(-1.7)*$ (-1.7) and it is a well-defined mathematical operation, so it is a valid operation in FORTRAN.

The above rules are useful in evaluating and writing arithmetic expressions in FORTRAN. While writing an arithmetic expression, a good thing to keep in mind is that excess parentheses are not detrimental if they help to clarify the true meaning of an expression. There is no penalty for the parentheses in FORTRAN even if they are not really necessary in an expression. Often, using parentheses liberally will lead to fewer mistakes and a clearer understanding of what is to be evaluated.

We now conclude with a number of examples that illustrate the use of the above rules for arithmetic expressions and operations.

Example (e)

The following expressions are invalid FORTRAN expressions for the reasons indicated:

    (a) A**—I   (Two operators together)
    (b) —2.0**B   (Real exponentiation of a negative quantity)
    (c) XY   (No operator between two operands)
    (d) A.B/(—C)   ("." is not a legal arithmetic operator)
    (e) (A+(B)/2   (Unbalanced parenthesis)

Example (f)

This example illustrates how several mathematical formulas can be implemented in FORTRAN using arithmetic expressions. A, B, C, D, X and Y are assumed to be real; I, J and K are assumed to be integer.

Mathematical formula	FORTRAN 77 expression
1. $\dfrac{a+b}{c+d}$	(A+B)/(C+D)
2. $a^2+b^3+c^{k^2}$	A**2+B**3+C**(K**2)
3. $\dfrac{1}{1+x^2}$	1.0/(1.0+X**2)
4. $\dfrac{(a+b+c)^i}{x-y}$	((A+B+C)**I)/(X—Y)
5. $xy - \dfrac{a}{j^4}$	X*Y—A/J**4
6. $\dfrac{x}{1+\dfrac{y}{a+b+c}}$	X/(1.0+Y/(A+B+C))

7. x^{y+1}. $d^a.c$ X**(Y+1.0)*D**A*C

8. $\left(\dfrac{1}{a}+\dfrac{2}{b}\right)^{c/4}$ (1.0/A+2.0/B)**(C/4.0)

Example (g)

This example shows how several arithmetic expressions are evaluated. It is assumed that A and B are real and that I and J are integer, and that

A = 1.0, B = 2.0, I = 3, and J = 4.

Expression	Result and Explanation
I/J*J	0, I/J = 3/4 = 0 (integer arithmetic)
I*J/I	4 (integer arithmetic)
I/J+J/I	1, I/J = 3/4 = 0 and J/I = 4/3 = 1 (integer arithmetic)
J/(I/B)	2.666667, I is converted to real before I/B is computed and J is converted to real before the second division is performed (mixed mode arithmetic)
I**(−I)/B**(−A)	0.0, I**(−I) is evaluated as 1/(3**3) = 1/27 = 0 (mixed mode arithmetic)
A+J/I+I/J*B	2.0, J/I = 4/3 = 1 and it is converted to real equivalent 1.0 while adding to A, I/J = 3/4 = 0 (mixed-mode arithmetic).

Example (h)

Assignment statements are executed in the order in which they appear in a program. In the following, indicate the values which are currently assigned to A, B, and C after each statement has been executed.

Statement	A	B	C
B = 0.0	?	0.0	?
C = 0	?	0.0	0.0
A = B*C+1	1.0	0.0	0.0
B = A+B*A	1.0	1.0	0.0
C = A+B	1.0	1.0	2.0
A = A**2	1.0	1.0	2.0
B = B/A+C/ (A+B+C)	1.0	1.5	2.0
A = A+B−C**2	−1.5	1.5	2.0
C = A**C	−*	−*	−*
A+B = C−A	−*	−*	−*
C = A*−B	−*	−*	−*

? Arbitrary initial value depending on computer.
* Error, invalid statement. The values of variables A, B and C remain unaffected.

Example (i)

The expression ISUM $= 6/2 + 3**(2*3) - 50*10$ is evaluated as shown in the following diagram:

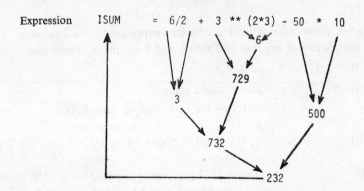

Example (j)

The expression x $= (9.0/6*3.0)**2 - (5/4)*3$ is evaluated as shown in the following diagram:

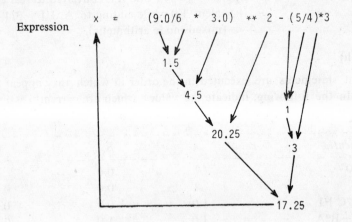

In Example (g) above, we have emphasized on the notions of integer arithmetic and mixed mode arithmetic. While evaluating the value of the expression on the right hand side, each term is calculated using either integer arithmetic, real arithmetic or mixed mode arithmetic, depending on the type of quantities involved in a term. If all quantities are of the integer type then integer arithmetic is used and so on. If, however, both real and integer quantities are involved in a term then all integer quantities are converted to the real type before performing an arithmetic operation as outlined in Rule 1. This is called mixed mode arithmetic.

3.9 MIXED MODE ASSIGNMENT STATEMENTS

A mixed mode assignment statement is an assignment in which the type of the variable on the left hand side (L.H.S.) is different from the type of the expression on the right hand side (R.H.S.). In this case, the type of the value of the expression is converted to the type of the variable on the L.H.S. before assigning the evaluated value to the variable. In other words, after evaluating the value of the expression on the R.H.S. the answer is assigned to the variable on the L.H.S. depending on its type. It must, however, be remembered that while evaluating the value of the expression no consideration to the type of the variable on the L.H.S. is given.

Example (a)

I = 4.5

The value assigned to I will be 4. When a real value on the R.H.S. is converted to integer, any fractional part is truncated.

Example (b)

K = 3.0/4 + 2.3

3.0/4 is 0.75 and the final value of the R.H.S. expression is 3.05. The value assigned to K is 3 after the truncating fractional part.

Example (c)

I = 3/4 + 4/5.0/8−2/3*4

The value of the first term (3/4) is 0; the value of the second term (4/5.0/8) is 0.1; and the value of the third term (2/3*4) is also 0. So the value of the entire expression is 0.1. The value assigned to I is, therefore, 0 (zero).

3.10 ELEMENTARY FORTRAN INTRINSIC FUNCTIONS

In scientific, engineering and business computations, it may often be necessary to evaluate several functions that are used quite frequently, such as square root, logarithms, exponentials, and trigonometric functions, etc. FORTRAN offers the facility of computing many such functions. A general form of writing an intrinsic function is

Function name (variable name or expression or constant)
$$\underbrace{\qquad\qquad\qquad\qquad\qquad\qquad}_{\text{argument}}$$

The argument type, whether real or integer, is often critical and it depends on the function being evaluated.

These functions produce a single result. These functions are a part of FORTRAN language and that is why they are called intrinsic functions or built-in functions. In this section, a list of only a few of the more common functions is given. Appendix A gives a detailed list of the functions prescribed by the 1977 FORTRAN standard.

Function	Mnemonic	Type of	
		Argument	Function
Absolute value, | x |	ABS (X)	Real	Real
arc sine, $\sin^{-1}x$	ASIN (X)	Real	Real
arc cosine, $\cos^{-1}x$	ACOS (X)	Real	Real
Arc tan, $\tan^{-1}x$	ATAN (X)	Real	Real
Exponential, e^x	EXP (X)	Real	Real
Logarithm to base 10, $\log_{10}x$	ALOG10 (X)	Real	Real
Natural logarithm, $\log_e x$	ALOG (X)	Real	Real
Square root, $\sqrt{x}$	SQRT (X)	Real	Real
Trigonometric sine, sin x	SIN (X)	Real	Real
Trigonometric cosine, cos x	COS (X)	Real	Real
Trigonometric tangent, tan x	TAN (X)	Real	Real
Length of character string S	LEN (S)	Character	Integer

Before using the above functions, the following points should be kept in mind:

1. The arc trigonometric functions return only the principal value:

   (a) $\sin^{-1}x$ $|x| \leqslant 1.0$, $-\pi/2 \leqslant$ result $\leqslant \pi/2$
   (b) $\cos^{-1}x$ $|x| \leqslant 1.0$, $0 \leqslant$ result $\leqslant \pi$
   (c) $\tan^{-1}x$ $-\pi/2 \leqslant$ result $\leqslant \pi/2$.

2. The value of the argument for a logarithmic function should be greater than zero.

3. The value of the argument for a square root function should be non-negative.

4. In the trigonometric sine, cosine and tangent functions, the argument x must be in radians, and not in degrees.

It is possible that the argument of a function may be an expression involving other mathematical operations and/or functions. In an arithmetic expression containing functions, the fuctions are evaluated first. The names of the functions cannot be used as names for normal variables in a program.

Example

Here are some algebraic expressions and their equivalent FORTRAN statements:

Algebraic Expression	FORTRAN 77 Statement
$Rl = (-b + \sqrt{b^2 - 4ac})/2a$	$Rl = (-B + SQRT(B**2 - 4.0*A*B))/(2.*A)$
$t = d/(v\cos\theta)$	$T = D/(V*COS(THETA))$
$h = vt\sin x - gt^2/2$	$H = V*T*SIN(X) - G*T*T/2.0$
$q = \exp(y\tan x)$	$Q = EXP(Y*TAN(X))$
$a = \log_{10}\sqrt{(|x|/y^z)}$	$A = ALOG10(SQRT(ABS(X)/(Y**Z)))$

3.11 FORTRAN STATEMENTS

The general statements that can be used in a FORTRAN program may be classified in the following four categories:

1. Arithmetic Assignment Statements
2. Input-Output Statements
3. Informational Statements
4. Flow of Control Statements

The last statement is discussed separately in the next chapter, while a brief description of the remaining three is given here.

3.11.1 Arithmetic Assignment Statements

The arithmetic assignment statement has been discussed in detail in Section 3.7. It may suffice to recall that the computer interprets an arithmetic statement as an operation in which expressions on the right hand side are evaluated and stored in the memory location indicated by the variable on the left hand side of the assignment (equal) sign. It is, therefore, necessary that all variables on the right hand side of the statement be available when the arithmetic assignment statement is executed, i.e. all right hand side variables must have numerical values available in their memory locations, otherwise an error will occur which may or may not be detected by a computer.

3.11.2 Input-output Statements

In order to solve a problem on a digital computer, it may be necessary to transfer the required data to its memory from one of its input units, e.g., card reader units, magnetic tape units, paper tape units, a console typewriter, or a cathode ray tube (CRT) terminal. In this book, we will confine our discussion to the most recent input unit, a CRT terminal. Therefore, two types of input statements, ACCEPT and READ, will be discussed in this book.

After a program is executed and the problem solved, the results are transferred from the memory of the computer to one of its output units. This transfer of results is done by using an output statement. We shall consider output statements such as TYPE or PRINT or WRITE, which are used when the output unit is a CRT terminal.

The input and the output data for a program may appear in a number of different layouts or formats. FORTRAN has a powerful facility by which a programmer can specify for an input data to be read in a suitable manner and similarly the output data can be printed in a desired manner by specifying a suitable format. That is, it is possible to specify exactly which positions (column numbers) in a line are to be occupied by a number to be printed and how many blanks should be left between two numbers, etc. These instructions are transmitted in FORTRAN via FORMAT specification statements, which are described in detail in Chapter 5.

A simpler way of reading or writing data is to use a "list directed" format statement. This will be used in this chapter and subsequent ones until we can learn more about format statements in Chapter 5. This is quite simple and can easily be used by beginners. The only disadvantage is that the programmer has little or practically no control over the form of data to be handled.

3.11.2.1 *List-Directed Input Statement*

(i) *The ACCEPT Statement*: In a FORTRAN program, one can use the "ACCEPT" statement to input data directly on the CRT terminal. A partial syntax form of the statement is:

$$ACCEPT^*, \text{ input list}$$

*(asterisk) implies list-directed formatting in the above statement.

Data are entered into each variable specified in the input list (a list of variables). Commas are used to separate the variable names in the input list. When an ACCEPT statement is executed, the input data must consist of FORTRAN constants separated by delimiter. A delimiter can be either a camma or a blank (or blanks). A comma with any number of preceding and succeeding blanks is interpreted as a single delimiter. An example of the ACCEPT statement is:

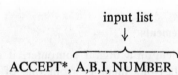

$$ACCEPT^*, A,B,I,NUMBER$$

If A = 1.0, B = 2.0, I = 3, NUMBER = 10, then various sets of input data could be

    1.0, 2.0, 3, 10
    1.0ƀ2.0ƀ3ƀ10
    1.0, ƀƀ2.0ƀ3ƀƀƀƀ, ƀƀƀƀ10

Note that all the above input data sets are valid (ƀ represents a blank space).

(ii) *The READ Statement*: The ACCEPT statement may not be available with some of the FORTRAN 77 compilers. In that case another input statement that can be used is READ statement. For the present, we will confine our discussion to the list-directed READ statement. A partial syntax form of the READ statement is:

READ (lun,*) input list.

where

Lun is a FORTRAN logical unit number (an integer which is implementation dependent), indicating the device from which data is to be read; as mentioned earlier, our input device is a CRT terminal which is designated by logical unit 5;

* implies list-directed formatting;

input list is a list of integer or real variables to which input data are to be assigned; while entering data on the terminal for the READ statement, one can follow the same guidelines as mentioned earlier for the ACCEPT statement.

The difference between the READ statement and the ACCEPT statement is that the READ statement is more versatile and can be used to read data from any of the input devices by specifying their logical unit numbers. The READ statement is also used while reading input data from a data file. This is discussed in detail in Chapter 5. The ACCEPT statement can only be used to read data from a CRT terminal. In the cases where the same input data may have to be used many times, it is recommended to store this data on a device. In this situation one has to use the READ statement to read data and one cannot use the ACCEPT statement.

An equivalent READ statement of the afore-mentioned example of the ACCEPT statement is:

logical unit number   input list

READ (5,*)   A, B, I, NUMBER

It may be noted that some of the FORTRAN compilers accept READ statement in the following form:

READ*, input list

In this case, users do not have to explicitly provide a logical unit number.

3.11.2.2 *List-Directed Output Statement*

(i) *The TYPE or the PRINT statement*: In a FORTRAN program, the TYPE or the PRINT statement is used to output the stored values of variables at the user's CRT terminal. A partial syntax form of the statement is:

TYPE*, output list

or

PRINT*, output list

Each TYPE or PRINT statement initiates a new line of output. The value of each item in the output list is printed in a sequence across the output line. Commas are used to separate items in an output list. These items may be FORTRAN constants, variables or expressions. Examples of the TYPE and the PRINT statements are:

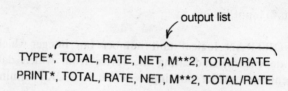

```
TYPE*, TOTAL, RATE, NET, M**2, TOTAL/RATE
PRINT*, TOTAL, RATE, NET, M**2, TOTAL/RATE
```

(ii) *The WRITE statement*: Again, statements TYPE or PRINT may not be available with all FORTRAN compilers. In that case, a more frequently used output statement is the WRITE statement. A partial syntax form of the list-directed WRITE statement is;

WRITE (lun,*) output list

where

lun is a FORTRAN logical unit number (an integer) that directs the printing of output results to a specific device (typically a CRT terminal or a line printer): our output device is a CRT terminal which is also an input device; for WRITE operation the logical unit number assigned to the CRT is 6; a CRT terminal can be used as both input and output device.

The difference between the WRITE statement and the TYPE or the PRINT statements is the same as that between the READ statement and the ACCEPT statement. The TYPE or the PRINT statements are used to print output data only on the CRT terminal, while the WRITE statement can be used to print output data on any output device and therefore a permanent storage of the output data can be done, if necessary.

An equivalent WRITE statement of the earlier noted example of the TYPE statement is:

```
        logical unit number      output list
WRITE(6,*) TOTAL, RATE, NET, M**2, TOTAL/RATE
```

An example that makes use of both the list-directed input and output statements in a typical FORTRAN 77 program fragment is given below:

Example (a)

Using the ACCEPT, TYPE and PRINT statements:

    TYPE*, 'ENTER VALUES OF X, Y AND I'
    ACCEPT*, X, Y, I
    Z = X + Y**I
    PRINT*, 'X = ', X, 'Y = ', Y, 'I = ', I 'X + Y**I = ', Z

When this program is executed, the prompt:

    ENTER VALUES OF X, Y AND I

is printed to tell the user to type in the values of X, Y and I on the terminal. If the user were to type:

    2.5, 3.0, 2

then the output would be:

$X = 2.5 \; Y = 3.0 \; I = 2 \; X + Y**I = 11.5$

Example (b)

Using the READ and WRITE statements:

The same program fragment using READ and WRITE statements is written as follows:

WRITE (6, X)' ENTER VALUES OF X, Y and I'
READ (5,*) X, Y, I
Z = X + Y**I
WRITE (6,*) 'X = ;, X, 'Y = ' Y, 'I = ', 'X + Y**I = ', Z

If this program is executed and the same input data is used, the output data would appear identical to what is mentioned above.

3.12 THE PARAMETER STATEMENT

A logical unit number is required in the READ and WRITE statements. The computer on which most of the examples included in this book are solved the logical units for the user's CRT terminal for the READ and WRITE statements are 5 and 6 respectively. However, if there are many READ and WRITE statements in a program, then it is not a good practice to use this integer constant in every input and output statement. If the program is to be executed on a different computer that uses different logical unit numbers or if different input/output devices are used for the same computer, then each READ and WRITE statement would have to be modified.

Alternatively, instead of using constants (such as 5), a FORTRAN 77 PARAMETER statement can be used. A parameter is merely a symbolic name for a constant. The general form of a PARAMETER statement is:

PARAMETER (pname$_1$ = const$_1$, pname$_2$ = const$_2$, . . .)

where

pname$_1$, pname$_2$ . . . are parameter names; these must follow the same rules as variable names (i.e. 6 character maximum and the type of the parameter names must be declared); and

const$_1$, const$_2$ . . . are constants of the same type as the associated parameters.

The PARAMETER statement is a nonexecutable statement. It must precede all statements that use the symbolic names. It must be noted that a symbolic name used as parameter may not be redefined via an assignment, READ, or another PARAMETER statement.

An example using the PARAMETER statement in a FORTRAN 77 program segment is given below:

INTEGER INLUN, OUTLUN
PARAMETER (INLUN = 5, OUTLUN = 6)
READ (INLUN, *)A

        WRITE (OUTLUN, *)A
        ⋮

If the logic unit number for input devices changes to 20 and for the output
device changes to 22, then only the second line of the program will be modified. The modified program is:

    INTEGER INLUN, OUTLUN
    PARAMETER (INLUN = 20, OUTLUN = 22)
    READ (INLUN, *)A
    WRITE (OUTLUN,*)A

The PARAMETER statement is a special feature of FORTRAN 77 and
this statement may not be used in the FORTRAN IV program.

3.13 STOP, PAUSE AND END STATEMENTS

Once all desired calculations have been performed and the results are
printed, the computer must be instructed to stop execution of the program.
The statement that directs the computer to "gracefully" terminate execution
is a single word:

    STOP

STOP is the last executable statement in the program that indicates the
logical end of the program. A program can have more than one STOP statement and it is not necessary for a STOP statement to appear at the end of
the program. It may appear anywhere in the body of a program. The STOP
statement returns control to the operating system program so that the terminal can be used to execute other jobs.

One of the difficulties with the STOP statement is that the computer
cannot conveniently be made to continue within the same program after the
STOP statement has been executed. The PAUSE statement allows the operator to overcome this difficulty. The PAUSE statement may be used at
any number of places in a program to temporarily halt the execution of the
program at desired strategic points. The PAUSE statement does, in fact, stop
the program execution, but it also allows restarting possibilities. This is usually
done by pressing a key on the computer console. The computer will resume the
execution of the program beginning with the statement just after the PAUSE
statement. The PAUSE statement may serve many useful purposes, such as
checking the intermediate results, mounting a new magnetic tape, or taking
some other possible actions.

The END statement is the very last statement of every FORTRAN program to indicate the physical end of a program. The statement signals to
the compiler that there are no more statements left to be translated. No program can have more than one END statement.

3.14 EXAMPLES OF SIMPLE FORTRAN 77 PROGRAMS

With the elementary FORTRAN 77 statements discussed so far, the reader must be able to write simple and complete FORTRAN 77 programs. In our previous two chapters, we have already discussed basic concepts associated with problem analysis, algorithm development and general program approach.

Before considering some illustrative examples, it may be useful to discuss one additional statement. This is the so-called comment line or *comment statement* or *informational statement*. These statements are descriptive comments and are listed with the program statements to aid the programmer in identifying or documenting the purpose of each section of the program. These statements are ignored by the compiler during the compilation of a program. These are nonexecutable statements and can contain any text desired. A totally blank line is also interpreted as a comment line. Careful placement of blank lines can make a program much easier to read and follow.

Now we shall discuss some simple examples that are written in FORTRAN 77.

Example 3.1

Write a computer program to compute and print the sum and average of two numbers.

In the above example, we are given two numbers which serve as input data. We are supposed to calculate the sum and the average of these numbers, so these are output data. After identifying input and output data, we can appropriately choose suitable variable names to represent them. These variable names are given in the data table.

Data Table for Example 3.1

Input Variables	Output Variables
NUM1: First number	SUM: Sum of two numbers
NUM2: Second number	AVG: Average of two numbers

The sum and the average of any two numbers is given by:

$$SUM = NUM1 + NUM2$$
$$AVG = SUM/2$$

Since the given numbers can either be real or integer, an explicit declaration is necessary to declare input variables NUM1 and NUM2 as real variables, or else NUM1 and NUM2 will be treated as integer variables.

A FORTRAN 77 program for computing the sum and the average is given below:

```
REAL NUM1, NUM2
TYPE*, 'WHAT ARE TWO NUMBERS, PLEASE TYPE IN'
ACCEPT*, NUM1, NUM2
SUM = NUM1 + NUM2
```

```
AVG = SUM/2.0
TYPE*, 'SUM OF TWO NUMBERS', NUM1, 'AND', NUM2,
'IS =', SUM
TYPE*, 'THEIR AVERAGE IS', AVG
STOP
END
```

The following flowchart describes the action of this program:

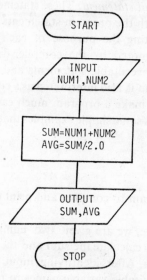

Figure 3.1: Flowchart for Example 3.1

Before this program can be run on the computer, it has to be entered into the computer by typing on the input device, a CRT terminal. One must follow certain guidelines to type in a program on a CRT terminal.

As seen above, the FORTRAN 77 statements are presented to the computer as a sequence of lines. A line consists of at least 72 columns and is partitioned as follows:

Column	Used for
1	Comment statement or special option. An asterisk (*) or letter (C) in column 1 indicates that the computer need not execute that line. The line is typed in as part of the program documentation and is used for explanatory comments.
1-5	Statement reference number (or statement label). A statement label is a one-to-five-digit unsigned integer that can be referenced by other FORTRAN statements. These statement numbers can appear anywhere in columns 1 through 5. These statement labels shall be discussed in detail in Chapter 4.

6	Continuation column. If a FORTRAN statement is too long and does not fit on a single line, it may be continued on the next line by putting a non-blank character (except the digit zero) in this column. For clarity, indent the statement on the continuation line.
7-72	FORTRAN statements. Indentations and spacing may be used for clarity. Blanks and tabs in these columns do not influence the execution of the program. If a statement is so long that more space is needed beyond column 72, then the next line must be a continuation line with a non-blank character appearing in column 6 and the continuation of the statement starting in column 7.
73-80	may be used for identification, but is often left blank. Columns 73 and beyond are ignored by a FORTRAN compiler.

Figure 3.2 shows a "FORTRAN coding form", which is useful in writing computer programs in the required format. These sheets may be used by beginners. Figure 3.3 shows a program listing of Example 3.1 on the FORTRAN coding form. Suitable comment statements have also been included in the program. After typing into the computer, the example program has been run. Computer program listing and results are shown in Figure 3.4.

Example 3.2

Given a four-digit integer, write a program that finds the sum of the individual digits. The program should also print the number in reverse order. For example, if the given number is 1234, the required sum is $1+2+3+4 = 10$ and the reverse order is 4321.

In the above example, it is required to find out the sum of individual digits of a four-digit number and it is also desired to print the number in the reverse order. In order to solve this problem, one should identify the four individual digits (0–9) that are contained in the number. The identification of a digit in a number is done by using integer arithmetic. The last digit, 4, in the number 1234 can be calculated, if we do the following calculations:

$$1234 - 1234/10*10$$

The second term 1234/10*10 gives 1230 because 1234/10 is calculated as 123 and not as 123.4. The third digit, 3, can be calculated in the same manner if the number is modified to 123 by throwing the last digit. This is obtained very easily by dividing the number by ten. Once these digits are known, one can easily compute the sum and a number in the reverse order can be found.

FORTRAN CODING FORM

Program _____
Coded By _____
Checked By _____
C FOR COMMENT

Date _____
Page ____ of ____
Keypunched _____

Identification
73   80

FORTRAN STATEMENT

```
C EXAMPLE PROGRAM #1
C SUM AND AVERAGE OF TWO NUMBERS
C
C DECLARATION
      REAL NUM1,NUM2
C READ INPUT DATA
      TYPE *,'WHAT ARE TWO NUMBERS, PLEASE TYPE IN'
      ACCEPT *,NUM1,NUM2
C PERFORM CALCULATIONS
      SUM=NUM1+NUM2
      AVG=SUM/2.0
C WRITE THE RESULTS
      TYPE*,'SUM OF TWO NUMBERS ',NUM1,' AND ',NUM2' IS= ',SUM
      TYPE*,'THEIR AVERAGE IS= ',AVG
      STOP
C END
```

Figure 3.2: FORTRAN Coding Form

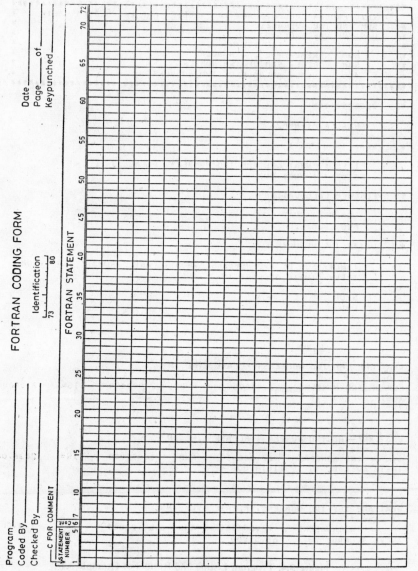

Figure 3.3: Program Listing of Example 3.1

```
*********************************************************************
*       THIS PROGRAM ACCEPTS ANY TWO NUMBERS AND CALCULATES THEIR   *
*       SUM AND THE AVERAGE.                                        *
*       LIST OF VARIABLES:                                         *
*          NUM1    REAL, THE 1st NUMBER                            *
*          NUM2    REAL, THE 2nd NUMBER                            *
*          SUM     REAL, SUM OF TWO NUMBERS                        *
*          AVG     REAL, AVERAGE OF TWO NUMBERS                    *
*********************************************************************

*       DECLARATION

           REAL NUM1,NUM2

*       READ INPUT DATA

           TYPE *,'WHAT ARE THE TWO NUMBERS, PLEASE TYPE IN'
           ACCEPT *,NUM1,NUM2

*       PERFORM CALCULATIONS

           SUM=NUM1+NUM2
           AVG= SUM/2.0

*       WRITE THE RESULTS

           TYPE*,'SUM OF TWO NUMBERS ',NUM1,' AND ',NUM2,' IS= ',SUM
           TYPE*,'THEIR AVERAGE IS= ',AVG

           STOP
           END




                        RUN I

WHAT ARE THE TWO NUMBERS, PLEASE TYPE IN
1.0 2.0
SUM OF TWO NUMBERS      1.000000      AND     2.000000     IS=     3.000000
THEIR AVERAGE IS=      1.500000

                        RUN II

WHAT ARE THE TWO NUMBERS, PLEASE TYPE IN
27.0 2009.0
SUM OF TWO NUMBERS      27.00000      AND     2009.000     IS=     2036.000
THEIR AVERAGE IS=      1018.000

                        RUN III

WHAT ARE THE TWO NUMBERS, PLEASE TYPE IN
76.8 56.2
SUM OF TWO NUMBERS      76.80000      AND     56.20000     IS=     133.0000
THEIR AVERAGE IS=      66.50000
```

Figure 3.4: Program Listing and Results of Example 3.1

```
*******************************************************************************
*     THIS PROGRAM ACCEPTS A FOUR DIGIT INTEGER NUMBER AND FINDS OUT         *
*     THE DIGITS WHICH CONSTITUTE THE NUMBER. IT ALSO COMPUTES THE           *
*     SUM OF THE DIGITS AND PRINTS THE NUMBER IN THE REVERSE ORDER.          *
*     LIST OF VARIABLES:                                                     *
*         NAME        TYPE                     USAGE                         *
*         ------      ------                   -------                       *
*         NUM1        INTEGER      THE GIVEN NUMBER                          *
*         NUM2        INTEGER      THE REVERSE OF THE GIVEN NUMBER           *
*         FSTDIG      INTEGER      FIRST DIGIT OF THE GIVEN NUMBER           *
*         SECDIG      INTEGER      SECOND DIGIT OF THE GIVEN NUMBER          *
*         THRDIG      INTEGER      THIRD DIGIT OF THE GIVEN NUMBER           *
*         FORDIG      INTEGER      FOURTH DIGIT OF THE GIVEN NUMBER          *
*         SUM         INTEGER      SUM OF THE DIGITS OF THE GIVEN NUMBER     *
*******************************************************************************
* DECLARATION
        INTEGER SUM,FSTDIG,SECDIG,THRDIG,FORDIG

* READ INPUT DATA
        PRINT *,'PLEASE TYPE IN THE 4 DIGITS NUMBER'
        READ *,NUM1

* INITIALIZATION
        SUM = 0
        NUM2 = 0
        NUM = NUM1

* PERFORM CALCULATIONS
        FORDIG = NUM - NUM / 10* 10
        NUM2 = NUM2 + FORDIG * 10**3
        SUM = SUM + FORDIG
        NUM = NUM / 10
*
        THRDIG = NUM - NUM / 10* 10
        NUM2 = NUM2 + THRDIG * 10**2
        SUM = SUM + THRDIG
        NUM = NUM / 10
*
        SECDIG = NUM - NUM / 10* 10
        NUM2 = NUM2 + SECDIG * 10
        SUM = SUM + SECDIG
        NUM = NUM / 10
*
        FSTDIG = NUM - NUM / 10* 10
        NUM2 = NUM2 + FSTDIG
        SUM = SUM + FSTDIG

* WRITE THE RESULTS
        PRINT*,'THE FIRST DIGIT OF THE NUMBER IS = ',FSTDIG
        PRINT*,'THE SECOND DIGIT OF THE NUMBER IS = ',SECDIG
        PRINT*,'THE THIRD DIGIT OF THE NUMBER IS = ',THRDIG
        PRINT*,'THE FOURTH DIGIT OF THE NUMBER IS = ',FORDIG
        PRINT*,'SUM OF THE DIGITS IN THE NUMBER IS = ',SUM
        PRINT*,'THE REVERSE NUMBER IS = ',NUM2
*
        STOP
        END
```

Figure 3.5: Program Listing of Example 3.2

Data Table for Example 3.2

Input Variables

NUMI: The given 4 digit number

Output Variables

SUM : Sum of the 4 digits

NUM2: The number in reverse order.

A program listing and the output of the above example are given in Fig. 3.5 and Fig. 3.6, respectively.

```
                              RUN I
WHAT IS THE 4 DIGITS NUMBER, PLEASE TYPE IN
1234
THE FIRST DIGIT OF THE NUMBER IS =               1
THE SECOND DIGIT OF THE NUMBER IS =               2
THE THIRD DIGIT OF THE NUMBER IS =               3
THE FOURTH DIGIT OF THE NUMBER IS =               4
SUM OF THE DIGITS IN THE NUMBER IS =              10
THE REVERSE NUMBER IS =         4321
```

```
                              RUN II
WHAT IS THE 4 DIGITS NUMBER, PLEASE TYPE IN
9876
THE FIRST DIGIT OF THE NUMBER IS =               9
THE SECOND DIGIT OF THE NUMBER IS =               8
THE THIRD DIGIT OF THE NUMBER IS =               7
THE FOURTH DIGIT OF THE NUMBER IS =               6
SUM OF THE DIGITS IN THE NUMBER IS =             30
THE REVERSE NUMBER IS =         6789
```

```
                              RUN III
WHAT IS THE 4 DIGITS NUMBER, PLEASE TYPE IN
1095
THE FIRST DIGIT OF THE NUMBER IS =               1
THE SECOND DIGIT OF THE NUMBER IS =               0
THE THIRD DIGIT OF THE NUMBER IS =               9
THE FOURTH DIGIT OF THE NUMBER IS =               5
SUM OF THE DIGITS IN THE NUMBER IS =             15
THE REVERSE NUMBER IS =         5901
```

Figure 3.6: Output Results of Example 3.2

Example 3.3

Given two sides and the included angle of a triangle, compute the other side, the other two angles and the area of the triangle.

This program requests data that specify the length of two sides and the included angle (in degrees) of a triangle. The value of the angle must be less than 180°. The program then computes the other side, the other two angles and the area of the triangle. Figure 3.7 shows a triangle whose two sides, a and b, are given and the included angle θ is given. It is required to calculate side c and angles α and β and the area of the triangle:

$$\text{side } c = (a^2+b^2-2ab \cos \theta)^{1/2}$$

$$\text{angle } \alpha = \cos^{-1}\left[\frac{c^2+b^2-a^2}{2bc}\right]$$

$$\text{angle } \beta = 180-(\alpha+\theta)$$

and

$$\text{area} = \tfrac{1}{2} ab \sin \theta$$

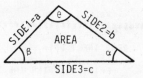

Figure 3.7

Data Table for Example 3.3

Input Variables	Output Variables
SIDE1 : Side a	SIDE3 : Side c
SIDE2 : Side b	ALPHA: Angle α
THETA: Angle θ	BETA : Angle β
	AREA : Area of the triangle.

A listing of a FORTRAN 77 program for the above example is shown in Figure 3.8, while the output results are shown in Figure 3.9.

3.15 ADDITIONAL DECLARATION STATEMENTS

Here is a brief description of declaration statements available with FORTRAN 77:

(1) DOUBLE PRECISION
(2) COMPLEX Constants and Variables
(3) LOGICAL Constants and Variables
(4) CHARACTER Constants and Variables
(5) The IMPLICIT Statement

3.15.1 Double Precision

On most computers, a real variable is accurate to seven or eight significant digits, depending on the wordlength of the machine. In some cases, there is a need for higher accuracy and more than eight significant digits are needed for calculating. In such cases, the double-precision feature of FORTRAN is employed to at least double the number of significant digits. The double-precision variable or constant name is declared by using a DOUBLE PRECISION type statement. Such a statement has a general form:

```
****************************************************************************
*    THIS PROGRAM ACCEPTS ANY TWO SIDES AND THE INCLUDED ANGLE OF A    *
*    TRIANGLE. IT THEN CALCULATES THE OTHER SIDE AND THE REMAINING TWO *
*    ANGLES. IT ALSO COMPUTES THE AREA OF THE TRIANGLE.                *
*    LIST OF VARIABLES:                                                 *
*        NAME         TYPE                 USAGE                        *
*        ------       ------               ------                      *
*        SIDE1        REAL          SIDE # 1                           *
*        SIDE2        REAL          SIDE # 2                           *
*        SIDE3        REAL          SIDE # 3                           *
*        THETA        REAL          ANGLE BETWEEN SIDE # 1 AND SIDE # 2 *
*        ALPHA        REAL          ANGLE BETWEEN SIDE # 2 AND SIDE # 3 *
*        BETA         REAL          ANGLE BETWEEN SIDE # 1 AND SIDE # 3 *
*        AREA         REAL          AREA OF THE TRIANGLE               *
*        PI           REAL          PIE = 22/7                         *
*        RADEGS       REAL          CONVERSION FACTOR, RADIANS PER DEGREE *
****************************************************************************

*    READ INPUT DATA

        PRINT *,'ENTER THE INPUT DATA'
        PRINT *,'SIDE # 1:'
        READ(5,*) SIDE1
        PRINT *,'SIDE # 2:'
        READ(5,*) SIDE2
        PRINT *,'ANGLE BETWEEN SIDE # 1 AND SIDE # 2:'
        READ(5,*) THETA

*    INITIALIZATION
        PI = 22.0 / 7.0
        RADEGS = PI / 180
*    PERFORM CALCULATIONS
        THETA = THETA * RADEGS
        SIDE3 = SQRT(SIDE1**2 + SIDE2**2 - 2*SIDE1*SIDE2*COS(THETA))
        ALPHA = ACOS((SIDE3**2 + SIDE2**2 - SIDE1**2)/(2*SIDE2*SIDE3))

        AREA = SIDE1 * SIDE2 * SIN(THETA) / 2

        THETA = THETA / RADEGS
        ALPHA = ALPHA / RADEGS
        BETA = 180 - THETA - ALPHA

*    WRITE THE RESULTS

        PRINT*,'THE RESULTS FOR THE TRIANGLE ARE:'
        PRINT*,'SIDE # 1:',SIDE1
        PRINT*,'SIDE # 2:',SIDE2
        PRINT*,'SIDE # 3:',SIDE3
        PRINT*,'ANGLE BETWEEN SIDE # 1 AND SIDE # 2 IS:',THETA
        PRINT*,'ANGLE BETWEEN SIDE # 2 AND SIDE # 3 IS:',ALPHA
        PRINT*,'ANGLE BETWEEN SIDE # 1 AND SIDE # 3 IS:',BETA
        PRINT*,'THE AREA OF THE TRIANGLE IS = ',AREA

        STOP
        END
```

Figure 3.8: Program Listing of Example 3.3

```
                        RUN I
ENTER THE INPUT DATA
SIDE # 1:
3.0
SIDE # 2:
4.0
ANGLE BETWEEN SIDE # 1 AND SIDE # 2:
90.0
THE RESULTS FOR THE TRIANGLE ARE:
SIDE # 1:    3.000000
SIDE # 2:    4.000000
SIDE # 3:    5.001517
ANGLE BETWEEN SIDE # 1 AND SIDE # 2 IS:    90.00000
ANGLE BETWEEN SIDE # 2 AND SIDE # 3 IS:    36.84203
ANGLE BETWEEN SIDE # 1 AND SIDE # 3 IS:    53.15797
THE AREA OF THE TRIANGLE IS =    5.999999
```

```
                       RUN II
ENTER THE INPUT DATA
SIDE # 1:
20.0
SIDE # 2:
25.5
ANGLE BETWEEN SIDE # 1 AND SIDE # 2:
64.8
THE RESULTS FOR THE TRIANGLE ARE:
SIDE # 1:    20.00000
SIDE # 2:    25.50000
SIDE # 3:    24.82691
ANGLE BETWEEN SIDE # 1 AND SIDE # 2 IS:    64.80000
ANGLE BETWEEN SIDE # 2 AND SIDE # 3 IS:    46.78920
ANGLE BETWEEN SIDE # 1 AND SIDE # 3 IS:    68.41080
THE AREA OF THE TRIANGLE IS =    230.7803
```

```
                       RUN III
ENTER THE INPUT DATA
SIDE # 1:
300.0
SIDE # 2:
409.0
ANGLE BETWEEN SIDE # 1 AND SIDE # 2:
120.0
THE RESULTS FOR THE TRIANGLE ARE:
SIDE # 1:    300.0000
SIDE # 2:    409.0000
SIDE # 3:    616.5712
ANGLE BETWEEN SIDE # 1 AND SIDE # 2 IS:    120.0000
ANGLE BETWEEN SIDE # 2 AND SIDE # 3 IS:    24.89842
ANGLE BETWEEN SIDE # 1 AND SIDE # 3 IS:    35.10158
THE AREA OF THE TRIANGLE IS =    53104.79
```

Figure 3.9: Output Results of Example 3.3

Examples

> DOUBLE PRECISION   list of variables
> DOUBLE PRECISION   THETA, MASS, BETA
> DOUBLE PRECISION   SUM, NUMBER, CONST

It should be noted that **DOUBLE PRECISION** affects only real numbers, not integer numbers. This feature does not exist for integers. In the above examples, MASS and NUMBER are double precision real variables although the first character of their names starts with M and N respectively.

There is also an exponential form for double precision constants. It is similar to the exponential form for real constants except that the character D is used in place of E.

Examples

> 12.0D + 8 has value 1200000000.00
> −0.25D − 02 has value −0.0025

In some computing machines, the one word **DOUBLE** may replace the pair of words **DOUBLE PRECISION**, but the effect is the same.

3.15.2 Complex Constants and Variables

A single complex number, in fact, comprises of two parts, one of which is the real part and the other, the imaginary part of the complex value. The general form of a complex number is $X + iY$ where X and Y are real, and $i^2 = -1$ so $i = \sqrt{-1}$. A FORTRAN complex constant of the complex number $X + iY$ is written as follows:

> (X,Y)

Examples

FORTRAN Constants	Value
(3.0, 4.0)	$3.0 + i4.0$
(2.3,–4.0)	$2.3 - i4.0$
(0.2,I)	Not valid, I is not a constant
3.0, 4.0	Not valid, parentheses are required
(3,4)	Not valid, Integers are not allowed

Before a complex variable can be processed in a FORTRAN program, it must be explicitly declared. An appropriate FORTRAN type statement to declare variables as complex variables is:

> COMPLEX THETA, VOLTAG, CURRNT

Complex numbers and complex variables are frequently encountered in complex algebra and in Electrical Engineering.

3.15.3 Logical Constants and Variables

A logical entity is one that can be either true or false. In FORTRAN, two logical entities—*logical constants* and *variables*—are commonly used. Logical entities are also known as *Boolean entities*. There are only two logical constants, represented as .TRUE. and .FALSE.. A logical variable can have either of the two values. An appropriate FORTRAN-type statement that declares variables as logical variables is:

LOGICAL FOUND, SEARCH, FLAG, CHECK

The above type statement specifies that FOUND, SEARCH, FLAG and CHECK are variables of the logical type. The only value that each of them can have is either .TRUE. or .FALSE.. Applications involving logical data are considered in subsequent chapters.

3.15.4 Character Constants and Variables

A character is a single letter (A. . . Z), digit (0. . . 9), or symbol (+ −*/, etc.). The collection of all the characters that a computer can represent is called the computer's *character set*. A *character string* is a sequence of one or more characters. A *character constant* in FORTRAN is a character string enclosed in apostrophes or single quotes ('). For example:

'XYZ'

is a character constant representing the character string XYZ. The number of characters in a character string is called the *length*. The 'XYZ' has length 3. Some more examples of valid character constants are:

Character string	length
'YOU'	3
'YOUƀARE'	7
'$2 =TEN'	6

Like integer and real variables which store integer and real values respectively, a character variable stores a *character string value*. The type statement to declare variables to be character variables is:

CHARACTER X*1, NAME*10

This statement declares variables X and NAME to be of type character. The length of X is 1 character while the length of NAME is 10 characters. It means that the variable X can store a character string whose length is one while the variable NAME can store a character string having a maximum length of ten. Some more examples of valid character type declarations are:

CHARACTER*5 X,Y,Z

Here, each character variable X,Y and Z has a length 5.

CHARACTER A*10, B*2, C*7

Here, the variables A, B and C are of character type having length 10, 2 and 7, respectively.

A detailed discussion on character constants, variables and their manipulations has been given in Chapter 8.

3.15.5 The Implicit Statement

In programs that make extensive use of integers and/or real variables, it becomes cumbersome to declare each variable in explicit mode (type REAL or INTEGER) declaration statements. For this reason, the IMPLICIT declaration statement allows you to declare the type of variables by specifying that names beginning with certain letters be of a certain type. Individual letters are given in parentheses. A range of letters can be specified by giving the first and last letters separated by a minus (−) sign. For instance, the statement

IMPLICIT REAL (I), INTEGER (A−E), LOGICAL (F−H, Z)

would cause all variable names beginning with I as real variable names, all those beginning with A, B, C, D, or E as integer variable names and all those beginning with F, G, H, or Z as logical. Variable names beginning with any letter not appearing in the IMPLICIT statement are covered by the usual I through N convention. Thus, in this example, names beginning with J, K, L, M and N will be integer names.

The general form of the IMPLICIT statement is:

IMPLICIT type (x, [,x] . . .) [, type (x [,x] . . .)] . . .

where

type specifies any of the permissible type variables, such as REAL, INTEGER, COMPLEX etc.

x   is a single alphabetic letter or a range of letters denoted by x_1-x_2, where x_1 and x_2 are single letters of the alphabet, x_1 and x_2 must be in alphabetic order. For example Q−M is not allowed.

The IMPLICIT statement must be the first of all the type declaration statements. This statement may not be available with all the FORTRAN compilers.

An explicit type statement will override the effect of an IMPLICIT statement. For instance, the statements

IMPLICIT INTEGER (A−C), REAL (M−N)
REAL   ALL, CAT
INTEGER   NUMBER

declare ALL and CAT as real variables even though the IMPLICIT statement declares variables beginning with A, B, or C as interger variables. Similarly, NUMBER is an integer variable.

3.16 SUMMARY

This chapter has introduced FORTRAN 77 statements necessary to write simple programs. A brief discussion of simple input and output statements, parameter statement, the termination and/or interruption statements that are necessary in the compilation and execution of a FORTRAN program and the type statements is given in this chapter. The application of most of these statements has been illustrated by some simple example programs.

By now you must have acquired sufficient skills to write simple FORTRAN programs. Rather than going on to more complex programs and getting involved in the complexities of large programs, the user should write many small programs. The programming exercises given in this chapter are structured with this in mind. The objective questions and the drill exercises are given to help the user assess his/her understanding of the basic features of FORTRAN.

Having gone through the subject content and the exercises of this chapter carefully, it will be desirable to develop some of the more powerful statements that exist in FORTRAN and to use them to write more complex programs. This will be the purpose of subsequent chapters.

OBJECTIVES QUESTIONS

(1) Which of the following constants does not represent a real number ?
  (a) 99.0E0
  (b) 99.
  (c) −99.000
  (d) 99
  (e) 9.9E + 01
(2) Which of the following is a grammatically correct integer variable identifier ?
  (a) LOT — TERY
  (b) IN*DIG
  (c) K123
  (d) 123K
  (e) RAT
(3) Which of the following is a grammatically correct real variable identifier ?
  (a) BANG + LORE
  (b) NEWDEL
  (c) BOMBAY
  (d) JN 420$
  (e) REAL A
(4) Which of the following declaration statements is valid ?
  (a) REAL   LUNG, ISA, MOON
     INTEGER PAY, COUNTR, ANGLE, THETA
  (b) REAL   INTEGER
     INTEGER REAL, COUNTER
  (c) REAL   LUNG, ISA, MOON,
     INTEGER PAY, COUNTER, ANGLE, THETA
  (d) REAL   1,2
     INTEGER 1.0, 2.0

(e) REAL   LUNG, ISA, MOON
     INTEGER PAY, COUNTER, LUNG, ANGLE

(5) Which of the following assignment statements results in the real number 2.5 being stored in memory location ALOC to machine accuracy ?

(a) ALOC = 5/2

(b) ALOC = 5./2./1./0.

(c) ALOC = 1 + 3/2

(d) ALOC = 2.0*1.24999999

(e) ALOC = 3/1.5 + 5/2.0

(6) If X = 1.0, Y = 2.0, I = 1, J = 2, which of the following expressions results in a 0.0 value ?

(a) J−2* I

(b) X/Y−I/J

(c) I/J

(d) X*I/J

(e) Y−J*X

(7) Which of the following FORTRAN expressions is not correct for writing

$$\frac{A}{C} - \frac{B}{D} \; ?$$

(a) ((A/C) − (B/D))

(b) A/C − B/D

(c) (A*D − B*C)/(C*D)

(d) (A − B*C/D)/C

(e) (A/C − B)/D

(8) Which of following is correctly represented by the FORTRAN statement (A/(C + B/D))−E ?

(a) $\dfrac{A}{C + B/D} - E$

(b) $\dfrac{A}{\dfrac{C + B}{D}} - E$

(c) $\dfrac{A}{C + \dfrac{B}{D} - E}$

(d) $\dfrac{A - E}{C + B/D}$

(e) $\dfrac{A}{C} + \dfrac{B}{D} - E$

(9) Which of the following is not a valid FORTRAN 77 BUILT-IN function ?

(a) DEXP

(b) ALOG

(c) CCOS

(d) INTEGR

(e) SQRT

(10) Which of the following I/0 statements is invalid ?

(a) ACCEPT*,A

(b) PRINT, *,A

(c) READ*, A, B, C, I, F, FORT

(d) TYPE*, A, B, C, I, F, FORT/A

(e) WRITE (6,*), A, B, C, I, F, FORT*A

(11) Which of the following FORTRAN 77 program segments is invalid?
   (a) ACCEPT*, A
      TYPE*, A
      STOP
      END
   (b) INTEGER A
      READ*, A
      STOP
      END
   (c) PARAMETER (IN = 5, OUT = 6)
      READ (IN, *),
      WRITE (OUT, *)A
      STOP
      END
   (d) ACCEPT*, B, A
      PRINT*, A/B
      STOP
      END
   (e) REAL A
      READ*, A
      STOP
      END

(12) Which of the following statements is true?
   (a) Integer variables that have not been explicitly declared must start with one of the letters I, J, K, L, M or N.
   (b) The statement STOP denotes the physical end of the program.
   (c) 1.0/2/3 evaluates to the same as 1.0/(2/3).
   (d) X = *(X) + 1 is a valid assignment statement.
   (e) X + Y = Z is a valid assignment statement.

(13) Which of the following are valid complex constants?
   (a) (0.0)
   (b) (6,4)
   (c) 3.0,2.0
   (d) (X,Y)
   (e) (3.0, − 4.77)

(14) Which of the following statements is false?
   (a) Double precision numbers also exist for integers.
   (b) The statement DOUBLE PRECISION X, Y, Z is valid.
   (c) The statement LOGICAL KK, I, J is valid.
   (d) The statement CHARACTER*5 DIE, BORN is valid.
   (e) A logical variable can have a value either .TRUE. or .FALSE.

(15) Which of the following constants is invalid?
   (a) '123*'
   (b) 123
   (c) A
   (d) (2.0, − 4.0)
   (e) (9.9E − 01,2.4)

(16) Fill in the blanks:
   (a) In a FORTRAN statement, columns one through five are used for—————, column six is used for—————, and the actual statement must be placed within columns—————through—————.
   (b) All declaration statements must appear before any—————statement.
   (c) An END statement is the—————–end of a program and it must be the——————statement of a program.

(d) A STOP statement is the————end of a program and it can appear———————in the program but before————statement.

(e) A variable can appear in only————type statement.

(f) Comments and blank lines in a program are————–statements and are generally used for enhancing the————of a program.

(g) Nested parenthesized subexpressions must be evaluated———————, with the————subexpression evaluated last.

(h) With real exponents, the number to be raised must be a————number.

(i) A FORTRAN variable must not contain more than————characters and the first character must be an————.

(j) It is————if the same variable appears on both sides of the equal (=) sign in a FORTRAN statement.

DRILL EXERCISES

(1) Identify the following numbers as valid or invalid FORTRAN constants. Represent valid constants as both integer and real constants:

(a) $-12{,}345$

(b) 8.0

(c) 99.99×10^2

(c) 10^{15}

(2) Write FORTRAN expressions to perform the following algebraic operations:

(a) $r + \dfrac{st}{u - v}$

(b) $k^2 + \left(\dfrac{nm}{2_i}\right)^{jk}$

(c) $\cos (r) + \dfrac{(ut)^4}{1 - v}$

(d) $\sqrt[4]{(x^2 + y^2 + 2^2)^3}$

(e) $e^{up} + \sqrt{DOWN} + \cos (FIRST)$

(f) $\log_{10} (x^2)/\ln(y^2)$

(3) If $I = 1, J = 2, A = 2, B = 3$, evaluate the following FORTRAN expressions:

(a) $- A**J + 3.5*I$

(b) $(A**J + 4.5)*I$

(c) $J**(-2) + 3*(I - 1)$

(d) $B/(J + A**I**2)$

(e) $A + B/J + I/J$

(f) $(A + B)/J + I$

(g) $(A + B)/(I + J)$

(h) $A + B/(1 + J)$

(4) Identify the error(s) in each of the following arithmetic assignment statements:

(a) $A = I**B$

(b) $Z = 29Y$

(c) $A = B + 3 = C + 4$

(d) $A*B = I**2$

(e) $3IJ = X - Y$

(f) $X = 2{,}000*A - (Y + Z)*4.$

(g) $C = 1.0 - E4* \pi$

(h) $\theta = 30 + B/A + C$

(i) $X + Y + Z$

(5) What values will be assigned to A and B as a result of the following statements:

(a) $A = 5.0$
$B = 99.0$
$B = B - A**4$
$A = A - B$

(b) $A = 10.0$
$B = 20.0$
$Z = A$
$B = A$
$A = B$

(c) A = 3.0
   B = 4.0
   Z = B
   B = A
   A = Z
(d) I = 5
   J = 6
   A = J/I
   B = I/J
   I = A + B + A*J/I*4
   A = I
   B = A/I + I*A/(J/I)

(6) Determine the value of the following expressions, given

X = .TRUE., Y = .FALSE., Z = (3.0,4.0), W = (− 1.0,2.0), assuming that X and Y are declared logical variables and Z and W are declared as complex variables:

U = X
V = Y
P = Z + W
Q = Z − P
R = Z*W
C = Q/Z

Determine the type of other Variables. Should they be declared in the program?

(7) A FORTRAN 77 program that computes the net salary of a person has been written as follows:

Column #   123456789......

```
      C     PROGRAM TO CACULATE NET SALARY
      C     GROSS = GROSS SALARY
            TAX = TAX PAID BY THE PERSON
      C     NET PAY = GROSS SALARY − TAX
      C     PROGRAM BEGINS
            REAL NET PAY GROSS, TAX
            ACCEPT*, GROSS*TAX
            NET PAY = GR*SS − TAX
            TYPE*, 'GROSS PAY = , GROSS
            TYPE, 'TAX = ', GROSS
            PRINT*, 'NET PAY OF THE PERSON', NET
      STOP
                        END
```

The program contains many syntax errors. Detect these errors and modify the program so that it computes the salary of the person correctly.

PROGRAMMING EXERCISES

(1) Write a FORTRAN 77 program to calculate the area of a triangle whose sides are a, b and c. The area of a triangle is given by

$$\text{area} = \sqrt{s(s − a)(s − b)(s − c)}$$

where $s = (a + b + c)/2$

(2) Write a FORTRAN 77 program to calculate the sum of the following series:

$$S = 1 + x + \frac{x^2}{2} + \frac{x^3}{3} + \frac{x^4}{4} + \frac{x^5}{5}.$$

(3) Write a FORTRAN 77 program to compute the average and the standard deviation of three real numbers x, y, and z. The formulae to calculate average and standard derivations are:

$$average = (x + y + x)/3$$

$$standard\ deviation = \sqrt{\{(x - avg)^2 + (y - avg)^2 + (z - avg)^2\}/3}$$

where avg is the average value.

(4) John borrowed a sum of $ 1,000,000 from a bank. The loan is to be paid in equal monthly instalments over a period of 30 years. The rate of interest is 20 % per annum. Write a FORTRAN 77 program to find out the amount of the first instalment and the interest paid by John. The formula for the regular instalment on a loan is given by:

$$R = \frac{ip/n}{1 - \left(\dfrac{i}{n} + 1\right)^{-ny}}$$

where

i = Absolute interest rate (not percentage)
p = Principal amount borrowed
n = Number of payments per year
y = Number of years
R = Regular instalment

and the amount of interest in the first instalment is given by ip/n.

(5) Write a FORTRAN 77 program to convert the weight of a person into kilograms from pounds.

(6) Write a FORTRAN 77 program that accepts a single value RADIUS, and then calculates and prints

  (i) the area of a circle having the given radius .(Area = πr^2)

  (ii) the volume of a sphere having the given radius.

$\left(\text{Volume} = \dfrac{4}{3}\ \pi r^3, \text{ where } \pi = 22/7 \text{ and r is the RADIUS.}\right)$

ANSWERS TO OBJECTIVE QUESTIONS

(1) d;	(2) c;	(3) c;
(4) a;	(5) d;	(6) e;
(7) e;	(8) a;	(9) d;
(10) b;	(11) c;	(12) a;
(13) e;	(14) a;	(15) c.

(16) (a) Statement label, continuation, 7, 72
  (b) Executable
  (c) Physical, very last
  (d) Logical, anywhere, END
  (e) One
  (f) Non-executable, clarity and readability
  (g) Inside-out, outermost
  (h) Non-negative
  (i) Six, alphabet
  (j) Valid/legal

Chapter 4

Control Structures

4.1 INTRODUCTION

In the programming exercises of the previous chapter, readers must have noticed that a FORTRAN program is executed statement after statement in sequence, until the last statement STOP is encountered. This simple "once-through" flow of program execution can be too restrictive in solving a variety of problems. In many situations, the programmer would like to skip certain statements in the program under one set of conditions, or execute those statements under another set of conditions. In many other situations, the programmer would like to repeatedly execute a segment of the program for a fixed number of times or until a specified condition is met. FORTRAN 77 provides the user with many techniques to control the logical flow of the program. The main objective of this chapter is to familiarize readers with control statements that are used in a FORTRAN structured program.

In a structured program, the logical flow is governed by three basic control structures:

1. Sequential
2. Selection or Decision
3. Repetition.

Sequential structure, as shown in Figure 4.1, refers to the execution of statements in the order in which they appear. The programming exercises of Chapter 3 are based on sequential structure. The other two control structures are discussed at length in this chapter.

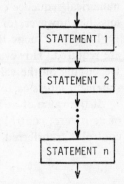

Figure 4.1: Sequential Structure

4.2 SELECTION OR DECISION STRUCTURE

The selection structure makes possible the selection and execution of one of a number of alternative actions. This enables the programmer to introduce decision points in program, that is, points at which a decision is made

75

during program execution to follow one of several courses of action. FORTRAN 77 features that allow the implementation of selection structures are IF statements. The three types of IF statements are:

(i) Arithmetic IF
(ii) Logical IF
(iii) Block IF (IF THEN, ELSE IF THEN, ELSE, END IF)

For each type, the decision to transfer control or to execute the statement or block of statements is based on the evaluation of an expression (arithmetic expression in the case of arithmetic IF and logical/relational expression in the cases of Logical IF and Block IF) within an IF statement. It must be noted that in structured programming, use of Arithmetic IF and/or Logical IF is not preferable, so only Block IF should be used. We will, however, include a brief description of both Arithmetic and Logical IF statements.

4.2.1 Arithmetic IF Statement

The arithmetic IF statement is a conditional transfer statement which evaluates the value of an arithmetic expression and transfers control to one of the three statements depending on the value or the algebraic sign of the arithmetic expression. The arithmetic IF statement has the form:

IF (ae) S1, S2, S3

where

ae is an arithmetic expression, and

S1, S2 and S3 are labels of executable statements or statement numbers.

A statement number is a positive integer ranging from 1 to 99999. To number or label a statement, the statement number can appear anywhere in columns one through five of the statement line. It is not necessary to maintain a numerical sequence of statement numbers in a program unit. It is not permissible, however, for any two statements to have the same statement number.

In an arithmetic IF statement all three numbers (labels), S1, S2 and S3, are required. However, they need not refer to three different statements. Depending on the value of ae, the control is transferred to one of the three statement labels as follows:

If the value of ae is less than zero, control passes to label S1. If the value of ae is zero, control goes to label S2. If the value of ae is greater than zero, control is transferred to label S3. This is illustrated in Figure 4.2.

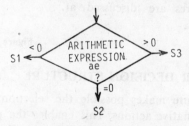

Figure 4.2: Arithmetic IF statement

Example (a)

IF (X–Y) 100, 200, 40

If X is less than Y, this statement transfer control to statement 100. If X is exactly equal to Y, the control is transferred to statement 200 and if X is greater than Y, then the control passes to statement 40.

Example (b)

IF (I–J) 10, 50, 50

This statement transfers control to statement 10 if I is less than J and to statement 50 if I is equal to or greater than J.

Example (c)

IF (Z) 100, 200, 100

This statement transfers control to statement 100 if Z is either negative or positive, i.e. the value of Z is either less than or greater than zero. If Z is equal to zero, control is transferred to statement 200.

4.2.2 Logical IF Statement

A logical IF statement employs a logical expression or a relational expression. It conditionally executes a single FORTRAN statement, depending on the value of a logical expression. The logical IF statement has a general form:

IF (e) S

where

e is a relational or logical expression, and
S is any statement except another logical IF statement, an arithmetic IF statement (allowable in some versions), a block IF statement, or a DO statement. (The DO statement is discussed later in this chapter.)

The logical IF statement first evaluates the expression e. If the value of the expression is true, statement S is executed and then the next statement following the logical IF statement is executed unless the statement S itself is an arithmetic IF statement (if allowed) or a GO TO statement (discussed later in this chapter) which would modify the normal sequence of execution. If e is false, control transfers to the next executable statement after the logical IF statement and statement S is not executed. This is illustrated in Figure, 4.3.

Before considering some examples, we must acquaint ourselves with relational and logical expressions.

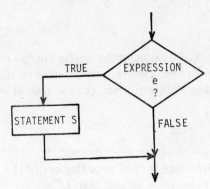

Figure 4.3: Logical IF Statement

4.2.2.1 *Relational Expressions*

Relational expressions involve a comparison of arithmetic expressions, the result of which can be only TRUE or FALSE. A relational expression has the form

    ae1 ro ae2

where

    ae1 and ae2 are two arithmetic expressions, and

    ro is a *relational operator*. A list of relational operators allowed in FORTRAN is given in Table 4.1.

Table 4.1: Relational Operators

Relational Operator in FORTRAN	Mathematical Symbol	Meaning
.LT.	$<$	Less than
.LE.	$\leq$	Less than or equal to
.EQ.	$=$	Equal to
.GT.	$>$	Greater than
.GE.	$\geqslant$	Greater than or equal to
.NE.	$\neq$	Not equal to

Examples of relational expressions:

    Let X = 2.0, Y = 4.0, I = 1 and J = 3 then

X.LT.Y	is true, because	$2.0 < 4.0$;
I.EQ.J	is false, because	$1 \neq 3$;
X.GT.Y/J	is true, because	$2.0 > 4.0/3$ or $2.0 > 1.333$;
(X*J) .EQ. (X+Y)	is true, because	$(2.0*3) = (2.0+4.0)$
X.LT.J	is true, because	$2.0 < 3$. In this example, the type of

arithmetic expressions differs because ae1 is real while ae2 is of integer type. In such a situation the relational expression is evaluated as

    (ae1−ae2) ro 0 (Zero)

where the type transformation rule applies to the arithmetic expression (ae1−ae2). If any of the terms involved is real, then the value of the expression is real, otherwise the value is of integer type. The value of 0 (zero) is of the same type as the type of the expression. The following are mixed mode expressions:

(X+Y).GT. (J+I)*J is false, because ((2.0+4.0)−(3+1)*3) .GT.0
or (−6.0.GT.0.0)   is false.
(Y/X.EQ. (J−I))   is true, because (4.0/2.0−(3−1)) .EQ.0 or
or (0.0 .EQ. 0.0)   is true.

When using the relational operators = (.EQ.) and ≠ (.NE.) to compare numeric quantities, it is important to remember that most real values cannot be stored exactly. As a result, relational expressions formed by comparing real quantities with .EQ. are often evaluated as false, even though these quantities are algebraically equal. This is illustrated by a simple progarm given in Figure 4.4.

4.2.2.2 *Logical Expressions*

A logical expression is formed by combining logical constants, logical variables, relational expressions and logical operators. The value of a logical expression is again either FALSE or TRUE. A list of logical operators allowed in FORTRAN is given in Table 4.2.

Table 4.2: Logical Operators

Logical Operator in FORTRAN	Logical Expression	Meaning
.NOT.	.NOT. re1	Negation of re1: .NOT. re1 is false if re1 is true and vice-versa.
.AND.	re1 .AND. re2	Conjunction of re1 and re2: re1 .AND. re2 is true if both re1 and re2 are true; it is false otherwise.
.OR.	re1 .OR. re2	Disjunction of re1 and re2: re1 .OR. re2 is true if either re1 or re2 or both are true; it is false otherwise.
.EQV.	re1 .EQV. re2	Equivalence of re1 and re2: re1 .EQV. re2 is true if both re1 and re2 are either true or false; it is false otherwise.
.NEQV.	re1 .NEQV. re2	Nonequivalence of re1 and re2: re1 .NEQV. re2 is true if either re1 is true and re2 is false or if either re1 is false and re2 is true: it is false otherwise. It is negation of equivalence .EQV.

```
***********************************************************************
*        THIS PROGRAM SHOWS INEXACT REPRESENTATION OF REALS          *
***********************************************************************
*
        INTEGER INLUN,OUTLUN
        PARAMETER (INLUN = 5, OUTLUN = 6)
* READ A NUMBER A
        WRITE(OUTLUN,*)' ENTER A REAL NUMBER'
        READ(INLUN,*)A
*
        B=A*0.33333356/0.33333356*0.00004667/0.00004667
* WRITE BOTH NUMBERS A & B
        WRITE(OUTLUN,*)' A=',A,' B=',B,' A-B=',A-B
        IF(B.EQ.A)WRITE(OUTLUN,*)' B IS EXACTLY EQUAL TO A'
        IF(B.NE.A)WRITE(OUTLUN,*)' B IS NOT EXACTLY EQUAL TO A'
        STOP
        END
***********************************************************************
```

RUN I

```
ENTER A REAL NUMBER
0.5
 A= 0.5000000      B= 0.5000000      A-B= 0.0000000E+00
B IS EXACTLY EQUAL TO A
```

RUN II

```
ENTER A REAL NUMBER
0.444
 A= 0.4440000      B= 0.4440000      A-B= -2.9802322E-08
B IS NOT EXACTLY EQUAL TO A
```

RUN III.

```
ENTER A REAL NUMBER
0.5567
 A= 0.5567000      B= 0.5567000      A-B= 0.0000000E+00
B IS EXACTLY EQUAL TO A
```

RUN IV

```
ENTER A REAL NUMBER
0.33333
 A= 0.3333300      B= 0.3333300      A-B= -2.9802322E-08
B IS NOT EXACTLY EQUAL TO A
```

Figure 4.4: Program Listing and Results to Show Inexact Representation of Reals

These meanings of logical operators are illustrated by the following truth tables, shown in Table 4.3, which display all possible values of expressions re1 and re2 and the corresponding values of the logical expression.

Table 4.3: Truth Tables for Logical Operators

re1	re2	.NOT. re1	re1 .AND. re2	re1 .OR. re2	re1 .EQV. re2	re1 .NEQV. re2
true	true	false	true	true	true	false
true	false	false	false	true	false	true
false	true	true	false	true	false	true
false	false	true	false	false	true	false

The *negation operator* (.NOT.) is a *unary operator* because it is used with only one relational expression. All other operators are *binary operators* since they are used with two relational expressions.

The hierarchy of the logical operators in the absence of parentheses is as follows:

1. .NOT.
2. .AND.
3. .OR.
4. .EQV. and .NEQV.

By using parentheses the hierarchy can be altered as in the case of arithmetic expressions. Operations at the same level are evaluated left to right. Logical operators have lower priority than relational operators when both are used in the same expression. Here are a few examples of logical operators:

Example

Consider the following program segment:

```
LOGICAL FOUND, SEARCH
FOUND = .TRUE.
SEARCH = .FALSE.
 I = 5
X = 2.0
Y = 5.0
```

then the following logical expressions are evaluated;

Logical Expression	Value
(i) (I .GT. X) .AND. FOUND	.TRUE.
(ii) .NOT. SEARCH .NEQV. (I*X .GT. Y)	.FALSE.
(iii) .FALSE. .OR. SEARCH	.FALSE.
(iv) (I .EQ. Y) .EQV. (Y .GT. I/X)	.TRUE.
(v) ((I .GT. X) .AND. (Y .NE. X)) .OR. (SEARCH)	.TRUE.

An expression may contain arithmetic, relational and logical operators. A summary of the rules for hierarchical precedence of these operators is as follows:

1. Expressions inside the parentheses are evaluated first. For a multiple set of (embedded) parentheses, the order is from innermost to outermost. The precedence levels for operators are as follows:

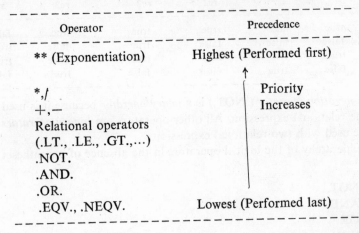

Operator	Precedence
** (Exponentiation)	Highest (Performed first)
*,/	
+,−	Priority Increases
Relational operators (.LT., .LE., .GT.,...)	
.NOT.	
.AND.	
.OR.	
.EQV., .NEQV.	Lowest (Performed last)

Operators at the same hierarchical level are performed left to right except for successive exponentiation operations, which are peformed right to left. The following examples illustrate precedence rules:

Example (a)

If A = 25.0, B = 30.0, I = 4 and J = 2, then the expression (A+B .LT. B*J .OR. I .LT. J .AND. A .NE. B/I) is evaluated as shown below:

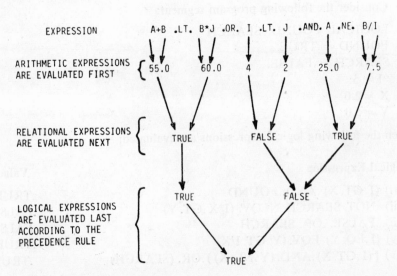

Example (b)

X/Y*Z+A .EQ. B .OR. I .GE. J**K**L .AND. I/5.0 .GT. X+Y.EQV..
.TRUE.

First of all, the arithmetic expressions are evaluated as follows:

(i)   X/Y*Z+A   as ((X/Y)*Z)+A = a
(ii) J**K**L   as J**(K**L)   = b
(iii) I/5.0   as (I/5.0)   = c
(iv) X+Y   as (X+Y)   = d

The expression can be now written in a simplified form as

a .EQ. B .OR. I .GE. b .AND. c .GT. d .EQV. .TRUE.

The relational operators are evaluated next, as shown below:

(i)   a .EQ. B = e (either true or false)
(ii) I .GE. b = f (either true or false)
(iii) c .GT. d = g (either true or false)

The expression can now be written as:

e .OR. f .AND. g .EQV. .TRUE.

The logical operators are evaluated last of all, as shown below:

(i)   f .AND. g   = h (either false or true)
(ii) e .OR. h   = i (either false or true)
(iii) i .EQV. .TRUE. = j (either false or true) Final Result.

Examples of Logical IF Statement

Example (a)

IF (I .GT. 4 .AND. J .EQ. K) BIG = A

If I is greater than 4 and J is equal to K, then the expression is true and BIG will be equal to A.

Example (b)

IF (N .NE. 4) GO TO 100

If N is not equal to 4, then control is transferred to statement 100. GO TO is a transfer statement which is described in a latter section.

Example (c)

IF (.NOT. FOUND) WRITE (1,100)

If .NOT. FOUND is true i.e. logical variable FOUND is false, then WRITE statement is executed.

Example (d)

IF ((X .GT. Y .OR. Y .LE. Z) .AND. (I .EQ. 3)) X = Y

If X is greater than Y or Y is less than or equal to Z and I is equal to 3, then X is assigned the same value as that of Y.

4.2.3 Block IF Statement

In a logical IF statement, if the expression is true, a single statement is executed. However, if there is more than one statement to be executed, one has to use GO TO statements. A more powerful IF statement is a *block IF statement*. The block IF statement is a special feature of FORTRAN 77 and is quite useful. Both arithmetic IF and logical IF statements can be simulated using a block IF statement. A general form of the block IF statement is:

        IF (1e) THEN
            block₁
        ELSE
            block₂
        END IF

where

1e is a logical expression,

block is a sequence of zero or more executable FORTRAN statements.

While typing a program using a block IF statement, the IF (1e) THEN construct must be on one line, the word ELSE must be on a separate line by itself, and the word END IF (or ENDIF i.e. no blank space between END and IF) must be on a single line too. The flow of control in a block IF construct is shown in Figure 4.5.

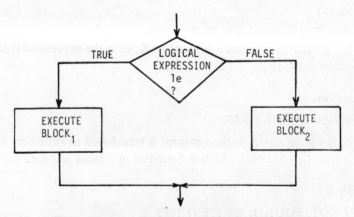

Figure 4.5: Block IF Statement (IF-THEN-ELSE)

The block IF statement is executed as follows:

Step (1) The logical expression (1e) is executed.

Step (2) If the logical expression (1e) is true, block₁ is executed and then control is transferred to the statement following the END IF, and therefore block₂ is not executed.

Step (3) If the 1e is false, then block₂ is executed and block₁ is skipped. Again on completion of the execution of block₂ the control is transferred to the statement following the END IF.

The following examples illustrate the block IF statement:

Example (a)

Consider the following program segment:

```
IF (MARKS .LE. 40) THEN
     WRITE (5,*), 'FAILED'   ! block₁
ELSE
     WRITE (5,*), 'PASSED'   ! block₂
END IF
```

If MARKS = 30, then expression (MARKS .LE. 40) is true, so block₁ is executed and the word FAILED is typed. If MARKS = 70, then the expression is false, so block₂ is executed and PASSED is typed.

Example (b)

Consider the following program segment:

```
IF(MAX.LT.NUMBER) THEN
     MAX = NUMBER
     NUMBER = NUMBER-1
ELSE
     MAX = NUMBER/2
END IF
```

Block₁ consists of two statements while block₂ consists of only one statement. If MAX is less than NUMBER, then block₁ is executed, MAX is assigned to the same value as that of NUMBER and NUMBER is decremented by 1. If MAX is less than NUMBER, block₂ is executed and MAX is equal to NUMBER/2.

A simpler form of the block IF statement is obtained by omitting ELSE block if it is not required. The form of the modified IF statement will be:

```
IF(le) THEN
     block₁
END IF
```

Block₂ is not present in this form and it contains only THEN block. The flow of control in this construct is shown in Figure 4.6.

In this case, Step (3) of IF-THEN-ELSE construct is not performed.

The following examples illustrate the IF-THEN construct:

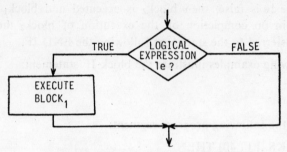

Figure 4.6: Block IF Statement (IF-THEN)

Example (a)

Consider the following program segment:

```
IF((I.GT.J).AND.(X.NE.Y)) THEN
    I = J+5
    Y = X
    J = I/2
END IF
```

If the logical expression is true, i.e., I is greater than J and X is not equal to Y, then the statement block is executed; I is equal to J+5, Y is assigned the value of X and J is equal to I/2. If the logical expression is false, then control transfers to the next executable statement after the END IF, and the block is not executed.

Example (b)

Consider the following program segment:

```
I = 5
IF(I.GE.1) THEN
    WRITE(5,*),I,I**4
    I = I–1
END IF
```

The value of I is 5, so the expression is true and therefore statements within IF-THEN block are executed. On the CRT terminal, 5 and 625 will appear and the value of I is then decreased by 1.

Readers must note that in a block IF statement, THEN block must be present while ELSE block may or may not be present.

4.2.4 Multialternative Selection Structure and Nested IF Statements

The logical IF and block IF statements considered in the preceding section involve selecting one of two alternatives. It is also possible to use the block IF construct to design selection structures that contain more than two alternatives. An arithmetic IF statement is a three-way selection structure in which selection is made depending on the algebraic value of the arithmetic expression.

Example

Consider the following program segment containing an arithmetic IF statement:

    IF(MARKS–60)10,20,30
    10 WRITE(5,*),'MARKS OBTAINED ARE LESS THAN 60'
    20 WRITE(5,*),'MARKS OBTAINED ARE EQUAL TO 60'
    30 WRITE(5,*),'MARKS OBTAINED ARE GREATER THAN 60'

The above program segment can be written with a block IF statement as:

    IF(MARKS.LT,60) THEN
        WRITE(5,*),'MARKS OBTAINED ARE LESS THAN 60'
    ELSE IF(MARKS.EQ.60) THEN
        WRITE(5,*),'MARKS OBTAINED ARE EQUAL TO 60'
    ELSE
        WRITE(5,*),'MARKS OBTAINED ARE GREATER THAN 60'
    END IF

This construct is an extension of the IF-THEN-ELSE construct. The ELSE block may not be present in such a construct. A general n-way selection construct is of the form:

    IF (lel) THEN
        block₁
    ELSE IF (le2) THEN
        block₂
    ELSE IF (le3) THEN
        block₃
        ⋮
    ELSE
        blockₙ
    END IF

If lel is true only block₁ is executed. The control is transferred to the statement following the END IF. If lel is false then one of the blocks, block₂, ...,blockₙ, is executed depending upon which expression is true. If le2 is true, then block₂ is executed; if le3 is true, block₃ is executed and so on... . If none of the conditions is true, then blockₙ is executed. In each case after block execution, control is transferred to the statement following the END IF. The flow of control in this construct is shown in Figure 4.7.

Such compound IF statements may be quite complex, and the correspondence between IFs and ELSEs may not be easily clear. A clear correspondence can be obtained while writing a program if indentation is used properly. The following example illustrates the use of a five-way block IF construct with a clear indentation.

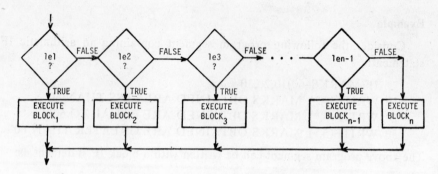

Figure 4.7: n–way Block IF Construct

Example

Consider the following program segment:

```
MIN = I
IF(I.GT.J) THEN
    MIN = J
ELSE IF (I.GT.K) THEN
    MIN = K
ELSE IF(I.GT.L) THEN
    MIN = L
ELSE IF(I.GT.M) THEN
    MIN = M
ELSE
    MIN = 0
END IF
```

If I is greater than J, MIN is assigned the value of J. If I is not greater than J but greater than K, then MIN is assigned the value of K. If I is not greater than J or K but greater than L, then MIN is assigned the value of L. If I is not greater than J, K or L but greater than M, then MIN is assigned the value of M. If I is not greater than J, K, L or M, then MIN is assigned a zero value. Readers must note that one and only one statement will be executed. Conditions are tested in the sequence in which they are written. For the above example, let I = 5, J = 6, K = 7, L = 8, M = 10, then the last statement is executed; so MIN = 0. If I = 5. J = 4, K = 3, M = 2, L = 1, then the first condition is executed; so MIN = 4. In this case, I is greater than J, K, L and M but MIN is assigned the value of J because the first condition (I.GT.J) is true and therefore, the control is transferred to the first executable statement following END IF.

Another way of multialternative selection is by using nested block IF constructs.

4.2.4.1 *Nested Block IF Construct*

A block IF construct may be included in a statement block of another block IF construct. A properly nested block IF construct is completely contained within a statement block of the outer IF construct, that is, for a nested block IF, IF and its matching ELSE (if present) and END IF must be in the same statement block; it must not overlap statement blocks of an outer block IF construct. Any statement block of a block IF construct may contain any number of block IF constructs. A general form of the nested IF statements is as follows:

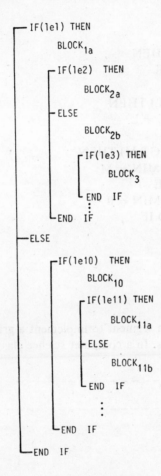

In this case block$_{1a}$ is executed if lel is true and block$_{2a}$ is executed if both lel and le2 are true. If lel is true but le2 is false block$_{2b}$ is executed. Irrespective of the value of le2, block$_1$ is executed as long as lel is true. The same logic can be applied to other blocks, e.g., block$_3$ is executed when lel is true, le2 is false and le3 is true. Block$_{11b}$ is executed if lel is false, le10 is true and lel1 is false.

In a nested IF construct, each block IF has its own END IF while the form of multialternative selection described in Section 4.2.4 has only one END IF.

Example (a)

The program segment for the previous example using nested IF statements can be written as follows:

```
MIN = I
IF(I.GT.J) THEN
    MIN = J
ELSE
    IF(I.GT.K) THEN
        MIN = K
    ELSE
        IF(I.GT.L) THEN
            MIN = L
        ELSE
            IF(I.GT.M) THEN
                MIN = M
            ELSE
                MIN = 0
            END IF
        END IF
    END IF
END IF
```

Example (b)

Let us write a program segment to implement a grade-assigning problem using nested IF statements. In a computer science class grades are assigned in the following manner:

Marks obtained out of 100	Grade
Marks $\geqslant$ 90	4.0
75 $\leq$ Marks < 90	3.0
60 $\leq$ Marks < 75	2.0
45 $\leq$ Marks < 60	1.0
Marks < 45	0.0

The program segment is as follows:

```
IF(MARKS.GE.90) THEN
    GRADE = 4.0
ELSE
```

```
        IF(MARKS.GE.75) THEN
            GRADE = 3.0
        ELSE
            IF(MARKS.GE.60) THEN
                GRADE = 2.0
            ELSE
                IF(MARKS.GE.45) THEN
                    GRADE = 1.0
                ELSE
                    GRADE = 0.0
                END IF
            END IF
        END IF
        END IF
```

Users must note that in both the above examples, the inner block IF construct is wholly contained in one of the blocks of its outermost block IF construct. To illustrate the use of arithmetic, logical and block IF constructs, here are some programming examples.

4.2.5 Programming Examples to Illustrate the Use of IF Statements

Example 4.1

This program determines the largest of three numbers, X, Y and Z. It then prints the largest number. Four versions of the program and the output results are given in Figure 4.8 making use of the arithmetic IF, logical IF, block IF and multi-alternative selection structure. The multi-alternative selection structure illustrates the use of compound conditions.

Example 4.2

This program accepts the lengths of the three sides, SIDE1, SIDE2, SIDE3, of a triangle and determines the type of triangle. It is based on the following cases:

Let X denote the largest of SIDE1, SIDE2 and SIDE3 and let Y and Z be the other two. Then,

(i) if $X \geqslant Y + Z$	no triangle is formed;
(ii) if $X = Y = Z$	an equilateral triangle is formed;
(iii) if $X^2 = Y^2 + Z^2$	a right-angled triangle is formed;
(iv) if $X^2 > (Y^2 + Z^2)$	an obtuse triangle is formed;
(v) if $X^2 < (Y^2 + Z^2)$	an acute triangle is formed.

An intrinsic function MAX is used to determine the largest side. One could have, however, included the program given in Example 4.1 to determine the largest side. The source program is given in Figure 4.9 which is self-explanatory. The output results are given in Figure 4.10 for various sets of input data.

```
**********************************************************************
*         THIS PROGRAM DETERMINES THE LARGEST OF THREE NUMBERS. FOUR   *
*         PROGRAM SEGMENTS USING DIFFERENT STATEMENTS ARE GIVEN TO     *
*         DETERMINE THE LARGEST NUMBER.                                *
*     LIST OF VARIABLES:                                               *
*         NAME                          USAGE                          *
*         ----                          -----                          *
*         X,Y,Z               THREE NUMBERS                            *
*         MAX                 LARGEST OF THE THREE NUMBERS             *
**********************************************************************
*
          INTEGER INLUN,OUTLUN
          PARAMETER (INLUN = 5, OUTLUN = 6)
          REAL MAX
'  READ THREE NUMBERS
          WRITE(OUTLUN,*)' ENTER THREE NUMBERS'
          READ(INLUN,*) X,Y,Z
*
*                         USING ARITHEMETIC IF
*
          MAX=X
          IF(Y-MAX)20,20,10
10        MAX=Y
20        IF(Z-MAX)40,40,30
30        MAX=Z
40        WRITE(OUTLUN,*)' THE LARGEST NUMBER IS= ',MAX
*
*                         USING LOGICAL IF
*
          MAX=X
          IF(Y.GT.MAX)MAX=Y
          IF(Z.GT.MAX)MAX=Z
          WRITE(OUTLUN,*)' THE LARGEST NUMBER IS= ',MAX
*
*                         USING BLOCK IF
*
          MAX=X
          IF(Y.GT.MAX)THEN
            MAX=Y
          END IF
          IF(Z.GT.MAX)THEN
            MAX=Z
          END IF
          WRITE(OUTLUN,*)' THE LARGEST NUMBER IS= ',MAX
*
*                         USING MULTIALTERNATIVE SELECTION
*
          IF(X.GE.Y.AND.X.GE.Z) THEN
            MAX=X
          ELSE IF(Y.GE.X.AND.Y.GE.Z)THEN
            MAX=Y
          ELSE
            MAX=Z
          END IF
          WRITE(OUTLUN,*)' THE LARGEST NUMBER IS= ',MAX
          STOP
          END
**********************************************************************
```

(Contd.)

```
                              RUN I
    ENTER THREE NUMBERS
    -8.0 6.0 -14.5
      THE LARGEST NUMBER IS=      6.000000
      THE LARGEST NUMBER IS=      6.000000
      THE LARGEST NUMBER IS=      6.000000
      THE LARGEST NUMBER IS=      6.000000


                             RUN II
    ENTER THREE NUMBERS
    -100.0 -500.78 -8654.0
      THE LARGEST NUMBER IS=     -100.0000
      THE LARGEST NUMBER IS=     -100.0000
      THE LARGEST NUMBER IS=     -100.0000
      THE LARGEST NUMBER IS=     -100.0000
```

Figure 4.8: Program Listing and Results of Example 4.1

```
**********************************************************************
*       THIS PROGRAM READS THREE SIDES OF A TRIANGLE. IT THEN        *
*       DETERMINES THE TYPE OF THE TRIANGLE.                         *
*       LIST OF VARIABLES:                                           *
*         NAME                      USAGE                            *
*         ----                      -----                            *
*         SIDE1           SIDE # 1 OF A TRIANGLE                     *
*         SIDE2           SIDE # 2 OF A TRIANGLE                     *
*         SIDE3           SIDE # 3 OF A TRIANGLE                     *
**********************************************************************
*
        INTEGER INLUN,OUTLUN
        PARAMETER(INLUN = 5, OUTLUN = 6)
* READ INPUT DATA
        WRITE(OUTLUN,*)' ENTER THREE SIDES OF A TRIANGLE'
        WRITE(OUTLUN,*)' SIDE # 1:'
        READ(INLUN,*)SIDE1
        WRITE(OUTLUN,*)' SIDE # 2:'
        READ(INLUN,*)SIDE2
        WRITE(OUTLUN,*)' SIDE # 3:'
        READ(INLUN,*)SIDE3
* DETERMINE LARGEST OF THE THREE SIDES
        X=MAX(SIDE1,SIDE2,SIDE3)
        IF(X.EQ.SIDE1)THEN
          Y=SIDE2
          Z=SIDE3
        ELSE
          IF(X.EQ.SIDE2)THEN
            Y=SIDE1
            Z=SIDE3
          ELSE
            Y=SIDE1
            Z=SIDE2
          END IF
        END IF
* DETERMINE THE TYPE OF THE TRIANGLE
        IF(X.GE.(Y+Z))THEN
          WRITE(OUTLUN,*)' NO TRIANGLE IS FORMED'
        ELSE IF(X.EQ.Y.AND.X.EQ.Z)THEN
          WRITE(OUTLUN,*)' AN EQUILATERAL TRIANGLE IS FORMED'
        ELSE IF(X*X.EQ.(Y*Y+Z*Z))THEN
          WRITE(OUTLUN,*)' A RIGHT ANGLE TRIANGLE IS FORMED'
        ELSE IF(X*X.GT.(Y*Y+Z*Z))THEN
          WRITE(OUTLUN,*)' AN OBTUSE TRIANGLE IS FORMED'
        ELSE IF(X*X.LT.(Y*Y+Z*Z))THEN
          WRITE(OUTLUN,*)' AN ACUTE TRIANGLE IS FORMED'
        END IF
        STOP
        END
**********************************************************************
```

Figure 4.9: Program Listing of Example 4.2

```
ENTER THREE SIDES OF A TRIANGLE
 SIDE # 1:
1.0
 SIDE # 2:
2.0
 SIDE # 3:
3.0
NO TRIANGLE IS FORMED
```

```
ENTER THREE SIDES OF A TRIANGLE
 SIDE # 1:
3.0
 SIDE # 2:
4.0
 SIDE # 3:
5.0
A RIGHT ANGLE TRIANGLE IS FORMED
```

```
ENTER THREE SIDES OF A TRIANGLE
 SIDE # 1:
10.0
 SIDE # 2:
10.0
 SIDE # 3:
10
AN EQUILATERAL TRIANGLE IS FORMED
```

```
ENTER THREE SIDES OF A TRIANGLE
 SIDE # 1:
1.0
 SIDE # 2:
2.0
 SIDE # 3:
1.5
AN OBTUSE TRIANGLE IS FORMED
```

Figure 4.10: Output Results of Example 4.2

4.3 GO TO STATEMENT

IF statements control the flow of a program after testing a condition. An unconditional branching around one or more statements is done by using another FORTRAN statement, GO TO (also written as GOTO). In a structured programming the GO TO statement is the least preferred and in a FORTRAN 77 program, it must be avoided wherever possible. Programs written in FORTRAN IV make extensive use of GO TO statements because it does not support many statements that may eliminate the use of GO TOs. An example is the implementation of block IF constructs using logical IF statements. FORTRAN IV does not support block IF constructs and one may therefore have to use GO TO statements in conjunction with logical IF statements. Consider the following program segment, which uses a block IF statement:

IF(X.GT.Y) THEN

$$
\left.\begin{array}{l}
Y = Y*X \\
Z = Z+Y \\
I = 3
\end{array}\right\} \text{block}_1
$$

ELSE

$$
\left.\begin{array}{l}
Y = Y/X \\
Y = Z-Y \\
I = 2
\end{array}\right\} \text{block}_2
$$

END IF

Each block contains three statements. Using a logical IF statement, the above program segment can be implemented thus:

IF(X.LE.Y) GO TO 100

$$
\left.\begin{array}{l}
Y = Y*X \\
Z = Z+Y \\
I = 3
\end{array}\right\} \text{block}_1
$$

GO TO 200

100 $\qquad$
$$
\left.\begin{array}{l}
Y = Y/X \\
Z = Z-Y \\
I = 2
\end{array}\right\} \text{block}_2
$$

200   CONTINUE

Note that the relational expression in the IF condition is changed from (X.GT.Y) to (X.LE.Y). If X is greater than Y, block$_1$ is executed; otherwise block$_2$ is executed. Using the GO TO's construct, condition (X.LE.Y) is tested.

If X is less than or equal to Y, then control is transferred to the statement with label 100. The program executes this statement and resumes its execution from this statement onwards, i.e. statements of block$_2$ are executed. The CONTINUE statement simply transfers control to the next executable statement. If X is greater than Y, then the condition (X.LE.Y) is false and the statements immediately after the IF statements are executed. The statement GO TO 200 unconditionally transfers control to statement 200, a CONTINUE statement. The purpose of providing this statement is to skip block$_2$. If this statement is not provided, then block$_2$ statements will also be executed. Readers must note that in a block IF construct, the same purpose is achieved by providing the ELSE statement.

GO TO statements can also be used to simulate repetitive structures, as you will see later in this section. We must again emphasize that GO TO statements should be avoided as far as possible. Excessive use of GO TO's in a program makes it difficult to read, test and amend. Nevertheless, we are including a brief discussion on various GO TO statements that are supported by FORTRAN IV. It might help those users who have access to a computer that supports a FORTRAN IV compiler.

The three types of GO TO statements are:

(1) Unconditional GO TO
(2) Computed GO TO
(3) Assigned GO TO

4.3.1 Unconditional GO TO Statement

A general form of unconditional GO TO statement is:

   GO TO S

where
   S is the label (or statement number) of an executable statement that must be present.

When a GO TO is encountered, the next statement to be executed will be the one numbered by statement label S. After statement S is executed, control continues with the statements following statement S. The earlier example explains the use of an unconditional GO TO statement. Some more examples of unconditional GO TO statements are:

Examples

   (a)   GO TO 10   (Control is transferred to the statement with label 10)

   (b)   GO TO 99259   (Control is transferred to the statement with label 99259).

   (c)   GO TO X   (Not valid, statement number must be a positive integer ranging from 1 to 99999).

4.3.2 Computed GO TO Statement

The unconditional GO TO statement transfers control to some other statement. Use of unconditional GO TO statement with a logical IF statement can achieve a two-way branching as explained in Section 4.3. One often encounters situations demanding a three-way, four-way (and so on) branching of control. These branchings can be achieved by using nested IF or multi-alternative selection structure. These can also be obtained by using unconditional GO TO and logical IF statements as shown below:

```
          IF(N.EQ.1) GO TO 100
          IF(N.EQ.2) GO TO 200
          IF(N.EQ.3) GO TO 300
          K = 1
          ⋮
     100  J = K + 1
          ⋮
     200  J = K - 1
          ⋮
     300  J = K
```

If N equals 1, control is transferred to statement number 100. If N equals 2, control is transferred to statement number 200 and if N equals 3 then control is transferred to statement number 300. The same branching can also be achieved by a single computed GO TO statement as shown below:

```
          GO TO(100,200,300),N
          K = 1
          ⋮
     100  J = K + 1
          ⋮
     200  J = K - 1
          ⋮
     300  J = K
```

The general from the computed GO TO statement is

$$GO\ TO(S1,S2,S3, \ldots ,SK),\ aie$$

where

S1,S2,S3. . . . SK are statement numbers, positive integers ranging from 1 to 99999,

aie is an arithmetic integer expression (could be a single integer variable) having a value in the range of 1 to K because there are K statement numbers in the GO TO statement.

Some examples of computed GO TO statements are as follows:

Example (a)

Consider the statement:

$$GO\ TO(10,20,30,40,100,1),ICOUNT$$

If the value of ICOUNT is 2, control is transferred to statement 20. IF ICOUNT is 6, control is transferred to the statement with label 1. If ICOUNT is less than 1 and greater than 6, control is transferred to the first executable statement after the computed GO TO statement. (Note that some compilers may cause termination of execution if ICOUNT is greater than 6 or less than 1.)

Example (b)

Consider the statement:

$$GO\ TO(999,2,36,44,99999),I+J+K$$

The arithmetic expression $I+J+K$ is evaluated and, depending on the value of the expression, control is accordingly transferred.

4.3.3 Assigned GO TO Statement

Most FORTRAN compilers provide for a third type of GO TO statement called assigned GO TO statement. The general form of the assigned GO TO statement is

$$GO\ TO\ I,(S1,S2,S3,.\ .\ .\ .\ ,SK)$$
where
I is an integer variable,
S1,S2,S3,. . . . ,SK are statement numbers.

An ASSIGN statement must be used to assign the value to the integer variable, I. The general form of the ASSIGN statement is

$$ASSIGN\ S\ TO\ I$$
where
S stands for the statement number of an executable statement.

The ASSIGN statement establishes a relationship between the variable I and a specific statement number. The assigned GO TO statement transfers control to the statement which has a label that was most recently assigned to variable I.

Example (a)

Consider the following statements:
    ASSIGN 99 TO K
    GO TO K
    This is equivalent to GO TO 99.

Example (b)

Consider the following statements:
    ASSIGN 99 TO ICOUNT
    GO TO ICOUNT, (20, 10, 5, 99)
This is equivalent to GO TO 99.

It must be noted that the value of the integer variable I must be set in the ASSIGN statement. The assigned GO TO statement is the most uncommonly used GO TO statement and the same purpose can be achieved by using the other two GO TO statements. To understand the use of GO TOs, study the following two programming examples.

4.3.4 Programming Examples to Illustrate the Use of GO TO Statements

Example 4.3

The program given in Example 4.1 to find the largest of three numbers is now given in figure 4.11 making use of a GO TO statement. The output is also given in Figure 4.11.

Example 4.4

In Example (b) of nested block IF statement, we showed how a grade assignment problem can be solved by using nested IF statements. The same problem is now solved by making use of a computed GO TO statement. The input data is marks obtained by a student (MARKS) and the output result is the corresponding grade that he/she will be assigned. The source program and the results are given in Figure 4.12. The crux of the problem using computed GO TOs is to somehow obtain aie (I in this example) in the range of 1 to K (K = 5 in this example). This is easily done by using the statement

$$I = \frac{(MARKS - 30)}{15} + 1$$

in this example.

Before we close our discussion on GO TOs and go on to discuss a very important control structure, let us study the following program segment:

```
        I = 1
        ISUM = 0

100     IF(I.GT.N) GO TO 99
            ISUM = ISUM+I
            I = I+1
            GO TO 100

99      WRITE (5,*), 'SUM OF NUMBERS  1...N', ISUM
```

The above program segment calculates the sum of 1 to N numbers. The first two statements are initializations. The third statement is a decision statement and if I ⩽ N, the three statements following the IF statement are executed. ISUM and I are updated. The GO TO 100 statement branches back

```
**********************************************************************
*        THIS PROGRAM DETERMINES THE LARGEST OF THREE NUMBERS USING  *
*        GO TO STATEMENTS.                                           *
*     LIST OF VARIABLES:                                             *
*       NAME                        USAGE                            *
*       ----                        -----                            *
*       X,Y,Z              THREE NUMBERS                             *
*       MAX                LARGEST OF THE THREE NUMBERS              *
**********************************************************************
*
         INTEGER INLUN,OUTLUN
         PARAMETER (INLUN = 5, OUTLUN = 6)
         REAL MAX
* READ THREE NUMBERS
         WRITE(OUTLUN,*)' ENTER THREE NUMBERS'
         READ(INLUN,*) X,Y,Z
*
         IF(X.GE.Y.AND.X.GE.Z) GO TO 100
         IF(Y.GE.X.AND.Y.GE.Z) GO TO 200
         MAX=Z
         GO TO 300
100      MAX=X
         GO TO 300
200      MAX=Y
300      WRITE(OUTLUN,*)' THE LARGEST NUMBER IS= ',MAX
         STOP
         END
**********************************************************************
```

```
                              RUN I

  ENTER THREE NUMBERS
 -8.0 6.0 -14.5
  THE LARGEST NUMBER IS=        6.000000


                              RUN II

  ENTER THREE NUMBERS
 -100.0 -500.78 -8654.0
  THE LARGEST NUMBER IS=       -100.0000
```

Figure 4.11: Program Listing and Output Results of Example 4.3.

```
*****************************************************************************
*        THIS PROGRAM ILLUSTRATES THE USE OF COMPUTED GO TO'S             *
*   LIST OF VARIABLES:                                                    *
*      NAME                      USAGE                                    *
*      ----                      -----                                    *
*      MARKS              MARKS OF A STUDENT                              *
*      I                  INTEGER INDEX USED IN COMPUTED GO TO STATEMENT  *
*      GRADE              GRADE ASSIGNED TO A STUDENT                     *
*****************************************************************************
*
       INTEGER INLUN,OUTLUN
       PARAMETER (INLUN = 5, OUTLUN = 6)
* READ INPUT DATA
       WRITE(OUTLUN,*)' PLEASE ENTER MARKS OBTAINED BY A STUDENT'
       READ(INLUN,*)MARKS
* PERFORM CALCULATIONS
       I=(MARKS-30)/15+1
       IF(I.LT.1)I=1
       GO TO (50,40,30,20,10) I
10     GRADE=4.0
       GO TO 60
20     GRADE=3.0
       GO TO 60
30     GRADE=2.0
       GO TO 60
40     GRADE=1.0
       GO TO 60
50     GRADE=0.0
60     WRITE(OUTLUN,*)' GRADES ASSIGNED TO THE STUDENT IS=',GRADE
       STOP
       END
*****************************************************************************
```

RUN I

```
PLEASE ENTER MARKS OBTAINED BY A STUDENT
90.0
GRADES ASSIGNED TO THE STUDENT IS=    4.000000
```

RUN II

```
PLEASE ENTER MARKS OBTAINED BY A STUDENT
59.0
GRADES ASSIGNED TO THE STUDENT IS=    1.000000
```

RUN III

```
PLEASE ENTER MARKS OBTAINED BY A STUDENT
60
GRADES ASSIGNED TO THE STUDENT IS=    2.000000
```

Figure 4.12: Source Program and Results of Example 4.4.

to the IF statement. Again, the IF statement is executed and if $I \leqslant N$, the three statements following the IF statement are executed. Again GO TO 100 transfers control to statement 100 and this procedure continues till I is greater than N. If I is greater than N, the IF condition is true, and so control is transferred to statement 99, which prints the sum of the first N positive integers.

The effect of providing the unconditional GO TO 100 statement in the above program segment is to repeatedly execute four statements. If the above pro-gram segment did not contain the logical IF statement, then the three state-ments would be executed for an infinite number of times since there is no way of coming out of the loop as shown in the following program segment:

```
      I = 1
      ISUM = 0
  100 ISUM = ISUM + 1
      I = I + 1
      GO TO 100
```

A repetitition structure must, therefore, contain a control feature so that statements are executed only a finite number of times. One can always use GO TOs to devise repetitive structures, but as noted earlier, use of GO TOs must be avoided as far as possible. FORTRAN 77 provides some repetitive structures that we will describe in the remaining part of this chapter.

4.4 REPETITION STRUCTURE

A repetition structure or loop makes possible repeated execution of one or more statements. This repetition must be controlled so that these state-ments are executed only a finite number of times. FORTRAN provides a very powerful and simple repetitive structure, the DO statement. Another powerful repetitive structure is WHILE (or DO WHILE) statement. The WHILE (or DO WHILE) structure is not, regrettably, part of standard FORTRAN 77 but some FORTRAN compilers support these structures; for instance, the WHILE statement is available in WATFIV. We will discuss the WHILE statement later in this section. Right now, we will discuss the DO statement.

4.4.1 The DO Statement

The DO statement provides iterative processing; that is, the statements in its range are repeatedly executed a specified number of times. In one statement, it provides for the initialization, incrementing and testing of a variable, plus repeated execution of a group of statements in its range. The basic form of the DO statement is:

```
      DO S[,]V = ae₁, ae₂ [,ae₃]
      ⋮                              Range of the DO statement
    S CONTINUE
```

where

S is the statement number; generally it is a CONTINUE statement but it can be any executable statement; this is the last statement in the range of the loop and is therefore called a terminal statement; the terminal statement must appear after the DO statement; the statements between the DO statement and the terminal statement are called the range of the DO statement; the comma indicated by [,] after S is optional;

V is a variable of type integer, real, or double precision; it is called the index variable or the DO variable.

ae_1, ae_2 and ae_3 (optional) are arithmetic expressions of type integer, real, or double precision; ae_1 represents the initial value assigned to the DO variable V; it is called initial parameter; ae_2 represents the limit (or terminal) value for the DO variable; it is called terminal parameter; ae_3 is optional and it represents the increment for the DO variable; it is called incrementing parameter; if ae_3 is omitted, it is assigned a default value of one; it is important to note that ae_3 must not be assigned a zero value; these parameters may be negative;

the COTINUE statement, as noted earlier, is the last statement in the range of a DO; this statement serves the function of a dummy line in a program; it may be omitted; some compilers also allow an END DO statement instead of CONTINUE as the terminal statement in the range of a DO.

The action of a DO loop is shown in Figure 4.13.

4.4.1.1 *Examples of DO Statements*

Example (a)

The following program segment implements the algorithm to calculate the sum of 1 to N integers:

```
      ISUM = 0
      DO 10 I = 1,N
         ISUM = ISUM + I  Range of the DO
   10 CONTINUE
      WRITE (5,*), 'SUM OF NUMBERS 1. . .N', ISUM
```

The DO statement causes the execution of the range N times, with index I taking on the values from 1 to N in succession. The indentation of the statement ISUM = ISUM + I within the range of the DO is highly recommended to increase the readability of the program.

Example (b)

Supposing we want to calculate the sum of the squares of odd integers with a value not greater than N. The following program segment evaluates the sum:

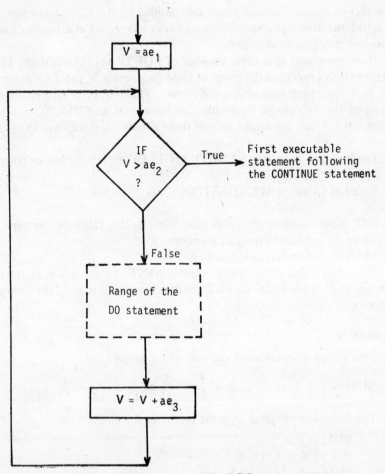

$$V = ae_1$$

$$\text{IF } V > ae_2 \, ?$$

True → First executable statement following the CONTINUE statement

False

Range of the DO statement

$$V = V + ae_3$$

Figure 4.13: Action of a DO Loop.

SUMOSQ = 0.0
DO 5 J = 1, N, 2
SUMOSQ = SUMOSQ + J**2 Range of the DO
5 CONTINUE
WRITE (5,*), 'SUM OF SQUARES OF THE ODD INTEGERS IS',
SUMOSQ

The DO index J is given the initial value 1 and then incremented by 2 after each execution of the range, until the index value is greater than N. Thus, if the value of N is 3, the range will be executed with J equal to 1 and then 3. If N is 5, the successive values of J will be 1, 3 and 5. Suppose N is 6; the successive values of J will also be 1, 3 and 5, since a further increment produces 7, which is greater than the terminal value. If the value of N is zero or negative, the range will not be executed at all. This is because a test is made at the beginning of the execution of the DO statement to determine how many executions of the range are specified by the DO parameters. This is called the *iteration count*. The range is not executed at all unless the iteration count is greater than zero.

Users must note that older versions of FORTRAN (FORTRAN IV and earlier) always executed the range at least once, even if the DO parameters are such that they logically specify zero. Thus, if N is zero in the above example, the DO range is executed at least once, so SUMOSQ will be 1.0 and not 0.0. Users must take care of these situations, if they use FORTRAN IV.

The iteration count for a FORTRAN 77 DO statement can be computed according to the formula

Iteration Count = MAX (INT($(ae_2 - ae_1 + ae_3)/ae_3$), 0)

where

INT is an intrinsic function that converts the value of the expression $(ae_2 - ae_1 + ae_3)/ae_3$ to integer, if necessary;

MAX is also an intrinsic function.

The larger value between the expression INT ($(ae_2 - ae_1 + ae_3)/ae_3$) and 0 is assigned to iteration count. If the iteration count is zero, the loop is not executed.

Example (c)

Suppose we want to calculate the sum of the series

$$SUM = 1 + \frac{1}{3} + \frac{1}{5} + \frac{1}{7} + \frac{1}{9} + \frac{1}{11} + \frac{1}{13} + \frac{1}{15} + \frac{1}{17} + \frac{1}{19}$$

The following program segment evaluates the sum

```
      SUM = 0.0
      DO 99 K = 1, 19, 2
      SUM = SUM + 1.0/K
  99  CONTINUE
```

Here $ae_1 = 1$, $ae_2 = 19$, $ae_3 = 2$, so iteration count is evaluated as

Iteration Count = MAX (INT ($(19 - 1 + 2)/2$), 0)
                = MAX (INT (10), 0)
                = MAX (10, 0)
                = 10

Example (d)

The following program segment evaluates

$$PRODKT = \sqrt{7.0} * \sqrt{6.0} * \sqrt{5.0} * \sqrt{4.0} * \sqrt{3.0} * \sqrt{2.0} * \sqrt{1.0}$$

```
      PRODKT = 1.0
      DO 100 X = 7.0, 1.0, - 10
      PRODKT = PRODKT*SQRT(X)
 100  CONTINUE
```

Here $ae_1 = 7.0$, $ae_2 = 1.0$, $ae_3 = -1.0$, so
$$\text{Iteration Count} = \text{MAX}(\text{INT}((1.0 - 7.0 - 1.0)/(-1.0)), 0)$$
$$= \text{MAX}(\text{INT}(7.0), 0)$$
$$= \text{MAX}(7,0)$$
$$= 7$$

Note that the DO variable is a real variable and ae_3 is negative. In this case the DO variable takes on values from 7.0 down to 1.0 in steps of 1.0.

The DO statement is subject to a few simple rules which are summarized here.

4.4.1.2 *Rules for DO Loops*

(1) The DO variable can be used in statements inside the range of the DO. After a normal exit from the top (when it has been completed), the value of the DO variable may not be available. However, under an abnormal exit, the current value of the DO variable is available for use outside the loop.

(2) It is not permissible to transfer control into the range of a DO other than by executing the DO itself, that is, DO loops must be entered only through the DO statement.

(3) It is permissible for the range of one DO (which we call the outer DO) to contain one or more DOs (which we call the inner DOs). The DO statements are then said to be nested. Nested DO loops are discussed in the next section.

(4) The last statement in the range of a DO must not be any of the following statements:

   (i) GO TO
   (ii) Block IF
   (iii) STOP
   (iv) END
   (v) Another DO statement

It is highly recommended that the last statement of a DO loop always be a CONTINUE statement.

(5) The DO variable V must not be altered by statements within the range of the DO. It is permissible, however, to alter any of the DO parameters ae_1, ae_2 and ae_3. If ae_1, ae_2, ae_3 are modified then the number of iterations that the loop makes will remain unchanged. The number of iterations is computed when the DO is first encountered, and so changes in the DO parameters would simply not be noticed.

(6) The DO variable V and the parameters ae_1, ae_2 and ae_3 may be of type REAL. However, it must be remembered that real arithmetic is subject to small errors. It is therefore possible that the iteration count computed as

$$\text{MAX}(\text{INT}) (ae_2 - ae_1 + ae_3)/ae_3), 0)$$

is different than expected because of rounding errors. Suppose $ae_1 = 1.0$, $ae_2 = 7.0$, $ae_3 = 0.5$ then

$$MAX(INT(\,(7.0 - 1.0 + 0.5)/0.5), 0)$$
$$= MAX(INT(13.0),0)$$
$$= 13$$

If the actual result of the real arithmetic were not 13.0 but 12.99999. . ., the integer would be 12 not 13. So use real DO parameters with caution.

4.4.2 Nested DO Loops

A DO loop can contain one or more than one complete DO loops. When this is done, it is essential that all statements in the range of an inner DO also be in the range of an outer DO; that is, the range of inner nested DO loop must be completely within the range of the next outer loop. Nested loops can share a CONTINUE statement. Figure 4.14 illustrates correctly and incorrectly nested DO loops:

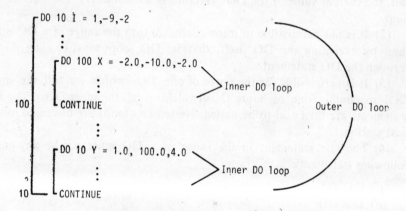

Figure 4.14.1: Correctly Nested DO Loops.

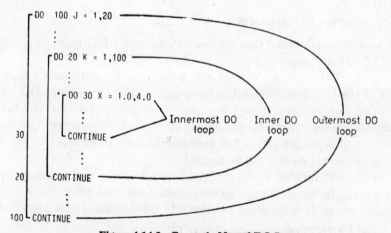

Figure 4.14.2: Correctly Nested DO Loops.

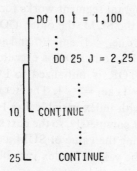

Figure 4.14.3: Incorrectly Nested DO Loops.

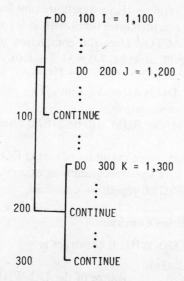

Figure 4.14.4: Incorrectly Nested DO Loops.

4.4.2.1 *Example of Nested DO Loops*

Suppose we want to calculate the sum of the following series:

SUM = 1! + 3! + 5! + 7!

where ! represents factorial; n! = n(n — 1)(n — 2)(n — 3). . . .3. 2. 1,
so 3! = 3 × 2 × 1 = 6. The following program segment evaluates the sum:

```
      SUM = 0.0
      DO 10 I = 1, 7, 2
      FACTOR = 1.0
      DO 20 J = I, 1, — 1
      FACTOR = FACTOR*J
   20 CONTINUE
      SUM = SUM + FACTOR
   10 CONTINUE
```

Let us see how the above program segment works for a few steps:

(1) After initialization of the SUM, the outer DO starts executing. The outer DO loop parameters are $ae_1 = 1$, $ae_2 = 7$ and $ae_3 = 2$. So the iteration count for the outer DO is 4. The outer DO is executed four time. In the first iteration, I will be 1. FACTOR is initialized to 1.0. The inner loop parameters are $ae_1 = I = 1$, $ae_2 = 1$, $ae_3 = -1$. The iteration count is 1, so the inner loop is executed once with index variable $J = 1$. FACTOR will be 1.0. The inner DO loop is executed completely, so the next statement SUM = SUM + FACTOR is executed, giving the value of SUM as 1.0. In the second iteration of the outer DO loop, the value of index variable I will be incremented to 3.

(2) $I = 3$, FACTOR is again initialized to 1.0. The inner DO parameters are $ae_1 = I = 3$, $ae_2 = 1$, $ae_3 = -1$, so iteration count for the inner DO is 3. This DO loop is therefore executed three times with index value as 3, 2, 1, respectively. The value of FACTOR after the completion of the loop will be $1.0*3*2*1 = 6.0$. SUM will now be $7.0 = (1.0 + 6.0)$. This completes the second iteration of the outer DO. The outer DO index is again increased to 5 and this time the inner DO is excuted 5 times. This process continues until the outer DO completes its execution.

(3) The final value of the SUM will be 5167.0 after the completion of the outer DO loop.

We will encounter many more examples of nested DO loops in the following Chapters. Before we give some programming examples, it will be worthwhile to study the DO-WHILE repetition construct.

4.4.3 DO-WHILE Repetition Construct

The general form of the DO-WHILE construct is

>   DO[S[,]] WHILE (1e)
>   ⋮   Range of the DO-WHILE statement
>   S CONTINUE

where

S is the statement number. It has same meaning as described in the DO statement. S is optional and may be omitted. If S is omitted, the terminal statement CONTINUE is replaced by END DO.

Comma following statement number is also optional.

1e is a logical expression.

The action of a DO-WHILE loop is shown in Figure 4.15.

The DO-WHILE statement is a conditional loop while the DO statement discussed earlier is a counted loop construct. The difference between the two is as follows:

(i) The DO-WHILE statement keeps executing as long as the logical expression (1e) continues to be true.

(ii) The DO statement executes definite number of iterations, whereas the DO-WHILE statement executes indefinite number of iterations.

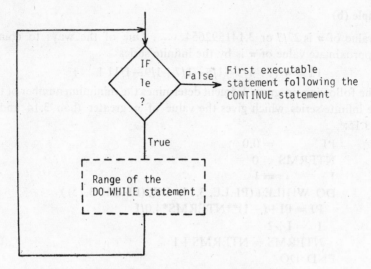

Figure 4.15: Action of a DO-WHILE Loop.

The DO-WHILE statement evaluates the logical expression (1e) at the beginning of each execution of the loop, including the first. If the value of the expression is true, the statements in the range of the DO-WHILE are executed; if the expression is false, no statement in the range of the DO-WHILE is executed and control is transferred to the statement following the last statement in the range of the DO-WHILE. Some examples of the DO-WHILE construct are given below.

4.4.3.1 *Examples of DO-WHILE Construct*

Example (a)

Consider the following program segment

```
      SUM   =   0.0
      TOTAL = 100.0
      I     = 5
      DO 10 WHILE (SUM .LT. TOTAL)
      SUM = SUM+I**2
      WRITE(5,*), SUM, I
      I = I+1
10    CONTINUE
```

The execution of the program segment produces the following output:

```
      25.0  5
      61.0  6
     110.0  7
```

Example (b)

The value of π is 22/7 or 3.141592654....... One of the ways to compute the approximate value of π is by the infinite series

$$PI = 4*(1 - 1/3 + 1/5 - 1/7 + 1/9 - 1/11 + ...)$$

The following program segment determines the minimum number of terms of the infinite series which gives the value of π greater than 3.14 and less than 3.15:

```
PI       = 0.0
NTERMS = 0
I        = 1
DO WHILE ((PI.LE. 3.14) .OR. (PI.GE. 3.15))
   PI = PI+(−1)**NTERMS*4.0/I
   I  = I+2
   NTERMS = NTERMS+1
END DO
WRITE (5,*), 'NUMBER OF TERMS = ', NTERMS
```

The condition ((PI.LE. 3.14).OR. (PI .GE. 3.15)) is tested at the beginning of the loop execution. If PI⩾3.14 or PI⩽3.15, then the condition is true and the loop is executed. Whenever the value of the PI is between 3.14 and 3.15, control is transfered to the WRITE statement.

A variation in the representation of this loop control has a general form:

```
WHILE (1e) DO
   ⋮                 Range of the loop
END WHILE
```

This is the WHILE-DO control construct supported by many compilers such as M77. There is no difference between the DO-WHILE construct and the WHILE-DO construct except that of its representation.

Regrettably, the standard FORTRAN 77 does not provide either DO-WHILE or WHILE-DO statements. Some compilers, e.g. WATFIV-S, VAX-11 FORTRAN, M77, etc., do support one of these repetitive constructs. Readers can, however, simulate this construct by using the block IF and the GO TO statement as shown below:

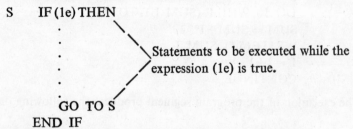

```
S     IF (1e) THEN
      ⋮
      ⋮              Statements to be executed while the
      ⋮              expression (1e) is true.
      ⋮
      GO TO S
      END IF
```

Note that the IF statement is labeled S and the GO TO S causes repeated evaluation of the logical expression until the expression is false.

Before we go on to programming examples for this chapter, let us see a few programming examples that make the use of repetition control structures, i.e. DO and DO-WHILE statements.

4.4.4 Programming Examples to Illustrate the Use of Repetition Constructs

Example 4.5

This program prints a table of integers, their squares, their square roots, their reciprocals, and their common algorithm (log to the base 10) values for all integer values between 1 and 50. The program makes use of a DO loop and intrinsic functions. The source program is shown in Figure 4.16 and the output in Figure 4.17. Readers may note that by changing the values of the DO parameters, similar tables can be printed for any range of integer numbers.

```
**************************************************************************
*       THIS PROGRAM PRINTS OUT A MATHEMATICAL TABLE                     *
*    LIST OF VARIABLES:                                                  *
*       NAME                    USAGE                                    *
*       ----                    -----                                    *
*       I               AN INTEGER BETWEEN 1 AND 50                      *
*       SQR             SQUARE OF THE INTEGER I                          *
*       SQROOT          SQUARE ROOT OF THE INTEGER I                     *
*       RECPRO          RECIPROCAL OF THE INTEGER I                      *
*       COMLOG          LOG TO THE BASE 10 OF THE INTEGER I              *
**************************************************************************
        INTEGER INLUN,OUTLUN
        PARAMETER (INLUN = 5, OUTLUN = 6)
* SET UP HEADINGS FOR THE TABLE
        WRITE(OUTLUN,*)'          I      SQUARE          SQUARE ROOT  ',
     1  ' RECIPROCAL     COMMON LOG'
        WRITE(OUTLUN,*)'          -      ------          -----------  ',
     1  ' ----------     ----------'
        DO 10 I=1,50
          SQR = I*I
          SQROOT=SQRT(I*1.0)
          RECPRO=1.0/I
          COMLOG=ALOG10(I*1.0)
          WRITE(OUTLUN,*)I,SQR,SQROOT,RECPRO,COMLOG
10      CONTINUE
        STOP
        END
**************************************************************************
```

Figure 4.16: Program Listing of Example 4.5.

RUN I

I	SQUARE	SQUARE ROOT	RECIPROCAL	COMMON LOG
-	------	-----------	----------	----------
1	1.000000	1.000000	1.000000	0.0000000E+00
2	4.000000	1.414214	0.5000000	0.3010300
3	9.000000	1.732051	0.3333333	0.4771213
4	16.00000	2.000000	0.2500000	0.6020600
5	25.00000	2.236068	0.2000000	0.6989700
6	36.00000	2.449490	0.1666667	0.7781513
7	49.00000	2.645751	0.1428571	0.8450980
8	64.00000	2.828427	0.1250000	0.9030900
9	81.00000	3.000000	0.1111111	0.9542425
10	100.0000	3.162278	0.1000000	1.000000
11	121.0000	3.316625	9.0909094E-02	1.041393
12	144.0000	3.464102	8.3333336E-02	1.079181
13	169.0000	3.605551	7.6923080E-02	1.113943
14	196.0000	3.741657	7.1428575E-02	1.146128
15	225.0000	3.872983	6.6666670E-02	1.176091
16	256.0000	4.000000	6.2500000E-02	1.204120
17	289.0000	4.123106	5.8823530E-02	1.230449
18	324.0000	4.242640	5.5555556E-02	1.255273
19	361.0000	4.358899	5.2631579E-02	1.278754
20	400.0000	4.472136	5.0000001E-02	1.301030
21	441.0000	4.582576	4.7619049E-02	1.322219
22	484.0000	4.690416	4.5454547E-02	1.342423
23	529.0000	4.795832	4.3478262E-02	1.361728
24	576.0000	4.898980	4.1666668E-02	1.380211
25	625.0000	5.000000	3.9999999E-02	1.397940
26	676.0000	5.099020	3.8461540E-02	1.414973
27	729.0000	5.196152	3.7037037E-02	1.431364
28	784.0000	5.291502	3.5714287E-02	1.447158
29	841.0000	5.385165	3.4482758E-02	1.462398
30	900.0000	5.477226	3.3333335E-02	1.477121
31	961.0000	5.567764	3.2258064E-02	1.491362
32	1024.000	5.656854	3.1250000E-02	1.505150
33	1089.000	5.744563	3.0303031E-02	1.518514
34	1156.000	5.830952	2.9411765E-02	1.531479
35	1225.000	5.916080	2.8571429E-02	1.544068
36	1296.000	6.000000	2.7777778E-02	1.556303
37	1369.000	6.082763	2.7027028E-02	1.568202
38	1444.000	6.164414	2.6315790E-02	1.579784
39	1521.000	6.244998	2.5641026E-02	1.591065
40	1600.000	6.324555	2.5000000E-02	1.602060
41	1681.000	6.403124	2.4390243E-02	1.612784
42	1764.000	6.480741	2.3809524E-02	1.623249
43	1849.000	6.557438	2.3255814E-02	1.633469
44	1936.000	6.633250	2.2727273E-02	1.643453
45	2025.000	6.708204	2.2222223E-02	1.653213
46	2116.000	6.782330	2.1739131E-02	1.662758
47	2209.000	6.855655	2.1276595E-02	1.672098
48	2304.000	6.928203	2.0833334E-02	1.681241
49	2401.000	7.000000	2.0408163E-02	1.690196
50	2500.000	7.071068	2.0000000E-02	1.698970

Figure 4.17: Output Results of Example 4.5.

Example 4.6

We want to compute the sum of the following series:

$$SUM = \sum_{i=1}^{20} \sum_{j=1}^{100} j+(i-5)*J/10.0$$

The program makes use of nested DO loops. The source program and the results are given in Figure 4.18.

```
*********************************************************************
*        THIS PROGRAM CALCULATES THE SUM OF A SERIES               *
*********************************************************************
*
         INTEGER OUTLUN
         PARAMETER (OUTLUN = 6)
*
         SUM=0.0
         DO 10 I=1,20
           DO 10 J=1,100
             SUM=SUM+J+(I-5)*J/10.0
10       CONTINUE
         WRITE(OUTLUN,*)' THE SUM OF THE SERIES IS=',SUM
         STOP
         END
*********************************************************************
```

                        RUN I

    THE SUM OF THE SERIES IS=   156550.0

Figure 4.18: Program Listing and Output Results of Example 4.6.

Example 4.7

Example 3.3 of Chapter 3 computes the area of a triangle. It requires two sides and the included angle as input. A student may, by mistake, type in incorrect values (e.g. negative numbers) for SIDE 1, SIDE 2 or angle THETA. This is undesirable because in a triangle, the sides should be positive and the angle should be between 0 degrees and 180 degrees (both exclusive). A negative value for any parameter will result in a negative value for the area. The program given in Figure 3.8 is modified to check these errors and display a suitable message. The program continues to ask the student to type in the correct values of these parameters. The program makes use of the DO-WHILE construct. The source program is given in Figure 4.19 and the input data and output results in Figure 4.20. Another feature that has also been added to the program is that it continues to execute any valid data set until it is terminated by typing zero values for all three parameters. Note that the program given in Figure 3.8 is to be run as many times as the number of data sets. This is a serious limitation of the program given in Figure 3.8 because a programmer does not have any control on when to stop the execution of the program.

```
*******************************************************************************
*       THIS PROGRAM READS ANY TWO SIDES AND THE INCLUDED ANGLE OF A          *
*       TRIANGLE. IT THEN CALCULATES THE OTHER SIDE AND THE REMAINING TWO     *
*       ANGLES. IT ALSO COMPUTES THE AREA OF THE TRIANGLE. THE PROGRAM        *
*       KEEPS ON ASKING DATA UNTIL THE USER ENTERS ZERO FOR ALL INPUT         *
*       DATA. IT ALSO CHECKS FOR ANY ERROR IN THE INPUT DATA.                 *
*       LIST OF VARIABLES:                                                    *
*       NAME                    USAGE                                         *
*       ----                    -----                                         *
*       SIDE1                   SIDE # 1                                      *
*       SIDE2                   SIDE # 2                                      *
*       SIDE3                   SIDE # 3                                      *
*       THETA                   ANGLE BETWEEN SIDE # 1 AND SIDE # 2           *
*       ALPHA                   ANGLE BETWEEN SIDE # 2 AND SIDE # 3           *
*       BETA                    ANGLE BETWEEN SIDE # 1 AND SIDE # 3           *
*       AREA                    AREA OF THE TRIANGLE                          *
*       PI                      PIE = 22/7                                    *
*       RADEGS                  CONVERSION FACTOR, RADIANS PER DEGREE         *
*******************************************************************************
*
        INTEGER INLUN,OUTLUN
        PARAMETER(INLUN = 5,OUTLUN = 6)
* INITIALIZE
        PI = 22.0 / 7.0
        RADEGS = PI / 180
* READ FIRST SET OF THE INPUT DATA
        WRITE(OUTLUN,*)' ENTER THE INPUT DATA'
        WRITE(OUTLUN,*)' SIDE # 1:'
        READ(INLUN,*)SIDE1
        WRITE(OUTLUN,*)' SIDE # 2:'
        READ(INLUN,*)SIDE2
        WRITE(OUTLUN,*)' ANGLE BETWEEN SIDE # 1 AND SIDE # 2:'
        READ(INLUN,*)THETA
        DO WHILE (SIDE1.NE.0.0.OR.SIDE2.NE.0.0.OR.THETA.NE.0.0)
* CHECK FOR ANY ERROR IN THE INPUT DATA
            DO WHILE (SIDE1.LE.0.0)
                WRITE(OUTLUN,*)' PLEASE ENTER A CORRECT VALUE FOR SIDE # 1'
                READ(INLUN,*)SIDE1
            END DO
            DO WHILE (SIDE2.LE.0.0)
                WRITE(OUTLUN,*)' PLEASE ENTER A CORRECT VALUE FOR SIDE # 2'
                READ(INLUN,*)SIDE2
            END DO
            DO WHILE (THETA.LE.0.0.OR.THETA.GE.180.0)
                WRITE(OUTLUN,*)' PLEASE ENTER A CORRECT VALUE FOR ANGLE'
                READ(INLUN,*)THETA
            END DO
* PERFORM CALCULATIONS
            THETA = THETA * RADEGS
            SIDE3 = SQRT(SIDE1**2 + SIDE2**2 - 2*SIDE1*SIDE2*COS(THETA))
            ALPHA = ACOS((SIDE3**2 + SIDE2**2 - SIDE1**2)/(2*SIDE2*SIDE3))
            AREA = SIDE1*SIDE2*SIN(THETA)/2
            THETA = THETA/RADEGS
            ALPHA = ALPHA/RADEGS
            BETA = 180 - THETA - ALPHA
*     WRITE OUTPUT RESULTS
            WRITE(OUTLUN,*)' THE RESULTS FOR THE TRIANGLE ARE:'
            WRITE(OUTLUN,*)' SIDE # 1:',SIDE1
            WRITE(OUTLUN,*)' SIDE # 2:',SIDE2
            WRITE(OUTLUN,*)' SIDE # 3:',SIDE3
```

—Contd.

```
              WRITE(OUTLUN,*)' ANGLE BETWEEN SIDE # 1 & SIDE # 2 IS:',THETA
              WRITE(OUTLUN,*)' ANGLE BETWEEN SIDE # 2 & SIDE # 3 IS:',ALPHA
              WRITE(OUTLUN,*)' ANGLE BETWEEN SIDE # 1 & SIDE # 3 IS:',BETA
              WRITE(OUTLUN,*)' THE AREA OF THE TRIANGLE IS = ',AREA
* READ NEXT SET OF THE INPUT DATA
              WRITE(OUTLUN,*)' ENTER THE INPUT DATA'
              WRITE(OUTLUN,*)' SIDE # 1:'
              READ(INLUN,*)SIDE1
              WRITE(OUTLUN,*)' SIDE # 2:'
              READ(INLUN,*)SIDE2
              WRITE(OUTLUN,*)' ANGLE BETWEEN SIDE # 1 AND SIDE # 2:'
              READ(INLUN,*)THETA
          END DO
          STOP
          END
************************************************************************
```

Figure 4.19: Program Listing of Example 4.7.

RUN I

```
 ENTER THE INPUT DATA
  SIDE # 1:
 0.0
  SIDE # 2:
 6.0
 ANGLE BETWEEN SIDE # 1 AND SIDE # 2:
 50.0
 PLEASE ENTER A CORRECT VALUE FOR SIDE # 1
 3.0
 THE RESULTS FOR THE TRIANGLE ARE:
 SIDE # 1:    3.000000
 SIDE # 2:    6.000000
 SIDE # 3:    4.676466
 ANGLE BETWEEN SIDE # 1 & SIDE # 2 IS:    50.00000
 ANGLE BETWEEN SIDE # 2 & SIDE # 3 IS:    29.43198
 ANGLE BETWEEN SIDE # 1 & SIDE # 3 IS:   100.5680
 THE AREA OF THE TRIANGLE IS =    6.896431
 ENTER THE INPUT DATA
  SIDE # 1:
 5.0
  SIDE # 2:
 -7.0
 ANGLE BETWEEN SIDE # 1 AND SIDE # 2:
 180.0
 PLEASE ENTER A CORRECT VALUE FOR SIDE # 2
 3.0
 PLEASE ENTER A CORRECT VALUE FOR ANGLE
 36.0
 THE RESULTS FOR THE TRIANGLE ARE:
 SIDE # 1:    5.000000
 SIDE # 2:    3.000000
 SIDE # 3:    3.119928
 ANGLE BETWEEN SIDE # 1 & SIDE # 2 IS:    36.00000
 ANGLE BETWEEN SIDE # 2 & SIDE # 3 IS:   109.5122
 ANGLE BETWEEN SIDE # 1 & SIDE # 3 IS:    34.48779
 THE AREA OF THE TRIANGLE IS =    4.409924
 ENTER THE INPUT DATA
  SIDE # 1:
 0.0
  SIDE # 2:
 0.0
 ANGLE BETWEEN SIDE # 1 AND SIDE # 2:
 0.0
```

Figure 4.20: Input and Output Results of Example 4.7.

4.5 PROGRAMMING EXAMPLES FOR THE CHAPTER

Example 4.8

The solution of a quadratic equation

$$ax^2 + bx + c = 0$$

is given by

$$x_{1,2} = \frac{-b \pm \sqrt{b^2 - 4ac}}{2a}$$

Based on the values of the coefficients a, b and c, the following cases may arise:

(1) If $(b^2 - 4ac) > 0$, roots are real and unequal and are given by

$$x_1 = \frac{-b + \sqrt{b^2 - 4ac}}{2a} \text{ and } x_2 \frac{-b - \sqrt{b^2 - 4ac}}{2a}$$

(2) If $(b^2 - 4ac) = 0$, roots are real and equal and are given by

$$x_1 = x_2 = -\frac{b}{2a}$$

(3) If $(b^2 - 4ac) < 0$, roots are complex and are given by

$$\left\{ \begin{array}{l} x_1 \\ \text{Real part} = -b/2a \\ \text{Imaginary part} = \sqrt{4ac - b^2}/2a \end{array} \right. \qquad \left\{ \begin{array}{l} x_2 \\ \text{Real part} = -b/2a \\ \text{Imaginary part} = -\sqrt{4ac - b^2}/2a \end{array} \right.$$

This program requests values for the coefficients (a, b and c) of the quadratic equation and calculates two roots. It prints two roots with a suitable massage for each case above. The program continues to execute until it is terminated by typing zeros for all the three coefficients.

Notice that the quantity $(b^2 - 4ac)$, sometimes called the *discriminant*, decides whether roots are real or complex. Therefore, this quantity is computed and stored in the variable called DISCRM for further use in calculating the roots. The source program is given in Figure 4.21 and the output results in Figure 4.22.

Example 4.9

This example is a good illustration of selecting various options and then carrying out necessary computations. The program converts various measurements in FPS system to SI system. It converts from either pound (1b) to kilogram (kg) (1 1b = 0.4536 kg), or from feet to meters (1 foot = 0.3048 meters) or from degree Fahrenheit (°F) to degree Celsius (°C) $(°C = \frac{(°F - 32)}{9} \times 5)$.

The program prints a menu of these options and asks the user to select one,

```
******************************************************************************
*        THIS PROGRAM CALCULATES ROOTS OF THE EQUATION:                      *
*             A*X**2 + B*X + C = 0.0                                         *
*   LIST OF VARIABLES:                                                       *
*     NAME                    USAGE                                          *
*     ----                    -----                                          *
*     A,B,C             COEFFICIENTS OF THE EQUATION                         *
*     DISCRM            DISCRIMINANT                                         *
*     ROOT1,ROOT2       TWO DISTINCT REAL ROOTS OF THE EQUATION             *
*     ROOT              EQUAL REAL ROOT OF THE EQUATION                      *
*     ROOT_R.           REAL PART OF THE COMPLEX ROOT                        *
*     ROOT_I            IMAGINARY PART OF THE COMPLEX ROOT                    *
******************************************************************************
*
        INTEGER INLUN,OUTLUN
        PARAMETER (INLUN = 5, OUTLUN = 6)
* READ INPUT DATA
        WRITE(OUTLUN,*)' ENTER COEFFICIENTS A,B & C'
        READ(INLUN,*)A,B,C
* PERFORM CALCULATIONS
        DO WHILE (A.NE.0.0.AND.B.NE.0.0.AND.C.NE.0.0)
           DISCRM=B**2-4.0*A*C
           IF(DISCRM.GT.0.0)THEN
* TWO DISTINCT REAL ROOTS
              WRITE(OUTLUN,*)' BOTH ROOTS ARE REAL AND GIVEN AS FOLLOWS:'
              ROOT1=(-B+SQRT(DISCRM))/(2.0*A)
              ROOT2=(-B-SQRT(DISCRM))/(2.0*A)
              WRITE(OUTLUN,*)' ROOT1=',ROOT1,' ROOT2=',ROOT2
           ELSE IF(DISCRM.EQ.0.0)THEN
* TWO EQUAL REAL ROOTS
              WRITE(OUTLUN,*)' BOTH ROOTS ARE REAL AND EQUAL AND GIVEN',
     1      ' AS FOLLOWS:'
              ROOT=-B/(2.0*A)
              WRITE(OUTLUN,*)' ROOT1= ROOT2=',ROOT
           ELSE
* TWO COMPLEX ROOTS
              WRITE(OUTLUN,*)' BOTH ROOTS ARE COMPLEX & GIVEN AS FOLLOWS:'
              ROOT_R=-B/(2.0*A)
              ROOT_I=SQRT(-DISCRM)
              WRITE(OUTLUN,*)'             ROOT1'
              WRITE(OUTLUN,*)' REAL PART      ',ROOT_R
              WRITE(OUTLUN,*)' IMAGINARY PART',ROOT_I
              WRITE(OUTLUN,*)'             ROOT2'
              WRITE(OUTLUN,*)' REAL PART      ',ROOT_R
              WRITE(OUTLUN,*)' IMAGINARY PART',-ROOT_I
           END IF
* READ NEXT INPUT DATA SET
           WRITE(OUTLUN,*)' ENTER COEFFICIENTS A,B & C'
           READ(INLUN,*)A,B,C
        END DO
        STOP
        END
******************************************************************************
```

Figure 4.21: Program Listing of Example 4.8.

```
                    RUN I

    ENTER COEFFICIENTS A,B & C
1.0 3.0 2.0
    BOTH ROOTS ARE REAL AND GIVEN AS FOLLOWS:
ROOT1=  -1.000000      ROOT2=  -2.000000
    ENTER COEFFICIENTS A,B & C
1.0 2.0 1.0
    BOTH ROOTS ARE REAL AND EQUAL AND GIVEN AS FOLLOWS:
ROOT1= ROOT2=  -1.000000
    ENTER COEFFICIENTS A,B & C
9.0,7.0,5.0
    BOTH ROOTS ARE COMPLEX & GIVEN AS FOLLOWS:
                ROOT1
REAL PART         -0.3888889
IMAGINARY PART    11.44552
                ROOT2
REAL PART         -0.3888889
IMAGINARY PART   -11.44552
    ENTER COEFFICIENTS A,B & C
0.0,0.0 0.0
```

Figure 4.22: Output Results of Example 4.8.

it uses a repetition structure to allow the user to make as many conversions as desired. The menu of options is:

1) Convert pound to kilogram
2) Convert feet to meters
3) Convert degree Fahrenheit to degree Celsius
4) Exit

The output is as follows:

WELCOME TO CONVERSION PROGRAM
THE MENU OF OPTIONS IS:
CONVERSION FROM POUNDS TO KILOGRAMS TYPE 1
CONVERSION FROM FEET TO METERS TYPE 2
CONVERSION FROM DEGREE FAHRENHEIT TO DEGREE CEL-
SIUS TYPE 3
IF YOU WANT TO EXIT, TYPE 4
ENTER MENU OPTION: 1, 2, 3, 4

If you enter 3

PLEATE ENTER DEGREES FAHRENHEIT

If you enter 32

EQUIVALENT DEGREES CELSIUS IS 0
ENTER MENU OPTION: 1, 2, 3, 4

If you enter 9

ERROR: 9 IS NOT A VALID MENU OPTION
PLEASE ENTER CORRECT MENU OPTION: 1, 2, 3, 4
$\vdots$

See the source program in Figure 4.23 and the output in Figure 4.24.

```
************************************************************************
*     THIS PROGRAM CONVERTS QUANTITIES IN F.P.S. SYSTEM TO S.I. SYSTEM *
*     LIST OF VARIABLES:                                               *
*       NAME                    USAGE                                  *
*       ----                    -----                                  *
*       MENU            MENU OPTION: 1,2,3 OR 4                         *
*       WEIGHT          WEIGHT                                         *
*       MEAZUR          MEASUREMENTS                                    *
*       TEMP            TEMPERATURE                                     *
************************************************************************
*
        INTEGER INLUN,OUTLUN
        PARAMETER(INLUN = 5, OUTLUN = 6)
        REAL MEAZUR
* PRINT A SUMMARY OF MENU OPTIONS
        WRITE(OUTLUN,*)' WELCOME TO CONVERSION PROGRAM'
        WRITE(OUTLUN,*)' THE MENU OF OPTIONS IS:'
        WRITE(OUTLUN,*)' CONVERSION FROM POUNDS TO KILOGRAMS TYPE 1'
        WRITE(OUTLUN,*)' CONVERSION FROM FEET TO METERS TYPE 2'
        WRITE(OUTLUN,*)' CONVERSION FROM DEGREE FAHRENHEIT TO DEGREE',
     1  ' CELSIUS TYPE 3'
        WRITE(OUTLUN,*)' IF YOU WANT TO EXIT, TYPE 4'
* READ INPUT DATA
        WRITE(OUTLUN,*)' ENTER MENU OPTION: 1, 2, 3, 4'
        READ(INLUN,*)MENU
* PERFORM CALCULATIONS
        DO WHILE (MENU.NE.4)
* CHECK FOR ANY ERROR IN THE INPUT DATA
          DO WHILE (MENU.LT.1.OR.MENU.GT.4)
            WRITE(OUTLUN,*)' ERROR:',MENU,' IS NOT A VALID MENU OPTION'
            WRITE(OUTLUN,*)' PLEASE ENTER CORRECT MENU OPTION: 1,2,3,4'
            READ(INLUN,*)MENU
          END DO
*
          IF(MENU.EQ.1)THEN
            WRITE(OUTLUN,*)' PLEASE ENTER WEIGHTS IN POUNDS'
            READ(INLUN,*)WEIGHT
            WEIGHT=WEIGHT*0.4536
            WRITE(OUTLUN,*)' EQUIVALENT WEIGHT IN KILOGRAMS IS:',WEIGHT
          ELSE IF(MENU.EQ.2)THEN
            WRITE(OUTLUN,*)' PLEASE ENTER MEASUREMENTS IN FEET'
            READ(INLUN,*)MEAZUR
            MEAZUR=MEAZUR*0.3048
            WRITE(OUTLUN,*)' EQUIVALENT MEASUREMENTS IN METERS IS:',
     1      MEAZUR
          ELSE IF(MENU.EQ.3)THEN
            WRITE(OUTLUN,*)' PLEASE ENTER DEGREES FAHRENHEIT'
            READ(INLUN,*)TEMP
            TEMP=(TEMP-32.0)*5.0/9.0
            WRITE(OUTLUN,*)' EQUIVALENT DEGREES CELSIUS IS:',TEMP
          END IF
          IF(MENU.NE.4)THEN
            WRITE(OUTLUN,*)' ENTER MENU OPTION 1, 2, 3, 4'
            READ(INLUN,*)MENU
          END IF
        END DO
        STOP
        END
************************************************************************
```

Figure 4.23: Program Listing of Example 4.9.

```
                              RUN I

    WELCOME TO CONVERSION PROGRAM
    THE MENU OF OPTIONS IS:
    CONVERSION FROM POUNDS TO KILOGRAMS TYPE 1
    CONVERSION FROM FEET TO METERS TYPE 2
    CONVERSION FROM DEGREE FAHRENHEIT TO DEGREE CELSIUS TYPE 3
    IF YOU WANT TO EXIT, TYPE 4
    ENTER MENU OPTION: 1, 2, 3, 4
    3
    PLEASE ENTER DEGREES FAHRENHEIT
    212
    EQUIVALENT DEGREES CELSIUS IS:    100.0000
    ENTER MENU OPTION 1, 2, 3, 4
    2
    PLEASE ENTER MEASUREMENTS IN FEET
    10.0
    EQUIVALENT MEASUREMENTS IN METERS IS:    3.048000
    ENTER MENU OPTION 1, 2, 3, 4
    5
    ERROR:            5 IS NOT A VALID MENU OPTION
    PLEASE ENTER CORRECT MENU OPTION: 1,2,3,4
    1
    PLEASE ENTER WEIGHTS IN POUNDS
    150.0
    EQUIVALENT WEIGHT IN KILOGRAMS IS:    68.04000
    ENTER MENU OPTION 1, 2, 3, 4
    9
    ERROR:            9 IS NOT A VALID MENU OPTION
    PLEASE ENTER CORRECT MENU OPTION: 1,2,3,4
    9
    ERROR:            9 IS NOT A VALID MENU OPTION
    PLEASE ENTER CORRECT MENU OPTION: 1,2,3,4
    4
```

Figure 4.24: Output Results of Example 4.9.

4.6 SUMMARY

This chapter has presented some of the most powerful statements available in FORTRAN. The selection or control statements have greatly expanded the range of problems that can be solved. The inclusion of the IF-THEN-ELSE-ENDIF statement in FORTRAN 77 provides programmers an opportunity to write structured programs. We strongly recommend the use of this statement wherever possible. The use of other control statements, such as the arithmetic IF, logical IF and GO TO statements, is strongly discouraged because they tend to cause multiple branches. These statements have, however, been discussed in detail keeping in view the fact that all users may not have access to a computer that supports the FORTRAN 77 compiler.

This chapter has also been devoted to another invaluable construct, the repetition statements. The DO statement and the WHILE statement provide a simple and convenient way to build iteration or counting loops. The DO statement combines the three steps of initializing a counter, incrementing the counter and testing the counter into one statement. The number of iterations that a DO statement makes is fixed and depends on the value of three parameters. The WHILE statement, on the other hand, iterates for an indefinite number of times as long as the logical expression contained in the WHILE statement is true.

The user should carefully study the example problems worked out in this chapter and try to solve the exercises given at the end of this chapter in order to gain complete confidence over these powerful statements.

In the next chapter, we will introduce the input/output statements provided in FORTRAN 77. The flexibility and the capabilities provided by these input/output statements would enable students to solve many complex problems involving large input data.

OBJECTIVE QUESTIONS

(1) Which of the following comments about logical expressions is false?
   (a) Parentheses must be used within expression to indicate those subexpressions that are to be evaluated first.
   (b) Expression will always be evaluated either as TRUE or FALSE.
   (c) Logical operators can be applied to numeric quantities.
   (d) In the absence of parentheses, the logical operator .NOT. has the highest priority (performed first) among logical operators.
   (e) Logical operators have lower priority than relational operators.

(2) Which of the following comments about a FORTRAN program is false?
   (a) When a GO TO is encountered, the execution is transferred to the statement referred to in the GO TO statement.
   (b) Excessive use of GO TOs results in efficient and neat programming.
   (c) The statement to which control is transferred by a GO TO statement must have a statement label.
   (d) The logical and relational operators must be within periods.
   (e) An arithmetic IF can always be replaced by logical IF statements.

(3) Which of the following comments about a FORTRAN program is true?
   (a) A FORTRAN program must contain a selection construct.
   (b) All FORTRAN statements must be numbered.
   (c) Statement numbers must be in a sequence.
   (d) Those statements which are referenced by another program statement must be numbered.
   (e) Statement numbers are related to line numbers.

(4) Which of the following IF statements is correct?
   (a) IF (X .GT. Y)
   (b) IF (X>Y) GO TO 20
   (c) IF (X .EQ. Y) THEN
       ELSE
           X = Y
       END IF
   (d) IF (X .EQ. Y) THEN Y = X
   (e) IF (X−Y) 10, 10, 20

(5) Which of the following block IF constructs is correct?

(a) IF X .GT. Y THEN	(b) (IF I .LE. J) THEN	(c) IF (I .LE. J)
X = Y	J = I	J = I
END IF	ELSE I = J	END IF

(d) IF (X .GT. Y) THEN   (e) IF (X .GT. Y) THEN
         Y = X   Y = X
     ELSE   ELSE IF (X .EQ. Y) THEN
     IF (X .EQ. Y) THEN   Y = X/2
         Y = X/2   END IF
     END IF   END IF
     END IF

(6) Which of the following DO statements is correct?

   (a) DO, 9345I = 1, 10
   (b) DO UNTIL I = 1
   (c) DO J = I*2, J*2, K/3.0
   (d) DO 5000 J = 1.0, 2.0,
   (e) DO 9345 K = I+M, M−I, M/2

(7) How many times would this DO statement be executed?
         DO 20 I = 1, 88, 10

   (a) 10
   (b) 9
   (c) 88
   (d) 20
   (e) 8

(8) For the following DO statement, which comment is false?
         DO 10 I = J, K, L

   (a) The iteration count is given by $(K−J+L)/L$.
   (b) J, K and L can have negative values.
   (c) The DO variable I can be used in an expression inside the DO range.
   (d) The loop is executed 10 times.
   (e) J, K and L must be assigned values before the execution of this statement.

(9) What is printed by this program segment?
         I = 0
         DO 99 J = 5, 1, −1
            I = I+J
      99 CONTINUE
         WRITE (5,*), I

   (a) I
   (b) 5
   (c) 99
   (d) 15
   (e) 0

(10) What is printed by this program segment ?
         J = 5
         DO 10 I = 1, J
            WRITE (5,*) J
            J = J−1

      10 CONTINUE
   (a) 1   (b) 5   (c) An Error Message   (d) 5   (e) 5
        2   4   5
        3   3   5
        4   2   5
        5   1   5

(11) What is printed by this program?

```
      DO 10 I = 1, 5
         WRITE (5,*) I
         I = I−1
10    CONTINUE
```

(a) 1   (b) 1   (c) An error message   (d) 5   (e) 0
   2   0   4   0
   3   0   3   0
   4   0   2   0
   5   0   1   0

(12) Which of the following program segments does not print the value of SUM as 10.0?

(a)
```
      SUM = 0.0
      DO 10 I = 1, 10
         SUM = SUM+1.0
10    CONTINUE
      WRITE (5,*) SUM
```

(b)
```
      SUM = 0.0
      DO 10 J = 1, 2
         DO 10 I = 5, 1, −1
            SUM = SUM  +1.0
10    CONTINUE
      WRITE (5,*) SUM
```

(c)
```
      SUM = 0.0
      DO 10 I = 1, 10
         SUM = SUM+I
10    CONTINUE
      WRITE (5,*) SUM
```

(d)
```
      SUM = 0.0
      DO WHILE (SUM .LT. 10.0)
         SUM = SUM+2.0
      END DO
      WRITE (5,*) SUM
```

(e)
```
      SUM = 0.0
10    SUM = SUM+2.0
      IF (SUM .LT. 10.0) GO TO 10
      WRITE (5,*) SUM
```

(13) Which of the following repetition constructs does not produce an infinite loop?

(a)
```
      x = 0.0
      DO WHILE (x .NE. 1.0)
         x = x+0.3
      WRITE (5,*), 'INFINITE LOOP'
      END DO
```

(b)
```
5     x = 0.0
      x = x+0.2
      IF (x .LE. 1.0) GO TO 5
```

(c)
```
      x = 0.0
      DO 10 WHILE (x .EQ. 0.0)
         y = x
10    CONTINUE
      x = x+0.2
```

(d)
```
      I = 1
10    IF (I .GT. 1) GO TO 20
      J = I+1
20    IF (J .EQ. 2) GO TO 10
```

(e)
```
      DO 10 I = 1, 1000
         DO 10 J = 1,1000
            DO 10 K = 1, 1000
               WRITE (5,*), 'INFINITE LOOP'
10    CONTINUE
```

(14) What is printed by this program?

```
      N = 0
      I = 0
      DO 9 J = 1, 10
         DO 9 K = 5, 1, −1
            I = I+1
            DO 9 M = 1, 2
               N = N+1
```

```
      9  CONTINUE
         WRITE (5,*) I, N
```

- (a)   0   0
- (b)   15   17
- (c)   50   52
- (d)   50 100
- (e) 150 150

(15) Which of the following statements is true?

- (a) A C in column 6 of a FORTRAN statement indicates a continuation from the preceding program line.
- (b) The statement GO TO LINE 3 is valid.
- (c) The statement DO 100 I*J = 1, K/J is valid.
- (d) The statement IF (X .NE. Y) GO TO 50 is valid.
- (e) Only one STOP statement is allowed in one program.

(16) Which of the following statements is false?

- (a) The DO variable can be a real variable.
- (b) The range of the DO statement will always be processed at least once.
- (c) After normal exit of the DO loop, the value of the DO variable becomes undefined.
- (d) A DO loop should always be entered at the DO statement.
- (e) A comment statement in the range of a DO loop is not executed and simply ignored.

(17) Which of the following statements is false?

- (a) The condition shown in a decision diamond of a flowchart is the basis for the logical expression in an IF statement.
- (b) When nesting block IF statements, a single END IF statement can be used as the last statement for two block IF statements
- (c) When nesting DO statements, a single CONTINUE statement can be used as the last statement for two DO statements.
- (d) The DO variable in a DO loop must not be modified by a statement in the range of the loop.
- (e) If a group of instructions are to be executed for a fixed number of times in a program, it is a good practice to use a DO loop.

DRILL EXERCISES

(1) If $I = 1, J = 2, K = 3, X = 1.0, Y = 2.0$ and $Z = 3.0$, evaluate the following logical expressions, whether TRUE or FALSE.

- (i) (I .GT. J*K) .AND. (Y .EQ. J*X)
- (ii) ((Z .NE. X+Y) .AND. (.NOT. (X .LT. Y))) .OR. (I .EQ. K)
- (iii) (.NOT. (Z .GT. Y) .AND. (I .NE. J)) .EQV. (I .LE. J)
- (iv) (I .LT. K) .AND. (J .LT. K) .AND. (Z .GE. Y+X) .AND. (X .EQ. I)
- (v) (I*J/K .EQ. J−2*I) .OR. ((Y*Z .EQ. 6.0) .AND. (X .LT. Y))

(2) Write a program segment using computed GO TOs to calculate the value of SUM that is given as follows:

```
IF I = 1 SUM = X+Y+Z
IF I = 2 SUM = (X+Y)*(Y+Z)
IF I = 3 SUM = (X−Y)/Z
IF I = 4 SUM = 0.0
IF I = 5 SUM = X/Y/Z
IF I = 6 SUM = 0.0
```

The program segment should ask for the values of I, X, Y and Z. It will then print the value of SUM.

(3) Study the following program segment:

```
IF (KOO .GT. 11) THEN
    IF (MEOW .EQ. 25) THEN
        IF (LOOG .EQ. 1) THEN
            WRITE (5.*), 'OH! GOD'
        ENDIF
    END IF
ELSE
WRITE (5,*), 'HI ! HI'
END IF
```

What will the above program segment print for the following values of KOO, LOOG, MEOW?

  (i) KOO = 24, LOOG = 1, MEOW = 25
 (ii) KOO = 1, LOOG = 1, MEOW = 150
(iii) KOO = 2000, LOOG = 1, MEOW = 150
(iv) KOO = 2000, LOOG = 5, MEOW = 25
 (v) KOO = 2000, LOOG = 2000, MEOW = 2000

(4) Study the following program segment and rewrite it using the multialternative selection structure, i.e. using ELSE IF statements:

```
IF (1e1) THEN
    IF (1e2) THEN
        block₁
    ELSE
        IF (1e3) THEN
            block₃
        END IF
        block₂
    END IF
ELSE
    IF (1e4) THEN
        block₄
    END IF
END IF
```

(5) Repeat Exercise 4 to write the program segment using logical IF and GO TOs. Now that you have three versions of the program segment, which one do you think is easy to understand?

(6) Write a FORTRAN 77 program segment for each of the following cases:
  (i) To calculate the value of COST when COST is a function of number of units (NUNITS):

If	$0 < NUNITS < 100$	COST = 1000 + 5*NUNITS
If	$100 \leq NUNITS < 500$	COST = 1100 + 4*NUNITS
If	$NUNITS \geqslant 500$	COST = 1350 + 3.5*NUNITS

 (ii) To calculate the safe load (S) of a certain type of load-bearing column. The safe load is a function of slimness ratio (R) of the column which is defined as the ratio of its length to its width. The safe load in pounds per square inch is given by two empirical formulae:

$$S = \begin{cases} 17000-0.485R^2 & \text{for } R < 120 \\ \dfrac{18000}{1+(R^2/18000)} & \text{for } R \geqslant 120 \end{cases}$$

(iii) To calculate the federal tax paid by a Canadian in 1985. Rates of federal income tax are given as follows:

Taxable Income (TI)	Tax ($)	Taxable Income (TI)	Tax ($)
TI≤ 1295	0.06*TI	12950<TI≤18130	3176+0.20(TI−12950)
1295<TI≤ 2590	78+0.16(TI−1295)	18130<TI≤23310	3212+0.23(TI 18130)
2590<TI≤ 5180	285+0.17(TI−2590)	23310<TI≤36260	4403+0.25(TI−23310)
5180<TI≤ 7770	725+0.18(TI−5180)	36260<TI≤62160	7641+0.30(TI−36260)
7770<TI≤12950	1191+0.19(TI−7770)	TI>62160	15411+0.34(TI−62160)

(iv) To assign grades on a grading scheme (commonly called 'grading on the curve') according to the following table:

X = MARKS OBTAINED	GRADES
$X < M - \dfrac{3}{2}\sigma$	0.0
$M - \dfrac{3}{2}\sigma \leq X < M - \dfrac{1}{2}\sigma$	1.0
$M - \dfrac{1}{2}\sigma \leq X < M + \dfrac{1}{2}\sigma$	2.0
$M + \dfrac{1}{2}\sigma \leq X < M + \dfrac{3}{2}\sigma$	3.0
$M + \dfrac{3}{2}\sigma \leq X$	4.0

where M is the average marks obtained, and σ is the standard deviation.

(v) To display the number of days in the month corresponding to a MONTH (1, 2,..., 12).

(vi) To calculate the sum of harmonic series

$$SUM = \sum_{K=1}^{100} \frac{1}{K}$$

(vii) To calculate the sum of the following series:

$$SUM = \sum_{i=1}^{100} \frac{6}{i^2}$$

(7) Write program segments using arithmetic IF, logical IF, GO TOs (don't use block IF and DO statements) for the cases (i), (iii), (iv) and (vii) of Exercise 6.

. (8) Analyze the following program and find out what is printed by the statement WRITE:

(i)
```
        DO 10 I = 1, 6, 2
            DO 10 J = 2, 4
                WRITE (5,*), I*J
    10  CONTINUE
```

(ii)
```
        J = 4
        I = 5
        DO WHILE (J .LE. 7)
            I = I+J
            WRITE (5,*), I, J
            J = J+1
        END DO
```

(iii)
```
        K = 3
        N = 100
        IF (K**2 .LE. N) THEN
            WRITE (5,*), K, N, K**2
            K = K+3
        END IF
        WRITE (5,*), K, N, K**2
```

(iv)
```
        X = 2.0
        Y = 3.0
        IF (X. LT. Y) TEMP = Y
        TEMP = X
        Y = TEMP
        IF (Y .GE. X) TEMP = X
        TEMP = Y
        X = TEMP
        WRITE (5,*), X, Y, TEMP
```

(9) Find mistakes in the following program segments:

(i)
```
        I = 2
        IF (I .GREATER. 1) THEN
            IF (I*5 .LE. 10)
            END IF
        ELSE
        END IF
```

(ii)
```
        N = 4.5
     10 IF (I .LT. N) THE
            I = I+1
            WRITE (5,*) I, N
            GO TO 20
        END IF
```

(iii)
```
        X = 1.0
        Y = 5.0
        DO 10 Z = Y, X, 2.0
            Z = Z+0.5
            Y = Y-5.0
            X = X+5.0
     10 WRITE (5, *), X, Y, Z
```

(iv) Add five numbers (1 to 5)
```
        DO 10 I = 1, 5
            ISUM = 0
            ISUM = ISUM+I
            I = 2*I
     20 CONTINUE
        WRITE (5,*) SUM
```

```
(v)        DO 1K I = 10,J,K
              J = 2
              K = 3
              DO 20 J = 1,10
                 IF (J .GT. K)
                    K = J
                 ELSE
                    1K = J
                 END
       1K   CONTINUE
              WRITE (5,*), J, I, K
       20   CONTINUE
```

(10) Which of these are valid nested DO constructs?

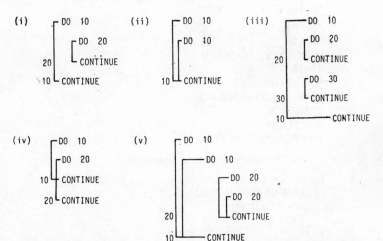

(11). Which of the following are permissible transfers in DO loops?

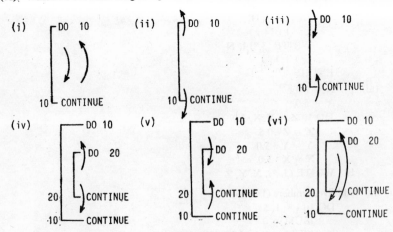

(12) Write a FORTRAN 77 program segment which requests an unknown number of integers and prints them out in the following sequence:

I2 I3 I4 .... I1

where integer I1 is accepted first, I2 is accepted next and so on .... In the output I2 is printed first, then I3, then I4 ... and then the last integer and then I1. The last integer is identified by a very large number, e.g. 9999999.

(13) Write a FORTRAN 77 program segment which counts non-zero digits in an integer number, e.g. the integer number 1001 contains two non-zero digits while in integer number 1234 all four are non-zero digits.

PROGRAMMING EXERCISES

(1) In a recent budget presented by the Finance Minister, the postal rates have been increased. The new rates for mailing letters are as follows:

    Rs 0.50 per 10 grams for the first 50 grams
    Rs 0.40 per 10 grams for the next 100 grams
    Rs 0.25 per 10 grams for the next 350 grams
    Rs 25 per kilogram for letters weighing more than 500 grams.

Prepare a FORTRAN 77 program that asks the weight of a letter and prints the postage to be paid.

(2) Air pressure is a function of altitude (h). Write a FORTRAN 77 program to compute the air pressure (p), which is given by

$$p = 14.7\, e^{-0.00038h}$$

at the following locations:

Location	Elevation (h in feet)
Everest	29,141
Nanda Devi	25,645
New York	55
New Delhi	760
Dead Sea	−1292

(3) GMT (Greenwich Mean Time) is taken as a reference to calculate the time around the world. Greenwich is situated at 0° longitude. For the purpose of calculating local time of a location, it is assumed that the longitude of a location east of Greenwich is positive and that of a location west of Greenwich is negative. The local time can then be computed by the following formula:

    Local time in hours = GMT in hours + Longitude of the location* 24/360

Write a FORTRAN 77 program to calculate the local time at the following locations if GMT = 12.00 hours:

Location	Longitude (degrees)
Calcutta	90
Melbourne	145
Madras	80
New York	−75
Beijing	120
Vancouver	−125
Brasilia	−50

(4) Birth control methods that are most widely used in North America are listed in the table below. An approximate probability of the effectiveness of each method is also given, that is, e.g. the probability of pills is 0.993, which means that out of 1,000 users, only seven can get pregnant. In a city, a survey was conducted on 1,000 couples to determine what methods they used. It was found that 50% couples used pills, 20% used condoms, 10% used the I.U.D., 7% used the diaphragm, 3% used chemical methods and the rest did not use any contraceptives. Write a FORTRAN 77 program to estimate the number of women likely to become pregnant.

S. No.	Method	Probability of Effectiveness
1	Pills	0.993
2	Condom	0.700
3	I.U.D.	0.980
4	Diaphragm	0.970
5	Chemical Methods	0.950
6	No contraceptive	0.400

(5) A projectile fired at an angle (θ) has a horizontal range (R) given by the following:

$$R = \frac{u^2 \sin 2\theta}{g}$$

where   u = initial velocity (m/sec.)
          g = 9.81 m/sec^2

Write a FORTRAN 77 program to compute R for each of the following values of u and θ.

u	θ
(i) 50	0° to 90° in steps of 15°
(ii) 2000	20° to 80° in steps of 20°

(6) Write a FORTRAN 77 program to accept a value of a and then print the value of the following integral:

$$\int_0^\pi \frac{x \sin x \, dx}{1 - 2a \cos x + a^2} = \begin{cases} \dfrac{\pi}{|a|} \ln(1 + |a|) & a < 1 \\ \pi \ln(1 + 1/a) & a > 1 \end{cases}$$

The program should stop if a is equal to zero, or a is equal to 1. Try for a$= -2.0$ to -0.2 in steps of 0.2 and a$=0.1$ to 1.0 in steps of 0.1.

(7) Write a FORTRAN 77 program to calculate and print the first 50 partial sums of the continued fraction

$$\text{SUM} = 1 + \cfrac{1}{1 + \cfrac{1}{1 + \cfrac{1}{1 + \cfrac{1}{1 + \cfrac{1}{1 + \cdot}}}}}$$

(8) Write a FORTRAN 77 program to evaluate the sum of each of the following infinite series:

(i) $\dfrac{1}{1^2} - \dfrac{1}{2^2} + \dfrac{1}{3^2} - \dfrac{1}{4^2} + \dfrac{1}{5^2} - \ldots\ldots$

(ii) $\dfrac{1}{1^2 2^2 3^2} + \dfrac{1}{2^2 3^2 4^2} + \dfrac{1}{3^2 4^2 5^2} + \ldots\ldots$

(iii) $x^2 - \dfrac{2^3 x^4}{4!} + \dfrac{2^5 x^6}{6!} - \ldots\ldots$ for $x = 2.0$

(iv) $(x-1) - \dfrac{(x-1)^2}{2} + \dfrac{(x-1)^3}{3} - \dfrac{(x-1)^4}{4} + \ldots\ldots$ for $x = 5.0$.

Your programs should print the sum after 5, 10, 50, 100 and 200 terms for each series.

(9) Write a FORTRAN 77 program to guess the minimum value of the quadratic equation

$$y = ax^2 + bx + c$$

in the interval between -5 and 10. Your program should do the following:

1. Request values for coefficients a, b and c from the user.
2. Initialize starting values for the variables
   XMIN and YMIN (use XMIN=0, YMIN = c).
3. Repeatedly generate a random guess for X and compute the corresponding value for Y. Test the value of Y against YMIN. If Y is smaller than YMIN, then replace XMIN and YMIN with the current values of X and Y.

To generate a random guess for X, you can use an intrinsic function RAN (SEED) where SEED is a large odd integer, e.g. 9999999. This gives a random number between 0 and 1.0. To get a random number between -5 and 10, you can use a statement

$$X = 15*RAN (SEED) -5$$

Repeat step (3) 200 times or more to obtain a reasonably good estimate for XMIN. If you increase the number of iterations to 500 do you expect to get a better estimate for XMIN. Test this statement.

(10) An approximation to the factorial is given by Stirling's approximation

$$n! = \sqrt{2\pi n}\ n^n\ e^{-n}$$

Write a FORTRAN 77 program to compute n! exactly, that is, using $n! = n(n-1)(n-2)\ldots 3.2.1$, and compare this value with the approximate value obtained by Stirling's formula. Compute the percentage relative error in the approximation. Your output should appear as follows:

N	EXACT VALUE	APPROXIMATE VALUE	% RELATIVE ERROR
1	1	0.9221	7.786
		$\vdots$	

The % relative error is given as follows:

$$\% \text{ relative error} = \frac{\text{exact value} - \text{approximate value}}{\text{exact value}} * 100.0$$

Print your output for n from 1 through 20.

(11) The mean arrival rate of persons at a cinema-house ticket window queue is λ and the mean service rate with which the ticket issuer can issue tickets is μ. If it is assumed that the arrival and the service (issuing of a ticket) process follow a Poisson distribution, then the mean number of persons waiting for service in a queue at the window is given by:

$$n = \frac{\lambda/\mu}{(1-\lambda/\mu)} \text{ if } \frac{\lambda}{\mu} < 1 \qquad (1)$$

and the probability that there are n persons waiting in the queue is

$$P_n = \left[\frac{\lambda}{\mu} \right]^n \left[1 - \frac{\lambda}{\mu} \right] \text{ if } \frac{\lambda}{\mu} < 1. \qquad (2)$$

Write a FORTRAN 77 program to do each of the following:

(i) For $\mu = 20$, compute and print the number of persons waiting in the queue for $\lambda = 0, 1, 2, \ldots, 19$.

(ii) For $\mu = 20$, and $\lambda = 4, 8, 12, 16$ compute P_n for $n = 0, 1, 2, 3, 4, \ldots, 20$.

(12) Write a FORTRAN 77 program to compute and print the value of each of the following series:

(i) $\dfrac{4}{\pi} \left[\dfrac{\sin x}{1} + \dfrac{\sin 3x}{3} + \dfrac{\sin 5x}{5} + \cdots + \dfrac{\sin 59x}{59} \right]$

for angles from $-180°$ to $180°$ in steps of $30°$.

(ii) $\dfrac{2}{\pi} - \dfrac{4}{\pi} \left[\dfrac{\cos 2x}{1.3} + \dfrac{\cos 4x}{3.5} + \dfrac{\cos 6x}{5.7} + \cdots + \dfrac{\cos 60x}{59.61} \right]$

for angles from $-180°$ to $180°$ in steps of $10°$.

(iii) $1 + x + \dfrac{x^2}{2!} + \dfrac{x^3}{3!} + \cdots + \dfrac{x^{99}}{99!} + \sin(x)$

for x from 0.0 to 1.0 in steps of 0.1.

(iv) $2 \left[\dfrac{x-1}{x+1} + \dfrac{1}{3} \left[\dfrac{x-1}{x+1} \right]^3 + \dfrac{1}{5} \left[\dfrac{x-1}{x+1} \right]^5 + \cdots + \dfrac{1}{99} \left[\dfrac{x-1}{x+1} \right]^{99} \right]$

for x from 1.0 to 4.0 in steps of 0.5.

ANSWERS TO OBJECTIVE QUESTIONS

(1) c	(2) b	(3) d	(4) e	(5) d	(6) e
(7) b	(8) d	(9) d	(10) b	(11) c	(12) c
(13) e	(14) d	(15) d	(16) b	(17) b	

Chapter 5

Files and Input/Output Operations

5.1 INTRODUCTION

Programs that we have written so far have involved relatively small amount of input/output data. In all of the examples, we have assumed that the input data were read from the input device such as a CRT terminal or a line printer. The output has also been directed to the output device such as a CRT terminal or a line printer. However, many applications involve large data sets, and these may be processed more conveniently if stored on magnetic tape or on a magnetic disk or on some other secondary (auxiliary) memory. The disks are the library of the computer system. During a computing session the memory (RAM) and the CPU are alive with data, calculations and programs. With disks or some other similar secondary storage devices, these things can be permanently recorded. Without them, all that you have done is forgotten when you log out (sign off).

Data stored in secondary memory can be processed in a FORTRAN program by using the structured data type called FILE. A file is a collection of related data items for input to or output by a program. The size of this collection is not fixed and is limited only by the amount of secondary memory available. Consequently, files are commonly used when there is too much data to store in main memory. The placement of input/output (I/O) data in a file is quite important. For clarity and better understanding of the I/O data it is necessary that the programmer has complete control over the form of printed output or of input data fields. The FORTRAN tool that provides this capability is FORMATted input/output.

In this chapter, file concepts, input/output operations and various format specifications are discussed at length. Example programs illustrating the use of files, input/output statements and formats are also included.

5.2 FILES

Data is transmitted to and from FORTRAN programs using files. A *file* is a collection of records, where each record is a contiguous stream of characters. The advantages of using files are:

1. The amount of data is so large that it is not possible to store it all in the computer's main memory.

135

2. The data can be easily used by processing one record at a time.
3. Several programs can access the same information when the information is stored in a file.
4. Any portion of the total amount of data can be easily accessed at any given time.
5. The user does not have to enter the data each time the program is executed, especially if the volume of data is large.

Figure 5.1 shows the path the data travels through a computer system when it is being written on the disk. When disk files are read, data follows

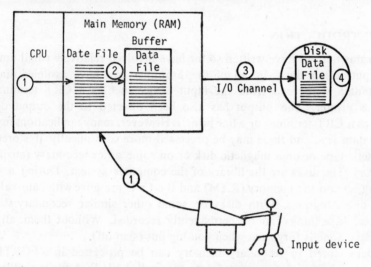

Figure 5.1: Flow of Data in a Disk-based Computer System.

the reverse path: from the disk over the *I/O channel* to the *buffer*, then to the RAM, and finally to an output device. A brief description of the flow of data is as follows:

1. Information created by a user at an input device (or a result produced by the CPU) is copied into the RAM.
2. As soon as the programmer's intention to store the information on the disk is known (end of data file editing session), the data is copied into a portion of RAM called the buffer. The buffer serves as a terminus for data transfer to and from the disk or magnetic tape.
3. Data traverses an I/O channel between the buffer and a designated disk file.
4. Data is coded onto the disk surface as tiny spots are magnetized in a clockwise or anti-clockwise direction. The data is stored on such disks in tracks arranged in concentric circles and is written onto or read from a disk using a disk drive. This device transfers information by means of a movable read/write head which is positioned over one of the tracks of the rotating disks. Magnetic tapes are also used for the storage of information.

In general, the data storage in a file can have either *sequential access* or *direct access*. With sequential access files, data must be read in the same order as it is written into the file. If the programmer wants to read fifth file record (line), the programmer must pass by the first four file records. On devices such as magnetic tapes, only sequential access files are possible. Direct access files allow a programmer to skip around, reading and updating file records without regard to their position in the file.

Sequential access files are easier to program and certainly the most efficient for a computer. These are preferred when the programmer wants to use almost all of the file data each time the file is opened, and its contents are very rarely changed. Direct access files are preferred if the programmer intends to frequently update the file records and wants to look at them out of sequence. Storing of mailing lists, theatre reservations and airline reservations are some of the application areas where direct access files are preferred.

Before discussing the programming processes needed to manipulate data files, it would be worthwhile to go through a brief discussion on records.

5.2.1 Records

The programmer's vocabulary includes two types of records: *physical records* and *file records*. A physical record is the smallest number of *bytes* that is transferred to or from the disk in one data transfer operation. The file buffer holds one physical record. Every WRITE operation writes out one record; every READ operation copies one physical record into the buffer. However, using formatted or list-directed I/O statements, it is possible to transfer data from or to more than one physical record. These records are termed as logical records. Thus, logical records are program-dependent while physical records are device-dependent. The distinction can be understood by considering a case where a record containing more than 80 characters is output to a terminal whose line width is 80. In this case, one logical record requires more than one physical record of 80 characters.

A file record is a conceptual unit of file information, and its size depends upon the programming project at hand. It is the entire package of information about an item in the file. A file record is composed of fields, or units of data, pertaining to the item. In an airline reservation file where the items are passengers, one file record contains all the information for one passenger. This record might be composed of several fields; a name field, an age field, a sex field, an address field, and a travelling-schedule field.

5.3 PROGRAMMING PROCESSES

Manipulating data files requires a computer program to accomplish five important tasks:

(a) "Connecting" to a file and declaring it OPEN: FORTRAN has an OPEN statement which takes care of this. OPEN associates FORTRAN logical units with files. It establishes a connection between a logical unit and a file or device.

(b)   Declaring the file OPEN for input or output: The computer needs to know whether the user will be writing into the file, or reading from the existing file.

(c)   Declaring the file for sequential or direct access: It makes a big difference to the computer whether the user plans to retrieve file data in sequence or whether an item will be retrieved directly without reading preceding items.

Tasks (b) and (c) and many others are accomplished by specifying suitable parameters in an OPEN statement.

(d)   Transferring data: The data is transferred by using READ and WRITE statements. Suitable parameters may be specified to accomplish desired processing.

(e)   Terminating the connection: The CLOSE statement terminates the connection between a logical unit and a file or device.

A brief description of the OPEN, CLOSE, READ, WRITE and other commonly used statements is given in the following sections.

5.4 OPEN STATEMENT

An OPEN statement either connects an existing file to a logical unit, or creates a new file and connects it to a logical unit. A partial syntax description of the FORTRAN 77 OPEN statement is as follows:

OPEN ([UNIT =] lun [,FILE = fname] [,ACCESS = acc] [,FORM = fmt] [,RECL = rlen] [,IOSTAT = ios] [,ERR = s] [,STATUS = sta])

Keyword specifications can appear in any order. Square brackets indicate optional parts; default values are provided in their absence. If the logical unit number (lun) is the first parameter in the list, the keyword identifier [UNIT =] is optional. lun is a non-negative integer unit number that must be unique for each file used in a program.

The FILE option, if specified, indicates the name of the file (fname) to be connected. If the file does not exist, most processors will create a file with the designated name. If this option is not specified, then the file is connected to a processor-determined file (i.e. the operating system assigns a file name of its choosing).

The ACCESS option is used to specify whether the file will be accessed sequentially or directly. If omitted, it is assumed that the file will be accessed sequentially. The associated character (acc) should be specified as DIRECT or SEQUENTIAL, as the case may be.

The FORM option is used to specify whether the file being opened is to be read or written using formatted or unformatted READ or WRITE statements. fmt is a character expression which can be either FORMATTED or

UNFORMATTED. For sequential access files, FORMATTED is the default while for direct access files UNFORMATTED is the default.

The RECL option is used to specify the maximum size of a logical record which can occur in the file. rlen is a numeric expression whose value must be greater than 0. For formatted files, the size is usually expressed as the number of characters in each record. For unformatted files, the size is the number of long words and it is always processor-dependent. This option is essential for direct access files and is ignored for sequential files.

The IOSTAT option is used to specify an integer variable to which a value will be assigned as indicating the status of the OPEN operation. It causes ios to be defined zero in a no-error condition, or as a positive integer if an error condition exists.

The ERR option is used to transfer control to the executable statement specified by statement label s when an error occurs in an OPEN statement. If an error occurs, no file is opened or created.

The STATUS option is used to specify the status of the file to be opened. sta is a character expression whose value is equal to OLD, NEW, SCRATCH, or UNKNOWN. If sta is OLD, the file must already exist. If sta is NEW, a new file is created. If sta is SCRATCH, a new file is created and it is deleted when the file is closed. If sta is UNKNOWN, the processor will first assume sta = OLD; if the file is not found, then sta = NEW, thereby creating a new file. The defeault is UNKNOWN.

Other specifiers are also possible in an OPEN statement. It is also true that not all the specifiers described above are available with all dialects of FORTRAN. Users are advised to consult the FORTRAN reference manual for the computing system on which they are working.

Examples

Here are some FORTRAN 77 OPEN statements with brief explanations.

(a) OPEN(UNIT = 1, FILE = 'XYZ.DAT', ACCESS = 'DIRECT')

This statement connects a direct access file XYZ.DAT to logical unit number 1.

(b) OPEN (1, FILE = 'ABC', STATUS = 'NEW', ERR = 10, IOSTAT = IOS)

This statement creates a new sequential access file ABC, which is connected to logical unit number 1. If there is an error in the opening of a file, IOS will be a positive integer and control will then be transferred to the statement whose label is 10. In case of an error, the file will not be opened at all.

(c) TYPE *. 'ENTER NAME OF THE FILE'
     ACCEPT *, FNAME
     OPEN (UNIT = 2, FILE = FNAME, ACCESS = 'DIRECT', FORM= 'FORMATTED', RECL = 100)

This statement uses the file name entered by the user and it is connected to unit 2 as a formatted direct access file with 100 characters per record.

5.5 CLOSE STATEMENT

The CLOSE statement disconnects a unit number from a specific file. A partial syntax form of the statement is

CLOSE([UNIT] = lun)

The required UNIT option indicates which unit is to be disconnected. Other parameters such as STATUS, ERR, IOSTAT etc. can also be specified. These have same meaning as described in OPEN statement and therefore, they are not discussed here.

Example

CLOSE (UNIT = 1)

This statement disconnects the file connected to logical unit number 1.

5.6 READ STATEMENT

The READ statement is used to transmit data from a file to a FORTRAN program. There are four classes of sequential READ statements: Formatted, list-directed, namelist-directed and unformatted. A partial syntax form of each of the READ statements in FORTRAN 77 is as follows:

(i) Formatted READ Statement:

READ([UNIT =]lun, [FMT] =]f [,IOSTAT = ios] [,ERR = s1] [,END = s2]) [list]

(ii) List-Directed READ Statement:

READ([UNIT =]lun,*[,IOSTAT = ios] [,ERR = s1] [,END = s2]) [list]

(iii) Unformatted READ Statement:

READ([UNIT =]lun[,IOSTAT = ios] [,ERR = s1] [,END = s2]) [list]

(iv) Namelist-Directed READ Statement:

READ([UNIT =]lun, [NML =]n[, IOSTAT = ios] [,ERR = s1] [,END = s2]) [list]

where

$$lun = \text{a logical unit number,}$$
$$f = \text{a format specifier,}$$
$$ios = \text{an integer variable,}$$
$$s1,s2 = \text{statement numbers (labels),}$$
$$n = \text{a namelist specifier,}$$
$$list = \text{a variable, an array element, an array,}$$
$$\text{or a combination of any of these.}$$

Options UNIT, IOSTAT and ERR have the same meaning as in an OPEN statement. The keyword UNIT is optional only if this is the first parameter. lun is an INTEGER constant or an expression which is used to determine the logical unit number.

The keyword FMT = is optional only if the format specifier is the second parameter. f, format specfier is either a FORMAT statement label or a character expression. A full discussion on FORMATS is given in Section 5.8. If f = *, then it specifies list-directed formatting. Users have already been familiarized with list-directed statement in Chapter 3.

The IOSTAT option is used to specify an integer variable to which a value will be assigned indicating whether an error or end-of-file condition exists. If ios = 0, no error or end-of-file condition exists. If ios is positive, an error condition does exist. If ios is negative, an end-of-file condition exists.

The ERR option is used to transfer control to the executable statement specified by statement label s1 when an error condition exists in READ statement.

The END option is used to transfer control to the executable statement specified by statement label s2 when an end-of-file condition exists.

Examples

The following are some valid FORTRAN 77 formatted and list-directed READ statements:

(a) READ (1,*) NUMBER
(b) READ (1,*,END = 10, ERR = 20, IOSTAT = IOS) VALUE, SUM
(c) READ (1,5,END = 10) RECORD, AVARGE
(d) READ (21,100,ERR = 300, IOSTAT = IOS, END = 40) A,B,C,I,J

5.6.1 Unformatted Read Statement

The unformatted sequential READ statement reads exactly one record (line) from the input file. It assigns the values contained in that record to the variables in the list in the order, left to right, in which these variables appear in the list. If there are more data values in a record (line) than the variables in the list, the remaining record is discarded. If the number of variables is greater than the number of values in the record, an error occurs.

The unformatted READ statement is different from the list directed READ statement as explained in the following example:

Example

Assuming that a record (line) contains the input data

$$1.0\ 2.0$$
$$3.0$$

the program segments

                    OPEN(UNIT = 2,FILE = 'JNK.DAT',STATUS = 'OLD')
                    READ(2) A, B

assign 1.0 and 2.0 to A and B respectively. If the READ statement is changed
to

                    READ(2) A
                    READ(2) B

then 1.0 and 3.0 are assigned to A and B respectively However, with the
list-directed READ statement, in both cases, 1.0 and 2.0 are assigned to A
and B respectively.

If a programmer wants to skip one record (line) during the read operation in this input file, it can be easily done by using an unformatted READ
statement:

                    READ(2)

5.6.2 Namelist-Directed READ Statement

This statement is not available with standard FORTRAN 77 compilers but
many compilers, such as WATFIV, support this statement. The NAME-
LIST statement is a convenient way to read and write a list of variables without an accompanying FORMAT statement. It is quite flexible, and in many
situations the preferable form of reading input data, particularly in scientific
applications where little I/O is required. In this option, the I/O list is declared
separately as a NAMELIST, with a list identifier name. The READ statement then contains the list identifier name in place of the statement label of
a FORMAT statement, and allows flexible input of some or all items of the
NAMELIST. No FORMAT statement is required with this READ statement.

The NAMELIST declaration statement has the general form:

                    NAMELIST/n/LIST

where

n is an identifier name (at most 6 alphanumeric characters, the first of
which is alphabetic) assigned to the I/O list 'LIST', which consists of variables or arrays. Each item name in the list is separated by comma. The
READ statement has the form:

                    READ([UNIT =]lun, [NML =]n[,IOSTAT = ios] [,ERR = s1]
                    [,END = s2]) [list]

The input for a namelist-directed READ statement is slightly different.
It consists of a record or records delimited by a special symbol, the dollar
sign ($), which starts in the second column of the first record. The first
column of every record is ignored. The namelist input has the form:

        Column # 1 2 3 4 5 . . . . . .
                    ⩝ $ n ⩝ list item = value [,list item = value, . . .] $ [END]

where

$ is a special symbol used to indicate the beginning or end of input. The ampersand (&) can be also used in place of the $ sign.

END is last delimiter, and optional part.

ƀ is a blank space.

Examples

Consider the program segments

NAMELIST/AMBER/A,B,C,I
OPEN(UNIT = 5, FILE = 'JNK.DAT', STATUS = 'OLD')
READ(5,AMBER)

An appropriate input record could be:

ƀ$AMBERƀA = 2.0, B = 3.0, C = − 4.08, I = 5$END

The above program segments assign 2.0, 3.0, −4.08 and 5 to A, B, C and I respectively. The data items (values) in the input record need not appear in the same order as the list items in the NAMELIST declaration. For example, another input set for the above READ statement might be:

ƀ$ AMBERƀB = 3.0, I = 5,
ƀC = − 4.08,ƀƀƀA = 2.0,ƀƀƀ$END

Here the input set uses two records, each starting in column 2.

In an input data set, the first blank column is followed by $ (or &) which denotes the beginning of the data group that belongs to the items in the list whose namelist identifier is AMBER. This is followed by a blank space and then data items. Each data item has either of these two forms:

1. Variable name = FORTRAN 77 constant.
2. Array name = a set of FORTRAN 77 constants, separated by commas.

The $END declares that this is the end of the namelist group AMBER.

This READ statement is tremendously important in minimizing errors while reading an input file. Furthermore, unlike the formatted READ statement, no fixed fields are necessary. Blanks are simply ignored. Compared to the list-directed READ statement, the namelist-directed READ statement has the advantage that the data iteme (values) need not correspond in precise sequence to the list items of the I/O list in the READ statement. That is, in a list-directed READ statement, all the list items in a READ statement must have a corresponding value in an input record. No variation is permitted in either the number of items-data and list, or in their sequence.

In the namelist-directed READ statement, it is not necessary that all the list items specified in the NAMELIST declaration statement be assigned input values. The statement does not change the values of those items that do not appear in the input data. As an example, another input set for the READ statement in earlier program segments might be:

ƀ$AMBERƀB = 3.0,I = 5$END

Here, only **B** and **I** are assigned input values while **A** and **C** are not, although they are declared in the NAMELIST declaration statement.

Before closing the discussion on namelist-directed READ statements, let us consider the following program segments:

```
NAMELIST/AMBER/A,B,/RED/I,C,K,SUM
NAMELIST/GREEN/NUMBER, MASS, FOUND, NAME
CHARACTER*7 NAME
COMPLEX A,B
LOGICAL FOUND
OPEN(UNIT = 1, FILE = 'JNK.DAT', STATUS = 'OLD')
READ(1,AMBER)
READ(1,GREEN)
READ(1,RED)
```

An appropriate input data set might be:

```
ƀ$AMBERƀB = (5.2,8.7), ƀƀ$END
ƀ$GREENƀNUMBER = 1,FOUND = .TRUE.,
ƀNAME = 'VIBGYOR'$END
ƀ$REDƀI = 3,K = 4,SUM = 0.0,C = −14.92$END
```

Until now, users must have been familiar with only two ways of assigning values to variables: (1) by reading the value of a variable; and (2) by equating via an arithmetic statement such as $I = 3$ or $A = 4.15$. There is also a third way of assigning a value to a variable. This is done by using a DATA statement. In some situations, it is preferable to use a DATA statement rather than other two methods. Consider a program in which the value of variable does not change from one run to the next. If the programmer uses as assignment statement such as $A = 4.15$, there are two disadvantages: (i) it is an executable statement and requires time to execute; and (ii) the storage requirement may be critical for large programs. Since A does not change, reading the value of A would be a nuisance. To simplify matters a nonexecutable DATA statement is used to assign numerical or alphanumeric characters to variables during the compilation phase of the program. The general form of the DATA statement is:

$$\text{DATA list}/d_1,d_2,\ldots\ldots d_N/,\text{list}/x_1,x_2,\ldots x_M/,\ldots$$

where

DATA is a FORTRAN term identifying the statement,

list is a list of variables to which values are to be assigned,

d_i,x_i are values assigned to the variables.

Both the variables and constants are separated by commas, and the list of constants begins and ends with a slash. The constants must correspond in number, type, and relative position in the list with the variables to which they will be assigned. Real constants may also be expressed in exponential form.

Examples

Assuming that A = 1.5, B = 0.019, I = 1, J = 2,C=1.5, either
of the following DATA statements may be used:
DATA A,B,I,J,C/1.5,1.9E-2,1,2,1.5/
DATA A,I/1.5,1/,B/1.9E-2/,J.C/2,1,5/
DATA A,C,B,I,J/2*1.5,1.9E-2,1,2/

In the last statement, the constant 1.5 is used twice (2*1.5), being assigned
to A and C, the first two variables in the list. The integer value ahead of the
asterisk (*) indicates how many times the constant following the asterisk is
used. Notice that the asterisk used in the DATA statement does not indicate multiplication.

Example (a)

Some of the valid FORTRAN data statements are:
  (a) DATA I, J, K, L, M/5*3/ {each variable is assigned a value of 3}
  (b) DATA R, B, Y/'RED', 'BLUE', 'YELLOW'/ {RED, BLUE and
       YELLOW are assigned to R, B, Y, respectively}
  (c) DATA R,B,Y/3*'*'/ {each variable is assigned character *}

Example (b)

Consider the program segments
DATA lunl, lun2/1,2/
      OPEN(UNIT = lunl, FILE = 'JNK.DAT'. STATUS = 'OLD')
      OPEN(UNIT = lun2, FILE = 'ABC', STATUS = 'OLD')
      READ(lunl,10)A,B
      READ(lun2,20)C,I,K

If, due to any reason, the logical unit numbers are to be changed to 21,
22, then in the absence of the DATA statement all the four remaining statements have to be modified. However, using the DATA statement, only this
statement is to be modified as:

      DATA lunl, lun2/21,22/

5.7 WRITE STATEMENT

The WRITE statement is used to transfer output data from internal storage,
such as magnetic core storage, to records contained in user-specified external
logic units i.e. to any of the I/O unit specified by the use. There are four
classes of sequential WRITE statements: formatted, list-directed, namelist-
directed and unformatted. Syntax forms of the WRITE statements are as
follows:

  (i) Formatted WRITE statement:

      WRITE([UNIT =]lun, [FMT =]f[,IOSTAT = ios][,ERR = s]) [list]

(ii) LIST-directed WRITE statement:
      WRITE ([UNIT =] lun,*[,IOSTAT = ios] [,ERR = s]) [list]
(iii)   Unformatted WRITE statement:
      WRITE([UNIT =] lun [,IOSTAT = ios] [,ERR = s]) [list]
(iv)   Namelist-directed WRITE statement:
      WRITE([UNIT =] lun, [NML =]n [,IOSTAT = ios] [,ERR =s])
      [list]

The WRITE operation is opposite to the READ operation and, at the same time, there is a great similarity between the two. The list in a WRITE statement may, however, contain any valid expression. In a READ statement the list must not contain an expression, except as a subscript expression in an array reference or as an expression in a substring reference. We will not go into a detailed discussion of each of the WRITE statements here. Users are advised to look into the corresponding READ statements for the syntactical rules that govern the use of WRITE statement parameters.

Example (a)

The following are some valid FORTRAN 77 WRITE statements:

   (i)   WRITE(1,10)VALUE,SUM,NUM   (Formatted)
  (ii) WRITE(1,*,IOSTAT = IOS,ERR = 20)A,B (List-directed)
 (iii) WRITE(1)   (Unformatted)
 (iv) WRITE(1,ERR = 20)X,Y,I,J,K   (Unformatted)
  (v) WRITE(1,AMBER)   (Namelist-directed)
 (vi) WRITE(2,RED, IOSTAT = IOS, ERR = 20) (Namelist-directed)

Example (b)

Assuming that A = 2.0, I = 3, C = 4.99, the program segments
   NAMELIST/KUMAR/A,I,C
   OPEN(UNIT = 1,FILE = 'JNK.OUT',STATUS = 'NEW')
   ⋮
   WRITE(1,KUMAR)

could give the following output.
   b$KUMAR
   bA = 2.0
   bI = 3
   bC = 4.99
   b$END

Before initiating a discussion on the FORMAT statement, a brief description of some of the additional I/0 statements may be quite appropriate. A general form of each of the statements is as follows:

   (i)   REWIND ([UNIT =] lun [,ERR = s] [,IOSTAT = ios])
  (ii) BACKSPACE([UNIT =]lun [,ERR = s] [,IOSTAT = ios])
 (iii) ENDFILE([UNIT =]lun [,ERR = s] [,IOSTAT = ios])

The parameters of each of the statements have the same meaning as defined earlier in READ statements.

The REWIND statement repositions the file connected to logical unit number lun to its beginning.

The BACKSPACE statement repositions the file connected to logical unit number lun to the beginning of the previous record. Thus, the preceding record is available for processing at the next I/O statement.

The ENDFILE statement writes a special 'END OF FILE' record to the file connected to logical unit lun.

5.8 FORMATS

Up to this point, readers have learnt four basic I/O operations—ACCEPT, READ, TYPE and WRITE. As described in earlier sections, these statements can be either formatted, list-directed or unformatted etc. List-directed and unformatted I/O statements are simple and easy to write, but unfortunately, these simple I/O statements have many drawbacks. The unformatted READ statement imposes severe limitations on the arrangement of the numerical values of the data list, and the unformatted WRITE statement allows a programmer no option in formatting the printed output. For example, a programmer wishes to print alphabets (A through Z) in one line with one blank between each character. With unformatted I/O, this desired output is not possible. A formatted WRITE statement, however, provides a programmer with this ability. Formatted I/O statements have a FORMAT statement associated with them that contains the format list that is used to control the form of output or input. A partial syntax form of formatted input statements is:

> ACCEPT f, inputlist

and

> READ(lun, f) inputlist

A partial syntax form of output statements is:

> PRINT f, outputlist

and

> WRITE(lun, f) outputlist

where

> lun is the logical unit number of the file (see OPEN statement),
> f is a format statement number,
> inputlist is a variable, array, character substring or array element,
> outputlist is a variable, array, character substring, array element or expression.

The associated FORMAT statement has the form:

> f   FORMAT (format list)

where

format list is a list of format *edit descriptors* usually separated by commas. A general form of format list is

(field$_1$, field$_2$, field$_3$, . . . , field$_n$)

in which

field is a *field descriptor* or a group of field descriptors enclosed in parentheses.

A field descriptor in a format specification has one of the following forms:

[r]c   [r]cw   [r]cw.m   [r]cw.d[Ee]

where

r is a repeat count for the field descriptor. Generally it is a non-zero unsigned integer constant indicating how many times field descriptor is to be repeated. If r is not present, the repeat count is assumed to be 1.

c is a format code. Some of the commonly used format codes are—
I, F, E, D, L, A, H, X, T, Q

The readers should consult a FORTRAN 77 reference manual for a complete list of format codes.

w is external field width, in characters.

m is minimum number of characters that must appear within the field (including leading zeros).

d is number of characters after decimal point.

E is an exponent field.

e is number of characters in the exponent.

The r term is optional; however, it cannot be used with H and Q format codes as described later. The terms r, w, m and d must all be unsigned integer constants or variable format expressions.

Some of the most commonly used field descriptors are:

(1) Integer — Iw, Iw.m
(2) Real and Complex — Fw.d, Ew.d, Ew.dEe, Dw.d
(3) Character — Aw
(4) Logical — Lw
(5) Edit— nX, Tn, Q
(6) Character and Hollerith Constants—nH, ' . . .' (Apostrophe Editing).
(7) Miscellaneous Edit descriptors.

A brief description of each of the field descriptors is given in the following sections.

5.8.1 I Field Descriptor

The I field descriptor or I format is used to read or write integer numbers. The general form of the I descriptor is:

Iw[.m]

The term m is optional. If m is present, the output consists of at least m digits, and is zero-field on the left, if necessary.

If the I descriptor is used with an input statement (READ and ACCEPT), the next w columns are read as an integer. These columns must have the form of an integer constant, it cannot contain a decimal point or exponent field. Any blanks within these columns are interpreted as zeros; hence the input must be right-justified. An entirely blank field is interpreted to be zero. If the first nonblank character in the field is a minus sign, the field is treated as a negative value. If the first nonblank character is a plus sign, or if no sign appears in the field, the field is treated as a positive value. Any non-numerical character other than the sign is taken to be an indication of error.

Example

Assuming that an input data line contains the following values

11b222b900bbb88

starting with column one, the statements

READ(lun, 10)NUMBER, ITOTAL, NSUM, IAVRAG
10   FORMAT(I2,I4,I4,I5)

result in the values 11, 222, 900 and 88 being assigned to NUMBER, ITOTAL, NSUM and IAVRAG. If the format statement

10   FORMAT(I4,I2,I8,I1)

is used then these values are 1102, 22, 9000008 and 8 respectively. However, if the format statement

10   FORMAT(I4,I2,I8,I2)

is encountered, an error in reading occurs because for IAVRAG field width is 2, while there is only one digit 8 left for reading.

If the I descriptor is used with an output statement (WRITE and PRINT), the value to be printed is right-justified in a field w columns wide. If the value does not fill the field, leading spaces are inserted; if the value exceeds the field width, a writing error occurs and the entire field may be filled with asterisks (*). If the value is negative, the field will have a minus sign as its leftmost, nonblank character. Care must be taken to provide a value of w such that a space for minus sign is available, when necessary. If the field descriptor Iw.m is used, the field consists of at least m digits. The value of m cannot be greater than w.

Example (a)

This example gives output for different integer numbers using various format specifications:

FORMAT	Integer Constant	Computer Output
		column # 1 2 3 4 5 6 . . . .
I4	123	♭ 1 2 3
I3	− 345	* * *
I4	− 345	− 3 4 5
I1	77	*
I3	3.4	Error (not permitted)
I3.3	2	0 0 2
I3.2	2	♭ 0 2
I3.4	2	Error (not permitted)

Example (b)

Assuming that the NUMBER, I TOTAL, NSUM, IAVRAG are assigned 32, 1234, –28 and 2, respectively, the statements

    WRITE (lun, 10) NUMBER, I TOTAL, NSUM, IAVRAG

    10 FORMAT (I2,I7,I5,I3)

would print the output as:

	I2		I7				I5				I3		
Column #	1	2	3 4 5 6 7 8 9				10 11 12 13 14				15	16	17
	3	2	♭ ♭ ♭ 1 2 3 4				♭ ♭ − 2 8				♭	♭	2
	NUMBER		ITOTAL				NSUM				IAVRAG		

If the format statement

    10 FORMAT (I2,I2,I5, I2.2)

is used, the output would be as follows:

	I2		I2		I5				I2.2	
Column #	1	2	3 4		5 6 7 8 9				10 11	
	1	2	* *		♭ ♭ − 2 8				0 2	
	NUMBER		Error for I TOTAL		NSUM				IAVRAG	

5.8.2 F Field Descriptor

F field descriptor or F format is used to read or write real numbers, or real/imaginary part of a complex number. The form of the F format is:

    Fw.d

If the descriptor is used with an input statement, the next w columns are read as a real number. If the field contains a decimal point, then this demical point is used; otherwise a decimal point is assumed d digits from the right of the number. Blanks in the field are treated in the same manner as discussed earlier in I field descriptor.

Example

Assuming that the input fields are:

      11ƀ222ƀ9.ƀƀƀ88

starting with column one, the statements

    READ (lun,10) AGE, TOTAL, SUM, AVRAGE
  10 FORMAT (F2.0,F4.2,F4.1, F4.0)

result in the values 11, 2.22, 9.0 and 88 being read into AGE, TOTAL, SUM and AVRAGE, respectively.

When the F descriptor is used with an output statement, the value to be printed is rounded to d demical positions, if necessary, and printed right-justified in a field w columns wide. If the value does not fill the field, leading spaces are inserted; if the value exceeds the field width, the entire field is filled with asterisks to indicate FORMAT OVER FLOW (on error).

The term w must be greater than or equal to $d+3$ in order to include a minus sign, if necessary; at least one digit to the left of the decimal point; and the decimal point.

Example

The following example illustrates the use of F field descriptor:

FORMAT	Real Constant	Computer Output
		column # 1 2 3 4 5 6 7 8 9 10
F3.1	543.4	* * *
F8.5	1.234567	ƀ 1 . 2 3 4 5 7
F8.6	1.234567	1 . 2 3 4 5 6 7
F8.3	−543.21	− 5 4 3 . 2 1 0
F5.2	−.9	− 0 . 9 0

5.8.3 E Field Descriptor

The E field is appropriate when a real value is to appear with a numerical value accompanied by an exponent. Exponent representation of a number is generally preferred when the number is either very small or very large. The general form for the E format is:

      Ew.d [Ee]

The term Ee in brackets is optional. Here, w indicates the total field width for the data item with d digits in the fractional part of the data item.

If the E field is used with an input statement, the data item associated with the E format can be any signed or unsigned real constant. If the constant has no decimal point, then a decimal point is assumed to be d digits from the right side of the field; otherwise, the given decimal point is used.

Example

Assuming that the input data is:

123.4E12ϸ5.3

the statements

READ (lun,10) NUMBER,SUM

10 FORMAT (E8.1,F4.1)

associates 123.4E12 and 5.3 with NUMBER and SUM, respectively. If the format statement, however, was:

10 FORMAT (E7.1, F5.1)

then 123.4E1 and 205.3 are associated with NUMBER and SUM, respectively. Note that for NUMBER only 7 digits are read and digit 2 is read for SUM. If the input data was

1234E12ϸ5.3

and the format statement

10 FORMAT (E8.1,F4.1)

was encountered, then 123.4E12 and 5.3 would be associated with NUMBER and SUM. Note that if no decimal point is present in the data, one is inserted according to the specification in the field descriptor. The number right to the decimal point in the field descriptor is used to determine the position of the decimal point.

If E field is used with an output statement, the value to be printed is rounded to d decimal positions, if necessary, and printed right-justified in a field w columns wide. The usual form of E-format numbers in the next w columns is

$$\pm 0.x_1x_2x_3 \ldots x_dE \pm YY$$

The leading zero before the decimal always appears. Plus signs are printed as blanks. Here, $x_1, x_2, \ldots, x_d$ are the specified digits and YY is the exponent.

In an E-field descriptor

$$w \geqslant d+7$$

i.e. the minimum field width w must be at least $d+7$. It can be easily seen from the above form. Leading sign (necessary only if negative), leading zero, decimal point, character E, sign of the exponent each needs 1 column while exponent digits need 2 columns, thus a total of 7 columns are needed in addition to d digits. If the field width is greater than $7+d$, then $w-(7+d)$ leading spaces will be provided. If the field width is insufficient, the field array be filled with asterisks (*) to indicate FORMAT OVERFLOW (an error).

As indicated earlier, the exponent field with Ee in the general form of E format is optional and if it is omitted, the value of e, by default, is two. If larger exponents are needed then e must be present. If $e>2$ then w must be equal to or greater than $d+5+e$.

Example

The following are some real numbers, a sample E-field descriptors, and the way in which the number would be printed.

FORMAT	Real Constant	Computer Output

FORMAT	Real Constant	column # 1	2	3	4	5	6	7	8	9	10	11
E9.2	123456.78	b̸	0	.	1	2	E	b̸	0	6		
E11.4	−1.23456	−	0	.	1	2	3	5	E	b̸	0	1
E10.3	0.00012	b̸	0	.	1	2	0	E	−	0	3	
E8.4	1234.678	*	*	*	*	*	*	*	*			
E11.2E4	−90.234	−	0	.	9	0	E	b̸	0	0	0	2
E11.3E3	0.163×10^{225}	b̸	0	.	1	6	3	E	b̸	2	2	5

5.8.4. D Field Descriptor

The D field descriptor is generally used when dealing with DOUBLE PRECISION values. The D format is identical to the E format except for the use of D in place of E. The general form of a D field is:

$$Dw.d$$

Example (a):

Input field example

Assuming that the input data is
$$123.4567890D{-}09\text{ b̸}5.3$$
the statements

READ (lun,10) NUMBER,SUM

10 FORMAT (D15.3,F4.1)

associate 123.4567890D-09 and 5.3 with NUMBER and SUM respectively.

Example (b)

Output field example

The following are some real numbers, a sample D-field descriptors, and the way in which the number would be printed.

FORMAT	Real Constant	Computer Output

```
                          column # 1 2 3 4 5 6 7 8 9 10 11 12 13 14 15 16
D16.9      123456.78925          ƀ 0 . 1 2 3 4 5 6 7 8  9  D  ƀ  0  6
D11.9      123456.78925          * * * * * * * * *  *  *
D15.4      0.0987654             ƀ ƀ ƀ ƀ ƀ 0 . 9 8  7  7  D  -  0  1
```

5.8.5 A Field Descriptor

The A field desrciptor is used for the input or output of character data. The general form is

$$A[w]$$

The field width w is optional. If the field width is omitted, then the default field width is the length of the associated data item.

If the format A[w] is used in an input statement, the next w characters are read. The maximum number of characters that can be stored for a variable depends on its type declaration. For character data type, the size is the length of the character data. For numeric variables the size depending on the data type is given in Table 5.1.

Table 5.1: Maximum Number of Characters for Each Data Type

Data Type	Maximum Number of characters
INTEGER	4
INTEGER*2	2
INTEGER*4	4
REAL	4
REAL*4	4
REAL*8 (DOUBLE PRECISION)	8
REAL*16	16
COMPLEX	8
COMPLEX*8	8
COMPLEX*16 (DOUBLE COMPLEX)	16
LOGICAL	4
LOGICAL*1	1
LOGICAL*2	2
LOGICAL*4	4
BYTE	1

If w is greater than the maximum number of characters that can be stored in the corresponding variable, only the rightmost characters are assigned to that variable and the leftmost excess characters are not read. If w is less than the number of characters (len) that can be stored, then w characters are read from the left, and trailing spaces (len-w) are added to the right.

Example (a)

Assuming that the input data is

                    TOGETHER

    the statements

                    CHARACTER*2 WORD1
                    CHARACTER*3 WORD2, WORD3
                    READ (lun,10) WORD1, WORD2, WORD3
            10   FORMAT (A2,2A3)

are executed, the variables WORD1, WORD2 and WORD3 are associated with TO, GET and HER. If the format statement, however, was

            10   FORMAT (A3,A2,A3)

then OG, ETƀ, HER are assigned to WORD1, WORD2 and WORD3;

Example (b)

Assuming that the input data is

                    USƀ$ = 12ƀRS

    if the statements

                    CHARACTER*1 EXRATE
                    READ (lun,10) EXRATE
            10   FORMAT (A10)

are executed, then S is assigned to EXRATE. If the first statement CHARAC-TER*1 is replaced by following type statements, the values assigned to EX-RATE shall be as follows:

First Statement	EXRATE
CHARACTER*7	$ = 12ƀRS
CHARACTER*10	USƀ$ = 12ƀRS
CHARACTER*12	USƀ$ = 12ƀRSƀƀ
CHARACTER*6	=12ƀRS
CHARACTER*4	2ƀRS

If the format A[w] is used in an output statement, then the output data item is printed in the next w columns. If w is greater than the size (len) of the data item, then the output consists of (w-len) blanks followed by the data item of size len. If w is less than len, then the output consists of the leftmost w characters of the data item. If w is omitted, then a default value, which is the length (len) of the data item, is supplied. If the data item is of numeric data type, the default value is the maximum number of characters that can be stored in a data item of that data type.

Example

The following are some data items, a sample A-field descriptors, and the way in which the data item would be printed.

FORMAT	Data Item	Computer Output
		column # 1 2 3 4 5 6 7 8 9 10
A6	INDIA	⌷ I N D I A
A6	BOMBAY	B O M B A Y
A6	FRIENDSHIP	F R I E N D

5.8.6 L Field Descriptor

L field descriptor is used for the input or output of logical data. The general form is:

Lw

If the format Lw is used in an input statement, the next w characters are scanned. If the first nonblank characters of the field are T, t, .T or .t, the value .TRUE. is assigned to the input data item; if the first nonblank characters are F, f, .F, .f, the value .FALSE. is assigned. An all-blank field is assigned the value .FALSE. Any other value in the field produces an error.

If the format Lw is used in an output statement, the field consists of w-1 blanks followed by the letter T (if the value is .TRUE.) or F (if the value is .FALSE.).

Example

Assuming that the input data is

⌷⌷⌷TRUE

the statements

```
         LOGICAL FOUND
         READ(1un,10) FOUND
10       FORMAT(L5)
         WRITE(1un,20) FOUND
20       FORMAT(L4)
```

associate ⌷⌷⌷T with FOUND. If the first format statement was

```
10       FORMAT(L3)
```

then ⌷⌷⌷F is associated with FOUND.

5.8.7 X and T Edit Descriptors

The X and T edit descriptors are used to control positioning within an input or output statement. The general form of the X edit descriptor is:

nX

This causes n (n $\geqslant$ 1) columns to be skipped on input or output from the current position. Initially, the current position is the first column of an input/output line.

Example (a)

Assuming that the input data is

12345678901234567890

the statements

```
        READ(1un,10) SUM,NUMBER
10      FORMAT(3X,F4.2,2X,I10)
        WRITE(1un,20) NUMBER,SUM
20      FORMAT(I10,5X,F4.1)
```

associate 45.67 and 123456789 with SUM and NUMBER respectively. The output will be printed as:

	I10			5X		F4.1	
Column #	1 2 3 4 5 6 7 8 9 10	11 12 13 14 15	16 17 18 19				
	ƀ 1 2 3 4 5 6 7 8 9	b ƀ ƀ ƀ ƀ	4 5 . 7				

The edit descriptor T has a general form:

Tn

It is used to read a value from a certain position or to write it at a certain position. The position is specified by n (n $\geqslant$ 1) which gives the column number at which position starts.

If the edit descriptor is used in an input statement, the data item is read from nth column position.

The T edit descriptor is extremely useful with prearranged data layouts where each field is known to start at a specified record (column) position.

Example (b)

Assuming that the input data is

123ƀƀABZ

the statements

```
        READ(1un,10) NUMBER,STRNG
10      FORMAT(A3,T6,A3)
```

would associate 123 and ABZ with NUMBER and STRNG. If the format statement was

    10   FORMAT(T6,A3,T1,A3)

then ABZ and 123 would be associated with NUMBER and STRNG.

If the edit descriptor is used in an output statement, the data item is written from columns n-1 because the first position is usually reserved for a carriage control character (discussed later), which is not printed.

Example (c)

In the above example, if two more statements

        WRITE(1un,20) STRNG,NUMBER
    20   FORMAT (T10,A3,T3,A3)

are added, then the output would be as follows:

Column # 1 2 3 4 5 6 7 8 9 10 11
         1 2 3   A B Z

Note that the X edit descriptor and the T edit descriptor are different. The X edit descriptor is used to skip columns while the T edit descriptor is used to specify a specific position in an I/O operation.

5.8.8 H Field Descriptor

The H field descriptor is used for including alphabetic, numeric or other data types in the printed output. These characters, listed in the FORMAT statement, are literally printed as part of the output. The general form for the H field is

    $nHc_1c_2...c_n$

where

    n is the number of characters to be printed
    c is an ASCII character

Example

Assuming I = 5, J = 1234, the statements

        WRITE(1un,10)I,J
    10   FORMAT(15HTWOϸNUMBERSϸARE,I2,I5)

will print

                                    15H
Column #   1 2 3 4 5 6 7 8 9 10 11 12 13 14 15
            T W O ϸ N U M B E R S ϸ A R E

                I2   I5
            16 17   18 19 20 21 22 23 24
                5   1   2   3   4

The main disadvantage of the field descriptor is that characters must be counted accurately to avoid an execution error. In order to alleviate the counting error, another field descriptor, character constants, is preferred.

5.8.9 Character Constants

This is also called *apostrophe editing* or *literal field descriptor*. Forming a literal field descriptor is simply a matter of enclosing the list of characters to be printed in quotation marks, using the apostrophe character (').

All characters, including blanks, between the leading and the closing apostrophe are literally printed in the output as they appear in the FORMAT field. Apostrophes are not printed. If an apostrophe is to be printed it is written as two apostrophes.

Example

The statements

$$\text{WRITE(1un,10)}$$
$$10 \quad \text{FORMAT('B' 'LOREƀISƀAƀNICEƀCITY')}$$

will print

```
Col #  1  2  3  4  5  6  7  8  9  10 11 12 13 14 15 16 17 18 19 20 21
       B  '  L  O  R  E  ƀ  I  S     ƀ  A  ƀ  N  I  C  E  ƀ  C  I  T  Y
```

5.8.10 Miscellaneous Edit Descriptors

Slash (/) editing

The slash edit descriptor is used to terminate input or output of the current record and initiates a new record. Generally, a record is a line of input or output to or from the user's terminal. Multiple slashes can be used to bypass input records or to output blank records. n slashes at the beginning or at the end of a format produce n blank records (lines). However, n slashes in the middle of a format produce (n-1) blank lines. Slashes need not be separated by commas.

Example

The statements

$$\text{WRITE(1un,10) I,J,K,L,}$$
$$10 \quad \text{FORMAT(2I4.4/I3,I2)}$$

are equivalent to

$$\text{WRITE(1un,10) I,J}$$
$$10 \quad \text{FORMAT(2I4.4)}$$
$$\text{WRITE(1un,20) K,L}$$
$$20 \quad \text{FORMAT(I3,I2)}$$

In the above example I and J are printed on one line, while K and L are printed on the next line.

A brief description of other edit descriptors is given in Table 5.2. For more details, users may consult a FORTRAN reference manual.

Table 5.2: A Brief Description of Various Edit Descriptors

Descriptor	Brief Explanation
BN,BZ	Used for treating non-leading blanks in an input field. These blanks can be treated as zeros or as null, in which case they are skipped.
S,SP,SS	Used for producing/suppressing a plus character (+) for numeric items.
Ow[.m]	Used to transmit information in unconverted, octal (base 8) form
Zw[.m]	Used to transmit information in unconverted, hexadecimal (base 16) form.
Gw.d[Ee]	Used to transfer real values in a suitable form, in effect, combines the F and E field descriptors. That is, it prints as F if the value will fit the field, otherwise it prints as E.
TLn,TRn	$n \geqslant 1$, same as T descriptor except that TL specifies for the tabbing left while TR specifies for the tabbing right.
Q	Used to obtain the number of characters in the input record remaining to be read during a READ operation.
$ (Dollar sign)	Used to modify carriage control.
: (Colon descriptor)	Used to terminate format control if no more items are left in the I/0 list.
nP	Used to specify a scale farctor for real data fields.

Before closing our discussion on FORMAT field descriptors, a brief mention of variable format expressions is worth noting.

5.8.11 Variable Format Expressions

This feature may not be available with all FORTRAN compilers. The standard FORTRAN 77 compilers do not support this format. However VAX-11 FORTRAN, WATFIV, IBM FORTRAN compilers do support this format. Users are advised to consult the language reference manual to check the availability of this format on their system. Variable format expressions or specifications are also known as *execution time formats* or *object-time format specifications*. A brief description of this format is included in this section. An expression in a FORTRAN statement can be used whenever an integer appears (except as the specification of the number of characters in the H field). The expression must be enclosed in single brackets. For example,

```
10 FORMAT(I<J*2>)
20 FORMAT(<I+3>F<J+I>.<K*2>)
```

An expression is evaluated each time it is encountered while writing data items. If the expression is not of integer data type, it is converted to integer data type before being used.

The variable format expression is especially useful in writing general programs involving arrays. Users will become more familiar with this format in the next chapter where its application is shown.

5.9 CARRIAGE CONTROL

The carriage on the high-speed line printer can be controlled in much the same fashion as the carriage on a typewriter. The first character in the format list of a FORMAT statement is usually a *carriage cantrol character*. These control characters allow the programmer better control over the vertical spacing of the computer output. The carriage control character is never printed and causes vertical spacing as described in Table 5.3.

Table 5.3: Carriage Control

Character	Action of Printer
' ' (Blank)	Single spacing; prints output at the beginning of the next line.
'0'	Double spacing; skips a line before printing output.
'1'	Paging or form feed; prints output at the top of a new page.
'+'	Overprinting; prints outputs at the beginning of the current line.

Any character other than those listed in Table 5.3 is treated as a blank, thus causing single spacing to occur. If the programmer accidentally omits the carriage control character, the first character of the record is not printed. A carriage control character can be used on its own, without any other data item. Some of the examples are:

```
10 FORMAT(' ', 'SINGLE SPACING')
20 FORMAT('SINGLE SPACING')
30 FORMAT('+SAME LINE')
40 FORMAT('0 DOUBLE SPACING')
50 FORMAT('1 NEXT PAGE')
60 FORMAT('0')
```

If a format statement is written as

$$FORMAT(I12,E16.4, I4.4,<J-1>F4.2)$$

then for the first integer variable, a field width of 11, not 12, is available. The reason is that the programmer has not specified a carriage control character and the first blank produced by the I12 format code is used as a blank control character. For correct fields, one must supply carriage control character explicitly as given below:

$$FORMAT(' ',I12,E16.4, I4.4,<J-1>F4.2)$$

Before summarizing this chapter some programming examples are given to illustrate the use of concepts discussed in this chapter.

5.10 PROGRAMMING EXAMPLES

Example 5.1

This example illustrates the accidental use of carriage control character. If either due to ignorance or by accident, the programmer allows a carriage control character to appear in print position 1, it will perform its intended function unnoticed until its surprising effects appear in the printed output. This example program shows the effect if 1 appears in print position 1. Figure 5.2 shows the program listing and the output of the program.

Starting with $N = 18$, and using format specification I2 for printing, 1 appears in print position 1, and the paper is advanced to the top of a new page. An 8 is printed in print position 2; the 1 in the first printing position is not printed. The succeeding two values of N with 1 as the first digit (14, 10) each has their second digits (4,0) printed in print position 2 at the top of a new page. For first two negative values minus sign is not printed and only their magnitude is printed. The last two values (-10 and -14) are not printed since they do not fit in the specified format I2. Format error occurs as shown by *.

Example 5.2

This example illustrates the use of FORMAT statements, using edit descriptors and character constant descriptors (apostrophe editing) to write messages. The program and the output is given in Figure 5.3. The program is quite simple to follow. Note the use of PARAMETER statement discussed in Chapter 3.

Example 5.3

A modern computing centre consists of four rooms with the following dimensions:

> Computer room — 15.0 meters × 10.0 meters
> Terminal room — 6.0 meters × 5.0 meters
> Managers room — 4.0 meters × 3.0 meters
> Store room — 5.5 meters × 4.0 meters

Write a FORTRAN 77 program to compute the area of each room and the total area of the Computing Centre. Present your results in a tabular form. The input data is given in an input data file EX5_3.DAT.

Figure 5.4 shows the source program. The program is quite straightforward and no explanation is needed for variable names. Figure 5.5 shows the input data and the output results.

```
***********************************************************
*        THIS PROGRAM SHOWS THE ACCIDENTAL USE OF CARRIAGE *
*        CONTROL CHARACTER                                 *
***********************************************************
         DATA LUN/2/
         OPEN(UNIT=LUN,FILE='EX5_1.OUT',STATUS='NEW')
         WRITE(LUN,100)
100      FORMAT(/' * OUTPUT *'/)
         N = 18
         DO 200 I = 1,N/2
                 WRITE(LUN,300) N
                 N = N-4
200      CONTINUE
300      FORMAT(I2)
         CLOSE(UNIT=LUN)
         STOP
         END
***********************************************************
```

```
* OUTPUT *
```

Top of second page
_____
```
8
```

Top of third page
_____
```
4
```

Top of fourth page
_____
```
0
6
2
2
6
*
*
```

Figure 5.2: Program Listing and Output of Example 5.1.

```
************************************************************
*       THIS PROGRAM ILLUSTRATES THE USE OF FORMAT        *
*       STATEMENTS FOR WRITING A MESSAGE                  *
************************************************************
        INTEGER LUN
        PARAMETER (LUN = 2)
        OPEN(UNIT=LUN,FILE='EX5_2.OUT',STATUS='NEW')
        WRITE(LUN,100)
        WRITE(LUN,200)
        WRITE(LUN,300)
        WRITE(LUN,400)
        WRITE(LUN,500)
        WRITE(LUN,600)
        WRITE(LUN,700)
        WRITE(LUN,800)
        WRITE(LUN,900)
        WRITE(LUN,1000)
100     FORMAT(T5,'*******   OUTPUT   *******'//)
200     FORMAT(T5,33('*'),/,T5,'*',31X,'*')
300     FORMAT(T5,'* IN THIS MONTH COMPUTER CENTER *')
400     FORMAT(T5,'* WILL BE CLOSED ON :           *')
500     FORMAT(T5,'* AUGUST 15,  INDEPENDENCE  DAY *')
600     FORMAT(T5,'* FROM  8.00 AM  TILL  MIDNIGHT *')
700     FORMAT(T5,'*              &                *')
800     FORMAT(T5,'* AUG 25,PREVENTIVE MAINTENANCE *')
900     FORMAT(T5,'* FROM  8.00 AM  TILL   3.00 PM *')
1000    FORMAT(T5,'*',31X,'*',/,T5,33('*'))
        CLOSE(UNIT=LUN)
        STOP
        END
************************************************************
```

```
*******   OUTPUT   *******


*********************************
*                               *
* IN THIS MONTH COMPUTER CENTER *
* WILL BE CLOSED ON :           *
* AUGUST 15,  INDEPENDENCE  DAY *
* FROM  8.00 AM  TILL  MIDNIGHT *
*              &                *
* AUG 25,PREVENTIVE MAINTENANCE *
* FROM  8.00 AM  TILL   3.00 PM *
*                               *
*********************************
```

Figure 5.3: Program Listing and Output of Example 5.2.

```
*****************************************************************
*          THIS PROGRAM READS IN NAME OF A ROOM, ITS LENGTH,    *
*          ITS WIDTH IN A COMPUTING CENTRE AND CALCULATES ITS   *
*          AREA. IT ALSO CALCULATES THE TOTAL AREA OF THE       *
*          COMPUTING CENTRE.                                    *
*****************************************************************
           CHARACTER* 13 NAME
           REAL LENGTH
           INTEGER INLUN,OUTLUN
           PARAMETER (INLUN = 1, OUTLUN = 2)
           OPEN(UNIT=INLUN,FILE='EX5_3.DAT',STATUS='OLD')
           OPEN(UNIT=OUTLUN,FILE='EX5_3.OUT',STATUS='NEW')
*
           TOTARA = 0.0
           WRITE(OUTLUN,100)
           WRITE(OUTLUN,200)
           WRITE(OUTLUN,300)
           WRITE(OUTLUN,200)
           DO 10 I = 1,4
               READ(INLUN,400)NAME,LENGTH,WIDTH
               AREA = LENGTH * WIDTH
               TOTARA = TOTARA + AREA
               WRITE(OUTLUN,500)NAME,LENGTH,WIDTH,AREA
10         CONTINUE
           WRITE(OUTLUN,200)
           WRITE(OUTLUN,600)TOTARA
           WRITE(OUTLUN,700)
100        FORMAT(' ',/,T22,'** OUTPUT **',//,T20,'COMPUTING CENTRE'/)
200        FORMAT(' ',52('-'))
300        FORMAT(5X,'ROOM',T20,'LENGTH',T34,'WIDTH',T49,'AREA')
400        FORMAT(A13,2F5.1)
500        FORMAT(' ',A,T18,F7.2,T32,F7.2,T44,F10.4)
600        FORMAT(' ',T32,'TOTAL AREA',T44,F10.4)
700        FORMAT(T32,22('-'))
           CLOSE(UNIT=INLUN)
           CLOSE(UNIT=OUTLUN)
           STOP
           END
*****************************************************************
```

Figure 5.4: Program Listing of Example 5.3.

Example 5.4

This FORTRAN 77 program illustrates the use of namelist-directed READ statement. It also shows the use of END, ERR and IOSTAT parameters in a READ statement.

Figure 5.6 gives the source program while Figure 5.7 shows three sets of input data and corresponding output results. Recall that in case the input file does not contain sufficient data, control is transferred to the statement label specified by the END parameter. Similarly, if there is an error in the input data file, the control is transferred to the statement label specified by the ERR parameter. The value of IOS (whether +ve or −ve) depends on the type of error.

Input Data

```
COMPUTER ROOM 15.00 10.00
TERMINAL ROOM  6.00  5.00
MANAGER  ROOM  4.00  3.50
STORE    ROOM  5.50  4.50
```

** OUTPUT **

COMPUTING CENTRE

ROOM	LENGTH	WIDTH	AREA
COMPUTER ROOM	15.00	10.00	150.0000
TERMINAL ROOM	6.00	5.00	30.0000
MANAGER ROOM	4.00	3.00	12.0000
STORE ROOM	5.50	4.00	22.0000
		TOTAL AREA	214.0000

Figure 5.5: Input Data and Output Results of Example 5.3.

The program is quite simple to follow and does not need any further explanation. Note the placement of FORMAT statements inside the body of the program. It is not needed to place a FORMAT statement after its corresponding READ/WRITE statement.

A value of 0.0 is assigned to variable D as it is not specified in the input file. Note the format for reading and writing namelist-directed READ/WRITE statements.

Example 5.5

The computer can serve as a tool for drawing pictures of simple as well as complex figures. Without really going into the complexities of the computer graphics, simple figures, sketches or maps can be drawn by making use of FORMAT statements. This example and the next example illustrate the use of FORMAT statements to draw simple figures.

This example shows how one can draw a Christmas tree using FORMAT statements.

Two FORTRAN programs have been given in Figures 5.8 and 5.9. Both programs draw the same Christmas tree that is shown in Figure 5.10. The program shown in Figure 5.9 makes use of variable FORMAT expressions by using DO loop counter. This program is quite short as compared to the one shown in Figure 5.8, which uses fixed FORMAT expressions. Users must note the distinct advantage of using variable FORMAT expressions in this case. Both the programs are quite easy to follow and no further explanation is required.

```
*******************************************************************
*          THIS PROGRAM ILLUSTRATES THE USE OF NAMELIST-DIRECTED    *
*          READ STATEMENT, AND THE APPLICATION OF READ PARAMETERS.  *
*******************************************************************
          NAMELIST/GREEN/A,B,C,D
          INTEGER INLUN,OUTLUN
          PARAMETER (INLUN = 1, OUTLUN = 2)
*  FORMAT STATEMENTS CAN BE PUT ANYWHERE IN THE PROGRAM
100       FORMAT(// ' THE OUTPUT IS AS FOLLOWS:'/)
200       FORMAT(' ',/,'    I = ',I5,'    J = ',I<J>.<J>,'    K = ',I5/)
300       FORMAT(3I4)
400       FORMAT(' END OF THE INPUT FILE DETECTED')
500       FORMAT(' ERROR IN THE INPUT FILE')
600       FORMAT(' THE VALUE OF IOS = ',T40,I7)
*
          OPEN(UNIT=INLUN,FILE='EX5_4.DAT',STATUS='OLD')
          OPEN(UNIT=OUTLUN,FILE='EX5_4.OUT',STATUS='NEW')
          READ(INLUN,*)I,J,K
          IF(I.GT.J) THEN
                READ(INLUN,GREEN)
                WRITE(OUTLUN,100)
                WRITE(OUTLUN,GREEN)
          END IF
          WRITE(OUTLUN,200)I,J,K
          READ(INLUN,300,END=10,ERR=20,IOSTAT=IOS)J,I,K
          WRITE(OUTLUN,200)I,J,K
          CLOSE(UNIT=INLUN)
          CLOSE(UNIT=OUTLUN)
          STOP
*
10        WRITE(OUTLUN,400)
          CLOSE(UNIT=INLUN)
          CLOSE(UNIT=OUTLUN)
          STOP
*
20        WRITE(OUTLUN,500)
          CLOSE(UNIT=INLUN)
          WRITE(OUTLUN,600)IOS
          CLOSE(UNIT=OUTLUN)
          STOP
          END
*******************************************************************
```

Figure 5.6: Program Listing of Example 5.4

Example 5.6

This example illustrates how one can draw a map of India by using FOR-MAT statements. The key to drawing the map is the determination of the data points that closely correspond to the boundary. Once the data points are known, it is quite easy to draw such a map using variable FORMAT expressions.

Figure 5.11 shows hand-drawn India map on a computer print-out giving the row and column position of a boundary point. The handwritten numbers on the right hand corner show the nearest column coordinate corresponding to a boundary point. An input data file is given in Figure 5.12. Note that

(i) **Input Data**

```
     5  4  10
     $GREEN A=1.0, B=2.0, C=3.0, D=4.0   $END
          4    3    1

     THE OUTPUT IS AS FOLLOWS:

     $GREEN
     A       =    1.000000      ,
     B       =    2.000000      ,
     C       =    3.000000      ,
     D       =    4.000000
     $END

       I =      5   J = 0004   K =      10


       I =      3   J = 0004   K =       1
```

(ii) **Input Data**

```
     5  4  10
     $GREEN A=1.0, B=2.0, C=3.0,   $END

     THE OUTPUT IS AS FOLLOWS:

     $GREEN
     A       =    1.000000      ,
     B       =    2.000000      ,
     C       =    3.000000      ,
     D       =    0.0000000E+00
     $END

       I =      5   J = 0004   K =      10

     END OF THE INPUT FILE DETECTED
```

(iii) **Input Data**

```
     5  4  10
     $GREEN A=1.0, B=2.0, C=3.0, D=4.0   $END
     4,3,*

     THE OUTPUT IS AS FOLLOWS:

     $GREEN
     A       =    1.000000      ,
     B       -    2.000000      ,
     C       =    3.000000      ,
     D       =    4.000000
     $END

       I =      5   J = 0004   K =      10

     ERROR IN THE INPUT FILE
     THE VALUE OF IOS =
```

Figure 5.7: Three Sets of Input Data and Output Results of Example 5.4.

```
*****************************************************************
*       USE OF FORMAT STATEMENTS FOR PRINTING A X-MAS TREE     *
*****************************************************************
        INTEGER LUN
        PARAMETER (LUN = 2)
        OPEN(UNIT=LUN,FILE='EX5_5.OUT',STATUS='NEW')
        WRITE(LUN,100)
        WRITE(LUN,200)
        WRITE(LUN,300)
        WRITE(LUN,400)
        WRITE(LUN,500)
        WRITE(LUN,600)
        WRITE(LUN,700)
        WRITE(LUN,800)
        WRITE(LUN,900)
        WRITE(LUN,1000)
        WRITE(LUN,1100)
        WRITE(LUN,200)
        WRITE(LUN,200)
        WRITE(LUN,200)
        WRITE(LUN,200)
100     FORMAT(//,T34,' A X-MAS TREE',///,T40,'*')
200     FORMAT(T39,'* *')
300     FORMAT(T38,'* * *')
400     FORMAT(T37,'* * * *')
500     FORMAT(T36,'* * * * *')
600     FORMAT(T35,'* * * * * *')
700     FORMAT(T34,'* * * * * * *')
800     FORMAT(T33,'* * * * * * * *')
900     FORMAT(T32,'* * * * * * * * *')
1000    FORMAT(T31,'* * * * * * * * * *')
1100    FORMAT(T30,'* * * * * * * * * * *')
        CLOSE(UNIT=LUN)
        STOP
        END
*****************************************************************
```

Figure 5.8: Program Listing of Example 5.5.

the number of data points in each row varies. The maximum number of data in a row is 9. There are many ways to read such a data file but one of the simplest ways is by using formatted READ statement as shown in Figure 5.13 which gives the source program.

The program is simple to follow. The data points are used to control the printer position in a row. Note the use of '+' carriage control character in the WRITE format statements.

```
***************************************************************
* USE OF VARAIBLE FORMAT STATEMENTS FOR PRINTING A X-MAS TREE*
***************************************************************
          INTEGER LUN
          PARAMETER (LUN = 2)
          OPEN(UNIT=LUN,FILE='EX5_51.OUT',STATUS='NEW')
          WRITE(LUN,100)
          DO 10 I = 0,10
          WRITE(LUN,200)
10        CONTINUE
          DO 20 I = 1,4
          WRITE(LUN,300)
20        CONTINUE
100       FORMAT(///,T34,' A X-MAS TREE'////)
200       FORMAT(T<40-I>,<I+1>('* '))
300       FORMAT(T39,2('* '))
          CLOSE(UNIT=LUN)
          STOP
          END
***************************************************************
```

Figure 5.9: Program Listing of Example 5.5.

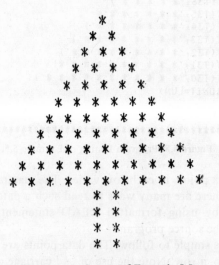

Figure 5.10: Output of Example 5.5.

The computer print-out is shown in Figure 5.14. Users may appreciate the limitations associated with the printing of the map. Using FORMAT statements, it is not possible to draw the exact map because of poor resolution of the printer. Using computer graphics, it is possible to draw an exact map. However, the simplicity involved with using FORMAT statements to draw simple figures should not be underemphasized.

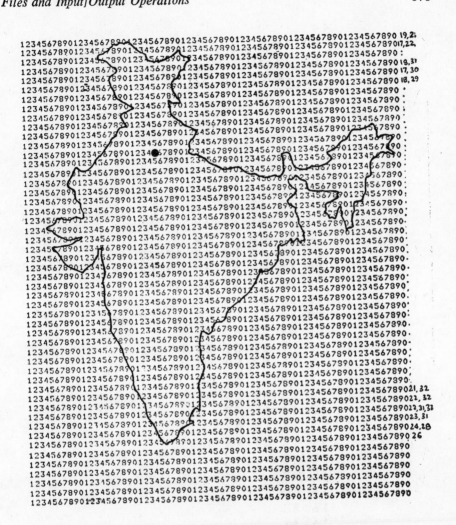

Figure 5.11 A Hand-drawn Map of India on Computer Print-out.

```
44
 19  21
 17  22  30
 15  24  26  28  32
 18  31
 17  30
 18  29
 18  29
 21  30
 19  28
 20  30
 18  33  65  66
 17  32  61  67  69
 15  25  31  59  68
 14  34  49  50  58  67  68  69
 10  12  37  39  49  50  53  55
  9  43  45  47  48  51  65
 10  50  53  64
 10  50  51  53  55  57  59  64
 11  49  58  62  63
  7   9  11  51  56  59  62
  5  51  57  58  59  61
  8  10  11  52  60  61
  6  15  49  50  51  52
  7  14  15  47
  8  13  15  47
 11  15  44  45  46
 15  43
 15  42
 15  40
 16  38
 16  37
 16  35
 17  32  33  34
 18  32
 18  32
 19  33
 20  33
 20  32
 21  32
 22  32
 22  31  32
 23  31
 24  28
 26
```

Figure 5.12: Input Data of Example 5.6.

```
************************************************************************
*         THIS PROGRAM DRAWS A MAP OF INDIA USING FORMAT STATEMENTS   *
************************************************************************
*
        CHARACTER*1,SYMBOL
        INTEGER INLUN,OUTLUN
        PARAMETER (INLUN = 1, OUTLUN = 2)
*
        OPEN(UNIT=INLUN,FILE='EX5_6.DAT',STATUS='OLD')
        OPEN(UNIT=OUTLUN,FILE='EX5_6.OUT',STATUS='NEW')
        PRINT*,' PLEASE TYPE IN THE SYMBOL FOR DRAWING THE MAP'
        READ(5,*)SYMBOL
        READ(INLUN,*)N
* READ POSITION OF POINTS AND DRAW THEM
        DO 10 I = 1,N
        READ(INLUN,100)N1,N2,N3,N4,N5,N6,N7,N8,N9
        WRITE(OUTLUN,200)SYMBOL
        IF(N2.NE.0)THEN
          WRITE(OUTLUN,300)SYMBOL
          IF(N3.NE.0)THEN
            WRITE(OUTLUN,400)SYMBOL
            IF(N4.NE.0)THEN
              WRITE(OUTLUN,500)SYMBOL
              IF(N5.NE.0)THEN
                WRITE(OUTLUN,600)SYMBOL
                IF(N6.NE.0)THEN
                  WRITE(OUTLUN,700)SYMBOL
                  IF(N7.NE.0)THEN
                    WRITE(OUTLUN,800)SYMBOL
                    IF(N8.NE.0)THEN
                      WRITE(OUTLUN,900)SYMBOL
                      IF(N9.NE.0)THEN
                        WRITE(OUTLUN,1000)SYMBOL
                      END IF
                    END IF
                  END IF
                END IF
              END IF
            END IF
          END IF
        END IF
*       WRITING DESIRED INFORMATION IN A MAP
        IF(I.EQ.13)THEN
          WRITE(OUTLUN,1100)
        END IF
        IF(I.EQ.14)THEN
          WRITE(OUTLUN,1200)
        END IF
        IF(I.EQ.22)THEN
          WRITE(OUTLUN,1300)
        END IF
10      CONTINUE
*
100     FORMAT(' ',9I3)
200     FORMAT(' ',T<N1>,A)
300     FORMAT('+',T<N2>,A)
400     FORMAT('+',T<N3>,A)
500     FORMAT('+',T<N4>,A)
600     FORMAT('+',T<N5>,A)
700     FORMAT('+',T<N6>,A)
```

—*Contd.*

```
800      FORMAT('+',T<N7>,A)
900      FORMAT('+',T<N8>,A)
1000     FORMAT('+',T<N9>,A)
1100     FORMAT('+',T25,'*')
1200     FORMAT('+',T21,'New Delhi')
1300     FORMAT('+',T21,'I   N   D   I   A')
*
         CLOSE(UNIT=INLUN)
         CLOSE(UNIT=OUTLUN)
         STOP
         END
```
****

Figure 5.13: Program Listing of Example 5.6.

PLEASE TYPE IN THE SYMBOL FOR DRAWING THE MAP

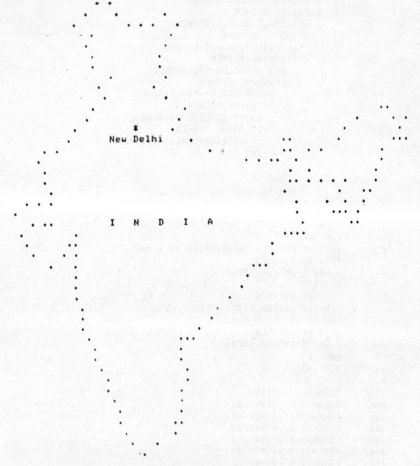

Figure 5.14: Computer Print-out of Example 5.6.

5.11 SUMMARY

The Communication between the programmer and the computer is an important part of programming. In order to facilitate better communication, various FORTRAN input/output statements have been introduced in this chapter. Starting with a discussion on file structure, necessary programming steps for manipulating data files are briefly described. A full length discussion on READ, WRITE and FORMAT statements must have provided readers with better ability to control the form of printed output and/or input data fields. Use of these statements to draw simple graphical figures is also illustrated. Not all I/O features are discussed in this chapter, but those that are described are the most commonly used. Before going to the next chapter which introduces a very powerful data structure, readers are advised to go through various exercises presented in this chapter. The drill and programming exercises given in this chapter should elucidate the use of the concepts discussed in this chapter.

OBJECTIVE QUESTIONS

(1) Which of the following READ statements is incorrect ?
  (a) READ (1,*) SUM, N, I
  (b) READ (1,20, END = 10, ERR = 20, IOSTAT = 30) SUM, N, I
  (c) READ (1)
  (d) READ (1, END = 10, FMT = 20) SUM, N, I
  (e) READ (1, 20, END = 10, ERR = 10) SUM, N, I
(2) Which of the following is not a correct way of assigning a value to A ?
  (a) DATA A/1.0/
  (b) READ (1, *) A
  (c) READ *,A,
  (d) NAMELIST/RED/ A
      READ (1, RED)
  (e) ACCEPT *,A,
(3) Which of the following program segments is correct ?
  (a) OPEN (UNIT = 1)
      READ (lun, *) A, B, I
  (b) OPEN (UNIT = 2, FILE = 'ABC', STATUS = 'NEW')
      READ (2, 10), A, B, I
      10 FORMAT (2F10.4, I3.2)
  (c) OPEN (UNIT = 2, IOSTAT = IOS, ERR = 10, STATUS = 'OLD',
      FILE = 'XYZ')
      WRITE (2, 10) A,B,I
      10 FORMAT (AE20, 13, I4)
  (d) OPEN (UNIT = 2, STATUS = 'OLD')
      ACCEPT *, A, B, I
  (e) OPEN (UNIT = 1, FILE = 'ABC', STATUS = 'NEW')
      TYPE (1, *) A, B, I
(4) Which of the following WRITE statements has a correct syntax form ?
  (a) WRITE (1, 2,) A, B, C
  (b) WRITE (2, 1), A, B, C,

    (c) WRITE (1, 2) A, B, C,

    (d) WRITE (1, 2) A, 1.0, C

    (e) WRITE (2, 1) A, B, C

(5) Which of the following FORMAT statements is correct ?

    (a) 1 FORMAT (12I30)

    (b) 1 FORMAT, (2I30, E14.3)

    (c) 1 FORMAT (F 10.12, I4)

    (d) 1 FORMAT (E 14.10, I4.4)

    (e) 1 FORMAT (5G14.5)

(6) Consider the following program segment

        OPN (1, I, ERR = 20, END = −30, FILE = '2BC', STATUS = 'KNOWN')

        READ, (1, $), A, B, 2

    10 FORM T (T, ANSWER, 2.5F6.2, C4),

    How many errors does the above segment have ?

    (a) 14

    (b) 13

    (c) 12

    (d) 15

    (e) 16

(7) Consider the program segment of Q. No. (6): Which of the following statements is true ?

    (a) OPEN statement has only 6 errors.

    (b) All statements have equal number of errors.

    (c) READ statement has only 4 errors.

    (d) FORMAT statement has the lowest number of errors.

    (e) FORMAT statement must precede READ statement.

(8) Which of the following statements prints

        HAPPY⊄DAYS⊄ARE⊄HERE⊄AGAIN

    (a) WRITE (1, 1) 'HAPPY', 'DAYS', 'ARE', 'HERE', 'AGAIN'

        1 FORMAT (' ', A5, X, A4, X, A3, X, A4, X, A5)

    (b) TYPE *, 'HAPPY⊄DAYS',/, 'ARE⊄HERE⊄AGAIN'

    (c) WRITE (1, 2) 'HAPPY', 'DAY', 'ARE', 'HERE', 'AGAIN'

        2 FORMAT (' ', A5, T8, A4, T13, A3, T17, A4, T25, A5)

    (d) WRITE (1,3) 'HAPPY', 'DAYS', 'ARE', 'HERE', 'AGAIN'

        3 FORMAT (' ', A5, X, A4, T13, A4, T17, A4, 2X, A5)

    (e) TYPE *, HAPPY⊄DAYS⊄ARE⊄HERE⊄AGAIN

(9) Which of the following FORMAT statements is not valid ?

    (a) 1 FORMAT (' ', 14, Q)

    (b) 2 FORMAT (' + ', T40, O10, Z20)

    (c) 3 FORMAT ('1', 5X, G10.3, TL5, 6X, I4.4)

    (d) 4 FORMAT ('0', 2Q, D14.3, E14.10)

    (e) 5 FORMAT (' ', F14.11, T16, 5X,/ , I4.3)

(10) What is the correct carriage control to put in a FORMAT statement to cause printing to occur on the next line ?

    (a) '0'

    (b) '+'

    (c) '1'

    (d) ' '

    (e) <0

(11) Which of the following statements about FORMAT statements is incorrect ?

    (a) F, E, I, D and G specifications can be placed in the same FORMAT statement.

    (b) A comma must be placed after every specification, including the last.

    (c) Character strings within quotation marks can occur in the same FORMAT statement as D, I and F specifications.

    (d) Horizontal spacing can be obtained by choosing a suitable value of field width w.

    (e) FORMAT statement must be labelled.

(12) The use of the edit descriptor 10X in a FORMAT statement will:

    (a) Print 10 X's.

    (b) Move the output to column 10.

    (c) Print 10 unknown numbers.

    (d) Move the next output 10 spaces to the right.

    (e) Move the next output 10 spaces to the left.

(13) What output results from the execution of the following program segment ?

```
        I = 99
        Z = 12.348
        TYPE 10, I, Z
   20   FORMAT (' ', I5, F7.2)
   10   FORMAT (' ', I7, F7.2)
```

    (a) ƀƀƀƀƀƀ99ƀƀ12.35

    (b) ƀƀƀƀƀ9912.34

    (c) ƀƀƀƀƀ99ƀ12.348

    (d) ƀƀƀ99ƀƀ12.35

    (e) ƀƀƀ99ƀƀ12.34

(14) Fill in the blanks:

    (a) The OPEN statement associates a file with a...................... . The unit number must be a.................. . For sequential access files, the default FORM option is.................while for direct access files, the default FORM option is......... .

    (b) The READ statement recognizes a file by its......................and UNIT option...................be specified.

    (c) The namelist-directed READ statement must be accompanied by a.................. statement which specifies the.............that.....................assigned input values.

    (d) The input data set for a namelist-directed READ statement must start in column.............with a..................sign or a..................sign.

    (e) The...............statement repositions the file to the first record while............... ....statement repositions the file to the beginning of the previous record.

    (f) The DATA statement is a.....................statement and it must, therefore, be placed before any..................statement.

    (g) The FORMAT statement can be placed...............in the body of the program.

    (h) The FORMAT field descriptors F, E and D provide specific ....and............ for numerics. Each field descriptor must correspond to a specific..................... in a READ/WRITE statement.

    (i) In a FORMAT statement, first character after the first quote is used for......... ....and is called as...................... . Double spacing is caused by......... ....while..................causes no vertical advance.

    (j) Two commonly used edit descriptors are..................and........................ If edit descriptor T (general from Tn) is used with a READ statement, the data item is read from..................character position but if it is used with a WRITE statement, the data item is witten from column............... .

DRILL EXERCISES

(1) Assuming

$$A = 0.99387E-5$$
$$B = 0.1234567E+15$$
$$C = 0.999999$$

D = 1.000001
I = 123
J = 405
K = 1209

What will be the computer output if following program segments are run?

(a) WRITE (1, 10) A, B, C, I, J, K
10 FORMAT (2E16.7, F10.3, 3I10)
(b) WRITE (1, 20) D, I/J, K/I, C*D
20 FORMAT (D20.12, 5X, 2I4.3,/, T40, G12.5)
(c) WRITE (1, 30) I, J
30 FORMAT ('0'//, 15HTWO NUMBERS ARE, I10, I2)

(2) Study the FORTRAN program given in Figure 5.15 and determine the output in the output file JNK.OUT

```
*******************************************************************
        INTEGER LUN
        PARAMETER (LUN=2)
        OPEN(UNIT=LUN,FILE='JNK.OUT',STATUS='NEW')
        X = 123.45
        Y = 0.12345
        Z = -0.12345
        WRITE(LUN,100) Y
        WRITE(LUN,200) X
        WRITE(LUN,300) Z
100     FORMAT(E11.5)
200     FORMAT(F6.2)
300     FORMAT(E12.5)
        CLOSE(UNIT=LUN)
        STOP
        END
*******************************************************************
```

Figure 5.15: Program Listing of Drill Exercise 2.

(3) Write FORTRAN 77 WRITE and FORMAT statements to print the following headings as specified:

(a)   A SUMMARY OF POPULATION SURVEY
    STATE   MALE   FEMALE   EMPLOYED   UNEMPLOYED

The first line should be the 4th line of a new page starting in column 20 and ending in column 61 with equal spacing between each word. There is one blank line between two lines. The second line should start in column 5 and end in column 80. The character M of word FEMALE should be in column 43 and spacing between each word should be nearly equal.

(b)   QUALITIES A GIRL MIGHT EXPECT IN HER BOYFRIEND
              (*** A SURVEY REPORT ***)
        ROMANTIC   INTELLIGENT   EXTROVERT
        RELIABLE   RICH

Every line should be centered on 40th column. The first and the last letters of each line except line 2 should be in column 2 and 79 respectively. The first letter of line 2 should be just below word A of line 1 and the last letter of line 2 should be just below letter R of word HER. Words in each line should be nearly equally-spaced. The gap between lines 1 and 2 should be one line while between lines 2 and 3 should be 3 lines.

(4) Consider the following program segment :

```
      READ (1, 100) A
100   FORMAT(f)
```

Where f is the format field specification. Determine the value stored in A after READ operation for the following format field specifications and input data.

Field Specification (f)	Input data Column #	1	2	3	4	5	6	7	8	9	10	11	12	13	14	15	Value of A
I5				4	5	0	.	0									
F10.4					−	3	2	.	7	8	4	9					
F13.6				2	4	5	.	6	7	8	E	+	0	9			
E10.1		1	2	3	.	4	5	6									
F15.13		0	.	0	0	0	0	0	0	0	0	0	0	0	0	1	

(5) What is printed by the following program segment:

```
      WRITE (5, 20)
20    FORMAT (' " ", XYZ)')
      WRITE (5, 30)
30    FORMAT (' + ', T40,' (" + ", A)/'1', T40,' (" − ", XYZ)')
      WRITE (5, 40)
40    FORMAT (' ', T8, 'IN')
      WRITE (5, 50)
50    FORMAT (' + ', T12, 'DIVERSITY')
      WRITE (5, 60)
60    FORMAT (' + ', 'UNITY')
```

(6) Consider the following program segment :

```
      I   =   5
      WRITE (2, 100)A
100   FORMAT (f)
```

where f is the format field specification. Determine the output printed by the computer for the following values of A and f:

Field Specification f	A	Value as printed out
I2.2	987	
F12.8	− 9.832E − 03	
E12.6	0.0000012345	
E11.4	− 0.000098765	
E11.2E4	9.17×10^{786}	
E9.5	5678.1234	
F < 2*I + 2>·<I − 1>	5678.1234	

(7) Consider the following program segment:

```
      LOGICAL SEARCH
      CHARACTER*7 NAME
      READ (1, 100) NAME, SEARCH
100   FORMAT (f₁, f₂)
```

where f_1 and f_2 are format field specifications. Determine the value stored in NAME and SEARCH after READ operation for the following format field specifications and input data set:

Field Specifications		Input data	Output data
f_1	f_2	Column numbers 1 2 3 4 5 6 7 8 9 10 11 12	SEARCH NAME
A7	L3	F O R T R A N ⌴ ⌴ ⌴	
A3	L2	F O R T ⌴ ⌴ R b F	
A9	L1	F O R T R A N 7 7 F	
A6	L4	P A S C A L ⌴ T ⌴ ⌴	
A5	L1	B A S I C ⌴ ⌴ T	

PROGRAMMING EXERCISES

(1) Write a FORTRAN 77 program to compute the values of trignometric functions sine, cosine, and tangent from 0 to 360 degrees in increments of 10 degrees. Present the results in a tabular form. For angle 90° and 270° print the message INFINITY for tangent function.

(2) The two roots of a quadratic equation $ax^2 + bx + c = 0$ are given by

$$x_{1,2} = \frac{-b \pm \sqrt{b^2 - 4ac}}{2a}$$

Note that roots may be real or complex. Write a FORTRAN 77 program to compute both the roots for any data set. The output for the possible cases should be arranged as shown:

(i)   COEFFICIENTS   VALUE
              A   1.0
              B   2.0
              C   1.0
      ROOTS ARE REAL AND EQUAL
          ROOT1 = ROOT2 = −1.0

(ii)   COEFFICIENTS   VALUE
              A   1.0
              B   − 3.0
              C   2.0
      ROOTS ARE REAL
          ROOT1 = 2.0
          ROOT2 = 1.0

(iii)   COEFFICIENTS   VALUE
              A   1.0
              B   2.0
              C   2.0

ROOTS ARE COMPLEX
REAL PART $= -1.0$
IMAGINARY PART $= +1.0$
CONJUGATE ROOT IS $-1.0 - j1.0$

(3) The area of a triangle is given by
    a b sinθ
    where a and b are any two sides of a triangle and θ is the angle between these two sides. Prepare a FORTRAN 77 program to calculate the area of a triangle. The input data is given in a file TRIANG. DAT. The number of data sets is unknown, however, the last data set is

    0.0 0.0 0.0

A sample of input data (a, b and θ in degrees) is given below:

    1.0 2.0 75.0
    3.0 4.0 90.0
    ⋮
    0.0 0.0   0.0

The program should print out the results as follows:

SIDE a	SIDE b	ANGLE	AREA
1.0	2.0	75.0	— —
3.0	4.0	90.0	— —
⋮			

Also determine the area of the largest triangle and print out the area, the sides and the angle of the largest triangle as:

LARGEST AREA =
SIDE a   =
SIDE b   =
ANGLE   =

(4) Prepare a FORTRAN 77 program to produce the following design

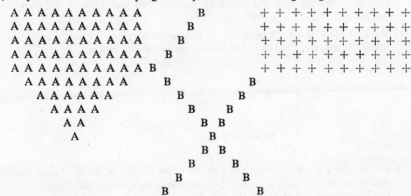

(5) Write a FORTRAN 77 program that will read any number of temperature values in degrees Celsius (°C). Terminate the program by choosing some hypothetical data such as

    -300.0

Compute the corresponding degree Fahrenheit (°F). °C and °F are related as follows:

$$°C = \frac{5}{9}(°F - 32)$$

Present your results in a tabular form. Also determine the value when both °C and °F are equal.

(6) The number of bacteria in a culture can be estimated by

$$N_0 e^{\lambda t}$$

where N_0 is the initial population, λ is the growth rate constant, and t is the time. Write a FORTRAN 77 program to calculate the number of bacteria present at time t for given values of λ and N_0. N_0, λ are to be read from an input file JNK.DAT. The input data in the file is as shown below

$\not b$$BACTRA$\not b$NO = 1000, ALAMDA = 0.20, $\not b\not b$$END

For t = 0 to 100 in increments of 5, present the results in the following form:

INITIAL POPULATION = 1000
GROWTH RATE   = 0.20

TIME	POPULATION
0	1000
⋮	⋮

(7) Write a FORTRAN 77 program that reads two four-digit numbers and then prints their product in the following format:

```
        1 2 3 4
        1 0 0 0
      _____
        0 0 0 0
        0 0 0 0
        0 0 0 0
        1 2 3 4
      _____
      1 2 3 4 0 0 0
      _____
```

Run the program with the following values: 7896 and 1234; − 1123 and 4501; − 1234 and − 5678; and 9999 and − 9999.

(8) Write a FORTRAN 77 program to generate and print the first 15 rows of the PASCAL triangle. Print the results in the format shown below:

```
1
1  1
1  2  1
1  3  3  1
1  4  6  4  1
1  5 10 10  5 1
⋮
```

(9) In Example 5.6 it was shown how one can draw a map of India. Using the input data given in the example modify the program to indicate the following:
(1) Mountains — Himalayas, Western Ghats
(2) Rivers — Ganges, Godavari, Brahmaputra
(3) Cities — Bombay, Madras, Calcutta, Bangalore
(4) Areas — Pakistan occupied Kashmir, Thar desert
    Use different symbols to show each of the above details.

(10) Write a FORTRAN 77 program to draw a map of your province. Locate four major cities and print their names adjacent to their location.

ANSWERS TO OBJECTIVE QUESTIONS

(1) b	(2) c	(3) d
(4) e	(5) e	(6) a
(7) c	(8) a	(9) d
(10) d	(11) b	(12) d
(13) a		

(14) (a) Logical unit number, non-negative integer, formatted, unformatted
 (b) Logical unit number, must
 (c) Declaration, variable or items, may be
 (d) 2, $, &
 (e) REWIND, BACKSPACE
 (f) Non-executable, executable
 (g) Anywhere
 (h) Fieldwidth, precision, variable name
 (i) Vertical spacing, carriage control character, 0, +
 (j) X, T, n, n − 1

Chapter 6

Arrays

6.1 INTRODUCTION

So far we have considered simple data types that represent single values. In many situations, however, it is necessary to process a collection of data that are related in some way. Processing such collection of data using only, simple data types can be extremely cumbersome. There are many ways of organizing data to make it easy to manipulate. The different organizing schemes are called data structures.

A simple but important data structure available in FORTRAN is an *array*. In this chapter we consider the implementation of arrays in FORTRAN and their applications in many problems.

6.2 STRUCTURE OF ARRAYS

In Chapter 5, we introduced files, which are collections of related data items used in the input/output operations. We also discussed how these data items can be retrieved (read) easily in a sequential manner. However, retrieving of data items in a nonsequential manner, together with the fact that they are usually stored in secondary memory, is rather slow and may not be practical in many applications.

In some cases, it is better to store data items in a sequence of main memory locations, each of which can be accessed directly. Such a data structure is called an array. An array is described by a single name or identifier, and each individual item or component in the array is referenced by a subscripted variable, formed by affixing to the array name a subscript or index enclosed in brackets. The term *subscript* has the same meaning here as in mathematical notations for matrices/arrays.

Let us now consider an example of processing test scores of students in a computational science class. The class has 10 students numbered 1,2,3, ... 10. Scores obtained by students are as follows:

Student Number	Score
1	90
2	73
3	50
4	99
5	40
6	85
7	91
8	65
9	64
10	45

By using the student number as an index or subscript, any element (i.e. score of a student) in a score array can be easily referenced. Let the name of the score array be SCORE, therefore, the Ith element of the array will be $SCORE_I$ or SCORE (I). For example, the score of student number 4 is SCORE (4) which is 99.

At this point, some users may wonder why different variable names are not used to represent the score of each student, e.g. SCOR1, SCOR2, . . . , SCOR10 to reference scores of student number 1,2, . . . , 10. There are some important advantages to using a subscripted variable like SCORE(1) OR SCORE(10), rather than separate names like SCOR1 or SCOR10. The most important of these is that the index variable in a DO loop may be used to determine the subscript. This allows different subscripted variables to appear in a repeat construct. It also avoids the need of using different variable names for each data item.

In FORTRAN, the computer must first be instructed to reserve a required number (in the above example it is ten) of memory locations for an array. The DIMENSION statement may be used to reserve these locations. These memory locations are allocated in sequence. The statement

DIMENSION   SCORE(10)

instructs the compiler to create an array with the name SCORE consisting of ten memory locations in which scores will be stored and to associate the subscripted variables SCORE(1), SCORE(2), . . . , SCORE(10) with these locations as shown in Figure 6.1.

Each subscripted variable references an individual memory location and hence can be used in much the same way as an ordinary variable. For example, the assignment statement

SCORE (3) = 50

stores the value 50 in the third location of the array SCORE; and the statement

WRITE (5, *), SCORE (7)

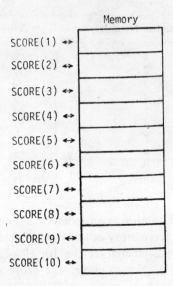

Figure 6.1: One-Dimensional Array SCORE.

displays the value stored in the seventh location of the array SCORE. There-fore, each item of the array SCORE can be accessed directly. This is one of the major advantages of using an array to store a set of data.

As noted earlier, a DIMENSION statement is used to reserve the requi-red number of memory locations. This is also called a *declaration of arrays* in FORTRAN. Besides the DIMENSION statement, there are other statements which can be used for declaring arrays in FORTRAN. These statements are discussed in the next section.

6.3 ARRAY DECLARATION STATEMENTS

A variable is declared as an array within a FORTRAN program using the standard explicit type declaration statements (INTEGER, REAL, LOGICAL, etc.), or it can be declared, as noted above, using a DIMENSION statement. An array declaration has the general form:

type $a([d_{l_1} :] d_{u_1} [, [d_{l_2} :] d_{u_2}] \dots)$

where

type is either an explicit type declaration statement such as INTEGER, REAL, LOGICAL, DOUBLE PRECISION, etc. or a DIMENSION statement;

a is a symbolic name of the array, that is, the array name;

d_l, d_u are dimension declarators or bound specifications for the array a;

d_l is the lower bound of the dimension while d_u is the upper-bound of the dimension; d_l is optional and if not specified it is assumed as 1; d_u is specified based on the number of memory locations desired to be reserved.

The value of d_l, the lower-bound dimension declarator, can be negative, zero or positive. The value of d_u, the upper-bound dimension declarator, must be greater than or equal to that of the corresponding d_l. In one-dimensional arrays d_{u_1} must necessarily be present, while d_{l_1} may or may not be. In two-dimensional arrays, d_{u_2} must be present, and d_{l_2} may or may not be present. Thus, the number of upper-bound dimension declarators indicates the number of dimensions in the array. In FORTRAN the number of dimensions can range from one to seven. In this chapter, we will mainly concern ourselves with up to two-dimensional arrays, with a brief introduction of arrays with three or more dimensions. In the following section, we will describe one-dimensional arrays. Multi-dimensional arrays are discussed in Section 6.5.

6.4 ONE-DIMENSIONAL ARRAYS

Some examples of declaration of one-dimensional arrays are:

DIMENSION	A (10)
REAL	NAME (100), Y (100:199)
INTEGER	Z(50), NUM (— 10:50)

The DIMENSION statement declares variable A to be array with the value of the lower-bound specification d_l as 1 and that of the upper-bound specification d_u as 10; that is, ten memory locations are reserved for array A. Thus, array A can contain 10 elements which are identified as A(1), A(2), A(3), . . . , A (10).

The REAL statement declares variables NAME and Y each to be an array of real type; that is, each element of these arrays is real. The REAL declaration statement serves two purposes: (i) it declares variables NAME and Y as real; and (ii) it declares NAME and Y to be arrays and instructs the computer to reserve the desired memory locations for each array. If we had used the DIMENSION statement in place of the REAL, then the array NAME would have been of the integer type and not of the REAL type. REAL declaration statements can, however, be replaced with the following statements:

REAL   NAME
DIMENSION NAME (100), Y (100:199)

The lower-bound specification for array Y is 100 and the upper-bound is 199, so the first element of array Y is Y (100) and not Y (1). The other elements of array Y will be Y (101), Y (102), . . . , Y (199). The number of elements is $100 = [199 - 100 + 1]$.

The INTEGER statement declares Z and NUM each to be an array of integer type.

The first element of NUM is NUM (— 10) and the total number of elements in the array NUM is 61 as shown in Figure 6.2.

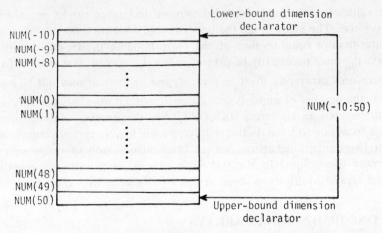

Figure 6.2 One-Dimensional Array NUM (−10:50).

Users are advised to follow some simple rules while using declaration statements in a FORTRAN program:

(1) A variable name can appear in only one type of declaration statement.

(2) Declaration statements must be placed at the beginning of the program in which they are used; that is, these statements must be placed before any executable statement in a FORTRAN program.

Some invalid declaration statements are:

   (a)   REAL NAME (100)
         DIMENSION NAME (100)
   (b)   DIMENSION X (10)
         DIMENSION Y (1000), X (10), Z (−100,0)
   (c)   REAL ICOUNT (10)
         ⋮
         SUM = A + B
         INTEGER MAX (100)
         ⋮

(a) and (b) violate rule (1) while (c) violates rule (2).

The following are some more examples of declaration statements for one-dimensional arrays:

   (a)   DIMENSION HEIGHT (100), WEIGHT (200), SUM (−10:40), NUMBER (100)
   (b)   REAL   LENGTH (−10:40), MEN (0:100), SCORE (100)
   (c)   INTEGER A(3), Y(15), Z(10:23)
   (d)   LOGICAL   SEARCH(10), FOUND(20)

Users must remember that if the DIMENSION statement is used for the declaration of arrays, the type of the array and its elements are decided by the name of the arrays. If the first letter of the array name is either I, J, K,

L, M or N, the array will be of type INTEGER, otherwise it will be of type REAL. In the DIMENSION statement of the above example, HEIGHT, WEIGHT, SUM will be of type REAL while NUMBER will be of type INTEGER.

In Section 6.2, we used the one-demensional array SCORE to store the test scores of a class of computational science students. This allowed us to access the score of any student by using a subscripted variable consisting of the array name SCORE followed by the index or subscript that indicated the student number. Now we want to process the students' scores to obtain the following information:

(1) Class Average
(2) Maximum marks obtained by a student
(3) Number of students whose score is greater than the class average

Before we attempt to write a FORTRAN program to obtain the above information, we must first of all store the students' scores in the array SCORE. Do not think that an array declaration statement automatically stores values in the array. It simply instructs the computer to reserve a specified number of memory locations for an array. You may reserve more memory locations than actually needed but what you should not do is to use the array memory beyond its range. For example, if we use the declaration statement

DIMENSION SCORE(5)

and then try to print the score obtained by student number 7 using

WRITE(5 *), SCORE(7)

the computer will flash an error message during execution. On the other hand, if we use the declaration statement

DIMENSION SCORE(15)

then the computer reserves 15 memory locations but we actually use ten locations only and, therefore, five locations are unused. Reserving more memory locations does not affect your program results except that it is a waste of computer memory. In many situations, the exact number of array elements may not be known in advance. In these cases, a reasonable overestimation should be made for reserving memory locations. Users must always avoid using array elements which are out of range. This is a common and serious programming error which causes the program to fail. As for the earlier example, since we know the number of students exactly, we will use the declaration statement

DIMENSION SCORE(10)

We will now describe how student scores in the array SCORE can be stored.

6.4.1 Input and Output of One-Dimensional Arrays

In Chapter 5 we discussed input/output (READ/WRITE) statements used with files. We assume that student scores are stored in a data file 'SCORE. DAT' in the following way:

                90
                73
                50
                99
                40
                85
                91
                65
                64
                45

The following program segment reads the array element:

```
DIMENSION SCORE(10)
OPEN(UNIT = 1, FILE = 'SCORE. DAT', STATUS = 'OLD')
READ(1, *) SCORE(1)
READ(1, *) SCORE(2)
READ(1, *) SCORE(3)
READ(1, *) SCORE(4)
      ⋮
READ(1, *) SCORE(10)
```

Since each element of an array is a unique variable, they are read just as any other variable. Another way of reading scores is:

```
DIMENSION SCORE(10)
OPEN (UNIT = 1, FILE = 'SCORE.DAT', STATUS = 'OLD')
READ(1, *) SCORE(1), SCORE(2), SCORE(3), . . . , SCORE(10)
```

If the number of students is quite large, say 100, then writing the READ statement in the above program segments would be an exhausting process. In fact, none of the above methods are normally used to read/write an array. The use of repeat constructs (DO loop and WHILE loop) to read/write an array element is quite common. FORTRAN also provides some short-cut methods for array input and output. We will describe these methods after we illustrate the use of repeat constructs for array input/output.

6.4.1.1 *Use of the DO Statement*

The following program segment reads students' scores by using the DO statement:

```
DIMENSION SCORE (10)
OPEN (UNIT = 1, FILE = 'SCORE.DAT', STATUS = 'OLD')
```

```
          DO 100 I = 1, 10
            READ(1, *) SCORE(I)
      100 CONTINUE
```

The DO loop is executed ten times. The initial value of the DO index I is one and the READ statement causes reading SCORE (1) in the first iteration of the DO loop. In the next iteration, I is increased to two and SCORE (2) is read, and so on. In the last iteration, SCORE(10) is read. If the number of students is increased to, say 100, then a simple modification in the DO statement accomplishes the reading of these many students' scores. The terminal parameter of the DO statement is changed to 100 as shown below:

```
          ⋮
          DO  100 I = 1, 100
             READ (1, *) SCORE (I)
      100 CONTINUE
```

6.4.1.2 *Use of the DO-While Statement*

The following program segment uses the DO-WHILE statement to read students' scores:

```
          DIMENSION SCORE (10)
          OPEN (UNIT = 1, FILE = 'SCORE. DAT', STATUS = 'OLD')
          I = 1
          DO WHILE (I. LE. 10)
            READ (1, *) SCORE (I)
            I = I + 1
          END DO
```

In addition to the above repeat constructs, FORTRAN provides two short-cut methods for array input and output. These are described in the following two subsections.

6.4.1.3 *Unsubscripted Array Name*

One method of array input/output is to simply give the array name as shown in the following program segment:

```
          DIMENSION SCORE (10)
          OPEN (UNIT = 1, FILE = 'SCORE. DAT', STATUS = 'OLD')
          READ (1, *) SCORE
```

The above segment causes the entire array (all the memory locations reserved for the array) to be read. There is a slight disadvantage in this method, since in many cases we don't want to read/write an entire array but only a part of it. In the above example, if we want to read scores of only those students whose student number is even, then we cannot use this simple method unless we modify the data file 'SCORE. DAT'. Another disadvantage of this method is that it requires prior knowledge of the number of elements to be read. The memory locations reserved through the declaration statement(s) should be equal to the number of entries to be read/written.

FORTRAN provides another short-cut method which is quite flexible and does not suffer from these disadvantages. This method for array input/output is called *implied DO list*.

6.4.1.4 *Implied DO List*

An implied DO list has a general form

$$.... (list, V = e_1, e_2[, e_3])$$

where

list is an input/output list (usually including array variables),

V is implied DO variable of type Integer or Real

e_1, e_2 and e_3 are parameters for the implied DO.

The variables V, e_1, e_2 and e_3 have the same forms and functions that they have in the DO statement as discussed in Chapter 4. In fact, an implied DO list is an I/O list that functions as though it were part of an I/O statement within a DO loop. The following program segment for reading students' scores shows how to use the implied DO list:

```
DIMENSION SCORE (10)
OPEN (UNIT = 1, FILE = 'SCORE.DAT', STATUS = 'OLD')
READ (1, *) (SCORE (I), I = 1, 10)
```

The list immediately preceding the DO variable (I, in the above example) is the range of the implied DO loop. The elements in the list can use the DO variable, but they must not change its value. The parentheses must enclose an implied DO as shown above. An implied DO list may contain another implied DO list nested within it as is the case with the nested DO loops. We will discuss nested implied DO lists with two-dimensional arrays.

The implied DO list is the method most preferred for arrays input/output. Input/output operations on the entire array or parts of the array can be easily performed by using the implied DO list. In many situations, when we do not know the input data arrangement (formatting), the implied DO list is the easiest way of reading data in arrays. For example, if the input data file 'SCORE.DAT' has scores arranged in the following manner:

```
90 73
50 99 40
85
91 65 64 45
```

that is, number of entries in each line is neither one nor fixed, the implied DO list reads these scores in the same manner as earlier. The first score 90 is stored in the memory location SCORE (1) and so on. However, the regular repeat constructs (DO loop or DO-WHILE loop) result in a reading error. The computer aborts the program and may even give a warning message:

"End of the file detected during read. . . .". The reason is that the READ statement in the DO range reads only one score from each line. The first score, 90 is read and stored in the memory location SCORE (1) because I is one. During the second iteration of the DO statement, SCORE (2) is read from the next line, thus storing 50 and not 73 in SCORE (2). Similarly, 85 is stored in SCORE (3) and 91 is stored in SCORE (4). The fifth iteration of the DO loop tries to read SCORE (5) from the fifth line of the data file. It results in a reading error because there are no more entries left to be read. It is, therefore, necessary to have only one input data in each line while using the DO or the WHILE statement for reading arrays.

The difference between the DO or the WHILE statement and the implied DO statement in reading/writing arrays is that the implied DO statement allows more than one input entry to appear on any line, while the DO or the DO-WHILE statements require only one input entry in any line. Similarly, the implied DO statement prints as many output entries in a line as can fit in the line, whereas the DO or the DO-WHILE statements result in one new line for each output entry. This is illustrated in the following program segment:

```
      DIMENSION SCORE (10)
      OPEN (UNIT = 1, FILE = 'SCORE.DAT', STATUS = 'OLD')
      OPEN (UNIT = 2, FILE = 'SCORE.OUT', STATUS = 'NEW')
      READ (1, *), (SCORE (I), I = 1, 10)
      WRITE (2, *) (SCORE (I), I = 1, 10)
      DO 10 I = 1, 10
          WRITE (2, *) SCORE (I)
   10 CONTINUE
```

In the above program segment, there are two WRITE statements, the first WRITE statement uses the implied DO list whereas the second WRITE statement is inside the DO range. The output in the file 'SCORE.OUT' may appear as follows:

90.0	73.0	50.0	99.0	44.0
85.0	91.0	65.0	64.0	45.0
90.0				
73.0				
50.0				
99.0				
44.0				
85.0				
91.0				
65.0				
64.0				
45.0				

Before we go back to our original problem of processing students' scores to obtain the desired information, let us list the various ways we have discussed to read/write arrays:

(a) Read/write each element of the array
(b) Read/write arrays using the DO/DO-WHILE statement
(c) Short-cut methods to read/write arrays:
   (i) Unsubscripted array name
   (ii) Implied DO list

Programming Examples 6.1, 6.2 and 6.3 illustrate the use of these methods. The source programs and output results are given in Figures 6.3, 6.4 and 6.5 respectively. Each program is run for two sets of input data given in Figure 6.6 and is quite easy to follow. Users must note the advantage of using the implied DO list in this case.

Coming back to our earlier problem, the information that we want to obtain by processing students' scores is:

(1) Class average
(2) Maximum marks obtained by a student
(3) Number of students whose score is greater than the class average.

The following program segment does the job:

```
      DIMENSION SCORE (10)
      OPEN (UNIT = 1, FILE = 'SCORE.DAT', STATUS = 'OLD')
      OPEN (UNIT = 2, FILE = 'SCORE.OUT', STATUS = 'NEW')
```

*Read students' scores

```
      READ (1, *) (SCORE(I), I = 1, 10)
```

*Calculate class average

```
      SUM = 0.0
      DO 10 I = 1, 10
         SUM = SUM + SCORE (I)
   10 CONTINUE
      AVERAG = SUM/10
      WRITE (2, 100) AVERAG
  100 FORMAT (' THE CLASS AVERAGE IS = ', F10.2)
```

*Calculate maximum marks obtained by a student

```
      AMAX = SCORE (1)
      DO 20 I = 2, 10
      IF (AMAX.LT.SCORE (I), THEN
         AMAX = SCORE (I)
      END IF
   20 CONTINUE
      WRITE (2, 200) AMEX
  200 FORMAT (' THE MAXIMUM MARKS OBTAINED =', F10.2)
```

```
********************************************************************************
*         THIS PROGRAM READS/WRITES STUDENTS' SCORES USING IMPLIED DO         *
*         LIST                                                                *
********************************************************************************
*
        DIMENSION SCORE(10)
        INTEGER INLUN,OUTLUN
        PARAMETER (INLUN = 1,OUTLUN = 2)
*
        OPEN(UNIT=INLUN,FILE='SCORE.DAT',STATUS='OLD')
        OPEN(UNIT=OUTLUN,FILE='SCORE.OUT',STATUS='NEW')
* READ NUMBER OF STUDENTS
        READ(INLUN,*)N_STU
* READ STUDENTS' SCORES
        READ(INLUN,*)(SCORE(I),I=1,N_STU)
* WRITE NUMBER OF STUDENTS
        WRITE(OUTLUN,100)N_STU
* WRITE STUDENTS' SCORES
        WRITE(OUTLUN,200)
        WRITE(OUTLUN,300)(SCORE(I),I=1,N_STU)
100     FORMAT(' NUMBER OF STUDENTS =',I6,/)
200     FORMAT(' ',10X,'STUDENTS'' SCORES',/)
300     FORMAT(' ',5F7.2)
        CLOSE(UNIT=INLUN)
        CLOSE(UNIT=OUTLUN)
        STOP
        END
********************************************************************************
```

Output Results for Input Data Set I

```
NUMBER OF STUDENTS =        10

            STUDENTS' SCORES

    93.00   73.00   50.00   99.00   40.00
    85.00   91.00   65.00   64.00   45.00
```

Output Results for Input Data Set II
```
NUMBER OF STUDENTS =        10

            STUDENTS' SCORES

    93.00   73.00   50.00   99 00   40.00
    85.00   91.00   65.00   64.00   45.00
```

Figure 6.3: Program Listing and Output Results of Example 6.1.

```
*****************************************************************************
*        THIS PROGRAM READ/WRITES STUDENTS' SCORES USING DO LOOP          *
*****************************************************************************
*
        DIMENSION SCORE(10)
        INTEGER INLUN,OUTLUN
        PARAMETER (INLUN = 1,OUTLUN = 2)
*
        OPEN(UNIT=INLUN,FILE='SCORE.DAT',STATUS='OLD')
        OPEN(UNIT=OUTLUN,FILE='SCORE.OUT',STATUS='NEW')
* READ NUMBER OF STUDENTS
        READ(INLUN,*)N_STU
* READ STUDENTS' SCORES
        DO 10 I=1,N_STU
          READ(INLUN,*)SCORE(I)
10      CONTINUE
* WRITE NUMBER OF STUDENTS
        WRITE(OUTLUN,100)N_STU
* WRITE STUDENTS' SCORES
        WRITE(OUTLUN,200)
        DO 20 I=1,N_STU
          WRITE(OUTLUN,300)SCORE(I)
20      CONTINUE
100     FORMAT(' NUMBER OF STUDENTS =',I6,/)
200     FORMAT(' STUDENTS'' SCORES',/)
300     FORMAT(' ',F7.2)
        CLOSE(UNIT=INLUN)
        CLOSE(UNIT=OUTLUN)
        STOP
        END
*****************************************************************************
```

Output Results for Input Data Set I

```
NUMBER OF STUDENTS =        10

STUDENTS' SCORES

    93.00
    73.00
    50.00
    99.00
    40.00
    85.00
    91.00
    65.00
    64.00
    45.00
```
Output Results for Input Data Set II

```
%FOR-F-ENDDURREA, end-of-file during read
```

Figure 6.4: Program Listing and Output Results of Example 6.2.

```
*****************************************************************************
*          THIS PROGRAM READ/WRITES STUDENTS' SCORES USING UNSUBSCRIPTED  *
*          ARRAY.                                                         *
*****************************************************************************
*
          DIMENSION SCORE(10)
          INTEGER INLUN,OUTLUN
          PARAMETER (INLUN = 1,OUTLUN = 2)
*
          OPEN(UNIT=INLUN,FILE='SCORE.DAT',STATUS='OLD')
          OPEN(UNIT=OUTLUN,FILE='SCORE.OUT',STATUS='NEW')
* READ NUMBER OF STUDENTS
          READ(INLUN,*)N_STU
* READ STUDENTS' SCORES
            READ(INLUN,*)SCORE
* WRITE NUMBER OF STUDENTS
          WRITE(OUTLUN,100)N_STU
* WRITE STUDENTS' SCORES
          WRITE(OUTLUN,200)
          WRITE(OUTLUN,300)SCORE
100       FORMAT(' NUMBER OF STUDENTS =',I6,/)
200       FORMAT('  ',10X,'STUDENTS'' SCORES',/)
300       FORMAT(' ',5F7.2)
          CLOSE(UNIT=INLUN)
          CLOSE(UNIT=OUTLUN)
          STOP
          END
*****************************************************************************
```

```
$FOR EX63
$LINK EX63
$RUN EX63
FORTRAN STOP
$              Output Results for Input Data Set I

$TYPE SCORE.OUT

NUMBER OF STUDENTS =     10

              STUDENTS' SCORES

   93.00   73.00   50.00   99.00   40.00
   85.00   91.00   65.00   64.00   45.00
$



$RUN EX63
FORTRAN STOP
$

$TYPE SCORE.OUT
              Output Results for Input Data Set II
NUMBER OF STUDENTS =     10

              STUDENTS' SCORES

   93.00   73.00   50.00   99.00   40.00
   85.00   91.00   65.00   64.00   45.00
$
```

Figure 6.5: Program Listing and Output Results of Example 6.3.

Input Data Set I

$TYPE SCORE.DAT

```
10
93
73
50
99
40
85
91
65
64
45
$
```

Input Data Set II

$TYPE SCORE.DAT

```
10
93 73
50 99 40
85
91 65 64   45
$
```

Figure 6.6: Input Data Sets of Examples 6.1, 6.2 and 6.3.

*Calculate number of students whose score is greater than the class average
    NUMBER = 0
    DO 30 I = 1, 10
       IF (SCORE(I).GT. AVERAG) THEN
          NUMBER = NUMBER + 1
       END IF
  30 CONTINUE
    WRITE (2,300) NUMBER
300 FORMAT (' NUMBER OF STUDENTS WITH SCORES GREATER
    THAN AVERAGE = ', I6)

This program segment reads students' scores using the implied DO list.
It then uses three DO statements to obtain the desired information. The first
DO statement calculates the sum of students' scores by adding all the array
elements SCORE (1), SCORE(2), . . . ,SCORE(10). The DO index I assists
in getting the required subscripts. The variable SUM is initialized to zero
outside the DO range and the first iteration adds SUM (which is zero) to
SCORE(1) because during the first iteration the value of the DO index I is
1. Therefore, SUM will be assigned the value stored in memory location
SCORE(1). The value of SUM will be 90.0. During the second iteration. I is

increased to two (note parameter e3 is one) and the value of SUM equals its old value plus the value stored in memory location SCORE(2); that is,

$$SUM = 90.0 + 85.0 = 175.0$$

This process continues for the DO index $I = 1, 2, 3, \ldots, 10$, and the final value of SUM will be equal to 881.0 which is the sum of students' scores; that is,

$$SUM = \sum_{i=1}^{10} score_i$$

The average value can then be easily calculated by dividing this sum by the total number of students.

The second DO loop calculates maximum marks (AMAX) obtained by a student. Initializing AMAX to the value stored in memory location SCORE (1), it then compares this value to the score of other students. Users should note that the initial value of the DO index I is two and not one and the DO loop repeats itself nine times. The IF-THEN statement checks if the value of AMAX is less than the value stored in memory location SCORE(I); I can have a value between 2 and 10. If for any value of I the IF condition is true, AMAX is assigned the value stored in memory location SCORE(I). After scanning through the entire array, the final value of AMAX will be the maximum marks obtained by a student. It is not necessary to have a separate DO statement for doing this part. In fact these statements can be put together with the statements of the first part, thus using only one DO statement. This has been done in Programming Example 6.4.

The third and final DO loop calculates the number of students whose score is greater than the class average. The FORTRAN statements to do this part are quite easy to follow so no further explanation is given. We will, however, answer one important question here: is it really necessary to store these scores in an array? The answer is yes. But if we are asked to simply calculate the class average and the maximum marks obtained by a student, we do not need to store students' scores. This is illustrated in the following program segment:

```
OPEN (UNIT = 1, FILE = 'SCORE.DAT', STATUS = 'OLD')
OPEN (UNIT = 2, FILE = 'SCORE.OUT', STATUS = 'NEW')
SUM = 0.0
AMAX = 0.0
DO 10 I = 1, 10
      READ (1, *), SCORE
      SUM = SUM + SCORE
      IF (AMAX.LT.SCORE) THEN
            AMAX = SCORE
      END IF
```

```
10   CONTINUE
     AVERAG = SUM/10
     WRITE (2, 100) AVERAG
     WRITE (2, 200) AMAX
100 . . .
200 . . .
```

The only constraint with this program segment is that the students' scores should appear one on each line in the input data file 'SCORE.DAT' because the READ statement is inside the DO statement. The reason for this has been explained earlier.

The above program segment reads each student score, SCORE, and then updates the SUM and AMAX. It does not store students' scores. The value of the variable SCORE changes in each iteration of the DO loop and the final value of the variable SCORE will be the last read value, which is 45 in our example. Now if we want to compute the number of students whose score is greater than the class average, we must first calculate the class average. The class average cannot be calculated until the program reads the scores of all the students. Once the program has read the students' scores and computed the average, there are two alternative ways of obtaining the number of students whose score is greater than the class average:

(i) While reading students' scores, store them so that they can be retrieved whenever required. This is exactly what an array accomplishes quite easily.

(ii) Do not store students' scores but again read the data file 'SCORE.-DAT'. So the data file is read twice: the first time for computing the class average and the maximum marks, and the second time for computing the number of students having scores greater than the class average. The problem with this solution is that every time the user wants to read the input file, he/she has to open and close it afresh. This results in a waste of computer time because each input/output operation tends to slow down the computer speed. There is another great disadvantage with this method. Consider the situation when a program requires only part of the data to be used again and therefore only that part needs to be read. But the computer reads a file only from the beginning. It is, however, possible to skip records but then it becomes quite a cumbersome process, particularly for large input files. To give you an idea, consider that we want to obtain the number of students whose score is greater than the class average and whose student number is greater than five. Well then, the second time you do not really need to read the first five students' scores and you start reading scores only from the sixth student. In such cases, the user is strongly advised against using this method.

Before we give some examples, here are a few suggestions on when to use arrays:

(i) If the input data is to be re-utilized then the use of the array structure is quite convenient and, in many situations, it is mandatory.

(ii) If a repetitious logic is used to process a collection of related data items.

(iii) If the programming problem quite naturally falls into the domain of matrices.

MORE EXAMPLES TO ILLUSTRATE THE USE OF IMPLIED DO LIST

Example (a)

This program segment shows how the implied DO list can be used to write only the odd elements of the array,

```
INTEGER SUM(20)
WRITE(1, *) (SUM(I), I = 1, 15, 2)
```

Example (b)

This program segment shows how the implied DO list can be used to print the following line,

$$-X-X-X-X-X-X-X-X$$
```
WRITE(1, *) ('-X', I = 1, 8)
```

Example (c)

This program segment shows how to read the students' scores in two subjects, if the data file is as follows:

95.0	88.0
25.0	30.0
100.0	40.0
50.0	90.0
60.0	70.0
33.0	45.0
⋮	⋮

Each row contains the scores of a student in Mathematics and English. The total number of students is 50.

```
REAL MATHS (50), ENGLIS (50)
N = 50
READ(1, *) (MATHS(I), ENGLIS(I), I = 1, N)
```

Example (d)

This program segment shows how to read the roll numbers of boys and girls in a class. The data is arranged as follows:

For boys   10   107   102   101   108 ...
For girls   20   201   205   220
                217   216   215 ... ...

The first element of the first row is the number of boys followed by the roll numbers of boys. The next element after the boys' roll numbers is the number of girls followed by their roll numbers.

```
INTEGER BOYS(50), GIRLS(50)
READ(1,*) NBOYS, (BOYS(I), I = 1, NBOYS)
READ(1, *) NGIRLS, (GIRLS(I), I = 1, NGIRLS)
```

The first READ statement reads number of boys, NBOYS and then the roll number of boys, BOYS. The second READ statement reads the number of girls, NGIRLS, and then their roll numbers and store them in an array GIRLS. Readers should note that the parameters of an implied DO loop can be read in the same statement. For example, the limiting parameters for both the loops (NBOYS and NGIRLS, respectively) are read in the same statement in which they are used. The only requirement is that the parameters must be read before the execution of the implied DO in which they are used. Therefore, it is not valid to use the following READ statements:

```
READ(1, *) (BOYS(I), I = 1, NBOYS), NBOYS
READ(1, *) (GIRLS(I), I = 1, NGIRLS), NGIRLS
```

The following READ statements, however, are valid:

```
READ(1, *) NBOYS, INCR, (BOYS(I), I = 1, NBOYS, INCR)
READ(1, *) NFIRST, NGIRLS, (GIRLS(I), I = NFIRST,
NGIRLS)
```

6.4.2 Programming Examples to Illustrate the Use of One Dimensional Array

Example 6.4

This example gives a FORTRAN 77 program for processing the scores of students in a computational science class. The program provides the following information:

(1) Class average
(2) Maximum marks obtained by a student
(3) Number of students whose scores are greater than the class average.

The input data is given in a file, 'EX6_4.DAT' and the output is to be written in an output file named 'EX6_4.OUT'. The first number in the data file is the number of students in the class. The remaining numbers in the data file are the scores of students. This problem has been discussed earlier and, therefore, no further explanation is needed. The source program is given in Figure 6.7 and the input and output files are shown in Figure 6.8.

Example 6.5

This example illustrates how to compute the *scalar product* (also called the *inner product*) of two one-dimensional arrays A and B. The maximum number of elements in each vector can be 50. The scalar product is defined as

$$\text{scalar product} \atop (\text{SCPROD}) = \sum_{i=1}^{N} A_i B_i$$

```
***********************************************************************
*         THIS PROGRAM PROCESSES STUDENTS' SCORES                     *
***********************************************************************
*
        REAL SCORE(100),MAX
        INTEGER INLUN,OUTLUN
        PARAMETER (INLUN = 1,OUTLUN = 2)
*
        OPEN(UNIT=INLUN,FILE='EX6_4.DAT',STATUS='OLD')
        OPEN(UNIT=OUTLUN,FILE='EX6_4.OUT',STATUS='NEW')
* READ STUDENTS' SCORES
        READ(INLUN,*)N_STU,(SCORE(I),I=1,N_STU)
* CALCULATE THE MAXIMUM SCORE OBTAINED BY A STUDENT AND THE CLASS
* AVERAGE
        SUM=0.0
        MAX=SCORE(1)
        DO 10 I=1,N_STU
          SUM=SUM+SCORE(I)
          IF(MAX.LT.SCORE(I))THEN
            MAX=SCORE(I)
          END IF
10      CONTINUE
        AVERAG=SUM/N_STU
* WRITE THE MAXIMUM SCORE AND THE CLASS AVERAGE
        WRITE(OUTLUN,100)AVERAG
100     FORMAT(' THE CLASS AVERAGE IS =',F10.2)
        WRITE(OUTLUN,200)MAX
200     FORMAT(' MAXIMUM MARKS OBTAINED BY A STUDENT =',F10.2)
* DETERMINE THE NUMBER OF STUDENTS WHOSE SCORES ARE GRAETER THAN THE
* CLASS AVERAGE
        NUMBER=0
        DO 20 I=1,N_STU
          IF(SCORE(I).GT.AVERAG)THEN
            NUMBER=NUMBER+1
          END IF
20      CONTINUE
        WRITE(OUTLUN,300)NUMBER
300     FORMAT(' NUMBER OF STUDENTS WITH SCORE GREATER THAN THE',
     1  ' CLASS AVERAGE =',I6)
        CLOSE(UNIT=INLUN)
        CLOSE(UNIT=OUTLUN)
        STOP
        END
***********************************************************************
```

Figure 6.7: Program Listing of Example 6.4.

```
25
88 77 56 89 100 99 55 35 78 65
69 83 71
38 95
33 49
79
10 89 59 46
60 87
92
```

```
THE CLASS AVERAGE IS =        68.16
MAXIMUM MARKS OBTAINED BY A STUDENT =     100.00
NUMBER OF STUDENTS WITH SCORE GREATER THAN THE CLASS AVERAGE =   14
```

Figure 6.8: Input and Output Results of Example 6.4.

```
*****************************************************************************
*         THIS PROGRAM COMPUTES SCALAR PRODUCT OF TWO VECTORS A & B         *
*****************************************************************************
*
        REAL A(50),B(50)
        INTEGER INLUN,OUTLUN
        PARAMETER (INLUN = 5,OUTLUN = 6)
* READ INPUT DATA
        WRITE(OUTLUN,*)' PLEASE ENTER # OF ELEMENTS IN VECTOR A & B'
        READ(INLUN,*)N
        WRITE(OUTLUN,*)' PLEASE ENTER ELEMENTS OF VECTOR A'
        READ(INLUN,*)(A(I),I=1,N)
        WRITE(OUTLUN,*)' PLEASE ENTER ELEMENTS OF VECTOR B'
        READ(INLUN,*)(B(I),I=1,N)
* CALCULATE SCALAR PRODUCT
        SCPROD=0.0
        DO 10 I=1,N
          SCPROD=SCPROD+A(I)*B(I)
10      CONTINUE
* WRITE OUTPUT RESULTS
        WRITE(OUTLUN,100)(A(I),I=1,N)
100     FORMAT(' THE VECTOR A IS:',<N>F7.2)
        WRITE(OUTLUN,200)(B(I),I=1,N)
200     FORMAT(' THE VECTOR B IS:',<N>F7.2)
        WRITE(OUTLUN,300)SCPROD
300     FORMAT(' THE SCALAR PRODUCT OF VECTORS A & B IS:',F10.4)
        STOP
        END
*****************************************************************************
```

```
PLEASE ENTER # OF ELEMENTS IN VECTOR A & B
4
 PLEASE ENTER ELEMENTS OF VECTOR A
1.0 2.0 3.0 4.0
 PLEASE ENTER ELEMENTS OF VECTOR B
1.0 0.0 0.0 0.0 0.0
THE VECTOR A IS:    1.00    2.00    3.00    4.00
THE VECTOR B IS:    1.00    0.00    0.00    0.00
THE SCALAR PRODUCT OF VECTORS A & B IS:     1.0000
```

```
PLEASE ENTER # OF ELEMENTS IN VECTOR A & B
5
 PLEASE ENTER ELEMENTS OF VECTOR A
2.0 2.5 3.9 4.8 6.5
 PLEASE ENTER ELEMENTS OF VECTOR B
3.8 7.3 4.3 -2.0 0.0
THE VECTOR A IS:    2.00    2.50    3.90    4.80    6.50
THE VECTOR B IS:    3.80    7.30    4.30   -2.00    0.00
THE SCALAR PRODUCT OF VECTORS A & B IS:    33.0200
```

Figure 6.9 Program Listing and Output Results of Example 6.5.

where N is the number of elements in each array. The program should read N, then the elements of array A and finally the elements of array B from the CRT terminal/line printer. The output should also appear on the CRT terminal/line printer.

A FORTRAN 77 source program to compute the inner product, along with input and output results is given in Figure 6.9.

Example 6.6

This program illustrates the use of a *histogram* to display the information graphically. A histogram is a graph that indicates the frequency of occurrences of a particular item in a group of items. For example, the frequency counts (total number of occurrences) of vowels a, e, i, o and u in the following statement,

algorithms + data structures = programs

could be displayed by the following histogram:

Letter	Number of Occurrences
a	****
e	*
i	*
o	**
u	**

where the number of asterisks indicates the number of occurrences of the associated letter. The items can also be grouped. For example, the following histogram displays another information:

Range of Letters	Number of Occurrences
a TO e	******* (7)
f TO m	******* (7)
n TO z	****************** (18)

This problem displays the grades of the students using histograms. The input data is the same as given in programming Example 6.4. The output should appear as follows:

Range of Grades	Number of Students
0—10	**** ...
11—20	***** ...
21—30	⋮
31—40	
41—50	
51—60	
61—70	
71—80	
81—90	
91—100	⋮

The source program is given in Figure 6.10 and the output in Figure 6.11. Note the use of another array NUMBER which has ten elements. NUMBER (1) stores the number of students whose scores fall within range 1, that is, the number of students whose scores are between 0 and 10. NUMBER (2) stores the number of students whose scores fall within range 2 ane so on. At this point users must be able to recognize the distinct advantages of using the array NUMBER rather than ten separate variables. This example also illustrates the advantage of using arrays in the output statement with a DO statement.

```
*********************************************************************
*       THIS PROGRAM DRAWS HISOGRAMS FOR STUDENTS' SCORES           *
*********************************************************************
*
        REAL SCORE(100)
        INTEGER INLUN,OUTLUN,UPPER,NUMBER(10)
        PARAMETER (INLUN = 1,OUTLUN = 2)
*
        OPEN(UNIT=INLUN,FILE='EX6_4.DAT',STATUS='OLD')
        OPEN(UNIT=OUTLUN,FILE='EX6_6.OUT',STATUS='NEW')
* READ INPUT DATA
        READ(INLUN,*)N_STU,(SCORE(I),I=1,N_STU)
* INITIALIZE
        DO 10 I=1,10
          NUMBER(I)=0
10      CONTINUE
* DETERMINE NUMBER OF STUDENTS IN EACH RANGE
        DO 20 I=1,N_STU
          J=(SCORE(I)-1)/10+1
          NUMBER(J)=NUMBER(J)+1
20      CONTINUE
* WRITE THE TITLE
        WRITE(OUTLUN,100)
100     FORMAT(' RANGE OF GRADES',T25,'NUMBERS OF STUDENTS',/)
* CALCULATE AND WRITE LOWER & UPPER, TWO VARIABLES USED TO REPRESENT
* LOWER AND UPPER RANGE OF THE GRADES. ALSO DRAW THE HISTOGRAM USING
* VARIABLE FORMAT SPECIFICATION
        LOWER=0
        UPPER=10
        DO 30 I=1,10
          J=NUMBER(I)
          IF(J.GT.0)THEN
            WRITE(OUTLUN,200)LOWER,UPPER
          ELSE
            WRITE(OUTLUN,300)LOWER,UPPER
          END IF
          IF(I.EQ.1)THEN
            LOWER=LOWER+11
          ELSE
            LOWER=LOWER+10
          END IF
          UPPER=UPPER+10
30      CONTINUE
200     FORMAT(' ',T5,I3,'-',I3,T28,<J>('*'))
300     FORMAT(' ',T5,I3,'-',I3)
        CLOSE(UNIT=INLUN)
        CLOSE(UNIT=OUTLUN)
        STOP
        END
*********************************************************************
```

Figure 6.10: Program Listing of Example 6.6.

```
$FOR EX66
$LINK EX66
$RUN EX66
FORTRAN STOP
$

$TYPE EX66.OUT

RANGE OF GRADES              NUMBERS OF STUDENTS

     0- 10                          *
    11- 20
    21- 30
    31- 40                         ***
    41- 50                         **
    51- 60                         ****
    61- 70                         **
    71- 80                         ****
    81- 90                         *****
    91-100                         ****
$
```

Figure 6.11: Output Results of Example 6.6.

6.5 MULTI-DIMENSIONAL ARRAYS

In Section 6.4 we considered one-dimensional arrays and illustrated their use to process input data. The elements in a one-dimensional array are simple (i.e. single numbers, truth values, etc.). The elements of an array may also be arrays. An array whose elements are one-dimensional arrays is called a *two-dimensional array*. Likewise, if the elements of a two-dimensional array are one-dimensional arrays, then the array is defined as a *three-dimensional array*, and so on. As noted earlier in the DIMENSION statement, FORTRAN 77 allows arrays of up to seven dimensions.

There are many problems in which the data being processed can be naturally organized in a two-dimensional, three-dimensional or multi-dimensional space. In the previous section, we considered the problem of processing students' scores in a computational science class. This problem can be further extended to writing a program for processing students' scores in other classes. The input data (scores) can be arranged in a table as given below:

Student Number	Classes			
	Computational science	Maths.	English	Physics
1	90	80	60	95
2	73	45	30	84
3	50	71	75	73
4	99	89	54	68
5	40	30	20	10
6	85	59	84	87
7	91	78	45	56
8	65	100	46	44
9	64	99	63	39
10	45	100	74	92

In the above table, there are ten rows and four columns for students' scores. The four scores of student 1 are in the first row, the four scores of students 2 in the second row, and so on.

One way of storing these scores is to use four one-dimensional arrays, one for each class. The declaration statement can be somewhat like this:

REAL COMSC(10), MATHS(10), ENGLIS(10), PHYZIX(10)

A more convenient way of storing these data items is to use a two-dimensional array. The declaration.

REAL SCORES(10,4)

reserves 40 memory locations for these data items. If the number of classes increases, say to ten, then the declaration statement can be easily modified as follows:

REAL SCORES(10,10)

On the other hand, using one-dimensional arrays, one has to declare ten separate arrays. In these cases, use of the multi-dimensional arrays is also convenient from a programming point of view. This will be clear after studying the programming examples given at the end of this section.

The elements of this two-dimensional array are identified by

SCORE(I,J)

which refers to the entry (memory location) in the ith row and jth column, that is, to the score earned by student i in class j. So the variable

SCORE(7,3)

refers to the score of student 7 in class 3 (English). The value of this variable is 45.0 as seen from the table.

To illustrate the use of multi-dimensional arrays, consider an example of maintaining an inventory of shirts by a retailer. There are several different brands of shirts and for each brand there are a variety of colors, collar sizes and sleeve lengths. A four-dimensional array can be used to record the inventory with each element of the array being the number of shirts of a particular brand, color, collar size, and sleeve length currently in stock. If there are four brands, ten different colors, three collar sizes and five sleeve lengths, then a declaration statement

DIMENSION INVENT(4,10,3,5)

reserves six hundred $(4 \times 10 \times 3 \times 5)$ memory locations for this array. A quadruply subscripted variable

INVENT(I,J,K,L)

is the number of shirts of brand I, color J, collar size K and sleeve length L.

In many situations, it may be required to declare more than four dimensions. We will, however, restrict our discussion to the three-dimensional arrays.

Some examples of two and three-dimensional array declaration statements are as follows:

(1) Two-dimensional arrays:

    (a) DIMENSION SCORE(10,10),CANDAT(100,2)
    (b) REAL   PRICE(100,−2:4),MARKS(−10:50,5)
    (c) INTEGER VECTR(3,2)SEX(100,10:40)

(2) Three-dimentional arrays:

    (a) DIMENSION NAME(100,2,3), A(−10:20,0:5,10)
    (b) REAL   I(0:2,−20:−10,−5:−2)
    (c) INTEGER X(4,3,2),Y(5,6,10)

We shall now briefly describe the structure for two- and three-dimensional arrays by giving suitable examples. The DIMENSION statement of two-dimensional arrays declares the SCORE to be a two-dimensional array. For each dimension, the lower-bound and upper-bound specifications are one and ten, respectively. Using the terminology of matrices, we can say that array SCORE contains ten rows and ten columns. The total number of memory locations (or elements in a matrix) reserved is 100 (10×10). A pictorial representation is given in Figure 6.12.

As observed earlier, this two-dimensional array may be considered to be a one-dimensional array of one-dimensional arrays (i.e., an array whose elements do not represent single value but a one-dimensional array). Each element in the two-dimensional array is, therefore, identified as SCORE(I,J), and it corresponds to the Ith row and Jth column element (memory location). Elements SCORE(1,1), SCORE(3,9) and SCORE(7,3) are shown in the Figure 6.12.

If we now extend the logic applied to two-dimensional arrays, a three-dimensional array may be considered to be a one-dimensional array whose elements are two-dimensional arrays. A pictorial representation for the

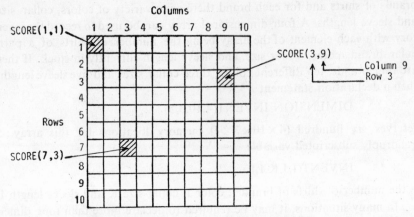

Figure 6.12: Two-dimensional Array SCORE.

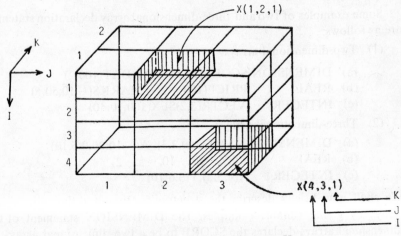

Figure 6.13. Three-Dimensional Array X.

INTEGER array X having upper bounds as 4, 3 and 2 and lower bounds as 1 is shown in Figure 6.13.

Each element is identified by X(I,J,K) as shown for the elements X(1,2,1) and X(4,3,1). Users must note that the computer does not store multi-dimensional arrays in a multi-dimensional memory space (or n-dimensional arrays in an n-dimensional memory space). The manipulation of these arrays in FORTRAN is straightforward. FORTRAN always stores an array in memory as a linear sequence of values. A one-dimensional array is stored with its first element in the first memory location and its last element in the last memory of the sequence. A two-dimensional array, by the FORTRAN 77 convention, is stored in columns. That is, the first column is stored as a one-dimensional array followed by the second column, and so forth. A two-dimensional SCORE(3,2), for example, would be stored in the following sequence:

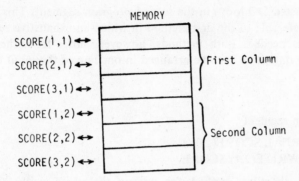

Note that the leftmost (first) subscript varies most rapidly in this storage scheme. This is called the *order of subscript progression*. The storage by order subscript progression may be cumbersome in some cases, especially for input and output operations for most two and three-dimensional arrays. However, the storage convention is of minor importance to us.

6.5.1 Input and Output of Two-Dimensional Arrays

Two-dimensional array input features in FORTRAN are very similar to those of one-dimensional arrays, already described in Section 6.4.1. There are however, a few additional features that are particularly suited to two-dimensional arrays. The following examples illustrate the use of these features in the input/output of arrays.

Example (a)

The following program segment:

```
REAL SCORE(2,3)
READ(1,*) SCORE(1,1)
READ(1,*) SCORE(1,2)
READ(1,*) SCORE(1,3)
READ(1,*) SCORE(2,1)
READ(1,*) SCORE(2,2)
READ(1,*) SCORE(2,3)
```

and the program segment:

```
REAL SCORE(2,3)
DO 10 I = 1,2
    DO 10 J = 1,3
        READ(1,*)SCORE(I,J)
10 CONTINUE
```

read the array SCORE. Only one-input value (data item) must appear on one line of the input file as in the case of one-dimensional arrays. Note the use of nested DO loops in the second program segment. This method is definitely preferable to the first method in which an exhaustive set of READ statements is needed. Both methods, however, suffer from the drawback that the one data item is to be arranged in one line of the input data file.

Example (b)

The program segment

```
REAL SCORE(2,3)
WRITE(2,*) SCORE
```

illustrates a short-cut method for writing the entire array SCORE. This method is, however, not as useful for two-dimensional arrays as it is for one-dimensional ones. The reason is that array elements will be written in the order in which they are stored, i.e. by columns as shown below:

```
SCORE(1,1),SCORE(2,1),SCORE(1,2),SCORE(2,2),SCORE(1,3),
   SCORE(2,3)
```

In fact, the following program segment does the same job:

```
REAL SCORE(2,3)
WRITE(2,*)SCORE(1,1),SCORE(2,1)SCORE(1,2),SCORE(2,2),
   SCORE(1,3),SCORE(2,3)
```

A more natural order of arrays input/output is by rows, and therefore the unsubscripted array input/output feature is not commonly used. Again, the most popular method of arrays input/output is to use a nested implied DO list.

6.5.1.1 *Nested Implied DO List*

The general form of the one-dimensional implied DO list as discussed in an earlier section is:

$$...(\text{list}, V = e_1,e_2[,e_3])$$

If the list itself contains an implied DO list, it results in a nested implied DO list. The following examples demonstrate the use of nested implied DO list.

Example (a)

The program segment

```
REAL SCORE(2,3)
READ(1,*) ((SCORE(I,J), J = 1,3), I = 1,2)
```

reads array SCORE by rows in the following manner:

```
SCORE(1,1)SCORE(1,2) SCORE(1,3),SCORE(2,1),
   SCORE(2,2),SCORE(2,3)
```

The inner implied DO list (SCORE(I,J), J = 1, 3) is the list of the general form of the one-dimensional implied DO list as shown above. For each value of the outer implied DO index I, the inner implied DO loop is repeated for all values of J, i.e. J = 1, 2 and 3. In other words, the variable of the innermost implied DO list varies more rapidly as explained below:

READ(1,*) ((SCORE(I,J),J = 1,3),I = 1,2)

The inner loop repeats rapidly

When I = 1, J runs through 1,2,3
When I = 2, J runs through 1,2,3

The outer loop repreats slowly
For each value of I, the inner loop
DO variable J runs from 1 to 3

The program segment

REAL SCORE(2,3)
WRITE(2,*) ((SCORE(I,J), I = 1,2), J = 1, 3)

is equivalent to the program segment

REAL SCORE(2,3)
WRITE(2,*)SCORE

which uses an unsubscripted array.

Example (b)

Let us consider that we have to solve three linear simultaneous equations given in the general form [A][X] = [B]:

$$\begin{bmatrix} 1 & 1 & 1 \\ 2 & -2 & 2 \\ 1 & 2 & 3 \end{bmatrix} \begin{bmatrix} x_1 \\ x_2 \\ x_3 \end{bmatrix} = \begin{bmatrix} 3 \\ 2 \\ 6 \end{bmatrix}$$

and the coefficients of matrix [A] and [B] are arranged in the following manner in a data file 'EQ.DAT':

3   ←number of equations

$$\left. \begin{array}{ccc} 1 & 1 & 1 \\ 2 & -2 & 2 \\ 1 & 2 & 3 \end{array} \right\}$$ Coefficients of matrix [A]

3   2   6]   Coefficients of matrix [B]

The following program segment reads the input data:

```
DIMENSION A(3,3), B(3)
OPEN(UNIT = 1, FILE = 'EQ.DAT', STATUS ='OLD')
READ(1,*)N
READ(1,*) ( (A(I,J), J = 1,N), I = 1,N)
READ(1,*) (B(I), I = 1,N)
```

The first READ statement reads a variable N. The other two READ statements read coefficients of matrices [A] and [B] respectively. The coefficients of vector [B] are arranged in the fourth row. If these coefficients are placed in the fourth column as shown below:

```
3        ← number of equations
1    1    1   3
2   -2    2   2
1    2    3   6
```
Coefficients   ↑ Coefficients of [B]
of [A]

then the following program segment can be used to read the input data:

```
DIMENSION A(3,3), B(3)
OPEN(UNIT = 1, FILE = 'EQ.DAT', STATUS = 'OLD')
READ(1,*)N, ( (A(I,J), J = 1,3), B(I), I = 1,3)
```

Another popular method for two-dimensional arrays input/output is to combine a regular DO statement with an implied DO list. For example, the following program segment does the same job as the above program segment:

```
      DIMENSION A(3,3), B(3)
OPEN(UNIT = 1, FILE = 'EQ.DAT', TYPE = 'OLD')
      READ(1,*)N
      DO 10 I = 1,N
          READ(1,*)(A(I,J), J = 1,N),B(I)
   10 CONTINUE
```

The use of the regular DO statement with an implied DO list is preferable in an array output using list-directed format. For example, if we want to print the matrix [A], then the following WRITE statement:

```
      DO 10 I = 1,N
          WRITE(2,*) (A(I,J),J = 1,N)
   10 CONTINUE
```

prints the output as follows:

```
1.0        1.0        1.0
2.0       -2.0        2.0
1.0        2.0        3.0
```

On the other hand, using a nested implied WRITE list,

$$\text{WRITE}(2,*) \ ((A(I,J), \ J = 1,N), \ I = 1,N)$$

may not print the matrix [A] as three rows of three elements. This depends on how the computer formats the data and one possible output form may be:

1.0	1.0	1.0	2.0	—2.0
2.0	1.0	2.0	3.0	

However, using nested implied DO lists in a formatted output can print the matrix [A] in three rows and three columns as shown below. The program segment

$$\text{WRITE}(2,100)(A((I,J), \ J = 1,N), \ I = 1,N)$$
$$100 \quad \text{FORMAT}(' \ ',<N>F \ 5.1)$$

prints matrix [A] as

Column # 1 2 3 4 5 6 7 8 9 10 11 12 13 14 15

1 . 0		1 .	0		1 . 0
2 . 0	— 2 .	0		2 .	0
1 . 0		2 .	0		3 . 0

6.5.2 Use and Manipulation of Two-Dimensional Arrays

We have earlier discussed the use of DO statements in the manipulation of one-dimensional arrays. For the manipulation of two-dimensonal arrays, DO statements are equally useful and, generally, nested DO statements are quite convenient. The two subscripts of a two-dimensional array (for example, subscripts I and J for an array A(I,J)) can be suitably manipulated with the nested DO index variables. For example, if [A] is given as follows:

$$[A] = \begin{bmatrix} 1 & 2 & 3 & 4 \\ 1 & 4 & 9 & 16 \\ 1 & 8 & 27 & 64 \\ 1 & 16 & 81 & 256 \end{bmatrix}$$

where

$$A(I,J) = J{**}I \text{ for } I,J = 1, 2, 3 \text{ and } 4,$$

the following FORTRAN 77 program segment generates it:

```
        DIMENSION A(4,4)
        DO 10 I = 1,4
          DO 20 J = 1,4
            A(I,J) = J**I
20        CONTINUE
10      CONTINUE
```

The inner loop DO 20 J = 1,4 is executed four times for each value of I from one to four in increments of one. For I = 1, the first row elements are generated; for I = 2, the second row elements are generated, and so on . . .

Array subscripts can be any valid integer arithmetic expression, whose value must lie within the declared subscript range. For example, if a matrix [A] is given as follows:

$$[A] = \begin{bmatrix} 1 & 2 & 3 & 4 \\ 2 & 3 & 4 & 5 \\ 3 & 4 & 5 & 6 \\ 4 & 5 & 6 & 7 \end{bmatrix}$$

and we want to obtain a matrix [B] from [A] such that:

(i)   B(I,J) = 0 for I,J = 1, 2, 3 and 4
(ii) B((I−1),(J−1)) = A(I,J) for I,J = 2, 3 and 4
(iii) B(4,J) = A(1,J) for J = 1, 2, 3 and 4

then [B] is given by

$$[B] = \begin{bmatrix} 3 & 4 & 5 & 0 \\ 4 & 5 & 6 & 0 \\ 5 & 6 & 7 & 0 \\ 1 & 2 & 3 & 4 \end{bmatrix}$$

The following FORTRAN 77 program segment does the job:

```
      DIMENSION A(4,4), B(4,4)
      DO 20 I = 1,4
        DO 10 J = 1,4
          B(I,J) = 0
          IF(I.GT.1.AND.J.GT.1)THEN
            B((I−1),(J−1)) = A(I,J)
          END IF
          IF(I.EQ.4) THEN
            B(I,J) = A(1,J)
          END IF
10      CONTINUE
20    CONTINUE
```

Note that the first statement B(I,J) = 0 inside the nested DO range satisfies condition (i). The first IF-THEN-END IF construct satisfies condition (ii), while the second IF-THEN-END IF construct satisfies condition (iii). Users must note that the integer expression for an array subscript can also appear on the l.h.s. as shown for the subscripts of matrix [B].

We now move on to programming examples which will help users a great deal in understanding the use of arrays to solve a variety of problems.

6.6 PROGRAMMING EXAMPLES FOR THE CHAPTER

Example 6.7

A computer manufacturing company sells ten different computer models and employs eight salespersons. A record of sales for each month can be represented by a table, the first row of which contains the sales of each model by salesperson 1, the second row contains the number of sales of each model by sales person 2, and so on. The sales table for a certain month can be as follows:

0	4	5	3	7	9	10	15	2	1
1	2	3	4	5	6	7	8	9	10
5	0	2	0	3	0	8	9	10	12
0	3	4	8	7	6	9	0	1	3
7	0	0	3	0	2	2	2	0	8
6	5	4	3	0	7	8	9	10	1
5	5	5	5	5	5	5	5	5	5
10	2	1	1	1	9	9	9	9	3

A FORTRAN 77 program is to be written to produce a monthly sales report, displaying the monthly sales in the following tabular form:

	COMPUTER MODEL									
SALESPERSON	1	2	3	4	5	6	7	8	9	10
1	0	4	5	3	7	9	10	15	2	1
2	1	2	3	4	5	6	7	8	9	10
3	5	0	2	0	3	0	8	9	10	12
4	0	3	4	8	7	6	9	0	1	3
5	7	0	0	3	0	2	2	2	0	8
6	6	5	4	3	0	7	8	9	10	1
7	5	5	5	5	5	5	5	5	5	5
8	10	2	1	1	1	9	9	9	9	3

and to print the total number of computers sold by each salesperson and the total number of each model sold by all salespersons. The program should also determine the salesperson who sold the maximum number of computers and which computer model had the maximum demand.

The input to the program is a sales table and the output is to be a report of the earlier indicated form.

The example requires the manipulation of the sales table. The table, an input, can be conveniently stored as a two-dimensional integer array SALES (I,J) where I identifies a salesperson and J indicates a computer model. For example, SALES(4,5) corresponds to number of computers of model five sold by salesperson 4. We also require two one-dimensional integer arrays: (i) COMPER(I), to store the number of computers sold by a salesperson I; and (ii) MODEL(J), to store the total number of computers of model J sold by all salespersons.

In fact, arrays COMPER and MODEL can be calcultated from array SALES as follows:

$$COMPER(I) = \sum_{J=1}^{10} SALES(I,J), \qquad I = 1,2. \ldots,8$$

and

$$MODEL(J) = \sum_{I=1}^{8} SALES(I,J) \qquad J = 1,2, \ldots,10$$

Once these two arrays are generated, the determination of the salesperson who sold the maximum number of computers and the model which had the maximum demand is straightforward, as shown in the source program in Figure 6.14. The input data and the output results are given in Figure 6.15.

Example 6.8

For the manipulation of matrices, ARRAY is the most convenient data structure available with FORTRAN. This programming example illustrates how this data structure can be used to multiply two matrices.

Suppose we want to multiply two two-dimensional matrices [A] and [B] where the matrix [A] is an $M \times N$ matrix (i.e. M rows and N columns) and the matrix [B] is an $N \times L$ matrix. Note that the number of columns of matrix [A] must be equal to the number of rows of matrix [B]. The product matrix [PROD] of matrices [A] and [B] will then be an $M \times L$ matrix with the entry PROD(I,J), which appears in the Ith row and the Jth column given by:

PROD(I,J) = the sum of the products of the entries in row I of matrix [A] with the entries of column J of matrix [B]

$$= A(I,1)*B(1,J)+A(I,2)*B(2,J)+\cdots+A(I,N)*B(N,J)$$

$$= \sum_{K=1}^{N} A(I,K)*B(K,J)$$

Suppose that matrix [A] is the 2×2 matrix and matrix [B] is the 2×3 matrix given as:

$$[A] = \begin{bmatrix} 1 & 2 \\ 3 & 4 \end{bmatrix} \qquad [B] = \begin{bmatrix} 1 & 0 & 2 \\ 3 & 5 & 4 \end{bmatrix}$$

```
****************************************************************************
*            THIS PROGRAM PROCESSES THE SALES OF COMPUTERS                  *
****************************************************************************
*
        INTEGER SALES(40,40),COMPER(40),MODEL(40)
        INTEGER INLUN,OUTLUN
        PARAMETER (INLUN = 1,OUTLUN = 2)
*
        OPEN(UNIT=INLUN,FILE='EX6_7.DAT',STATUS='OLD')
        OPEN(UNIT=OUTLUN,FILE='EX6_7.OUT',STATUS='NEW')
* READ INPUT DATA
        READ(INLUN,*)N_MOD,N_SPER,((SALES(I,J),J=1,N_MOD),I=1,N_SPER)
* CALCULATE NUMBER OF COMPUTERS SOLD BY EACH SALESPERSON
        DO 10 I=1,N_SPER
          COMPER(I)=0
          DO 10 J=1,N_MOD
            COMPER(I)=COMPER(I)+SALES(I,J)
10      CONTINUE
* CALCULATE NUMBER OF COMPUTERS SOLD OF EACH MODEL
        DO 20 J=1,N_MOD
          MODEL(J)=0
          DO 20 I=1,N_SPER
            MODEL(J)=MODEL(J)+SALES(I,J)
20      CONTINUE
* DETERMINE THE SALESPERSON WHO SOLD MAXIMUM NUMBER OF COMPUTERS
        MAXPER=1
        MAXCMP=COMPER(1)
        DO 30 I=2,N_SPER
          IF(MAXCMP.LT.COMPER(I))THEN
            MAXCMP=COMPER(I)
            MAXPER=I
          END IF
30      CONTINUE
* DETERMINE THE MODEL WHOSE DEMAND WAS MAXIMUM
        MAXMOD=1
        MAXCMM=MODEL(1)
        DO 40 J=2,N_MOD
          IF(MAXCMM.LT.MODEL(J))THEN
            MAXCMM=MODEL(J)
            MAXMOD=J
          END IF
40      CONTINUE
* WRITE COMPUTER SALES IN A TABULAR FORM
        WRITE(OUTLUN,100)
100     FORMAT(' ',T25,'COMPUTER MODEL')
        WRITE(OUTLUN,200)(J,J=1,N_MOD)
200     FORMAT(' SALESPERSON',T15,':',<N_MOD>I5,/,<15+5*N_MOD>('-'))
        WRITE(OUTLUN,300)(I,(SALES(I,J),J=1,N_MOD),I=1,N_SPER)
300     FORMAT(' ',I7,T15,':',<N_MOD>I5)
        WRITE(OUTLUN,400)
400     FORMAT(' ',<15+5*N_MOD>('-'))
        WRITE(OUTLUN,500)(I,COMPER(I),I=1,N_SPER)
500     FORMAT(' SALES OF SALESPERSON',I3,' :',I6)
        WRITE(OUTLUN,600)(J,MODEL(J),J=1,N_MOD)
600     FORMAT(' SALES OF MODEL',I3,' :',I6)
        WRITE(OUTLUN,700)MAXCMP,MAXPER
700     FORMAT(' ',/,' MAXIMUM # OF COMPUTERS',I6,' WERE SOLD BY',
     1   ' SALESPERSON:',I3,/)
        WRITE(OUTLUN,800)MAXCMM,MAXMOD
800     FORMAT(' MAXIMUM # OF COMPUTERS',I6,' WERE SOLD OF MODEL:',I3)
```

Contd.

```
      CLOSE(UNIT=INLUN)
      CLOSE(UNIT=OUTLUN)
      STOP
      END
**********************************,*****************************************************
```

Figure 6.14: Program Listing of Example 6.7.

```
   10 8
0   4  5  3  7  9 10 15  2  1
1   2  3  4  5  6  7  8  9 10
5   0  2  0  3  0  8  9 10 12
0   3  4  8  7  6  9  0  1  3
7   0  0  3  0  2  2  2  0  8
6   5  4  3  0  7  8  9 10  1
5   5  5  5  5  5  5  5  5  5
10  2  1  1  1  9  9  9  9  3
```

		COMPUTER MODEL									
SALESPERSON	:	1	2	3	4	5	6	7	8	9	10
1	:	0	4	5	3	7	9	10	15	2	1
2	:	1	2	3	4	5	6	7	8	9	10
3	:	5	0	2	0	3	0	8	9	10	12
4	:	0	3	4	8	7	6	9	0	1	3
5	:	7	0	0	3	0	2	2	2	0	8
6	:	6	5	4	3	0	7	8	9	10	1
7	:	5	5	5	5	5	5	5	5	5	5
8	:	10	2	1	1	1	9	9	9	9	3

```
SALES OF SALESPERSON    1 :     56
SALES OF SALESPERSON    2 :     55
SALES OF SALESPERSON    3 :     49
SALES OF SALESPERSON    4 :     41
SALES OF SALESPERSON    5 :     24
SALES OF SALESPERSON    6 :     53
SALES OF SALESPERSON    7 :     50
SALES OF SALESPERSON    8 :     54
SALES OF MODEL    1 :     34
SALES OF MODEL    2 :     21
SALES OF MODEL    3 :     24
SALES OF MODEL    4 :     27
SALES OF MODEL    5 :     28
SALES OF MODEL    6 :     44
SALES OF MODEL    7 :     58
SALES OF MODEL    8 :     57
SALES OF MODEL    9 :     46
SALES OF MODEL   10 :     43

MAXIMUM # OF COMPUTERS    56 WERE SOLD BY SALESPERSON:   *

MAXIMUM # OF COMPUTERS    58 WERE SOLD OF MODEL:   7
```

Figure 6.15: Input and Output Results of Example 6.7.

then the matrix [PROD] will be a 2×3 matrix. The entry in the first row and first column PROD (1,1) is:

$$1*1+2*3 = 7$$

Similarly, the entry PROD(1,2) is:

$$1*0+2*5 = 10$$

The complete product matrix [PROD] is given by:

$$[\text{PROD}] = \begin{bmatrix} 7 & 10 & 10 \\ 15 & 20 & 22 \end{bmatrix}$$

A FORTRAN 77 program to multiply two matrices is given in Figure 6.16. The two sets of input data and the corresponding output results are given in Figure 6.17. The program is quite easy to follow. It first reads matrix [A] and then matrix [B] and then calculates the PROD(I,J) according to the earlier defined equation:

$$\text{PROD(I,J)} = \sum_{K=1}^{N} A(I,K)*B(K,J)$$

Example 6.9

This example illustrates how arrays can be used to simulate some physical phenomenon. The Game of Life, invented by mathematician John H. Conway, is intended to model life of a hypothetical organism that is capable of reproduction.

The organisms live in a two-dimensional world that is represented by a rectangular grid (see Figure 6.18). Each cell in the grid represents a possible site for an organism and may not be occupied by more than one organism at a time. The presence of an organism is represented by placing '*' in a cell and 'O' in an unoccupied cell. If the grid extends indefinitely in both directions, then each cell has eight neighbours, as indicated in Figure 6.18 for cell 'A'.

If an organism occupies a site, it may survive to the next generation or it may die, depending on the number of neighbouring sites that are occupied by other organisms. Births and deaths occur according to the following rules:

(1) An organism is born in any empty cell having exactly three neighbours (Figure 6.19).
(2) An organism dies from isolation if it has less than two neighbours (Figure 6.20).
(3) An organism dies from overcrowding if it has more than three neighbours (Figure 6.21).
(4) All other organisms survive to the next generation.

```
*****************************************************************************
*        THIS PROGRAM COMPUTES MULTIPLICATION OF TWO MATRICES A & B        *
*****************************************************************************
*
        REAL A(10,10),B(10,10),PROD(10,10)
        INTEGER INLUN,OUTLUN
        PARAMETER (INLUN = 1,OUTLUN = 2)
*
        OPEN(UNIT=INLUN,FILE='EX6_8.DAT',STATUS='OLD')
        OPEN(UNIT=OUTLUN,FILE='EX6_8.OUT',STATUS='NEW')
* READ TWO MATRICES
        READ(INLUN,*)M,N,((A(I,J),J=1,N),I=1,M)
        READ(INLUN,*)N,L,((B(I,J),J=1,L),I=1,N)
* CALCULATE THE PRODUCT OF TWO MATRICES
        DO 10 I=1,M
          DO 10 J=1,L
            PROD(I,J)=0.0
            DO 10 K=1,N
              PROD(I,J)=PROD(I,J)+A(I,K)*B(K,J)
10      CONTINUE
* WRITE BOTH MATRICES AND THEIR PRODUCT
        WRITE(OUTLUN,100)
        WRITE(OUTLUN,200)((A(I,J),J=1,N),I=1,M)
100     FORMAT(' THE MATRIX A IS:',/)
200     FORMAT(' ',<N>F7.3)
        WRITE(OUTLUN,300)
        WRITE(OUTLUN,400)((B(I,J),J=1,L),I=1,N)
300     FORMAT(' THE MATRIX B IS:',/)
400     FORMAT(' ',<L>F7.3)
        WRITE(OUTLUN,500)
        WRITE(OUTLUN,600)((PROD(I,J),J=1,L),I=1,M)
500     FORMAT(' THE PRODUCT OF MATRICES A & B IS:',/)
600     FORMAT(' ',<L>F7.3)
        CLOSE(UNIT=INLUN)
        CLOSE(UNIT=OUTLUN)
        STOP
        END
*****************************************************************************
```

Figure 6.16: Program Listing of Example 6.8.

Set I

```
2 2
1 2
3 4
2 3
1 0 2
3 5 4
```

```
THE MATRIX A IS:

  1.000   2.000
  3.000   4.000
THE MATRIX B IS:

  1.000   0.000   2.000
  3.000   5.000   4.000
THE PRODUCT OF MATRICES A & B IS:

  7.000  10.000  10.000
 15.000  20.000  22.000
```

Set II

```
2 3
1 0 2
3 0 4
3 4
4 2 5 9
6 4 1 8
9 0 0 2
```

```
THE MATRIX A IS:

  1.000   0.000   2.000
  3.000   0.000   4.000
THE MATRIX B IS:

  4.000   2.000   5.000   9.000
  6.000   4.000   1.000   8.000
  9.000   0.000   0.000   2.000
THE PRODUCT OF MATRICES A & B IS:

 22.000   2.000   5.000  13.000
 48.000   6.000  15.000  35.000
```

Figure 6.17: Input and Output Results of Example 6.8.

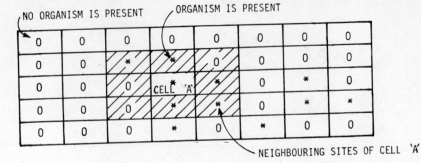

Figure 6.18: The two-dimensional world of the organisms in the life simulation game.

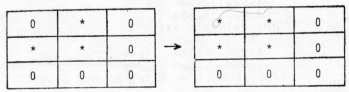

Figure 6.19: A new organism is born.

0	0	0		0	0	0
0	*	0	→	0	0	0
0	0	0		0	0	0·

Figure 6.20: The organism dies from isolation.

0	*	*		0	*	*
0	*	0	→	0	0	0
*	*	0		*	*	0

Figure 6.21: The organism in the central square dies from crowding.

0	*	0		0	0	0
*	0	0	→	*	*	0
*	0	0		0	0	0

Figure 6.22: A new organism is born in the central square while at the same time the upper and the lower organisms each having one neighbour die of isolation.

To illustrate the birth and death process of organisms, the first four generations for a particular initial configuration of organisms are shown below. Note that the organism dies in the fifth generation.

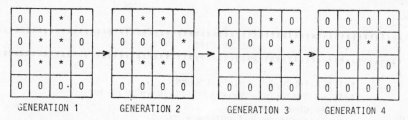

GENERATION 1   GENERATION 2   GENERATION 3   GENERATION 4

A FORTRAN 77 source program to play the Game of Life and to investigate the patterns produced by various initial configurations is given in Figure 6.22. Two sets of input data and output results are given in Figures 6.23 and 6.24. The program uses three two-dimensional arrays: INITAL, NEBORS and NEW. The number of rows and the number of columns in each array are M and N respectively. For this program these values are assumed as ten and thirty respectively. Readers must note that, the program is written such that the row (M+1) is reflected back as row 1 and row (0) is reflected as row (M) and the same is true for columns. The array INITAL represents the initial configuration at the start of a generation IGEN and the array NEW represents the configuration at the finish of a generation. The value of elements in both arrays INITAL and NEW is either 0 or 1 where 1 represents the presence of an organism and 0 represents the absence of an organism. The array NEBORS is used to calculate the number of occupied neighbouring cells for each cell which is the most intricate part of the program. This is done in a loop using four nested DO statements. For a cell (I,J) the neighbouring cells will be (I−1,J−1), (I−1,J), (I−1,J+1), (I,J−1), (I,J+1), (I+1,J−1), (I+1,J), and (I+1,J+1). The row and column displacements for these cells are obtained by the two innermost DO statements. IPOS and JPOS variables used in the program represent the row and column position of a neighbouring cell (I,J). The cell (I,J) is not a neighbouring cell to itself, so an IF (IPOS. NE.I.OR.JPOS.NE.J) THEN statement is used to avoid the counting of this cell. With the help of the array NEBORS, the array NEW is constructed on the basis of the rules outlined above. The program stops after specified number of generations are examined or if there is no change from one generation to the next, or if no organism survives.

6.7 SUMMARY

In this chapter we learned how to use an array—a group of memory locations that can all be identified with a common name but are distinguished by one or more subscripts. The use of arrays provides one of the most powerful tools available to a FORTRAN programmer since it allows a programmer to handle very large amounts of data with a minimum of programming effort. The use of the DO statements in arrays provides one of the most potent combinations available to FORTRAN programmers.

Because of the above reasons, the reader must go through all the solved example problems and should make honest efforts to solve a large number of problems given at the end of this chapter.

```
*****************************************************************
*                        GAME OF LIFE                          *
*****************************************************************
*
       INTEGER INLUN,OUTLUN,ROW,COLUMN
       INTEGER INITAL(10,30),NEBORS(10,30),NEW(10,30)
       LOGICAL CHANGE,ALLKIL
       PARAMETER (INLUN = 1,OUTLUN = 2)
       OPEN(UNIT=INLUN,FILE='EX6_9.DAT',STATUS='OLD')
       OPEN(UNIT=OUTLUN,FILE='EX6_9.OUT',STATUS='NEW')
* INITIALIZE
       M=10
       N=30
       DO 10 I = 1,M
         DO 10 J = 1,M
           INITAL(I,J)=0
10     CONTINUE
* READ NUMBER OF GENERATIONS TO BE EXAMINED
       READ(INLUN,*)NGEN
* READ INITIAL CONFIGURATION, THE ROW AND COLUMN INDICIES IN WHICH AN
* ORGANISM LIVES
       DO 30 I=1,M*N
         READ(INLUN,*,END=40)ROW,COLUMN
         INITAL(ROW,COLUMN) = 1
30     CONTINUE
* WRITE INITIAL CONFIGURATION; TAKE A NOTE OF THE WRITE STATEMENTS
40     WRITE(OUTLUN,500)
       DO 60 I=1,M
         DO 50 J=1,N
           IF(INITAL(I,J).NE.0)THEN
             WRITE(OUTLUN,600)
           END IF
50       CONTINUE
         WRITE(OUTLUN,700)
60     CONTINUE
* CALCULATE MATRIX NEBORS
       DO 120 IGEN=1,NGEN
         DO 70 I=1,M
           DO 70 J=1,N
             NEBORS(I,J)=0
             DO 70 K=-1,1
               IPOS=I+K
               DO 70 L=-1,1
                 JPOS=J+L
                 IF(IPOS.NE.I.OR.JPOS.NE.J)THEN
                   IF(IPOS.GT.M)THEN
                     IPOS=1
                   END IF
                   IF(IPOS.LT.1)THEN
                     IPOS=M
                   END IF
                   IF(JPOS.GT.N)THEN
                     JPOS=1
                   END IF
                   IF(JPOS.LT.1)THEN
                     JPOS=N
                   END IF
                   NEBORS(I,J)=NEBORS(I,J)+INITAL(IPOS,JPOS)
                 END IF
70           CONTINUE
```

—*Contd.*

```
* DETERMINE A NEW CONFIGURATION AND CHECK IF AT LEAST ONE ORGANISM
* SURVIVES
          ALLKIL=.TRUE.
          DO 80 I = 1,M
            DO 80 J =1,N
            NEW(I,J)=0
            IF(INITAL(I,J).EQ.0.AND.NEBORS(I,J).EQ.3)THEN
              ALLKIL=.FALSE.
              NEW(I,J)=1
            END IF
            IF(INITAL(I,J).EQ.1.AND.(NEBORS(I,J).EQ.2.OR.
     1      NEBORS(I,J).EQ.3))THEN
              ALLKIL=.FALSE.
              NEW(I,J)=1
            END IF
80  -     CONTINUE
* RESTORE NEW CONFIGURATION TO THE ARRAY INITAL AND CHECK IF THERE
* IS ANY CHANGE IN THE CONFIGURATION FROM THE PREVIOUS ONE
          CHANGE=.FALSE.
          DO 90 I = 1,M
            DO 90 J =1,N
            IF(NEW(I,J).NE.INITAL(I,J))THEN
              INITAL(I,J)=NEW(I,J)
              CHANGE=.TRUE.
            END IF
90        CONTINUE
* WRITE NEW COFIGURATION
          WRITE(OUTLUN,800)IGEN
          DO 110 I=1,M
            DO 100 J=1,N
            IF(INITAL(I,J).NE.0)THEN
              WRITE(OUTLUN,600)
            END IF
100       CONTINUE
            WRITE(OUTLUN,700)
110       CONTINUE
* STOP,IF NO ORGANISM SURVIVES
          IF(ALLKIL)THEN
            WRITE(OUTLUN,900),IGEN
            STOP
          END IF
* STOP,IF NO CHANGE IN THE CONFIGURATION
          IF(.NOT.CHANGE)THEN
            WRITE(OUTLUN,1000),IGEN
            STOP
          END IF
120       CONTINUE
*
500       FORMAT(' GENERATION #   0 (INITIAL CONFIGURATION)',/)
600       FORMAT('+',T<J>,'*')
700       FORMAT(' ')
800       FORMAT(' ','GENERATION #',I3,/)
900       FORMAT(' ALL ORGANISMS ARE KILLED AFTER',I5,' GENERATIONS,',
     1    ' HENCE STOPPED')
1000      FORMAT(' NO CHANGE AFTER',I5,' GENERATIONS, HENCE STOPPED')
          CLOSE(UNIT=INLUN)
          CLOSE(UNIT=OUTLUN)
          STOP
          END
```

****

Figure 6.22: Program Listing of Example 6.9.

```
10
4  4
5  3
5  4
6  3
6  ⌐
```

GENERATION # 0 (INITIAL CONFIGURATION)


```
   *
   **
   **
```


GENERATION # 1


```
  **
   *
  **
```


GENERATION # 2


```
   *
    *
   *
```


GENERATION # 3

GENERATION # 4

ALL ORGANISMS ARE KILLED AFTER   4 GENERATIONS, HENCE STOPPED

Figure 6.23: Input Data and Output Results of Example 6.9.

```
  7
4 3
4 4
4 5
5 4
```

GENERATION # 0 (INITIAL CONFIGURATION)

```
***
 *
```

GENERATION # 1

```
 *
***
***
```

GENERATION # 2

```
***

* *
 *
```

GENERATION # 3

```
 *
 *
* *
 *
 *
```

—Contd.

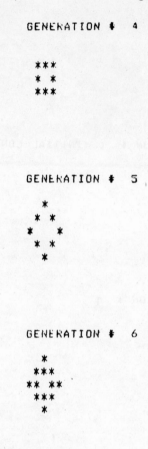

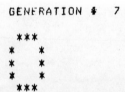

Figure 6.24: Input Data and Output Results of Example 6.9.

OBJECTIVE QUESTIONS

(1) Which of the following statements is false?
   (a) Real and integer arrays can be dimensioned in the same DIMENSION statement.
   (b) DIMENSION statements must be placed before any executable statement in a program unit.
   (c) Several DIMENSION statements can be used in one program unit.
   (d) The maximum number of memory locations reserved for each array declared in a DIMENSION statement varies from one computer machine to another.

(e) No array variable can be declared in two DIMENSION statements in a program unit.

2) Which of the following statements about a subscript is true?
   (a) It must be an integer variable name.
   (b) It can be an integer arithmetic expression.
   (c) The value of a subscript is always positive.
   (d) If the value of a subscript is negative, the subscript is assumed to be the absolute value (i.e. the negative sign is ignored).
   (e) It must be an integer number.

(3) An integer variable IFF is to be used to calculate a subscript according to the following rule:

IFF	Required Subscript
1–20	1
21–40	2
41–60	3
61–80	4
81–100	5

Which of the following expressions could be used to calculate the required subscript?
   (a) IFF/20
   (b) IFF/20+1
   (c) (IFF−1)/20
   (d) (IFF+1)/20+1
   (e) (IFF−100)/20+5

(4) What is printed by the following program segment?

```
      INTEGER NUM(10), SUM(10)
      DO 100 I = 1, 5
          NUM (I) = 100−I*10
  100 CONTINUE
      DO 10 J = 1, 5
          SUM (J) = NUM (6−J)
   10 CONTINUE
      WRITE (5,*), NUM (4), SUM (5)
```
   (a)   4   5
   (b) 60   5
   (c) 60 90
   (d)   4 90
   (e) 10 10

(5) Which of the following segments is the correct program segment to swap values of X (1) and X (ISWAP)?
   (a) X (1) = X (ISWAP)
        X (ISWAP) = X (1)
   (b) X (1) = TEMP
        TEMP = X (ISWAP)
        X (ISWAP) = TEMP
   (c) TEMP = X (ISWAP)
        X (1) = TEMP
        X (ISWAP) = X (1)
   (d) TEMP = X (ISWAP)
        X (ISWAP) = X (I)
        X (1) = TEMP

(e) TEMP = X (1)
     X (1) = X (ISWAP)
     X (ISWAP) = X (1)

(6) Which of the following statements about multi-dimensional arrays is false?
     (a) All the elements of an array must be assigned a value before any element can
          be used.
     (b) Arrays can be declared using a DIMENSION statement.
     (c) FORTRAN 77 allows arrays only up to seven dimensions.
     (d) The value of an array element can be assigned, or read from a file.
     (e) It is not necessary to use all the elements of an array in a program segment.

(7) Which of the following declaration statements set in a program unit is not allowed?
     (a) DIMENSION A (10, 10)
     (b) REAL NUMBER
          DIMENSION NUMBER (−10 : 100), X (1, 2, 3)
     (c) DIMENSION X (10, 10, 2, 2, 2, 10, 10), Y (−10 : 2, 2 : 4)
     (d) DIMENSION ZUPP (10, 3), X (4, 5)
          INTEGER X (10), Y (10, 10)
     (e) LOGICAL SEARCH(10), FOUND(10)
          DIMENSION X (10)
          LOGICAL X

(8) How many elements can be stored in each of the following arrays?
     INTEGER A (0 : 5), B (1, 5), C (−8 : 8, 2 : 3)
     (a) 6, 5, 17
     (b) 5, 5, 16
     (c) 6, 5, 34
     (d) 0, 1, 8
     (e) 5, 5, 34

(9) What is printed by the following program segment?
     DIMENSION MATRIX (3, 3)
     DO 10 I = 1, 3
         DO 20 J = 1, I
             MATRIX (I, J) = 0
     20   CONTINUE
         DO 30 J = I+1, 3
             MATRIX (I, J) = −1
     30   CONTINUE
     10 CONTINUE
         *, MATRIX (1, 1), MATRIX (2, 3), MATRIX (3, 3)
     (a)   1   2   3
     (b)   0   0   0
     (c) −1 −1   0
     (d)   0 −1   0
     (e)   0 −1 −1

(10) Consider the following program segment
     DIMENSION IA (3, 2)
     READ (1, *) ((IA (I, J), J = 1, 2), I = 1, 3)
     WRITE (2, 100) ((IA (I, J), J = 1, 2), I = 1, 3)
     100 FORMAT (' ', 2 I 3)
     The input data in a file whose logical unit number is 1 is given as follows:
     0 1 2
     3 4 5

What will be written in the file whose logical unit number is 2?
(a) 0 1 2 3 4 5
(b) 0 1
   2 3
   4 5
(c) 0 3
   1 4
   2 5
(d) 0 1 2
   3 4 5
(e) 0 1
   3 4
   0 0

(11) If the WRITE and the corresponding FORMAT statements in the above program are changed to
    WRITE (2, 200) ((IA (J, I), J = 1, 3), I = 1, 2)
    200 FORMAT (' ', 3I3)
What will be written in the file whose logical unit number is 2?
(a) 0 1 2 3 4 5
(b) 0 1 2
   3 4 5
(c) 0 2 4
   1 3 5
(d) 0 1
   2 3
   4 5
(e) An error message

(12) Data is stored in an unformatted form in a data file 'JNK .DAT'. If the values are stored in order (1, 1), (1, 2), (1, 3), (2, 1),··· etc., which is the most preferable and the correct form to read the data in a two-dimensional array INPUT (5, 3)?
(a) READ (1,*) ((INPUT (I, J), J = 1, 3), I = 1, 5)
(b) READ (1,*) ((INPUT (I, J), I = 1, 5), J = 1, 3)
(c) READ (1,*) ((INPUT (J, I), I = 1, 5), J = 1, 3)
(d)   DO 10 I = 1, 5
        READ (1,*) (INPUT (I, J), J = 1, 3)
    10 CONTINUE
(e)   READ (1, 100) ((INPUT (I, J), J = 1, 3), I = 1, 5)
    100 FORMAT (3I10)

(13) In what order will the following program segment print out the subscripted variables from a three-dimensional array?
    LOGICAL A (2, 2, 2)
    DO 10 I = 1, 2
      DO 10 J = 1, 2
        DO 10 K = 1, 2
          WRITE (1,*) A (I, K, J)
 10 CONTINUE
(a) A(1,1,1), A(1,1,2), A(1,2,1), A(1,2,2), A(2,1,1), A(2,1,2), A(2,2,1), A(2,2,2)
(b) A(1,1,1), A(1,2,1), A(1,1,2), A(1,2,2), A(2,1,1), A(2,2,1), A(2,1,2), A(2,2,2)
(c) A(1,1,1), A(2,2,2)
(d) A(1,1,1), A(2,1,1), A(1,2,1), A(2,2,1), A(1,1,2), A(2,1,2), A(1,2,2), A(2,2,2)
(e) A(1,1,1), A(1,2,1), A(1,1,2), A(1,2,2), A(2,1,1), A(2,2,2)

DRILL EXERCISES

(1) Consider the following declaration statements:

              DIMENSION A (100), B (−1 : 5)

              INTEGER   SUM (100,−2 : 0)

              REAL   NUMBER (1000, 2 : 5, 3), X (100, 100, 100)

              LOGICAL   SEARCH (−5 : 0, 0 : 5, 5 : 10)

How many elements can be stored in the following arrays:

              A, B, SUM, NUMBER, X, SEARCH

(2) Determine the number of lines printed by

              WRITE (6, 100) (ABC (I), I = 1, 4), XYZ, (BOY (J), J = 1, 5)

using the following format specifications :

(a) 100 FORMAT (' ', F 5.1)

(b) 100 FORMAT (' ', 5F5.1)

(c) 100 FORMAT (' ', 10F5.1)

(d) 100 FORMAT (' ', 4F10.4, 6F3.2)

(e) 100 FORMAT (' ', 10I5)

(3) Find as many syntax errors as you can in the following program segment :

```
        COMPLEX X (10)
        REAL ABC (10), INK
  20    DIMENSION PUT (I)
        READ (5, 100) (ABC (I), I = 1, 20)
  100   FORMAT (' ', <N>F10.4)
        DO 100 I = 1, 10
            IF (ABC (I) .EQ. 0.0) THEN X (I) = (ABC (I), ABC (10−I) )
            IF (ABC (I) .NE. 0.0) THEN
                X (I) = (ABC (I) )
  100   CONTINUE
        IF (INK .EQ. 4 .AND. ABC (10) = INK) THEN GO TO 20
        END
        STOP
```

(4) What will the following program segments do?

(a)
```
    REAL NUMBER (10), DIFF (10)
    DO 10 I = 1, 10
        READ (1,*) NUMBER (I)
10  CONTINUE
    DO 15 I = 1, 9
        DIFF (I) = NUMBER (I+1)−NUMBER (I)
15  CONTINUE
```

(b)
```
    INTEGER MATRIX (10, 20)
    N = 10
    M = 20
    DO 10 I = 1, N
        DO 10 J = 1, M
            IF (I .LT. J) THEN
                MATRIX (1, J) = −1
            ELSE IF (I .EQ. J) THEN
                MATRIX (I, J) = 0
            ELSE
                MATRIX (I, J) = 1
            END IF
10  CONTINUE
    WRITE (1,*) ( (MATRIX (I, J), J = 1, M), 1 = 1, N)
    WRITE (1,*) ( (MATRIX (1, J), I = 1, N), J = 1, M)
```

```
(c)      REAL ADD (10, 10)
             DO 10 I = 1, 2
                DO 20 J = 6, 1, −1
                   SUM=0.0
                   SUM = SUM+ADD (I, J)
      20           CONTINUE
                ADD (I, J) = SUM
                WRITE (2,*) (ADD (I, J), J = 1, 6)
      10        CONTINUE
(d)      REAL ADD (100)
             SUM = 0.0
             DO 10 I = 1, 100
                SUM = SUM+ADD (I)
      10    CONTINUE
             WRITE (2,*) SUM
             AVRAG= SUM/100
             SUMSQ = 0.0
             DO 20 I = 1,100
                SUMSQ = SUMSQ+(ADD (I)−AVRAG)**2
      20    CONTINUE
             STDDEV = SQRT (SUMSQ/100)
             WRITE (2,*) STDDEV
(e)      INTEGER MATRIX (10, 10), DIAG (10)
             DO 10 I = 10, 1, −1
             DIAG (I) = MATRIX (I, I)
      10    CONTINUE
             WRITE (2,*) (DIAG (I), I = 1, 10)
```

(5) Write a FORTRAN 77 program segment that finds the first non-zero value in an array. For example, if array A is a five-element array, where A (1) = 0, A (2) = 0, A (3) = 1, A (4) = 0, A (5) = 2, then the first non-zero value is A (3) which is 1.

(6) An integer array NUMBER contains 100 elements. Write a FORTRAN 77 program to interchange the 1st and the 100th elements, the 2nd the 99th elements, and so on, of the array NUMBER. The program should stop after interchanging the 50th and 51st elements.

(7) An integer array named CHANGE contains 21 elements. Write a FORTRAN 77 program to accomplish the following:
(a) Replace the second element by the product of the first and the last element.
(b) Replace the middle element by the average value of all array elements.
(c) Replace all negative values by zeros.
(d) Print the array CHANGE.

(8) Write a FORTRAN program segment to calculate the transpose of a matrix [A]. The transpose of matrix [A] is obtained by interchanging its rows and columns, that is, the transpose of matrix A(I, J) is $A^T(J, I)$ for each value of I and J. For example, the transpose of a matrix A

$$[A] = \begin{bmatrix} 1 & 2 & 3 \\ 4 & 5 & 6 \end{bmatrix}$$

is given by

$$[A]^T = \begin{bmatrix} 1 & 4 \\ 2 & 5 \\ 3 & 6 \end{bmatrix}$$

(9) Write a FORTRAN 77 program segment to compare the corresponding elements of two one-dimensional arrays, A and B. The size of each array is 100. If more than half the elements of array A are greater than the corresponding elements of array B, write a message "ARRAY A IS GREAT", otherwise write a message "DON'T KNOW".

(10) Modify the program given in programming Example 6.4 so that it can calculate the standard deviation of students' scores. The standard deviation for n numbers x_1, x_2, x_3,..., x_n is given by

$$\text{standard deviation} = \sqrt{\frac{1}{n} \sum_{i=1}^{n} (x_i - \bar{x})^2}$$

where $\bar{x}$ is the average value of the n numbers x_1, x_2,..., x_n.

(11) A one-dimensional array NUMBER contains six elements, such that NUMBER (1) = 1, NUMBER (2) = 2,..., NUMBER (6) = 6. Using implied DO lists, write FORTRAN 77 program segments to print the following patterns:

```
(a) 1 2 3 4 5 6      (b) 1                    (c) 1
    2 3 4 5 6            1 2                       1 3
    3 4 5 6              1 2 3                     1 3 5
    4 5 6                1 2 3 4                   2 4 6
    5 6                  1 2 3 4 5                 2 4
    6                    1 2 3 4 5 6               2
```

(12) Write a FORTRAN 77 program segment to declare an array ZUNKU to be 10 by 10, and assign values to ZUNKU (I, J) such that:

$$\text{ZUNKU (I, J)} = \begin{cases} \text{I*J} & \text{if J is odd} \\ \text{I+J} & \text{if I is even} \\ 0, & \text{otherwise} \end{cases}$$

(13) For each of the following, write appropriate declaration statements:
   (a) A one-dimensional array A whose subscripts are intergers from 0 through 5.
   (b) A two-dimensional array B (I, J) whose subscript I is from −5 through 5 and J is from 10 through 15. The array B is of logical type.
   (c) A one-dimensional array A whose subscripts start from −50. The number of elements in the array is 20.
   (d) An array to represent a four-dimensional space (I, J, K, L), the lower-bound value of each subscript is zero while the upperbound values for I. J, K and L are 10, 15, 2 and 8, respectively.

(14) Which of the following statements is true?
   (a) If BOY (I) = BOY (J), then I = J.
   (b) If BOY (I+J, K+L) = 4, then it is always true that
       BOY (I, K)+BOY (J, L) = 4.
   (c) BOY (X (Y (2)), Z(X (Y (2)))) is invalid.
   (d) The statement REAL BOY (1, 2, 3, 4, 5, 6, 7) is valid.
   (e) If BOY is an array, then READ (5, 100) BOY will cause reading of just BOY (1).

PROGRAMMING EXERCISES

(1) Somewhere in this universe there exists another race of intelligent persons. They have 200 basic numerical digits (we have only ten digits 0, 1, 2,..., 9) in their number theory. These 200 digits may be assumed to be the same as our first 200 numbers 0, 1, 2, 3, 4,..., 199. Long ago, when we did not have any computing machine, a student from that place visited this planet. He posed a puzzle to an undergraduate class of mathematics students. He said that he had 200 stones, each

engraved with the digit of his number system. He said they could assume that the stones were numbered 0 through 199. All the stones were placed in a row with all the numbers face up. Beginning with the first stone, he turned every even-numbered stone face down. Next, beginning with the second stone, he turned every other stone over; in other words, turned it face up, if it was face down, and turned it face down if it was face up. He repeated this procedure with every third stone, then every fourth stone and so on. He wanted to know how many stones would be faced down when the process was complete and what would be their numbers. He gave a time limit of five minutes. No graduate student could solve the puzzle in five minutes. Can you do it now? Write a FORTRAN 77 program to solve this puzzle. Do you have any idea how much time will your computer take to solve this puzzle?

(2) Write a FORTRAN 77 program to reverse the order of integers in an array INTGR. The total number of elements in the array is 100.

(3) Write a FORTRAN 77 program to sum two matrices [A] and [B]. Each matrix has m rows and n columns. The output should display all the three matrices, [A], [B] and their sum matrix.

(4) Write a FORTRAN 77 program to check whether a square matrix [A] of dimensions $N \times N$ is: (i) symmetrical about the main diagonal, (ii) lower-triangular, i.e. every element above the main diagonal is zero. The main diagonal is the one which runs from A (1, 1) to A (N, N).

(5) Write a FORTRAN 77 program to read the high and low temperatures of each day from a file 'TEMP.DAT', and store them in an array (30, 2). Find the highest high temperature and the average high temperature. Also calculate the largest variation in the temperature (high-low) on a day. The input data in file 'TEMP.DAT' is given as follows:

```
35    20
37    10
45    20
 5     0
      ⋮
-100  -100
```

The first column indicates the high temperatures and the second column gives the low temperatures. The maximum number of rows in the file is 30 but the exact number of rows is not known. The last entry (a dummy entry) in the input file is -100 for both high and low temperatures.

(6) On a chessboard, the queen can attack any chesspiece that is on the same row, column, or diagonal to the queen. The problem is to position n queens on an $n \times n$ chessboard so that no queen can attack any other. Write a FORTRAN 77 program to simulate this chessboard problem for a given value of n.

(7) The correlation coefficient (r) for a set of n data points (X, Y) is given by

$$r = \frac{n\Sigma XY - (\Sigma X)(\Sigma Y)}{\sqrt{[n\Sigma X^2 - (\Sigma X)^2][n\Sigma Y^2 - (\Sigma Y)^2]}}$$

Write a FORTRAN 77 program to computer for the following two data sets:

(8) There are many interesting problem in the number theory. One interesting problem is to find integer numbers that can be written as the sum of two squares in two different ways. One such number is 221, because

$$221 = 10^2 + 11^2 = 5^2 + 14^2$$

Write a FORTRAN 77 program to find these numbers between 1 and 1000. An extension to this problem is the determination of integer numbers that can be written as the sum of two cubes. In fact there is an interesting story about it. The

Set 1		Set 2	
X	Y	X	Y
1.0	0.8	34.2	102.4
2.0	1.5	40.0	100.0
3.0	2.2	42.0	97.5
4.0	3.1	43.2	97.8
5.0	3.5	40.0	98.0
6.0	4.0	53.0	100.0
7.0	4.8	54.0	97.1
8.0	5.7	55.0	95.0

famous mathematician G.H. Hardy once mentioned to the great Indian mathematician Ramanujam that he had just ridden in a taxi whose number he considered a very dull number. Ramanujam promptly replied that, on the contrary, the number was very interesting because it was the smallest positive integer that could be written in the form of the sum of two cubes (i.e. i^3+j^3) in two different ways. Write a FORTRAN 77 program to find the number of Hardy's taxi.

(9) The classical algorithm discussed in Programming Example 6.8 for matrix multiplication $[C]_{m\times n} = [A]_{m\times p} [B]_{p\times n}$ requires mnp multiplications and mn (p−1) additions. You should verify this by slightly modifying the FORTRAN program given in Figure 6.15. A more efficient method, Winograd's method, of matrix multiplication reduces the number of multiplications to about half with the following formula:

$$C_{ij} = \sum_{k=1}^{p/2} [(a_{i,\,2k}+b_{2k-1,j})*(a_{i,\,2k-1}+b_{2k,\,j})\,]-d_i+e_j+a_{ip}*b_{pn}$$

where

$$d_i = \sum_{k=1}^{p/2} a_{i,\,2k}*a_{i,\,2k-1} \text{ and } e_j = \sum_{k=1}^{p/2} b_{2k-1,\,j}*b_{2k,\,j}$$

and the last term $(a_{ip}*b_{pn})$ is present only if p is odd. Write a FORTRAN 77 program to calculate the product of two matrices using Winograd's method.

(10) A car dealer keeps a record of all his sales in the form of a file, with each line having a fixed format as follows:

(i) The first eight positions are used for the car registration number, an integer number (0−99999999).

(ii) The next position is used to identify the model of the car (0−9).

(iii) The next six positions are used for the date on which a car is sold. The first of these two positions are for the day (1−30, every month is assumed to be of 30 days), the next two are used for the months (1−12) and the last two are for the year (1−99). Each item is right-justified, for example

Column #	1	2	3	4	5	6	7	8	9	10	11	12	13	14	15
					4	0	9	2	0	5	1	1	7	8
		3	2	5	1	0	7	9	1	7	0	9	8	6
	⋮													

Write a FORTRAN 77 program which will read such data and output the details (the registration number and the sale date) of each model sold from August 15, 1947 (150847) till June 7, 1958 (070658), both inclusive.

(11) The following table gives a set of data that represents power generated in megawatts from a power plant over a period of ten weeks. Each row represents one week's data, each column represents data taken from the same day of the week.

Table: Power Generated at a Power Plant

	DAY1	DAY2	DAY3	DAY4	DAY5	DAY6	DAY7
Week1	400.	500	503	600	250	300	550
Week2	402	615	353	434	441	298	446
Week3	330	180	373	530	207	242	320
Week4	240	192	265	600	351	561	370
Week5	250	370	299	400	451	534	367
Week6	500	420	404	500	403	600	441
Week7	602	444	555	333	408	175	321
Week8	218	279	205	291	396	212	293
Week9	400	369	201	383	496	313	372
Week10	600	459	209	421	373	335	555

Write a FORTRAN 77 program to read the information and compute the following results:
  (i) Average daily power output.
 (ii) Maximum power generated by the plant on any day.
(iii) Number of days on which there was above-average power output.
 (iv) Overall efficiency of the plant, if the installed capacity of the plant is 700 mw.
  (v) The week in which maximum power was generated.

(12) One of the papers in the preliminary examination for Indian Civil Services (ICS.) contains 100 multiple-choice questions. Each question has five choices and only one choice is correct. The examination results and the students' answers can be represented as follows:
  (i) An integer array CORANS (100) contains the correct answers (digit 1, 2, 3, 4 or 5) to the questions.
 (ii) An integer array RESPON (500, 100) contains the responses to the 100 questions by 500 students. That is, each row of the array RESPON contains the answers for one student. Again the student answers are coded as 1, 2, 3, 4 or 5. Assume that no student marked more than one choice and no question is left unanswered by a student.

Write a FORTRAN 77 program to read these two arrays and compute the following:
  (a) How many students qualify for the final exam if the minimum passing score is 60?
  (b) How many students get the correct answer to all the questions whose answer is the first choice (i.e. 1)?

(13) Mr. Ramaswamy has the following portfolio of stocks at the start of a period and makes the given set of transactions during the period.

Starting Portfolio

Stock Number	# of Shares	Price/Share
1	50	15.0
2	100	25.0
3	200	20.0
4	600	5.0
5	200	10.0

Transactions

Stock Number	Action	Shares	Price/Share
6	Buy	300	15.00
3	Sell	100	25.00
5	Sell	200	9.50
7	Buy	400	12.50

Final Prices

Stock Number	Price/Share	Stock Number	Price/Share
1	12.50	6	18.00
2	30.00	7	15.00
3	22.50		
4	7.50		
5	9.00		

Write a FORTRAN 77 program to display his starting portfolio, a summary of his transactions and his final portfolio. Also, compute the net profit/loss accrued to Mr. Ramaswamy as a result of these transactions.

ANSWERS TO OBJECTIVE QUESTIONS

(1) d;   (2) b;   (3) e;   (4) c;   (5) d;   (6) a;
(7) d;   (8) c;   (9) d;   (10) b;   (11) c;   (12) a;
(13) b;   (14) d.

Chapter 7

Subprograms

7.1 INTRODUCTION

A brief discussion on modular design and structured programming has been given in Section 2.9 of Chapter 2. The basic philosophy is one of 'divide and conquer' by which complicated tasks or subjects are successively divided into simpler and more manageable parts which can be easily handled. A FORTRAN program can be divided into smaller subprograms that can be developed and tested separately. This is called a *modular design approach*.

A *subprogram*, as the name implies, is a sequence of instructions that forms part of a program. These instructions are contained in a separate program that performs a specific task under the direction of another program from which the program is called. Some subprograms are included in the FORTRAN language as intrinsic functions. Intrinsic functions such as EXP, SQRT, SIN, ALOG, etc. have already been discussed in Chapter 3. These functions are really subprograms that evaluate the appropriate mathematical function.

The FORTRAN library does not contain all functions needed for various applications. In fact, it covers only a few common mathematical functions. A programmer may well have to write *blocks* (modules of the code) which perform simple or specialized functions. This capability of writing separate blocks or subprograms is a very important feature of the FORTRAN language. These subprograms are separate, independent program units and can be combined with any program.

There are two basic types of subprograms in FORTRAN:
(i) FUNCTION subprograms
(ii) SUBROUTINE subprograms

FUNCTIONS are appropriate when a single value is returned from the subprogram and SUBROUTINES are a better choice when the subprogram returns a number of values each time it is called. These functions and subroutines are written only once but may be called at several locations in a program to avoid unnecessary duplication of the code.

We begin this chapter by discussing an example that illustrates the use of subprograms and we will then go on to describe the functions and subroutine subprograms.

Example

We want to write a FORTRAN program to calculate the binomial co-efficient:

$$C(n, m) = \frac{n!}{n!\,(n-m)!} \qquad n, m \geqslant 0$$

where n! represents factorial n.

In this example, one has to basically calculate three factorials: factorial n, factorial m and factorial (n−m). A FORTRAN program to do the job could be somewhat like this:

```
* Initialization
      FACN = 1.0
      FACM = 1.0
      FACNM = 1.0
* Calculation of Factorials
      DO 10 I = 1, N
      FACN = FACN*I
10 CONTINUE
      DO 20 I = 1, M
      FACM = FACM*I
20 CONTINUE
      DO 30 I = 1, (N—M)
      FACNM = FACNM*I
30 CONTINUE
* Calculation of C(n, m)
      BICOFF = FACN/(FACM*FACNM)
      STOP
      END
```

Notice that the above program listing has three initialization statements and three DO loops which basically perform the same task. In this situation, one can write a subprogram to calculate the factorial of a quantity and call it three times to calculate the binomial coefficient. A FORTRAN program to do this job is somewhat like this:

```
* MAIN (CALLING) program
      BICOFF = FACT(N) / (FACT(M) * FACT(N—M))
      STOP
      END
* FUNCTION subprogram
      FUNCTION FACT (K)
```

```
              FACT = 1.0
              DO 10 I = 1, K
                 FACT = FACT*I
      10  CONTINUE
              RETURN
              END
```

Users may compare the above two versions and decide which is better, more economical and desirable. From all aspects, it is preferable to use the second version which uses a function subprogram. For this example, writing a function subprogram is more appropriate, but we will nevertheless write a subroutine subprogram to illustrate its use.

```
      *  MAIN (CALLING) program
              CALL FACTOR (N, FACN)
              CALL FACTOR (M, FACM)
              CALL FACTOR (N−M, FACNM)
              BICOFF = FACN / (FACM*FACNM)
              STOP
              END
      *  Subroutine Subprograms
              SUBROUTINE FACTOR (K, FAC)
              FAC = 1.0
              DO 10 I = 1, K
                 FAC = FAC*I
      10  CONTINUE
              RETURN
              END
```

Users may note the difference between the last two versions of the FORTRAN program. The syntax form of a function subprogram or a subroutine subprogram is quite different and it is called in different manners. These differences are compared in Table 7.1. The user is advised to refer to this chart while reading the rest of this chapter:

Table 7.1: A Comparison of Function and Subroutine Subprograms

Subprogram	Form of Subprogram	Method of Calling the Subprograms	Number of Values Returned
FUNCTION	FUNCTION name (arguments) ⋮ RETURN ⋮ RETURN END	Use the name (with arguments) in the R.H.S. of any expression	1
SUBROUTINE	SUBROUTINE name (arguments) ⋮ RETURN ⋮ RETURN END	Call the name (arguments)	0 or more than zero

The program that creates the whole program and normally calls the sub-programs is referred to as the *main program* or *mainline program*. A main program must contain a STOP statement. Only one main program is allowed in one FORTRAN job. A complete FORTRAN program may, however, contain more than one subprogram. A subprogram may be called from any program unit except from itself. A FORTRAN subprogram must not call itself as FORTRAN does not allow recursion. The term *program unit* means any type of program (i.e., a main program or a subprogram). The term *calling program* refers to the program unit that is invoking (using) a subprogram. As mentioned earlier, a subroutine is called by using a CALL statement while a function is called simply by using its name. As soon as a subprogram is called from a program unit, control is transferred to the subprogram and the computer continues performing instructions in the subprogram until it is returned to the calling program by a RETURN statement. Control is returned to the very next instruction in the calling program from where it was called. The following diagram shows how control passes from one program unit to another program unit:

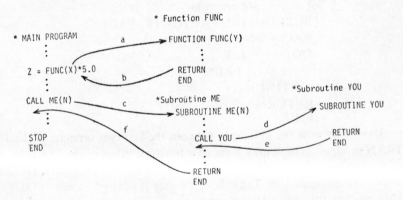

The statement $Z = FUNC(X) * 5.0$ in the main program contains a function FUNC (X). Control is, therefore, transferred to the function subprogram (arrow 'a'). Statements in the function FUNC (Y) are executed until a RETURN statement is encountered. Control is then transferred to the main program (arrow 'b') where the value of the function is multiplied by 5.0 and the result is stored in variable Z. Control then passes to the next statement from where the execution continues. Again, when the statement CALL ME (N) in the main program is encountered, control passes to the subroutine ME (arrow 'c'). The statements in the subroutine ME are executed until the statement CALL YOU is encountered. The statement transfers control to the subroutine YOU (arrow 'd'). The statements in the subroutine YOU are executed until a RETURN statement is encountered which transfers control back to subroutine ME (arrow 'e'). The statements in this subroutine continue to be executed till a RETURN statement in the subroutine ME is encountered which transfers control back to the main program (arrow 'f'). The statements following the statement CALL ME (N) in the main program are then executed till the program encounters a STOP statement in the main program.

We will now discuss each of the subprograms in the remaining part of this Chapter. We must remember that subprograms should be viewed as modules of a total FORTRAN program that might consist of numerous subprograms.

7.2 FUNCTION SUBPROGRAMS

A function subprogram is used in the same way as an intrinsic function is used. The difference is that we write the function subprogram ourselves while intrinsic functions are available in the FORTRAN language library. The function subprogram is not really a complete program as the prefix sub- in the subprogram implies; if it were executed by itself it would not produce meaningful results. As explained earlier, it is called by another program. In the earlier section, we have discussed briefly the form of a subprogram and the way it is called from a calling program. We will now discuss this in detail.

7.2.1 The Function Invocation (Calling) Statement

The general form of a function invocation statement is:

function name $([a_1, a_2, a_3, \ldots , a_n])$

where

function name is the name of the function (any valid variable name); and $a_1, a_2, a_3, \ldots , a_n$ are an optional list of arguments to be passed to the function subprogram; the arguments can be valid variables, subscripted variable names, array names, expressions, constants, or function names; these arguments are called *actual arguments*.

The value of the function is returned through the name of the function (acting as a variable). The type of the function value (whether real, integer, etc.) depends on the type of the function name. If the function is not typed the value returned by the function is implicitly typed by the function name. If the name begins with I, J, K, L, M or N, the function value is integer; otherwise it is real.

Example (a)

In the factorial example the statement

$$BICOFF = FACT (N) / (FACT (M) * FACT (N-M))$$

contains three calls for the function FACT. The function has one argument.

Example (b)

Consider the following statement:

$$Z = A(M, N, T) + P(X(2), X**4, 2.5, Y/2.0)$$

The statement has two functions, A and P. Function A has three arguments while function P has four arguments. Arguments can be variable, arrays, array elements, constants, expressions and/or functions too.

Users may wonder how the computer differentiates between a function and a reference to an array. For example, FACT(N) could be a reference to the Nth element of array FACT. If the variable FACT is declared as an array, then FACT is an array, otherwise it is treated as a reference to a function subprogram. If the user does not define FACT as a function subprogram then a compilation error will occur. The same principle applies to the arguments of a function. In the above example, if the user has defined X to be an array then X(2) is the second element of array X, otherwise X is treated to be a reference to the function X with one argument whose value is 2.

7.2.2 The Function Definition Statement

The first statement in every function subprogram must be the FUNCTION statement which has a general form:

[type] FUNCTION function name ($[p_1, p_2, p_3, \ldots, p_n]$)

where

function name is the name of the function;

$p_1, p_2, p_3, \ldots, p_n$ is optional list of dummy arguments used to pass the data to and from the calling program; the arguments can either be variable names, expressions, array names, or function names; these arguments cannot be either subscripted variables or constants; type is the optional type declaration for the function results; function can be typed as REAL, INTEGER, CHARACTER, DOUBLE PRECISION, LOGICAL and COMPLEX; if type is omitted, the function value is implicitly defined by the function name; if the name starts with I, J, K, L, M or N, the value is integer; otherwise it is real.

The dummy arguments used in the subprogram are dummy names for the actual arguments listed in the invocation statement. When the function subprogram is executed, the value of each actual argument replaces the value of the corresponding dummy argument. The argument names used may be the same or different. An important rule to remember is that the arguments in the invocation statement (i.e. actual arguments) should correspond in number, order and type with the dummy arguments of the FUNCTION statement. There must be a one-to-one correspondence between the two sets of arguments.

Example

In the calling program,

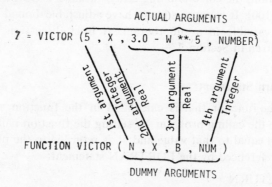

In the function subprogram N is the same as 5, (N = 5), X is the same as X, B is the same as 3.0-W**5 and NUM is the same as NUMBER.

The type of dummy arguments is determined either by the first character of the variable (integer or real) or by the type statements in the subprograms. For example, if a subprogram begins with the statements:

INTEGER FUNCTION ANKIT (N, A, B)
INTEGER N, A
REAL   B

then N and A are integer variables in the subprogram, and B is a real variable. It is incorrect to reference this function with a statement such as

Z = ANKIT (5, 1.0, 2.0)

since 1.0 is the real constant, and the function requires the second argument to be an integer. The user should be careful about the number of arguments while writing subprograms. Another thing to remember is that if an argument in a function subprogram is an array name, the array name must be declared in a DIMENSION or type statement in the function subprogram. For example, consider the following program segment:

```
* MAIN PROGRAM
      DIMENSION NUMBER (100)
        ⋮
      Z = LOVIN (50, NUMBER)
        ⋮
      STOP
      END
* FUNCTION Subprogram
      FUNCTION LOVIN (N, NUM)
      DIMENSION NUM(N)
        ⋮
```

The array variable NUM in the subprogram is declared to be an array. Note that the array variable NUM is not declared as NUM(100) while in the main program, the corresponding array variable NUMBER is declared as NUMBER(100). It is permissible to have adjustable bound specifications for an array variable in a subprogram. A brief discussion on adjustable dimension is given in Section 7.7.

7.2.3 The Return Statement

The value of the function that is calculated in the function subprogram is passed back to the calling program by setting the function name all by itself (no arguments) equal to that value and it is returned to the place where the function was referenced by the FORTRAN statement:

> RETURN

For example, in the following subprogram segment:

> FUNCTION FACT(N)
>   IF (N.LT.0) RETURN

if the value of N is less than zero, control is passed back to the statement in the calling program where the invocation was made. Many RETURN statements can be included in a function subprogram.

The very last statement in a subprogram is the END statement. It is similar to the END statement in a main program.

We will now illustrate the use of function subprograms by giving a few examples.

7.2.4 Examples of Function Subprogram

Example (a)

Function AVG returns the average of three numbers.

Calling Program	Function Subprogram
	REAL FUNCTION AVG (NUM1, NUM2, NUM3)
AVRAG 1 = AVG (10, 20, 30)	
	AVG = (NUMI+NUM2+NUM3)/3.0
AVRAG 2 = AVG (M, N, L)	RETURN
	END

Example (b)

Real function LARGE returns the larger value of any two arguments.

Calling Program	Function Subprogram
REAL LARGE	REAL FUNCTION LARGE (P,Q)
$\vdots$	IF (P.GT.Q) THEN
X = LARGE (A, B)	LARGE = P
$\vdots$	ELSE
IF (Y.LT. LARGE (X, Z)) THEN	
	LARGE = Q
$\vdots$	END IF
	RETURN
	END

Example (c)

In this example real function LARGE returns the largest element in a real array of size 50.

Calling Program	Function Subprogram
REAL X (50), Y (50), LARGE	REAL FUNCTION LARGE (A)
$\vdots$	REAL A (50)
XLARGE = LARGE (X)	LARGE = A (1)
YLARGE = LARGE (Y)	DO 10 I = 2, 50
$\vdots$	IF (LARGE.LT.A (I))
	LARGE = A (I)
	10 CONTINUE
	RETURN
	END

Example (d)

This example gives a complete program to print a table of factorials of number from 1 to N.

```
* Main Program
      DO 10 I = 1, N
      WRITE (6, *) 'NUMBER', I, 'FACTORIAL = ', FACT (I)
10    CONTINUE
      STOP
      END
* Function Subprogram
      FUNCTION FACT (K)
      FACT = 1
      DO 10 I = 2, K
      FACT = FACT*I
10    CONTINUE
      RETURN
      END
```

Note that the function FACT is referenced in the WRITE statement in the main program and it is called N times inside the DO loop.

7.2.5 Communication of Variables

Since subprograms are separate programs that are treated independently by the compiler, identical variable names that are totally unrelated, can be used in the calling and called (subprograms) programs with no risk of confusion. It is also permissible to use same statement numbers in the calling and called programs because both programs are compiled separately. For this reason, if a programmer wishes to refer in a subprogram to a variable that is used in a calling program, he (she) cannot use the same name and hope that it will refer to the variable with the identical name in the calling program. For example, in the above example, variable I is used as DO variables in both main program and subprogram. The variable I in the main program and the variable I in the subprogram are totally unrelated and have no connection whatsoever. The same is the case with statement number 10 which is used in both main program and subprogram. The only way to *communicate* variables between called and calling programs is either through the common statement (discussed in Section 7.9) or by passing the variable name as an argument of a sub-program. Only these variables are global variables both to calling and called program, otherwise all other variables are local variables and are accessible in the program unit in which they are defined. In the above example, the only variables common to the two programs are I (in main program) and K (in subprogram).

The concept of communication of variables between the called and the calling program is very important from the programming point of view. Here is an example to illustrate this concept.

Example

The cartesian coordinates of point P (see Figure 7.1) are given by (x, y). We want to convert cartesian coordinates into polar coordinates (r, θ). The formulae that relate the polar coordinates with the cartesian coordinates are

$$r = \sqrt{x^2 + y^2},$$
$$\theta = \tan^{-1}(y/x).$$

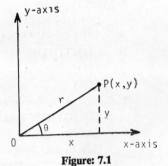

Figure: 7.1

The function subprogram returns a single value, so to calculate r and θ_i we should write two function subprograms, one for calculating r and the other for calculating θ. This is shown below:

```
*Main Program
X = 3.0
Y = 4.0
R = ARG(X,Y)
THETA = ANGLE(X,Y)
STOP
END
*ARG Function Subprogram
FUNCTION ARG(XCORD,YCORD)
ARG = SQRT(XCORD**2+YCORD**2)
RETURN
END
*ANGLE Function Subprogram
FUNCTION ANGLE(XCORD,YCORD)
ANGLE = ATAN(YCORD/XCORD)*180.0/3.1427
RETURN
END
```

In this example variables common to the main program and the subprogram are given as follows:

Main Program	Subprogram ARG	Subprogram ANGLE
X	XCORD	
Y	YCORD	
X		XCORD
Y		YCORD

Note that the variable XCORD and YCORD of subprogram ARG have no relation with the variable XCORD and YCORD of subprogram ANGLE.

Instead of writing two function subprograms, we can write only one function subprogram, CONVRT. We can return one value through the value of the function and the other value as an argument of the function. This is shown below:

```
*Main Program
X = 3.0
Y = 4.0
R = CONVRT(X,Y,THETA)
STOP
END
*CONVRT Function Subprogram
FUNCTION CONVRT(XCORD,YCORD,BETA)
CONVRT = SQRT(XCORD**2+YCORD**2)
BETA = ATAN(YCORD/XCORD)*180.0/3.1427
RETURN
END
```

In this example, the value of R is returned via the function name CONVRT and THETA can be returned via argument BETA. The variable THETA (in the main program) corresponding to variable BETA (in the subprogram) is undefined upon calling, but is defined upon return. One should remember that the communication link between the calling program and the called programs revolves around addresses of storage locations rather than the numerical values of the arguments. For example, consider the statements

    R = CONVRT(X,Y,THETA)
    FUNCTION CONVRT(XCORD,YCORD,BETA)

appearing in the main program and subprogram, respectively. In the main program, storage locations are established for X, Y, and THETA as shown below:

X -------------------☐

Y -------------------☐

THETA ----------------☐

Memory Locations

The arguments XCORD, YCORD, and BETA in the FUNCTION statement are dummies, and no storage locations are established explicitly for these variables. When the FUNCTION is called, the addresses of the storage locations of the arguments (in this case X, Y, and THETA) in the calling statements are used by the subprogram to obtain and/or store the value of its arguments (in this case, XCORD, YCORD, and BETA):

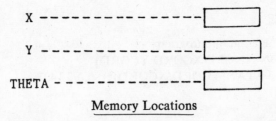

Actual Arguments	Memory Locations	Dummy Arguments
X ----------------	3.0	----------- XCORD
Y ----------------	4.0	----------- YCORD
THETA -----------	53.13	----------- BETA

Main Program   Subprogram

In the above example, the values of X and Y are 3.0 and 4.0, respectively defined in the main program. The variables XCORD and YCORD in the subprogram will also have same values. The value of THETA is undefined, so the value of BETA when the function is called is also undefined. However, the value of BETA is calculated in the subprogram by the statement

    BETA = ATAN(YCORD/XCORD)*180.0/3.1427

This gives the value of BETA as 53.13 degrees. The variable THETA now has the same value as that of BETA which is 53.13. Thus the subprogram can manipulate the quantities in the storage at will, and upon return of control to the main program, the values in these storage locations remain as last defined by the subprogram. One should be careful in writing subprograms when a function subprogram changes the value of one or more of its arguments.

Before we give a programming example using function subprograms, some examples of invalid function invocation should help a reader in avoiding to make these potential mistakes.

Table 7.2: Examples Involving Invalid Function Subprograms

Calling Program	Function Subprogram	Error Description
K = KON(A,B*2,3.0)	FUNCTION KON(C,D)	Arguments disagree in number
K = LAVIKA(4.0,1,3.0)	FUNCTION LAVIKA(C,D,E)	"1" is integer and "D" is real. Argument type mismatch
X = SUM(Y(3),Z)	FUNCTION SUM(X,Z)	Function cannot invoke inself. Recursion is not allowed in
	A = SUM(2.0,4.0)	FORTRAN
REAL KON ⋮ X = KON(X,Y)	FUNCTION KON(A,B)	KON should be declared as REAL in the subprogram
INTEGER X(50) P = ANV(X(1),−2)	FUNCTION ANV(G(2),4) INTEGER G(50)	Function arguments may not be subscripted variable names and/or constant
INTEGER GOD REAL NUM(10) I = GOD(A,NUM)	FUNCTION GOD(B,C) INTEGER GOD	Function type must precede the word FUNCTION. C must be declared as an array in function subprogram

7.2.6 Programming Example Using Function Subprograms

Example 7.1

A new computer selling store distributes lucky cards to each of its potential customers. Each card has three numbers on it in the range of 1 to 1000. The store manager then draws at random a number from 1 to 1000. If the number drawn by the manager matches any one of the customer's card numbers, the customer gets a discount in rupees equal to his lucky number. Write a FORTRAN program to read a lucky card and determine the discount that the customer receives. For example, if the lucky card contains the numbers 100, 150, 500 and the manager draws the number 150, the customer receives a discount of Rs. 150. To solve this problem, we will write:

(i) A function called RANDOM to generate a random number between two specified integers named LOW and HIGH. The function makes use of an intrinsic function RAN. The argument SEED of the function RAN is an input data. Depending upon the value of SEED, a random number is generated between 0.0 and 1.0 by the function RAN.

(ii) A function called CHECK to determine whether the customer has a lucky number and if so, the function returns the amount won by the customer.

The complete program listing for this is given in Figure 7.2. A sample run is given in Figure 7.3.

7.3 STATEMENT FUNCTIONS

Users now know how to define a function subprogram. The function subprogram, in general, may contain several FORTRAN statements and may produce more than one answer. In cases where the function is so simple that it can be defined with a single FORTRAN statement and produces only one answer, the statement functions can be used as a better choice. Statement functions are generally used when a particular expression needs to be evaluated for different values of variables at different locations in a program unit. These statement functions are defined in the program unit in which they are used. A statement function is nonexecutable and it is evaluated whenever it is referenced in the program. For example, if the function $(x^2 + 1)/(x^3 - 1)$ appears in several different locations throughout the program, a statement function named EQN, can be written as:

$$EQN(X) = (X**2+1.0)/(X**3-1.0)$$

The variable name X used in the definition of the function could have been any real variable name. It is called a *dummy argument* or *dummy variable*, for it serves to define the function and to give the type of the argument for the function. It may be used as a variable elsewhere in the program. For example, the statement function could be written as:

$$EQN(Y) = (Y**2+1.0)/(Y**3-1.0)$$

by replacing dummy variable X by Y. The value to the dummy argument is supplied by the actual argument when it is invoked. The following points should be kept in mind regarding statement functions:

(1) All statement functions must precede the first executable statement of the program but follow all DIMENSION and type declaration statements.

```
***********************************************************************
*          COMPUTER SALES PROMOTION -- LOTTERY PROBLEM                *
***********************************************************************
        INTEGER RANDOM,RANNUM,CARNUM(3)
        CHARACTER*3 RESPON
        RESPON = 'YES'
        DO WHILE(RESPON(1:1).EQ. Y .OR.RESPON(1:1).EQ. y )
          WRITE(6,100)
          READ(5,200) RESPON
          IF (RESPON(1:1).EQ. Y .OR.RESPON(1:1).EQ. y ) THEN
            WRITE(6,300)
            READ(5,*)(CARNUM(I),I=1,3)
* FUNCTION RANDOM IS REFERENCED
            RANNUM = RANDOM(1,1000)
* FUNCTION CHECK IS CALLED
            AMOUNT = CHECK(CARNUM,RANNUM)
            WRITE(6,400)RANNUM,AMOUNT
          END IF
        END DO
100     FORMAT(' TO MATCH A NUMBER, TYPE YES')
200     FORMAT(A3)
300     FORMAT(' ENTER THREE NUMBERS FROM 1 TO 1000')
400     FORMAT(' THE LUCKY NUMBER IS = ',I6,/,
     1  ' THE CUSTOMER WINS Rs. = ',F10.0)
        STOP
        END
*
***********************************************************************
*                        FUNCTION RANDOM                             *
*  THIS FUNCTION GENERATES A RANDOM NUMBER BETWEEN THE INTEGER        *
*  VALUES LOW AND HIGH                                               *
***********************************************************************
*
        INTEGER FUNCTION RANDOM(LOW,HIGH)
        INTEGER LOW,HIGH,SEED
        WRITE(6,100)
        READ(5,*) SEED
        SEED = SEED * 2 + 9999999
        RAND = RAN(SEED)
        RAND = RAND * (HIGH - LOW + 1) + LOW
        RANDOM = RAND
100     FORMAT(  ENTER AN INTEGER NUMBER OF NOT MORE THAN 9 DIGITS
        RETURN
        END
*
***********************************************************************
*                        FUNCTION CHECK                              *
*  THIS FUNCTION CHECKS IF THE CUSTOMER'S NUMBER MATCHES THE         *
*  RANDOM NUMBER AND RETURNS THE AMOUNT THAT IS WON BY HIM/HER.      *
***********************************************************************
*
        FUNCTION CHECK(CARDN,NUM)
        INTEGER CARDN(3)
        CHECK = 0.0
        DO 10 I = 1,3
          IF(CARDN(I).EQ.NUM) CHECK = NUM
10      CONTINUE
        RETURN
        END
***********************************************************************
```

Figure 7.2: Program Listing of Example 7.1.

```
TO MATCH A NUMBER: TYPE YES
YES
ENTER THREE NUMBERS FROM 1 TO 1000
489 294 500
ENTER AN INTEGER NUMBER OF NOT MORE THAN 9 DIGITS
777777777
THE LUCKY NUMBER IS =    294
THE CUSTOMER WINS Rs. =        294.
TO MATCH A NUMBER, TYPE YES
Y
ENTER THREE NUMBERS FROM 1 TO 1000
400 300 538
ENTER AN INTEGER NUMBER OF NOT MORE THAN 9 DIGITS
999998683
THE LUCKY NUMBER IS =    538
THE CUSTOMER WINS Rs. =        538.
TO MATCH A NUMBER, TYPE YES
Wes
ENTER THREE NUMBERS FROM 1 TO 1000
200 300 999
ENTER AN INTEGER NUMBER OF NOT MORE THAN 9 DIGITS
206789279
THE LUCKY NUMBER IS =    866
THE CUSTOMER WINS Rs. =        0.
TO MATCH A NUMBER, TYPE YES
NO
```

Figure 7.3: A Sample Run of Example 7.1.

(2) The statement function may use FORTRAN intrinsic functions, other statement functions defined previously, or function subprograms.

(3) The statement function only defines the function, so it is non-executable.

(4) Execution occurs when the function is invoked at the time of the execution of the FORTRAN statement in which function appears. For example, the function EQN may be used in any of the following manners:

    (a) Z = EQN(3.14)
    (b) Z = EQN(X)+EQN(Y)
    (c) Z = EQN(X+SQRT(5.0)/2.0)+4.0
    (d)   D 10 I = 1,100
           Z = EQN(A(I))
     10   CONTINUE

(5) The statement function must contain at least one argument. It may, however, contain more than one argument. They are separated by commas and like function subprograms, dummy arguments and actual arguments must be consistent with each other.

(6) The statement function may be defined by using variables that do not appear in the argument list of the function. For example, the

function statement to evaluate the quadratic expression $Z = ax^2 + bx + c$ can be written as:

$$Z(X) = A*X*X + B*X + C$$

The variables A, B and C do not appear as arguments, and their current values at the time of calling are used in the function evaluation. So, at the time of invoking the function statement, variables A, B and C must be defined. Variable X is a dummy variable, but A, B and C are not.

(7) A function may not be defined in terms of itself and no recursion is allowed.

(8) Names that are declared as array names in DIMENSION or type statements must not be used as function names. We should not use the names of intrinsic functions as names of the functions we define.

The general form of the statement function definition is:

function name $(a_1[, a_2, a_3, \ldots, a_n]) =$ expression

where

function name is the name of the function (any variable name); $a_1, a_2, \ldots, a_n$ are dummy arguments that must be nonsubscripted variable names; at least one argument must be present; and expression is any arithmetic expression that contains dummy arguments, and possibly other constants, variables, array elements, or intrinsic functions, function subprograms or previously defined statement functions.

7.3.1 Examples of Statement Functions

The following are some examples that illustrate the use of the statement functions.

Example (a)

Consider the program segment

$$IJK(N) = N*(N+1)/2$$
$$\vdots$$

$I = IJK(2)$ The value of I will be 3.
$N = 4$
$J = IJK(N)$ The value of J will be 10.

Note the use of variable N which is used as a dummy argument in the function definition and also used as an ordinary variable in the program.

Example (b)

Consider the program segment

$$EQN(X,Y) = A*X*X+B*X+SQRT(Y)$$
$$\vdots$$

A = 1.0
B = 2.0
Z = EQN(2.0,4.0)
A = 4.0
P(1) = 25.0
U = EQN(3.0,P(1))

The value of Z will be:

$$1.0*2.0*2.0+2.0*2.0+\sqrt{4.0} = 10.0$$

The value of U will be:

$$4.0*3.0*3.0+2.0*3.0+\sqrt{25.0} = 47.0$$

Note the use of intrinsic function SQRT in these function definitions. Current values of A and B are used when a function statement is invoked. The value of the variable A at the first call of the function is 1.0 and at the second call it is changed to 4.0. The value of the variable B at both calls is 2.0.

Example (c)

The following example shows invalid statement function definition or invalid invocation to statement functions:

Description	Reason
IJK = N*(N+1)/2 $\vdots$ I = IJK(N)	Argument needed for IJK
EQN(3.0,X(1)) = 3.0/X(1)	Constants or subscripted variables not allowed
EQN(X,Y) = X + Y $\vdots$ X = EQN(I*J)	Arguments different in number and type
IJK(N) = N + IJK(K)	Recursion not allowed. A function cannot refer to itself.

Example (d)

This example gives a complete program listing to read two values A and B, and prints the larger of (A^2+B^2+4AB) and (A^2+B^2-4AB). The statement functions, F1 and F2, are used to evaluate the expressions (A^2+B^2+4AB) and (A^2+B^2-4AB).

$$F1(X,Y) = X*X+Y*Y+4.0*X*Y$$
$$F2(X,Y) = X*X+Y*Y-4.0*X*Y$$

```
        READ(5,*)A,B
        IF(F1(A,B).GE.F2(A,B))THEN
            X = F1(A,B)
        ELSE
            X = F2(A,B)
        END IF
        WRITE(G,*)A,B,X
        STOP
        END
```

If A = 2.0 and B = 3.0, then F1 = 37.0 and F2 = −11.0, The value of X will be 37.0.

Example (e)

Write a FORTRAN program to calculate the approximate number of days that have elapsed between two dates—D1, M1, Y1 and D2, M2, Y2 where D, M and Y refer to day, month and year. It is assumed that there are an average of 365.25 days in each year and an average of 30.44 days in each month.

We use two statement functions: ITOTAL to calculate the total number of days that have elapsed from the date 0,0,0 to a date D,N,Y; and, IELAPS to calculate the days elapsed between two days:

```
        INTEGER D,M,Y,D1,M1,Y1,D2,M2,Y2
        ITOTAL (D,M,Y) = D+(M-1.0)*30.44+Y*365.25
        IELAPS(D1,M1,Y1,D2,M2, Y2)  = ABS(ITOTAL(D1,M1,Y1)-
        ITOTAL(D2,M2, Y2))
        READ(5,*)D1,M1,Y1,D2,M2,Y2
        NDAYS = IELAPS(D1,M1,Y1,D2,M2,Y2)
        WRITE(6,*) NDAYS
        STOP
        END
```

Note that the statement function IELAPS uses an intrinsic function ABS and a statement function ITOTAL. The statement function ITOTAL has been defined in an earlier line. Both statement functions follow the type statement.

7.4 SUBROUTINE SUBPROGRAMS

We have so far discussed function subprograms. If a subprogram calculates a single value, but does nothing more, the customary practice is to write it as a function subprogram; otherwise, it is written as a subroutine subprogram. The SUBROUTINE differs from the FUNCTION subprogram in the following respects:

(1) The name of the subroutine does not return any numerical value. It is, therefore. not necessary to follow any type declaration convention

while naming a subroutine. The name, however, should be a valid variable name.

(2) In the naming of the subprogram, the word SUBROUTINE replaces the word FUNCTION in the definition statement. The general form of the SUBROUTINE statement is:

SUBROUTINE subroutine name [(p₁,p₂,p₃, . . . ,pₙ)]

The dummy arguments $p_1, p_2, \ldots, p_n$ have the same meaning as defined in the FUNCTION definition statement. These arguments including the parentheses are optional and may be omitted. However, in the FUNCTION definition statement parentheses are not optional and must be provided. The following program segment gives a SUB-ROUTINE subprogram for calculating the factorial of a number:

```
    SUBROUTINE FACT (K, IFACT)
    IFACT = 1
    DO 10 I = 1,K
        IFACT = IFACT*I
 10 CONTINUE
    RETURN
    END
```

(3) The only means of communicating with the subroutine is via either the arguments or the common block. So we need an additional variable IFACT as an argument of the SUBROUTINE FACT in order to transfer the factorial of K back to the calling program.

(4) A subroutine is accessed (or called) from another program through the CALL statement. The subroutine cannot be used in an arithmetic assignment statement as no numerical value is associated with its name. The general form of the CALL statement is:

CALL subroutine name [(a₁,a₂,a₃, . . . ,aₙ)]

where

CALL is a required keyword;

$a_1, a_2, \ldots, a_n$ are actual arguments, and have the same meaning as defined in the FUNCTION INVOCATION (CALLING) STATEMENT described in Section 7.3.

Examples

```
    CALL FACT(N, IFACT)
    CALL ANGLE(X,Y, THETA,ARG)
    CALL PLUS(A,B (2), SIN (X), 4*K+N,NAVG)
```

The CALL statement is an executable statement. Whenever a subroutine is to be called, a transfer is made to that subroutine through the CALL statement. Upon exiting from the subroutine the control is transferred to the statement immediately following the CALL statement in the calling program.

The SUBROUTINE subprogram follows more or less the same rules as the FUNCTION subprogram. These are listed as follows:

(1) The logical end of a SUBROUTINE (or exit from a SUBROUTINE) is the RETURN statement. Many RETURN statements can be included in a subroutine.

(2) The physical end of a SUBROUTINE is an END statement.

(3) A SUBROUTINE may not call itself and no recursion is allowed.

(4) The concept of "communication" of variables between the called and the calling program is analogous to the one described in the FUNCTION subprogram.

(5) Use of subscripted variables in the SUBROUTINE and in the FUNCTION is analogous.

(6) The arguments in the CALL statement should correspond in number, order and type to the dummy arguments. of the SUBROUTINE statement. The same is true of the FUNCTION subprograms.

(7) Identical variable names and statement numbers can appear in both the calling and the called program with no risk of confusion.

7.4.1 Examples of Subroutine Subprograms

To illustrate the differences and similarities discussed above and the concepts involved with SUBROUTINES, three examples of subroutine subprograms are given below:

(a) a subroutine that uses no arguments.

(b) a subroutine that uses arguments.

(c) a subroutine that uses an array.

Example (a)

Let us write a subroutine that prints a row of fifty asterisks. The name of the subroutine is ASTRSK.

Subroutine	Main Program
SUBROUTINE ASTRSK	———————
WRITE (6,100)	———————
100 FORMAT(' ', 50 ('*'))	CALL ASTRSK
RETURN	———————
END	———————
	CALL ASTRSK
	———————
	END

Each time the statement
CALL ASTRSK

is encountered during the program execution, a row of fifty asterisks will be printed.

Example (b)
We will write a subroutine SWAP(X, Y) that interchanges the values of its
two arguments. That is, it sets X equal to the old value of Y, and sets Y
equal to the old value of X.

Subroutine	Main Program
SUBROUTINE SWAP(X,Y)	————————
TEMP = X	————————
X = Y	CALL SWAP (A, B)
Y = TEMP	————————
RETURN	————————
END	END

Whenever the statement
        CALL SWAP (A,B)

is encountered during program execution, the values of A and B are interchanged. Note that A and B must be variables, not constants, since SWAP
changes the values of its arguments. One must remember that if a subroutine
changes the value of a dummy argument, the corresponding actual arguments
must be a variable and neither a constant nor an expression. This is also true
of function subprograms.

What would happen if the statement
        CALL SWAP (5.0,3.0)

is used in the main program?
When the above statement is encountered during the execution of the
program, control is transferred to the subroutine SWAP and the dummy
arguments X and Y are assigned values. 5.0 and 3.0, respectively. The statement

        TEMP = X

then assigns variable TEMP a value of 5.0. The next statement

        X = Y

gives

        5.0 = 3.0

which is an invalid equality and it does not comply with the FORTRAN
expression rules. One must, therefore, exercise extreme care in the use of
arguments in a subprogram. A dummy argument may be one of the three
types:

(1) Input arguments—that provide values to the subprogram to use in
    its operation and are **not** modified by the subprogram.
(2) Output argument—that the subprogram calculates and returns to the
    calling program.
(3) Input/Output arguments—that furnish values to the subroutine, are
    modified in the subroutine, and are passed back to the calling pro-
    gram. Input/Output arguments are also known as *mixed arguments*.

The actual arguments corresponding to the output dummy arguments and/ or input/output dummy arguments should be neither constants nor expressions. In the earlier example, dummy arguments X and Y are input/output arguments and therefore corresponding actual arguments must not be either constants or expressions.

Example (c)

To illustrate a subroutine that uses an array, let us consider a subroutine named TRANSP, which transposes a square matrix. The array name and the size of the array are passed to the subroutine as the arguments. For example, for a square array A(N,N), the name of the array is A and its size is N. The transpose of an array is obtained by interchanging the elements of the corresponding rows and columns. The transpose of a 3×3 matrix is shown below:

$$A = \begin{bmatrix} 1 & 2 & 3 \\ 4 & 5 & 6 \\ 7 & 8 & 9 \end{bmatrix} \qquad A^T = \begin{bmatrix} 1 & 4 & 7 \\ 2 & 5 & 8 \\ 3 & 6 & 9 \end{bmatrix}$$

where A^T is the transpose of matrix A. Note that diagonal entries remain unchanged and the other entries are given by

$$A^T(I,J) = A(J,I).$$

The subroutine and the main program are:

```
Subroutine                      Main Program
SUBROUTINE TRANSP (A,N)         DIMENSION X(3,3),Y(2,2)
DIMENSION A(N,N)                    ⋮
DO 10 I = 1,N                   CALL TRANSP (X,3)
    DO 10 J = I+1,N                 ⋮
                                CALL TRANSP (Y,2)
        TEMP = A(I,J)               ⋮
        A(I,J) = A (J,I)        STOP
        A(J,I) = TEMP           END
10  CONTINUE
    RETURN
    END
```

The two CALL statements in the main program result in two calls on the SUBROUTINE TRANSP. At the first call, the matrix X is transposed, while at the second call, matrix Y is transposed. The subroutine receives the value of these matrices under the matrix name A. The matrix A is dimensioned as an N by N, while the dimensions of matrices X and Y are 3 by 3 and 2 by 2 respectively. Note that the dimensions of the matrix A match the dimensions of the matrices X and Y. It is quite valid to declare a matrix in the subprogram having variable dimensions. We shall discuss this at length in a later section. Variable N is an input argument and that is why it is permissible to supply the constant as an actual argument. On the other hand, the array variable is an input/output argument and therefore the corresponding actual argument cannot be a constant or expression.

It may be noticed that the statements inside the DO loops basically interchange two variables A(I,J) and A(J,I). These statements could have been replaced by calling the subroutine SWAP described earlier. The modified subroutine will be as follows:

```
      SUBROUTINE TRANSP(A,N)
      DIMENSION A(20,20)
      DO 10 I = 1,N
        DO 10 J = I + 1,N
          CALL SWAP(A(I,J),A(J,I))
   10 CONTINUE
      RETURN
      END
```

These examples should help the user understand the many ways in which subroutine subprograms can be used. Subprograms are very powerful tools in FORTRAN and they make programming jobs quite easy. They should be used wherever feasible, to provide a modular approach to programming and to make a program more understandable and easier to debug. The advantage of the modular approach is that once a module of a program has been tested and debugged, one can forget about it and concentrate on testing other modules.

The next section briefly describes subprogram structure diagrams.

7.5. SUBPROGRAM STRUCTURE DIAGRAMS

In FORTRAN programs, particularly large and complex programs, using subprograms it is often useful to show the relationship between the called program(s) and calling program(s) with a diagram. The common method is to represent each program or subprogram by a rectangular box and to draw a line between boxes to represent a *subroutine call* or a *function reference*. The relation between a main program calling subroutine A is shown in Figure 7.4

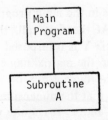

Figure 7.4: Subprogram Structure Diagram.

The structure diagram for transposing a square matrix is shown in Figure 7.5. The main program calls the subroutine TRANSP and the subroutine TRANSP calls the subroutine SWAP. Depending on the size of a program, subprogram structure diagrams can be quite complex. Figure 7.6 shows one such diagram. The calling sequence is also given.

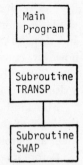

Figure 7.5: Subprogram Structure Diagram for Transposing a Matrix.

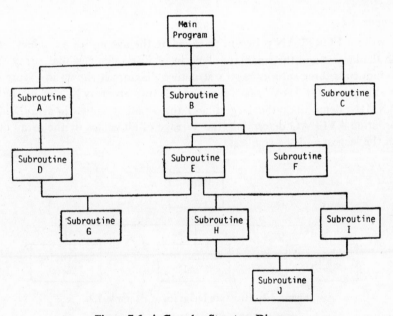

Figure 7.6: A Complex Structure Diagram.

Calling Program(s)		*Called Program(s)*
Main program	calls	subroutine A, B and C
subroutine A	calls	subroutine D
subroutine B	calls	subroutines E and F
subroutine D	calls	subroutine G
subroutine E	calls	subroutines G, H and I
subroutine H	calls	subroutine J
subroutine I	calls	subroutine J

Notice that the subroutine G is called by both subroutines D and E and similarly subroutine J is called by subroutines H and I. This is quite valid and this situation arises in many practical programming jobs. Many people, however, consider this as a dangerous practice, since a change in subroutine G would affect both subroutines D and E. One must, however, be careful if such a situation is ever encountered.

This kind of subprogram structure diagram does not show anything about the logic of the subprogram, but it clearly illustrates the relationship among them and greatly helps in developing a structure design for a problem.

Before discussing some more important concepts associated with the subprograms, we will give a programming example that illustrates the use of subroutines.

7.6 PROGRAMMING EXAMPLE
USING SUBROUTINE SUBPROGRAMS

Example 7.2

We write a FORTRAN program to calculate the average of all values other than the largest and the smallest values in a single dimensional array. The program calls three subroutines. A structure diagram is shown in Figure 7.7. The subroutine GETDAT reads input values into an array X. The subroutine MAXMIN determines the largest and the smallest values in array X. The subroutine AVERAG determines the average of all values in the array other than the largest and the smallest.

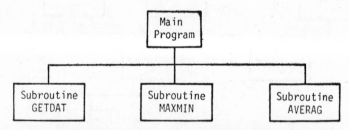

Figure 7.7: Structure Diagram of Example 7.2.

The complete program is shown in Figure 7.8. The input data and the output results are given in Figure 7.9.

7.7 VARIABLE ARRAY DIMENSIONS

These are also called *adjustable array declarations* or *object time dimensions*. Arrays that are passed from one program to another must be declared as arrays in the subprograms through appropriate type declaration statements. In the calling program, it is necessary to specify the dimention size of arrays as a numeric constant, so that the proper amount of adjacent storage locations are assigned during compilation. Within the called program, however, we can

```
*********************************************************************
*  THIS PROGRAM CALCULATES THE AVERAGE OF ALL VALUES OTHER THAN   *
*  THE LARGEST AND THE SMALLEST VALUES IN A VECTOR X.             *
*********************************************************************
         REAL X(1000)
*  CALL TO SUBROUTINE GETDAT
         CALL GETDAT(X,N)
*  CALL TO SUBROUTINE MAXMIN
         CALL MAXMIN(X,N,BIG,SMALL)
*  CALL TO SUBROUTINE AVERAG
         CALL AVERAG(X,N,BIG,SMALL,AVG)
         WRITE(6,100)N,BIG,SMALL,AVG
100      FORMAT(' TOTAL NUMBER OF VALUSES READ =',I6,/,
     1   ' THE LARGEST   VALUE = ',F10.3,/,
     1   ' THE SMALLEST VALUE = ',F10.3,/,
     1   ' THE  AVERAGE   VALUE = ',F10.3)
         STOP
         END
*
*********************************************************************
*                        SUBROUTINE GETDAT                        *
*  THIS SUBROUTINE READS THE INPUT VALUES INTO AN ARRAY X. IT     *
*  CHECKS FOR AN ERROR IN THE NUMBER OF INPUT VALUES. NOTE THE    *
*  USE OF THE STOP STATEMENT IN THE SUBROUTINE                    *
*********************************************************************
*
         SUBROUTINE GETDAT(X,N)
         REAL X(1000)
         OPEN(UNIT=1,FILE='EX7_2.DAT',STATUS='OLD')
         READ(1,*)N
         IF(N.LT.1.OR.N.GT.1000) STOP
         READ(1,*)(X(I),I=1,N)
         CLOSE(UNIT=1)
         RETURN
         END
*
*********************************************************************
*                        SUBROUTINE MAXMIN                        *
*  THIS SUBROUTINE DETERMINES THE LARGEST (BIG) AND THE SMALLEST  *
*  (SMALL) ENTERIES IN ARRAY X OF SIZE N. NOTE THE USE OF VARIABLE*
*  ARRAY DIMENSION.                                               *
*********************************************************************
*
         SUBROUTINE MAXMIN(X,N,BIG,SMALL)
         REAL X(N)
         BIG = X(1)
         SMALL = X(1)
         DO 10 I = 1,N
           IF(BIG.LT.X(I)) THEN
             BIG = X(I)
           ELSE IF(SMALL.GT.X(I)) THEN
             SMALL = X(I)
           END IF
10       CONTINUE
         RETURN
         END
*
```

(Figure 7.8—Contd.)

```
**************************************************************************
*                     SUBROUTINE AVERAG                                 ,
*  THIS SUBROUTINE DETERMINES THE AVERAGE OF ALL VALUES OTHER           *
*  THAN THE LARGEST AND THE SMALLEST VALUES.                            ,
**************************************************************************
*
         SUBROUTINE AVERAG(X,N,BIG,SMALL,AVG)
         REAL X(N)
         SUM = 0.0
         NUM = 0
         DO 10 I = 1,N
           IF(X(I).NE.BIG.AND.X(I).NE.SMALL) THEN
             SUM = SUM + X(I)
             NUM = NUM + 1
           END IF
10       CONTINUE
         AVG = SUM / NUM
         RETURN
         END
**************************************************************************
```

Figure 7.8: Program Listing of Example 7.2.

```
   30
   1.0 3.0 5.4 6.0 4.0 13.0 4.9 3.6 0.2 45.0
   3.7 5.8 3.2 1.8 3.6 43.0 3.7 5.9 2.5 12.0
   2.8 3.1 9.7 3.2 3.7 26.8 4.7 4.9 3.9 39.8
```

Figure 7.9.1: Input Data of Example 7.2.

```
   TOTAL NUMBER OF VALUSES READ =      30
   THE LARGEST   VALUE =     45.000
   THE SMALLEST  VALUE =      0.200
   THE AVERAGE   VALUE =      8.179
   FORTRAN STOP
```

Figure 7.9.2: Output Results of Example 7.2.

postpone declaring the dimension size of arrays until execution time; that is, we can specify the dimension size of arrays in the called program as a variable. For example, in a subprogram, we can write:

DIMENSION A(N)

where the value of N is not provided until the execution of the subprogram. This type of declaration feature is quite useful in writing subprograms that have to process arrays of different dimensions. Consider the example of transposing a square matrix discussed earlier. Had we declared matrix A in the subroutine of size 3 by 3 using the statement

DIMENSION A(3,3)
in place of the statement
DIMENSION A(N,N)

in the subroutine, there would have been no problem in transposing matrix X, because both matrices X and A have same dimension. But let us see what happens when the statement

CALL TRANSP(Y,2)

is executed. Assume that matrix X is given as follows:

$$Y = \begin{bmatrix} 1 & 2 \\ 3 & 4 \end{bmatrix}$$

In Chapter, 6, we noted that a two dimensional array, by convention in FORTRAN 77, is stored by columns. The entries of Y are stored in the following column-by-column order:

```
Y(1,1)[    1    ]
Y(2,1)[    3    ] } Column 1
Y(1,2)[    2    ]
Y(2,2)[    4    ] } Column 2
```

When the statement

CALL TRANSP(Y,2)

is encountered, control passes to the subroutine with the following correspondence being set-up:

A(1,1)$\longleftrightarrow$Y(1,1), and the rest of the entries correspond in the column-by-column order

N$\longrightarrow$2

The size of matrix A is 3 by 3, and A(1,1) and Y(1,1) share the same storage unit, so we obtain the following correspondence between arrays A and Y:

```
                  Array_Y              Array_A
column 1 { Y(1,1) [   1   ]   A(1,1) }
           Y(2,1) [   3   ]   A(2,1) } column 1
column 2 { Y(1,2) [   2   ]   A(3,1) }
           Y(2,2) [   4   ]   A(1,2) }
                  [  :    ]   A(2,2) } column 2
                  [  :    ]     :    }
                              :    } column 3
```

One can immediately see the mismatching between the elements of matrix A and Y. Depending on the compiler, one will either receive an error message or the remaining five entries of matrix A will be assigned as zeros. So matrix A will be as follows:

$$A = \begin{bmatrix} 1 & 4 & 0 \\ 3 & 0 & 0 \\ 2 & 0 & 0 \end{bmatrix}$$

After executing the DO loops, matrix A will be modified as follows:

$$A = \begin{bmatrix} 1 & 3 & 0 \\ 4 & 0 & 0 \\ 2 & 0 & 0 \end{bmatrix}$$

Notice that $N = 2$, so the last row and the last column are not interchanged. After returning from the subroutine, the transpose of matrix Y will be given as follows:

$$Y^T = \begin{bmatrix} 1 & 2 \\ 4 & 3 \end{bmatrix}$$

This is not correct because the transpose of matrix Y should be:

$$Y^T = \begin{bmatrix} 1 & 3 \\ 2 & 4 \end{bmatrix}$$

The difficulty in this program is due to the different dimensions assigned to matrices Y and A. To avoid this difficulty one must dimension the dummy array A just as the array Y is dimensioned in the main program. This is accomplished by using the variable array dimension feature; which allows the user to adjust the size of the array in the subprogram to the size of the corresponding array in the main program (or calling program). Using this feature, it is possible to write subprograms that can be used, without modification, for many different programming tasks. A question that may arise here is what happens if matrices involved are not square matrices? In that situation, it is necessary to match both the dimensions of both matrices (dummy and actual), since the number of rows is not equal to the number of columns.

The general rule is that the first $n-1$ (n minus 1, where n is the number of dimensions) subscripts of the subprogram's DIMENSION statements must correspond to the dimensions in the main program. For a two-dimensional array (or a matrix), the first (row) subscript must have the same dimension as the corresponding actual array argument in the main program. The size of the second (column) subscript in the subprogram need not agree with the size of the second subscript in the main program. For three-dimensional arrays in a subprogram, the first two (row and column) subscripts must have the same size as the array being passed by the main program. For a one-dimensional array in a subprogram, according to the general rule, it is not necessary to have the same dimension as the corresponding actual array argument in the main program.

In the next section the EQUIVALENCE statement is discussed. This statement allows multiple variables to be assigned the same memory location.

7.8 THE EQUIVALENCE STATEMENT

The EQUIVALENCE statement is a non-executable statement that can be used to share storage location; it assigns two or more variables in the same program unit to the same storage location in the computer's memory. For example, the statement

EQUIVALENCE (X,Y)

causes the variables X and Y to share the same storage location, and hence, have the same value. Changing the value of either X or Y changes the value of both. X and Y should be thought of as different names for the same memory location.

Similarly, the statement

EQUIVALENCE (A,B), (NO,N), (X,XX,XXX,XXXX)

specifies that the variables A and B share the same memory location. NO and N occupy the same storage locations and X, XX, XXX, XXXX all refer to the same memory locations. The general form of an EQUIVALENCE statement is:

EQUIVALENCE (namel, name2,…,namen), (namel,…namem),…

where

name represents a variable or a subscripted array element; all names within the same set of parentheses refer to the same storage location; if name represents an array name, the subscript must be an integer constant.

It is allowable to have equivalence variables of different types. This may cause problems, however, due to the different internal representations of numbers.

The EQUIVALENCE statement can be helpful in at least two ways:

(1) In a program, if two different names (or different spellings of the same name) are used to denote the same quantity, we can use an EQUI-VALENCE statement—instead of changing the program—to associate both the names with the same storage location. For example, if variables RESIS and OHM both represent resistance, the statement

EQUIVALENCE (RESIS,OHM)

causes both to refer to the same memory location. That means variables RESIS and OHM will be equivalent and changing the value of one changes the value of the other.

(2) The second use of the EQUIVALENCE statement is to minimize the amount of memory space required to execute a program. This applies especially for arrays than for nonsubscripted variables. Suppose, that in the early portion of a program, a single-dimensional array, NUM, is required and later in the program, after all references to NUM are concluded, another single

dimensional array, KEEP, is needed. If we use the same storage locations for both of these arrays, we can save a great deal of memory space. For example, if arrays NUM and KEEP are of sizes 500 and 400 respectively, we can write:

DIMENSION NUM(500),KEEP(400)
EQUIVALENCE (NUM(1),KEEP(1))

The EQUIVALENCE statement equalizes the first element in each array, but since each array is stored sequentially, 500 memory locations will be reserved, as needed for the array NUM, and the first 400 of these will be used for the array KEEP. So the number of locations is reduced by 400. The correspondence between the entries in two arrays is schematically shown as follows:

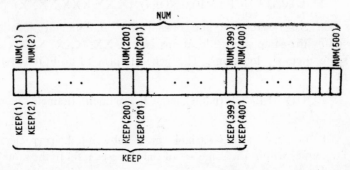

EQUIVALENCE statements can be used to associate any of the entries (not just the first entries) in two arrays with the same storage location. For example, if elements NUM(50) and KEEP(25) are equivalenced, the storage scheme appears as follows:

Similarly, it is possible to equalize higher-dimensional arrays with one-dimensional array. For example, the statements

DIMENSION A(4,3),B(3),C(2,2),D(5)
EQUIVALENCE (A(1,1),B(1)),(A(1,2),C(2,1)),(A(4,2),D(1))

cause storage to be arranged as follows:

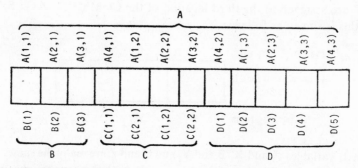

Note that for higher dimensional arrays, the first subscript varies most rapidly, while the latter ones are varied the least rapidly, because arrays are stored by columns as explained in Chapter 6. These concepts are quite useful in conjunction with the COMMON statement discussed in the next section.

7.9 THE COMMON STATEMENT

Up to this point we have emphasized that subroutine and function subprograms are independent program units, compiled separately from the main program. This means that variable names that appear in a program unit are local to that program unit. The only way for communication (passing values) of variables between program units so far seems to be through the correspondence set up between dummy and actual arguments. But there is another way by which program units can communicate with each other. This is COMMON STORAGE AREA (called a COMMON BLOCK), which is used by means of the COMMON statement. Variables and/or arrays to be stored among program units are declared in a COMMON statement. The common block may be thought of as a block of memory locations that can be accessed by proaram units containing a COMMON statement. A COMMON statement must be included in every program unit that is to share variables and arrays.

Suppose the three variables A, B and C are to be assigned to the common storage area and these are to be accessed by different program units. The COMMON statement

COMMON A,B,C

would be included in each program unit that needs to reference these variables. The names of variables used in the COMMON statement may, however, be different in various program units—the ordering and length of the variables in the COMMON statement determines which names in one program unit will be associated with which names in another program unit. If the above statement is included in the main program, and the statement

COMMON X,Y,Z

is included in a subroutine subprogram, then A and X are assigned to the first location of the common block, B and Y refer to the second location, and

C and Z are assigned to the third location of the COMMON block. Schematically, this is shown as follows:

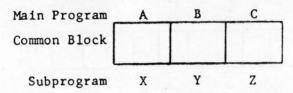

In fact, variables A and X, B and Y, and C and Z are really the same. If the main program assigns a value of 2.0 to variable A, then when the subroutine is called, X will also have the value 2.0, since X is on the same memory location as A. Now if the value of X is altered to 4.0 in the subprogram, then that would become the current value of A when control is returned to the main program.

The general form of the COMMON statement is:

COMMON name1, name 2, ..., namen

where name1,...,namen are variable names or array names.

The COMMON statement is a non-executable declaration which must be placed at the beginning of the programming unit, before the first executable statement. The following example illustrates the use of COMMON statement:

Example

Main Program	Subprogram
DIMENSION X(4), Y(2,2)	SUBROUTINE SUB (D,E)
COMMON X,A,N,Y,J	DIMENSION U(3), V(2,2)
⋮	COMMON U,A,AA,I,V
CALL SUB (B,C)	⋮
⋮	RETURN
STOP	
	END
END	

The COMMON statement in the main program sets up the following common block:

```
X(1)
X(2)
X(3)
X(4)
A
N
Y(1,1)
Y(2,1)
Y(1,2)
Y(2,2)
J
```

The COMMON statement in the subroutine subprograms sets up the following correspondence:

```
X(1)  ┌────────────┐  U(1)
X(2)  │            │  U(2)
X(3)  │            │  U(3)
X(4)  │            │  A
   A  │            │  AA
   N  │            │  I
Y(1,1)│            │  V(1,1)
Y(2,1)│            │  V(2,1)
Y(1,2)│            │  V(1,2)
Y(2,2)│            │  V(2,2)
   J  └────────────┘
```

Note that variable A in the subroutine and the variable A in the main program are not the same. Variable A in the subroutine and X(4) in the main program refer to the same memory location, while variable A in the main program and the variable AA in the subroutine refer to the same memory location. The same is true for other variables. J refers to the last memory location of the block. It is not used by the subroutine SUB; it could be used by another subprogram. The COMMON statement can also be used with the FUNCTION subprograms.

Three important points that govern the use of COMMON statements are:

(1) A program unit may have several COMMON statements, but only one common block is set up. For example, the pair of statements

COMMON A,B,C,M
COMMON X(10), LIST(100), D

is equivalent to the single statement

COMMON A,B,C,M,X(10), LIST(100), D

(2) The COMMON statement can be used instead of a type or DIMENSION statement to declare arrays. The following three program segments have the same effect:

DIMENSION X(100)
COMMON   X

or

REAL   X(100)
COMMON   X

or

COMMON   X(100)

However,

REAL   X(100)
COMMON   X(100)

is illegal.

(3) The memory location in the common block can be associated with different variable names in different program units.

A COMMON statement is different from the EQUIVALENCE statement, which treats only variables within the same program unit. The COMMON statement causes variables in different program units to be stored in the same memory location.

Program units may communicate via either the COMMON statement or the arguments, but a variable or an array must not be accessed by both methods. That is, a variable used as a dummy argument must not appear in the COMMON statement. The use of the COMMON statement not only eliminates the necessity of establishing an argument list but also provides a more efficient technique.

The type of common block discussed above is called BLANK COMMON or UNLABELED COMMON, since no name is assigned to the common block. Only one blank common block can be established in a FORTRAN program. In situations where more than one common block is required, labeled COMMON statements may be used. These are discussed in the following section.

7.9.1 Labeled (Named) Common Blocks

Variables and arrays declared in a COMMON statement are available to any program unit in which the COMMON statement appears. In many instances, the number of variables contained in the COMMON statement is large and all program units do not require access to all variables. For example, consider a main program with two subprograms. Variables X, Y and Z are to be in COMMON with one subprogram and variables X, TOT(4), N, NUM(2) are to be in COMMON with the other subprogram. In such a case it is possible to construct labeled blocks of COMMON. These labeled or named COMMON blocks allow subprograms to access only those COMMON blocks that are needed. The following code shows such an arrangement:

Main program	Subprogram
COMMON/BLK1/X	SUBROUTINE SUB1
COMMON/BLK2/Y,Z	COMMON/BLK1/XX
COMMON/BLK3/TOT(4), N,	
NUM(2)	COMMON/BLK2/X, ZZ
⋮	⋮
CALL SUB1	END
⋮	SUBROUTINE SUB2
CALL SUB2	
⋮	COMMON/BLK1/X
END	COMMON/BLK3/TOT(4), N,
	NUMBER(2)
	⋮
	END

The association of variables with the memory locations in these labeled common blocks is as follows:

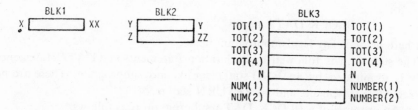

Variable name may differ between program units, but label names must be the same. No variable can be in more than one labeled COMMON, and therefore we have to use a separate COMMON block for X. Two or more labeled COMMON blocks may be written in only one COMMON statement, as illustrated below for the main program in the above example:

COMMON/BLK1/X/BLK2/Y, Z/BLK3/TOT(4), N, NUM(2)

The general form of the labeled COMMON statement is:

COMMON/block namel/namel, . . ., namen/block name2/namel, . . .

where

block name is the name of the common block;
name is the name of a variable or an array; and
slashes (/) are a required part of the statement.

Both blank common items and labeled common blocks may be listed in the same COMMON statement. For example:

COMMON X, Y/BLK1/X (10), ME (20), I

This statement can also be written as:

COMMON / / X, Y/BLK1/X (10), ME (20), I

The double slash (/ /) appearing after COMMON indicates the absence of a label for the first common block.

The next section discusses a special type of subprogram called BLOCK DATA.

7.10 BLOCK DATA SUBPROGRAMS

In Chapter 5, you have seen how the nonexecutable DATA statement can be used to initialize program variables and arrays. DATA statements alone are not adequate for initializing variables or arrays associated with the labeled or named COMMON blocks. Instead, a small subprogram beginning with the words BLOCK DATA must be used. The BLOCK DATA subprogram contains no executable statements. Only declaration statements (such as INTEGER DIMENSION, labeled COMMON blocks, etc.) and

DATA statements may be used. The BLOCK DATA subprogram begins with the statement

        BLOCK DATA

    or

        BLOCK DATA name

where name is any legal subprogram name.
The statement is followed by declaration statements and DATA statements. It is terminated by an END statement like any subprogram. There are no executable statements and no RETURN statements.

    An example of a BLOCK DATA subprogram is as follows:

        BLOCK DATA
        INTEGER X, Y
        REAL NUM, I, II
        DIMENSION ANT(5), B(2)
        COMMON/BLK1/TOT, ANT, X, NUM, P, Q
        COMMON/BLK2/Y, I, B
        DATA X, Y/5, 6/TOT/0.5/
        DATA ANT(1), ANT(2), ANT(3), ANT(4), ANT(5) /5*0.0/,
        II/4.6/
        DATA B(1), B(2)/4.0, 5.0/
        EQUIVALENCE (I,II)
        END

The above subprogram initializes variables as shown below:

	BLK1			BLK2	
TOT	0.5		Y	6	
ANT(1)	0.0		I	4.6	II
ANT(2)	0.0		B(1)	4.0	
ANT(3)	0.0		B(2)	5.0	
ANT(4)	0.0				
ANT(5)	0.0				
X	5				
NUM					
P					
Q					

    It is not necessary to initialize all variables in a labeled COMMON block. For example, variables NUM, P and Q are not initialized.

7.11 EXTERNAL AND INTRINSIC STATEMENTS

A dummy argument of a function or a subroutine subprogram may itself be a subprogram name. For example, the argument FUNC in the following function definition is a function itself.

        REAL FUNCTION GET (FUNC, Z, Y)
        GET = FUNC (Z+Y)
        RETURN
        END

If the main program contains the statement

X = GET (FUN, A, B)

where FUN is some function subprogram name, it must have a way of informing the FORTRAN compiler that FUN is a subprogram name, rather than a variable, so that the argument can be passed correctly. It does so by declaring the user written function FUN by an EXTERNAL statement of the form

EXTERNAL FUN

If FUN is available in the FORTRAN language library (an intrinsic function such as SIN, SQRT, TAN, etc.) the declaration is then made by using INTRINSIC statement:

INTRINSIC FUN

In general, when an actual argument to a subprogram is a subprogram name or an intrinsic function name, the calling program must declare the argument by including an EXTERNAL or INTRINSIC statement. Note that these statements are included in the calling program and not in the program unit that is being called.

The general from of the INTRINSIC and EXTERNAL statements are:

EXTERNAL name$_1$, name$_2$, ...

INTRINSIC name$_a$, name$_b$, ...

where

name$_1$, name$_2$, . . . are the names of user written subprograms to be used as arguments;

name$_a$, name$_b$, . . . are the names of intrinsic functions to be used as arguments.

7.12 MULTIPLE ENTRY AND RETURN

The normal entry into a subprogram (SUBROUTINE or FUNCTION) occurs where the subprogram is referenced. The subprogram is entered into at the very first executable statement following the FUNCTION or SUBROUTINE definition statement. There are times when one may wish to enter a subprogram at a point different from the first statement. The ENTRY statement allows the user to enter a subprogram at different points in the subprogram. The general form of this statement, which appears in the subprogram, is:

ENTRY name (p$_1$, p$_2$, p$_3$, . . . , p$_n$)

where

name is the name of the entry point into the subprogram; it can be any valid variable name (in a function subprogram, this name returns a value to the calling program); and

p$_1$, p$_2$ . . . are dummy arguments analogous to the arguments in a FUNCTION or SUBROUTINE statement.

The ENTRY statement is a nonexecutable statement, and the entry into the subprogram is at the first executable statement following the ENTRY statement. An ENTRY statement, however, must not be placed within the range of a DO loop. The arguments in the ENTRY statement may or may not be identical to the arguments in the FUNCTION or SUBPROGRAM statement.

Consider the following example where FUNCTION POLY calculates the value of the polynomial $Y = AX^3 + BX^2 + CX + D$. Also, the first time when the FUNCTION is called, the value of A, B, C and D must be read and returned to the calling program. The function subprogram is given as follows:

```
FUNCTION POLY (A, B, C, D, X)
READ (5, *) A, B, C, D
ENTRY POLYNM(X)
POLY = D+X*(C+X*(B+X*A))
RETURN
END
```

A plausible main program for calling above function could be:

```
*Main Program
    ⋮
Y = POLY (A, B, C, D, X)
    ⋮
Z = POLYNM (X)
    ⋮
END
```

The first reference to the statement $Y = POLY(A, B, C, D, X)$ in the main program is to FUNCTION POLY. This causes variables A, B, C and D to be read, and then executes the arithmetic statement ignoring the ENTRY statement because it is a nonexecutable statement. The second reference in the statement

$$Z = POLYNM(X)$$

is to POLYNM. This causes execution to start at the first executable statement after ENTRY statement. It therefore calculates the function POLY without reading variables A, B, C, and D. Notice that the ENTRY statements are not the same as the FUNCTION statements.

The diagram on the next page shows the sequence of operations:

Just as it may be desirable to enter a subprogram at different points, it may also be desirable to return to some statement other than the statement immediately following the CALL statements (multiple returns apply only to SUBROUTINE subprograms).

The general form of the multiple return is:

$$\text{CALL name } (a_1, a_2, *s_1, a_3, *s_2, \ldots)$$

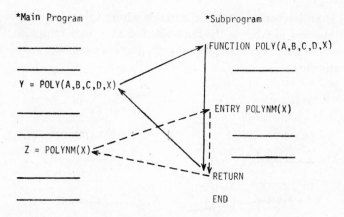

```
*Main Program                    *Subprogram

_____                          ↗ FUNCTION POLY(A,B,C,D,X)
_____                          _____

Y = POLY(A,B,C,D,X)               _____

_____                          ↗ ENTRY POLYNM(X)

_____                          _____

Z = POLYNM(X)                     _____

_____                          RETURN

_____                          END
```

where

> name is a valid subroutine name;
>
> $a_1, a_2, \ldots$ are actual arguments analogous to the arguments in a CALL statement;
>
> $s_1, s_2, \ldots$ are statement numbers of statements in the calling program where control is to be returned [these must be preceded by the asterisk (*) or the ampersand (&) symbol in the argument list to differentiate them from integer constants]; these can be specified in any order in the CALL argument list.

In the SUBROUTINE subprograms, the following format is used:

> SUBROUTINE name $(p_1, p_2, *, p_3, *, \ldots)$
>
> $\vdots$
>
> RETURN1
>
> $\vdots$
>
> RETURN3
>
> $\vdots$
>
> RETURN2
>
> $\vdots$
>
> RETURN
> END

where

> asterisks (*) are used to correspond with the $*s_1, *s_2, \ldots$ in the calling program's CALL argument list;
>
> RETURN1 means execution returns to the calling program to the statement corresponding to the first * encountered in the CALL argument list; RETURN2 means returning to the second * in the argument list; and so on.

Notice that the RETURN statement is of the form:

> RETURNi

where i is an integer constant or variable whose value denotes the location of the statement number in the argument list at which return to the main program is to be made. The following program segment shows the sequence of operations:

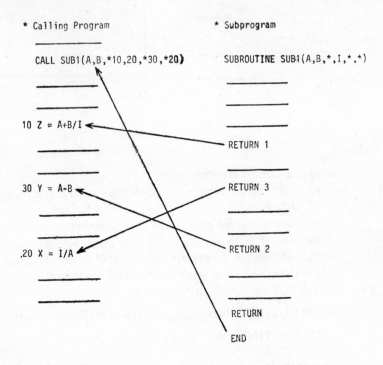

```
* Calling Program                    * Subprogram
_____                      _____

  CALL SUB1(A,B,*10,20,*30,*20)         SUBROUTINE SUB1(A,B,*,I,*,*)
  _____                       _____

  _____                       _____

10 Z = A+B/I                            _____

  _____                          RETURN 1

  _____                       _____

30 Y = A-B                                 RETURN 3

  _____                       _____

.20 X = I/A                                RETURN 2

  _____                       _____

  _____                          RETURN

                                         END
```

7.13 THE SAVE STATEMENT

The SAVE statement is a declarative statement used to specify that the values of certain variables in a subprogram are to remain defined even after the subprogram executes a RETURN or an END statement. Normally when a subprogram returns, the values of all variables in the subprogram become undefined except for the following:

1. Variables in the argument list
2. Variables in blank COMMON
3. Variables in a labeled COMMON block that appears in the subprogram and in at least one program unit that is calling the subprogram. The general form of the SAVE statement is:

    SAV [var₁ [,var₂],...]

where var is a variable name, an array name or a labeled COMMON block. The labeled COMMON block name must be preceded and followed by a slash.

Note that var must not be a part of a labeled COMMON block, but the entire COMMON block can be saved, as mentioned above, with the following statement

SAVE /BLK1/

where BLK1 is the name of the block.

The brackets ([and]) are optional, if no list is given for the SAVE statement, all variables, arrays and labeled COMMON blocks will be saved; that is, all entities in the program unit in which the SAVE statement appears will be saved. The SAVE statement is included in a subprogram after the subprogram statement SUBROUTINE or FUNCTION statement.

7.14 PROGRAMMING EXAMPLES FOR THE CHAPTER

Example 7.3

This example illustrates how to determine the length and the equation of a straight line. The length and the equation of a line with endpoints coordinates as (x_1, y_1) and (x_2, y_2) are given by:

$$\text{length} = \sqrt{(x_1 - x_2)^2 + (y_1 - y_2)^2}$$

equation of a line

$$y = mx + c$$

where slope $m = \left[\dfrac{y_2 - y_1}{x_2 - x_1} \right]$ and intercept $c = (y_1 - mx_1)$

A structure diagram is shown in Figure 7.10. The complete program listing is given in Figure 7.11. A sample run of the program is given in Figure 7.12.

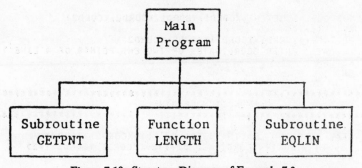

Figure 7.10: Structure Diagram of Example 7.3.

Example 7.4

This example has been discussed in Example 6.7 in Chapter 6. The program given in Figure 7.13 makes use of subroutine subprograms. This example provides an excellent opportunity to compare two versions—with and without the use of subroutine subprograms. The input data and output results are the same as shown in Figure 6.15.

```
***************************************************************
*  THIS PROGRAM DETERMINES THE LENGTH AND THE EQUATION OF A LINE.  *
*  THE LINE IS SPECIFIED BY ITS ENDPOINTS' COORDINATES. THE       *
*  PROGRAM IS EXECUTED IN AN INTERACTIVE MODE.                    *
***************************************************************
        REAL LEN,LENGTH
        CHARACTER*3 RESPON,ANSWER
        RESPON = 'YES'
        DO WHILE(RESPON(1:1).EQ.'Y'.OR.RESPON(1:1).EQ.'y')
          WRITE(6,100)
          READ(5,200) RESPON
          IF (RESPON(1:1).EQ.'Y'.OR.RESPON(1:1).EQ.'y') THEN
* CALL TO SUBROUTINE GETPNT
            CALL GETPNT(X1,Y1,X2,Y2)
            WRITE(6,300)
            READ(5,200) ANSWER
            IF (ANSWER(1:1).EQ.'Y'.OR.ANSWER(1:1).EQ.'y') THEN
* FUNCTION LENGTH IS CALLED
              LEN = LENGTH(X1,Y1,X2,Y2)
              WRITE(6,400) LEN
            END IF
            WRITE(6,500)
            READ(5,200) ANSWER
            IF (ANSWER(1:1).EQ.'Y'.OR.ANSWER(1:1).EQ.'y') THEN
* CALL TO SUBROUTINE EQLIN
              CALL EQLIN(X1,Y1,X2,Y2)
            END IF
          END IF
        END DO
100     FORMAT(' TO ENTER COORDINATES OF A LINE, TYPE YES')
200     FORMAT(A3)
300     FORMAT(' TO FIND THE LENGTH OF THE LINE, TYPE YES')
400     FORMAT(' THE LENGTH OF THE LINE = ',F10.3)
500     FORMAT(' TO FIND THE EQUATION OF THE LINE, TYPE YES')
        STOP
        END
*
***************************************************************
*                   SUBROUTINE GETPNT                         *
***************************************************************
*
        SUBROUTINE GETPNT(XCORD1,YCORD1,XCORD2,YCORD2)
        WRITE(6,100)
        READ(5,*)XCORD1,YCORD1,XCORD2,YCORD2
100     FORMAT(' ENTER COORDINATES OF TWO END POINTS OF A LINE')
        RETURN
        END
*
***************************************************************
*                   FUNCTION LENGTH                          *
***************************************************************
*
        REAL FUNCTION LENGTH(XCORD1,YCORD1,XCORD2,YCORD2)
        LENGTH = SQRT((XCORD1-XCORD2)**2+(YCORD1-YCORD2)**2)
        RETURN
        END
*
```

(Figure 7.11—Contd.)

```
***************************************************************
*                    SUBROUTINE EQLIN                         *
***************************************************************
*
      SUBROUTINE EQLIN(XCORD1,YCORD1,XCORD2,YCORD2)
      REAL INCEPT
      SLOPE = (YCORD2-YCORD1)/(XCORD2-XCORD1)
      INCEPT = YCORD1-SLOPE*XCORD1
      IF(INCEPT.GE.0.0)THEN
         WRITE(6,100)SLOPE,INCEPT
      ELSE
         WRITE(6,200)SLOPE,INCEPT
      END IF
100   FORMAT(' EQUATION OF THE LINE IS: Y = ',F6.2,' * X +',F6.2)
200   FORMAT(' EQUATION OF THE LINE IS: Y = ',F6.2,' * X ',F6.2)
      RETURN
      END
***************************************************************
```

Figure 7.11: Program Listing of Example 7.3.

```
TO ENTER COORDINATES OF A LINE, TYPE YES
Y
ENTER COORDINATES OF TWO END POINTS OF A LINE
0.0 0.0 2.0 2.0
TO FIND THE LENGTH OF THE LINE, TYPE YES
YES
THE LENGTH OF THE LINE =      2.828
TO FIND THE EQUATION OF THE LINE, TYPE YES
YES
EQUATION OF THE LINE IS: Y =   1.00 * X +  0.00
TO ENTER COORDINATES OF A LINE, TYPE YES
Y
ENTER COORDINATES OF TWO END POINTS OF A LINE
-2.7 6.4 -4.8 -2.1
TO FIND THE LENGTH OF THE LINE, TYPE YES
Y
THE LENGTH OF THE LINE =      9.352
TO FIND THE EQUATION OF THE LINE, TYPE YES
Y
EQUATION OF THE LINE IS: Y =  -2.18 * X -12.56
TO ENTER COORDINATES OF A LINE, TYPE YES
YES
ENTER COORDINATES OF TWO END POINTS OF A LINE
2.7 -0.1 9.4 5.4
TO FIND THE LENGTH OF THE LINE, TYPE YES
Y
THE LENGTH OF THE LINE =      8.215
TO FIND THE EQUATION OF THE LINE, TYPE YES
YES
EQUATION OF THE LINE IS: Y =  -0.90 * X +  2.65
TO ENTER COORDINATES OF A LINE, TYPE YES
No
```

Figure 7.12: A Sample Run of Example 7.3.

```
*****************************************************************
*   THIS PROGRAM PROCESSES THE SALES OF COMPUTERS. ANOTHER VERSION *
*   OF THIS PROGRAM IS GIVEN IN EXAMPLE 6.7 OF CHAPTER 6. THIS     *
*   PROGRAM SHOWS THE ADVANTAGE OF USING SUBROUTINE SUBPROGRAMS.   *
*   NOTE THE USE OF COMMON BLOCK.                                  *
*****************************************************************
        INTEGER SALES(40,40),COMPER(40),MODEL(40),FLAG
        COMMON/BLK1/SALES
        INTEGER INLUN,OUTLUN
        PARAMETER (INLUN = 1,OUTLUN = 2)
        OPEN(UNIT=INLUN,FILE='EX6_7.DAT',STATUS='OLD')
        OPEN(UNIT=OUTLUN,FILE='EX7_4.OUT',STATUS='NEW')
*   READ INPUT DATA
        READ(INLUN,*)N_MOD,N_SPER,((SALES(I,J),J=1,N_MOD),I=1,N_SPER)
*   CALCULATE NUMBER OF COMPUTERS SOLD BY EACH SALESPERSON
        FLAG=0
        CALL N_COMP(N_SPER,N_MOD,FLAG,COMPER)
*   CALCULATE NUMBER OF COMPUTERS SOLD OF EACH MODEL
        FLAG=1
        CALL N_COMP(N_MOD,N_SPER,FLAG,MODEL)
*   DETERMINE THE SALESPERSON WHO SOLD MAXIMUM NUMBER OF COMPUTERS
        CALL MAXMUM(COMPER,N_SPER,MAXPER,MAXCMP)
*   DETERMINE THE MODEL WHOSE DEMAND WAS MAXIMUM
        CALL MAXMUM(MODEL,N_MOD,MAXMOD,MAXCMM)
*   WRITE COMPUTER SALES IN A TABULAR FORM
        WRITE(OUTLUN,100)
100     FORMAT(' ',T25,'COMPUTER MODEL')
        WRITE(OUTLUN,200)(J,J=1,N_MOD)
200     FORMAT(' SALESPERSON',T15,':',<N_MOD>I5,/,<15+5*N_MOD>('-'))
        WRITE(OUTLUN,300)(I,(SALES(I,J),J=1,N_MOD),I=1,N_SPER)
300     FORMAT(' ',I7,T15,':',<N_MOD>I5)
        WRITE(OUTLUN,400)
400     FORMAT(' ',<15+5*N_MOD>('-'))
        WRITE(OUTLUN,500)(I,COMPER(I),I=1,N_SPER)
500     FORMAT(' SALES OF SALESPERSON',I3,' :',I6)
        WRITE(OUTLUN,600)(J,MODEL(J),J=1,N_MOD)
600     FORMAT(' SALES OF MODEL',I3,' :',I6)
        WRITE(OUTLUN,700)MAXCMP,MAXPER
700     FORMAT(' ',/,' MAXIMUM # OF COMPUTERS',I6,' WERE SOLD BY',
     1  ' SALESPERSON:',I3,/)
        WRITE(OUTLUN,800)MAXCMM,MAXMOD
800     FORMAT(' MAXIMUM # OF COMPUTERS',I6,' WERE SOLD OF MODEL:',I3)
        CLOSE(UNIT=INLUN)
        CLOSE(UNIT=OUTLUN)
        STOP
        END
*
*****************************************************************
*                      SUBROUTINE MAXMUM                          *
*****************************************************************
        SUBROUTINE MAXMUM(NUM,N,MAX1,MAX2)
        INTEGER NUM(40)
        MAX1=1
        MAX2=NUM(1)
        DO 10 I=2,N
          IF(MAX2.LT.NUM(I))THEN
            MAX2=NUM(I)
            MAX1=I
          END IF
10      CONTINUE
        RETURN
        END
```

(Figure 7.13—Contd.)

```
****************************************************************************
*                         SUBROUTINE N_COMP                              *
*   IF FLAG=0 THEN THIS SUBROUTINE CALCULATES THE NUMBER OF              *
*   COMPUTERS SOLD BY EACH SALESPERSON. IF FLAG=1, THE SUBROUTINE       *
*   DETERMINES THE NUMBER OF COMPUTERS SOLD OF EACH MODEL.              *
****************************************************************************
*
        SUBROUTINE N_COMP(N,M,FLAG,NUM)
        COMMON/BLK1/SALES
        INTEGER NUM(40),SALES(40,40),FLAG
        DO 10 I=1,N
          NUM(I)=0
          DO 10 J=1,M
            IF(FLAG.EQ.0)NUM(I)=NUM(I)+SALES(I,J)
            IF(FLAG.EQ.1)NUM(I)=NUM(I)+SALES(J,I)
10      CONTINUE
        RETURN
        END
****************************************************************************
```

Figure 7.13: Program Listing of Example 7.4.

Example 7.5

We want to write a FORTRAN program to plot the function y = sin (x) for values of x ranging from $-\pi$ to π. We know that the values of y will be in the range from -1.0 to 1.0. The graph of y = sin (x) is shown in Figure 7.14.

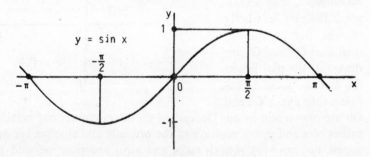

Figure 7.14: Plot of y = sin (x).

The graph is obtained by plotting various points (x, y) belonging to the curve and then joining these points together. We calculate the value of y for various values of x and plot the corresponding points as shown in Figure 7.14.

It is more difficult to print the graph on computer than one may expect, because the printer paper moves in a vertical direction while the x-axis runs horizontally. It is also not possible to obtain a smooth curve due to the poor resolution of the printer. Nevertheless, we will describe a technique that will help the user do the plotting quite satisfactorily. The following is a description of steps involved in plotting a function:

(1) The basic idea is to store various points of a curve in a two-dimensional array of appropriate size. We choose a two-dimensional character array PLOT (20,70) which has 20 rows and 70 columns reserved for plotting. Every entry of the array is initialized to a blank space.

(2) The next step is to determine a proper scaling for x values. If x_{MAX} and x_{MIN} represent the maximum value of x and the minimum value of x, respectively, then the increment x_{INT} from one column to the next column is given by

$$x_{INT} = \frac{x_{MAX} - x_{MIN}}{70}$$

since there are 70 columns reserved for plotting.

(3) Similarly, we should determine a proper scaling for y values. In order to do this, we should calculate y_{MAX} and y_{MIN} and again using the formula

$$y_{INT} = \frac{y_{MAX} - y_{MIN}}{20}$$

we can calculate y_{INT}. Note that y_{MAX} and y_{MIN} may not correspond to x_{MAX} and x_{MIN}, respectively.

(4) The next step is to draw the x-axis (abscissa) and the y-axis (ordinate). Depending on where the plot lies, axes are drawn accordingly. For example, if the plot lies wholly in the first quadrant, then axes Oa and Ob are drawn. If the plot lies in the first and second quadrant, then axes a'Oa and

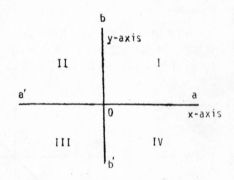

Ob are drawn and so on. Depending on the minimum and maximum values of x and y, the position of the ordinate and abscissa are determined. For example, if both x_{MAX} and x_{MIN} are positive, and both y_{MAX} and y_{MIN} are postive (that is the curve lies wholly in the first quadrant) then the abscissa Oa will be drawn from point PLOT (20,1) to point PLOT (20,70), that is the last row of the array. The ordinate will be the first column of the array. Similarly the positions of the ordinate and of the abscissa can be determined for other values of x_{MAX}, x_{MIN}, y_{MAX} and y_{MIN}. The column position x_{MID} of the ordinate can be determined as follows:

$x_{MID} = 1$, if $x_{MAX} * x_{MIN}$ is $+$ve

$x_{MID} = |x_{MIN}/x_{INT}|$, if $x_{MAX} * x_{MIN}$ is $-$ve.

Similarly the row position y_{MID} of the abscissa can be determined as follows:

$y_{MID} = 20$, if $y_{MAX} * y_{MIN}$ is $+$ve

$y_{MID} = |y_{MAX}/y_{INT}|$, if $y_{MAX} * y_{MIN}$ is $-$ve.

The ordinates and the abscissa are then stored in array PLOT corresponding to the column x_{MID} and the row y_{MID}, respectively.

(5) Finally, the coordinates for the plot are calculated and stored in the array PLOT. The array PLOT is then printed. Figure 7.15 gives a source program to plot the function y = sin (x). The plot is shown in Figure 7.16.

```
**************************************************************************
*                        GRAPH PLOTTING                                 *
**************************************************************************
        CHARACTER *1 PLOT(21,71)
        COMMON/BLK1/ PLOT
* DEFINE THE FUNCTION TO BE PLOTTED
        FCNPLT(X) = SIN(X)
* INITIALIZE ARRAY PLOT
        CALL INITLZ
        WRITE(6,100)
* READ RANGE OF X VALUES
        READ(5,*) XLOW,XHIGH
* DETERMINE X-SCALING
        CALL SCALE(XLOW,XHIGH,XMAX,XMIN,XINT,71)
* CALCULATE RANGE OF Y VALUES
        YLOW = FCNPLT(XLOW)
        YHIGH = FCNPLT(XHIGH)
        DO 10 I = 0,69
          X = I * XINT + XMIN
          Y = FCNPLT(X)
          IF (Y.GT.YHIGH)THEN
            YHIGH = Y
          ELSE IF (Y.LT.YLOW)THEN
            YLOW = Y
          END IF
10        CONTINUE
* DETERMINE Y SCALING
        CALL SCALE(YLOW,YHIGH,YMAX,YMIN,YINT,21)
        MIDX = 1
* DETERMINE POSITION OF ORDINATE
        CALL POS_OA(XMIN,XMAX,XINT,MIDX,71)
        MIDY = 21
* DETERMINE POSITION OF ABSCISSA
        CALL POS_OA(YMIN,YMAX,YINT,MIDY,21)
* STORE ORDINATE POINTS
        DO 20 I =1,21
          PLOT(I,MIDX) = 'I'
20      CONTINUE
* STORE ABSCISSA POINTS
        DO 30 J =1,71
          PLOT(MIDY,J) = '-'
30      CONTINUE
* STORE THE CROSSING POINT (ORIGIN)
        PLOT(MIDY,MIDX) = '+'
* STORE PLOTTING POINTS
        DO 40 J = 1,71
          X = XMIN + (J-1) * XINT
          IY = INT(MIDY-FCNPLT(X)/YINT)
          IF(IY.LE.0) IY=1
          IF(IY.GT.21) IY=21
          PLOT(IY,J)='*'
40      CONTINUE
* DRAW PLOT
        DO 50 I =1,21
        WRITE(6,200)(PLOT(I,J),J=1,71)
50      CONTINUE
100     FORMAT(' ENTER THE RANGE OF X VALUES')
200     FORMAT(T2,71A1)
        STOP
        END
*
```

(Figure 7.15 Contd.)

```
********************************************************************
*                       SUBROUTINE INITLZ                         *
********************************************************************
*
      SUBROUTINE INITLZ
      CHARACTER *1 PLOT(21,71)
      COMMON/BLK1/ PLOT
      DO 10 I =1, 21
        DO 10 J =1,71
          PLOT(I,J)= '
10    CONTINUE
      RETURN
      END

*
********************************************************************
*                       SUBROUTINE SCALE                          *
*  THIS SUBROUTINE DETERMINES THE SCALING FOR THE AXES. THE        *
*  SUBROUTINE CALLS ANOTHER SUBROUTINE MAXMIN WHICH DETERMINES     *
*  MAXIMUM AND MINIMUM VALUES.                                     *
********************************************************************
*
      SUBROUTINE SCALE(LOW,HIGH,MAX,MIN,INIT,N)
      REAL LOW,HIGH,MAX,MIN,INIT
      CALL MAXMIN(LOW,HIGH,MAX,MIN)
      INIT = (MAX-MIN)/N
      RETURN
      END

*
********************************************************************
*                       SUBROUTINE MAXMIN                         *
********************************************************************
*
      SUBROUTINE MAXMIN(LOW,HIGH,MAX,MIN)
      REAL LOW,HIGH,MAX,MIN
      IF(LOW.LT.HIGH)THEN
        MAX=HIGH
        MIN=LOW
      ELSE
        MAX=LOW
        MIN=HIGH
      END IF
      RETURN
      END

*
********************************************************************
*                       SUBROUTINE POS_OA                         *
*  THIS SUBROUTINE DETERMINES THE POSITION OF THE ORDINATE AND     *
*  ABSCISSA.                                                       *
********************************************************************
*
      SUBROUTINE POS_OA(MIN,MAX,INIT,MID,N)
      REAL MAX,MIN,INIT
      IF(MAX*MIN.LT.0.0)THEN
        IF(N.EQ.71)MID = INT(ABS(MIN/INIT))+1
        IF(N.EQ.21)MID = INT(ABS(MAX/INIT))+1
        IF(MID.LT.1)MID=1
        IF(MID.GT.N)MID=N
      END IF
      RETURN
      END
********************************************************************
```

Figure 7.15: Program Listing of Example 7.5.

The program given in Figure 7.15 is quite general and, in fact, can be used to plot a variety of functions. One may have to change the function statement that defines the function to be plotted.

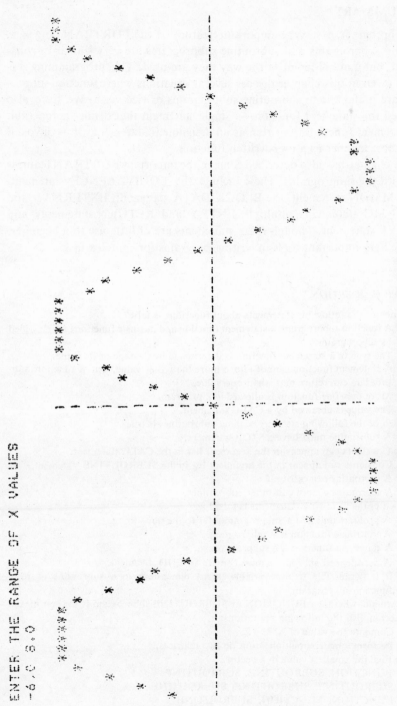

Figure 7.16: Plot of SIN (X) Printed by Example 7.5.

7.15 SUMMARY

The subprogram is a very important feature of the FORTRAN language. Function subprograms and subroutine subprograms are very similar in construction, but quite different in the way they are used. The programming examples given in this chapter discuss several situations where function subprograms are preferable to subroutine subprograms or vice versa. We have also discussed the statement function—a single statement that defines a function. The statement function is written as an assignment statement. It is invoked in the same manner as a user-written function.

The chapter has also described some of the important FORTRAN features used with the subprograms. These include the EQUIVALENCE statement, the COMMON statement, the BLOCK DATA statement, EXTERNAL and INTRINSIC statements, multiple ENTRY and RETURN statements, and the SAVE statement. Though these statements are of little use to a beginner, they are very important tools in writing programs for complex tasks.

OBJECTIVE QUESTIONS

(1) Which of the following statements about functions is false?
  (a) A function subprogram, a statement function and intrinsic functions are classified as subprograms.
  (b) The type of a statement function is determined by the type of its name.
  (c) A statement function cannot return more than one value, but a function subprogram can return more than one value.
  (d) More than one function is allowed in a program.
  (e) The value is obtained by a CALL statement.
(2) Which of the following statements about subroutines is true?
  (a) A subroutine must have a STOP statement.
  (b) Constants can appear in the argument list in the CALL statement.
  (c) Constants can appear in the argument list in the SUBROUTINE statement.
  (d) A subroutine can call itself.
  (e) A subroutine cannot call other subroutines.
(3) Which of the following statements is false?
  (a) A program unit and a subprogram refer to the same thing.
  (b) An intrinsic function is a subprogram.
  (c) A statement function is a subprogram.
  (d) A user defined subroutine must contain an END statement.
  (e) It is permissible to use variable array dimensions in a subroutine or in a function subprogram.
(4) Determine whether a FUNCTION or SUBROUTINE subprogram is the best means to accomplish the following operations:
  (i) Compute the value of $X**3+Z$.
  (ii) Perform a matrix multiplication on two matrices.
  (iii) Find the smallest value in a vector.
  (a) FUNCTION, SUBROUTINE, SUBROUTINE
  (b) SUBROUTINE, SUBROUTINE, SUBROUTINE
  (c) FUNCTION, FUNCTION, SUBROUTINE
  (d) FUNCTION, SUBROUTINE, FUNCTION
  (e) FUNCTION, FUNCTION, FUNCTION

(5) Which of the following statements is true?
   (a) The END statement in some cases is not needed in a subprogram.
   (b) Function subprograms can return only one value to the calling program.
   (c) The statement N = FUN (2.0, 3) is invalid.
   (d) Since only one value can be returned by a function subprogram, only one RETURN statement is allowed in the subprogram.
   (e) A statement function can be coded in only one statement.

(6) Which of the following statements cannot be replaced by referencing the statement function

$$FUN (X, Y, Z) = X*Y*Z+SQRT (X+Y)-Z?$$

   (a) Z = 1.0+Y+3.0+SQRT (1.0+Y)-3.0
   (b) S = A (1)*A(2)*A(3)+SQRT (A (1)+A (2))-A (3)
   (c) IF ((8.0*17.0*Z+5.0-Z) .GT. 0.0) GO TO 10
   (d) T = X*Y*X+SQRT (X+Y)-X
   (e) U = 3.0+SQRT (2.0)-1.0

(7) The statement REAL A (N) will be valid in
   (a) a main program, a subroutine and in a function subprogram.
   (b) a subroutine or a function subprogram.
   (c) both in a main program and a subroutine subprogram.
   (d) both in a main program and a function subprogram.
   (e) only in a main program.

(8) Which of the following statements is false?
   (a) Statement functions are referenced in exactly the same way as the intrinsic functions are referenced.
   (b) The function statement A (X, Y) = F*X+G*Y is correct.
   (c) If FUNC(X) is defined in a function statement, the expression FUNC(SQRT(A)) is a valid function reference but SQRT(FUNC (B)) is not.
   (d) Function statements are non-executable statements.
   (e) The function statement FUNC(X) = X+FUNC(Y) is not valid.

(9) Which of the following statements is false?
   (a) Actual and dummy arguments must always agree in number and type.
   (b) Subroutine names cannot have more than six characters.
   (c) More than one common statement is allowed in a subroutine.
   (d) It is possible for subroutines to have no arguments.
   (e) Arguments in a subroutine or function arguments list can be declared in a COMMON statement.

(10) Which of the following statements is false?
   (a) The expressions COMMON BLOCK and COMMON STORAGE AREA are used synonymously.
   (b) The statement EQUIVALENCE (A(5), B, C(10)) is a valid statement.
   (c) COMMON statements provide a means of communication between program units.
   (d) BLOCK DATA subprograms must contain only nonexecutable statements.
   (e) BLOCK DATA subprograms serve only one purpose—when executed, they assign values to variables.

(11) How many memory locations are reserved in unlabeled COMMON by each of the following sets of statements?
   (i) COMMON   X, Y, Z
   (ii) COMMON   A, B, C (20), I, J
   (iii) DIMENSION A(10), B(20), C(50)

            COMMON A, B
            COMMON X, N

(iv) DIMENSION A(100), B(50, 2)
     COMMON A, Q
     EQUIVALENCE (A (1), B (1, 1), Q)

(a) 3, 24, 32, 100
(b) 3, 5, 4, 2
(c) 3, 24, 4, 2
(d) 3, 24, 32, 101
(e) 3, 24, 32, 51

(12) Study the following program segment:

```
* Main Program
  EXTERNAL SQRT
  S = 36.0
  X = 25.0
  Y = Z (S, SQRT)+4.8
  STOP
  END
* Function Subprogram
  FUNCTION Z (X, FX)
  Z = FX (X)
  RETURN
  END
```

What is the value of Y?

(a) 9.8
(b) 10.8
(c) 4.8
(d) 40.8
(e) undefined

(13) Study the following program segment:

```
* Main Program
  I = 3
  J = 2
  CALL SUB (I, J, N, P, Q)
  A = 4.0
  WRITE (6, *), I, J, N, P, Q
  STOP
  END
* Subroutine Subprogram
  SUBROUTINE SUB (J, I, K, A, B)
  A = I
  B = A*I
  K = J/I
  I = J
  RETURN
  END
```

What is printed by the WRITE statement in the main program?

(a) 3, 2, 1, 2.0, 4.0
(b) 2, 3, 0, 4.0, 4.0
(c) 3, 3, 1, 2.0, 4.0
(d) 2, 2, 1, 4.0, 4.0
(e) 3, 2, 0, 4.0, 4.0

(14) What will be printed when the following program is executed?

```
COMMON/XX/I, J, K, L, M/YY/N (2)
EQUIVALENCE (I, J, K) (L, M)
```

```
        I = 5
        M = 2
        N(1) = J
        N(2) = L
        CALL SUB (X)
        WRITE (6, *) I, J, K, L, M, N(1), N(2), X
        STOP
        END
        SUBROUTINE SUB(X)
        COMMON/XX/J, I, K, L, M/YY/N(2)
        I = N(1) + L−N (2)−I
        J = 4 + M
        X = K/2.0
        RETURN
        END
```

(a) 0, 6, 5, 2, 2, 5, 2, 2.5

(b) 6, 0, 5, 2, 2, 5, 2, 2.5

(c) Undefined

(d) 5, 5, 5, 2, 2, 5, 2, 2.5

(e) 5, 5, 5, 5, 5, 5, 2, 2.5

(15) What is printed by this program?

```
        COMMON I, J
        I = 2
        J = 3
        K = 5
        L = 4
        M = 2
        CALL SUB (K, L, M)
        WRITE (6, *) I, J, K, L, M
        STOP
        END
        SUBROUTINE SUB (L, M, I)
        COMMON J, K
        I = J+K+L+M
        J = K+L+M
        K = L+M
        RETURN
        END
```

(a) 12, 9, 5, 4, 14

(b) 2, 3, 5, 4, 2

(c) 2, 9, 5, 4, 2

(d) 12, 9, 5, 4, 2

(e) 2, 3, 5, 4, 14

ANSWERS TO OBJECTIVE QUESTIONS

(1) e;	(2) b;	(3) a;	(4) d;	(5) e;
(6) e;	(7) b;	(8) c;	(9) e;	(10) e;
(11) a;	(12) b;	(13) c;	(14) b;	(15) a.

DRILL EXERCISES

(1) Write FORTRAN statements to perform each of the following instructions:

   (i) Write the FUNCTION definition statement for an integer FUNC with the array named X and the variables Y, Z, I, J as arguments.

   (ii) Write the SUBROUTINE statement for a subroutine named SUB that calculates the sum of three input arguments X, Y and Z. The computed sum is passed back under the dummy argument SUM.

   (iii) Write the CALL statement for a subroutine named COUNT that counts the number of occurrences of a value X in the array A. The camputed count is received back under the argument N.

   (iv) Write a BLOCK DATA subprogram to initialize variables X, Y and I in a labeled COMMON block named BLK1 to 1.0, 2.0 and 3, respectively.

(2) Which of the following program segments contain invalid statements? Explain the reason if a statement is not valid:

   (i) SUBROUTINE CAL (X, Y, A, I)
       DIMENSION X(I), A (N)

   (ii) FUNCTION X (X, Y, Z)

   (iii) FUNCTION FUNCTION (3, A+B, D (1))
        DIMENSION X (100)

   (iv) FUN (I) = SQRT (MIN (I, 5))
        Z = FUN (4.9)+4.0

   (v) SUM (A, B, C) = A+B+C+D
       Z = SUM (A+B, Z)

   (vi) F = FUN (X, FUN (X, Y))
        $\vdots$
        FUNCTION FUN (X, Y)

   (vii) SUBROUTINE (A, B, C, D)

   (viii) SUBROUTINE SUB (X, Y)
         REAL X(10), Y(10)
         EQUIVALENCE/X(5), Y(5)/

(3) Consider the following program segment:

```
* Main Program
  COMMON/XX/A(100), X, Y, Z
  _____
  _____
  STOP
  END
  FUNCTION F(X, Y, I)
  COMMON/XY/P, Q
  _____
  _____
  RETURN
  END
  SUBROUTINE FIND (B, C, N)
  COMMON/XX/A(100), X,Y, Z
  COMMON/XY/P, Q
  _____
  _____
  RETURN
  END
```

(a) Determine whether each of the following statements can be used in the main program? If it cannot be used, explain why?

   (i) CALL F (X, Y, I)

   (ii) Z = F (A, B, N,)*X/Y

(iii) Z = FIND (C, D, I)

(iv) IF (F (B, C, I) .GT. 0.0) GO TO 10

(v) I = F (3, 4, 2)/F (1, 2, 3)

(vi) P = Q*F (C, D, N)

(vii) CALL FIND (P, Q, N)

(b) Determine whether each of the following statements can be used in the function subprogram? If not, why?

(i) F = X*P+Y/I+A/B

(ii) CALL FIND (B, C, N)

(iii) Y = F (1.0, 2.0, 3)

(iv) CALL FIND (B+C, C+N, N/2)

(c) Determine whether each of the following statements can be used in the sub-routine subprogram. If not, why?

(i) EQUIVALENCE (P, X)

    Z = F (1.0, 2.0, 3)

(ii) CALL FIND (D, E, I)

(iii) STOP

(4) Write a function/subroutine subprogram or a statement function (whichever you think is the most appropriate) to perform the following operations:

(i) To compute the determinant of a 2×2 matrix.

(ii) To compute the length of the hypotenuse of a right angle triangle, given sides A and B. Hypotenuse is given by $\sqrt{A^2+B^2}$.

(iii) To compute the distance between the two points (x_1, y_1) and (x_2, y_2).

(iv) To compute the mean and the standard deviation of a set of measurements contained in a one-dimensional array of variable length.

(v) To calculate the difference in absolute value between the largest and smallest elements of an array of size N.

(vi) To compute the cube root $\left(\sqrt[3]{x} = \dfrac{|x|^{4/3}}{x}\right)$ of a number.

(vii) To convert miles to kilometers.

(5) What output will be printed by the following program segments?

```
(i) READ (5, *) I, J, K
    DO 10 L = 1, I
        IX = (10-L)*FUNC (I, J, K,-L)
10  WRITE (6, *), IX
    STOP
    END
    INTEGER FUNCTION FUNC (L, M, N, I)
    FUNC = I+L+M+N
    RETURN
    END
```
Assume values of I, J and K as 4, 2 and 3 respectively.

```
(ii) DIMENSION A (10)
     N = 5
     DO 10 I = 1, N
         A (I) = I
10   CONTINUE
     DO 20 I = 5,0, -1
         Z = FUNC (N, A, I)
         WRITE (6, *) I, Z
20   CONTINUE
     STOP
     END
```

```
          FUNCTION FUNC (N, A, I)
          DIMENSION A(N)
          FUNC = 0.0
          DO 10 J = 1, N
              FUNC = FUNC+A(J)*I
   10   CONTINUE
          RETURN
          END
(iii) READ(5, *) A, B, C
          CALL ROOT (A, *10, B, C, *20, *30)
          DISCRM = SQRT (B*B−4.0*A*C)
          R1 = (−B—DISCRM) / (2.0*A)
          R2 = (−B+DISCRM) / (2.0*A)
          WRITE (6, *) R1, R2
          STOP
   10   R = −C/B
          WRITE (6, *) R
          STOP
   20   WRITE (6,*), 'COMPLEX ROOTS'
          STOP
   30   R = −B / (2.0*A)
          WRITE (6,*) R, R
          STOP
          END
          SUBROUTINE ROOT (A, *, B, C, *, *)
          IF (A .EQ. 0.0 .AND. B .NE. 0.0) RETURN 1
          DISC = B*B−4.0*A*C
          IF (DISC .EQ. 0.0) RETURN 3
          IF (DISC .LT. 0.0) RETURN 2
          RETURN
          END
```

Calculate the output for the following values of A, B and C.

(a) 1.0, 2.0, 3.0
(b) 0.0, 2.0, 1.0
(c) 1.0, −2.0, 1.0
(d) −1.0, −2.0, 1.0

```
(iv) FUNCA(I) = I+J
          FUNCB(J) = J+3
          DO  10  K = 1, 4
                   M = FUNCB (FUNCA (K))
   10   WRITE (6,*) K, M
          STOP
          END
(v)  K = 4
          CALL SUB2 (K, X)
          WRITE (6,*)K, X
          I = FUNC (2, 3, 4)
          CALL SUB 2 (I, Y)
          WRITE(6,*) I, Y
          STOP
          END
```

```
      SUBROUTINE SUB1 (I, J, K, L, M)
      M = K
      I = J
      IF(K .GT. J) THEN
         L = K
      ELSE
         L = J
      END IF
      RETURN
      END
      INTEGER FUNC(I, J, K)
      FUNC = 0
      DO 10 L = I, J, K
         FUNC = FUNC+L
10    CONTINUE
      RETURN
      END
      SUBROUTINE SUB2 (I, A)
         J = I+3
         K = I*J
         CALL SUB1 (I, K, J, M, N)
         A = (M+N) / 2.0
         I = FUNC (J, K, M)
         RETURN
      END
(vi)  COMMON/BLK1/I, J, K, L
      COMMON/BLK2/M, N
      CALL SUB1 (X)
      CALL SUB2 (X, Y)
      WRITE(6,*) I, J, X, Y
      STOP
      END
      SUBROUTINE SUB1 (Y)
      COMMON/BLK1/K, L, J, I
      K = L+I
      L = J*I
      Y = (I+J+K+L)/2.0
      RETURN
      END
      SUBROUTINE SUB2 (X, Y)
      COMMON/BLK2/I, J
         I = I+J
         Y = I*5.0
      RETURN
      END
      BLOCK DATA
      COMMON/BLK1/II (2), JJ(2)
      COMMON/BLK2/MM(2)
      DATA II/1, 2/, JJ/2*3/, MM/4,5/
      END
```

PROGRAMMING EXERCISES

(1) Write a logical function CHECK that has three arguments: (i) number of students in a class, (ii) an integer array containing the students roll number; and (iii) an integer variable which stores the number of a student. The function CHECK should return the value TRUE, if the roll number of the student appears in the array, and FALSE, otherwise.

(2) In cold climates, it is very important to know the combined effect of wind and temperature on the human body. An index known as wind-chill factor is calculated that gives an indication how fast the skin may get affected. The relevant formulas to calculate wind-chill factor are:

X = 0.279 times windspeed in km/hr.

$Y = (10.45 + 10\sqrt{\overline{X}} - X) *(33.0 - TEMP)$

Wind-Chill temperature = 33.0 − (Y/22.034)

where TEMP is the temperature in Celsius. Write a FORTRAN program to calculate wind-chill-temperature. Use three function subprogram each to calculate X, Y and wind-chill-temperature.

(3) Write a FORTRAN program to insert an element ITEM at location LOC in a one-dimensional array LIST of size N. The value of LOC is between 1 and N both inclusive. After inserting the element in location LOC, the size of the array LIST increases to N+1 and values in locations LOC, LOC+1, LOC+2, . . . N moves to location LOC+1, LOC+2, LOC+3, . . ., N+1 respectively. Your program should make use of a subroutine:

INSERT (LIST, N, ITEM, LOC).

(4) An operation opposite to the one described in Exercise 3 is called deletion. Extend your program of Exercise 3 to delete an element ITEM from the array LIST from location LOC using the subroutine

DELETE (LIST, N, ITEM, LOC)

After deleting the element from the location LOC, values in location LOC+1, LOC+2, . . . , N move to LOC, LOC+1. . . . ,N−1 respectively, thus reducing the size of the array to N−1.

(5) Write a FORTRAN program that calculates for any date in the 20th century the day of the week on which a particular date has occurred or will occur. You must include a function subprogram to do the job.

(6) A complex number is a number of the form x+iy, where x and y are real numbers and $i^2 = -1$. Write a menu-driven FORTRAN program that reads two complex numbers and allows the user to select one of the operations of addition, subtraction, multiplication, or division to be performed. The program should then call an appropriate function or subroutine subprogram to perform the specified operation and display the result. The four operations are defined as follows:

Sum: (x+iy)+(u+iw) = (x+u)+i (y+w)
Subtraction: (x+iy)−(u+iw) = (x−u)+i (y−w)
Multiplication: (x+iy)*(u+iw) = (xu−yw)+i (xw+yu)

Division $(x+iy)/(u+iw) = \left(\dfrac{xu+yw}{u^2+w^2} \right) + i \left(\dfrac{yu-xw}{u^2+w^2} \right)$

(7) The classical model often referred to as the EOQ (economic order quantity) model is the simplest of the inventory models. Using the EOQ model, the optimal quantity ordered Q_{opt} is given by

$$Q_{opt} = \sqrt{\frac{2C_oD}{C_c}}$$

where C_o is the ordering costs per order, C_e is the carrying cost per unit per year and D is demand for goods in inventory. The optimal total cost TC_{opt} is given by

$$TC_{opt} = \sqrt{2C_o\,C_e\,D}$$

Write a FORTRAN program that should include two function subprograms, each for calculating Q_{opt} and TC_{opt}. Test your program for the following data:

(i) $C_o = $ Rs. 300/order   (ii) $C_o = $ Rs. 150/-order
       $C_e = $ Rs. 15/unit $C_e = $ Rs. 12/-unit
       D = 20,000 units/year   D = 1,500 units/year

(8) A good method of solving an equation

$$f(x) = 0$$

is the technique of interval halving. Suppose that $a < b$, $f(a) < 0$ and $f(b) > 0$ (see Figure 7.17). Then there must be some number X between a and b that solves the equation. Consider the midpoint of the interval

$$c = \frac{a+b}{2}$$

if $f(c) < 0$, then X must be between c and b.

If $f(c) > 0$, then X must be between a and c.

Thus, the interval is reduced in which the unknown X lies to half of its original size. Again apply the same technique to pinpoint the location of X to any desired degree of accuracy.

Write a function

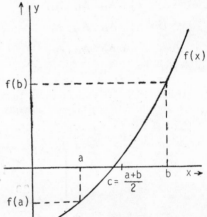

Figure 7.17.

     EQN (F, A, B, EPSLAN)

that returns a value of X solving

$$F(X) = 0$$

in the interval A to B to an accuracy of EPSLAN. Test your function by finding a solution of

$$1.5X^4 - 39.83X^3 + 0.83X^2 - 0.53X + 20.43 = 0$$

between 1.0 and 50.0. You may have to include an EXTERNAL statement in the program that calls EQN, because F is a function.

(9) An interesting practical example where linear simultaneous equations must be solved is the determination of loop currents in an electrical network. Consider the network shown in Figure 7.18. The network contains two d.c. supplies represented by circle. The voltage of each supply is 10 volts and 5 volts, respectively. There are four resistors of known value. The loop currents in three loops are designated as I_1, I_2, and I_3. Using the Kirchhoff Voltage Law, the following three equations can be written:

$$\begin{array}{rcl} 6I_1 - 4I_2 - 2I_3 & = & 10 \\ -4I_1 + 7I_2 - 3I_3 & = & -5 \quad \text{or} \\ -2I_1 - 3I_2 + 6I_3 & = & 0 \end{array} \qquad \begin{bmatrix} 6 & -4 & -2 \\ -4 & 7 & -3 \\ -2 & -3 & 6 \end{bmatrix} \begin{bmatrix} I_1 \\ I_2 \\ I_3 \end{bmatrix} = \begin{bmatrix} 10 \\ -5 \\ 0 \end{bmatrix}$$

These equations can be solved by using Cramer's rule:

$$I_1 = \frac{D_1}{D}, \quad I_2 = \frac{D_2}{D} \quad \text{and} \quad I_3 = \frac{D_3}{D}$$

where

$$D_1 = \begin{vmatrix} 10 & -4 & -2 \\ -5 & 7 & -3 \\ 0 & -3 & 6 \end{vmatrix} \qquad D_2 = \begin{vmatrix} 6 & 10 & -2 \\ -4 & -5 & -3 \\ -2 & 0 & 6 \end{vmatrix}$$

$$D_3 = \begin{vmatrix} 6 & -4 & 10 \\ -4 & 7 & -5 \\ -2 & -3 & 0 \end{vmatrix} \qquad D = \begin{vmatrix} 6 & -4 & -2 \\ -4 & 7 & -3 \\ -2 & -3 & 6 \end{vmatrix}$$

The D's represent determinants. The calculation of a determinant having the form

$$D = \begin{vmatrix} A_{11} & A_{12} & A_{13} \\ A_{21} & A_{22} & A_{23} \\ A_{31} & A_{32} & A_{33} \end{vmatrix}$$

is given by

$$D = A_{11}(A_{22}A_{33} - A_{23}A_{32}) - A_{12}(A_{21}A_{33} - A_{23}A_{31}) + A_{13}(A_{21}A_{32} - A_{22}A_{31})$$

Using a FUNCTION subprogram to determine the determinants, write a FORTRAN program to calculate the loop currents.

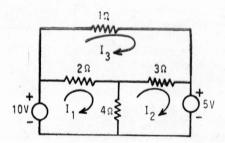

Figure 7.18.

Chapter 8

Character String Data Types

8.1 INTRODUCTION

The word compute usually suggests arithmetic operations performed on numerical data; thus computers are sometimes thought to be mere "number crunchers" whose only function is to process numeric information. In modern computing, however, most computer utilization involves information handling which requires processing of non-numeric items or character data types. In Chapter 3, we introduced the character data type and in subsequent chapters, we discussed some of the character-processing capabilities of FORTRAN 77. In this chapter, we extend our study to the whole range of FORTRAN 77 capabilities for character manipulation.

Character manipulation of any kind is rather difficult in FORTRAN, as the language was not originally designed for such an application. It is nevertheless possible to write programs which will do all the necessary character manipulation.

8.2 COMPUTER REPRESENTATION OF CHARACTERS

In Chapter 1, we learned that computers internally use binary language (0's and 1's). Numeric data types such as integers and real numbers are converted into binary numbers when they are used in a computer. Similarly characters are also converted into a binary form, or a *binary string*. There are several codes for converting character information into binary strings, but most computers use ASCII (American Standard Code for Information Interchange) or EBCDIC (Extended Binary-Coded-Decimal Interchange Code). For the most part, you do not need to know about these codes for writing FORTRAN programs. You do, however, need to be aware of the fact that there is a significant difference in the standard storage schemes between character strings and numeric strings that are to be used in arithmetic computations. For example, the integer number 7 and the character 7 will not be stored in the same manner. Thus, it is not possible to use arithmetic computations with character data even if the characters represent numbers.

8.3 CHARACTER STRING CONSTANTS AND VARIABLES

In earlier chapters, we have already come across character constants and character variables. For the sake of continuity, these are discussed here again briefly. In many respects, you can think of using character strings in the same manner as using numeric data. A *character constant* is any nonempty string of characters enclosed in apostrophes. These apostrophes are not counted as a part of the string. If two consecutive apostrophes (not a double quote) are encountered within a character constant they represent a single apostrophe. Thus the character constant DON'T is 'DON''T'. The list below gives several examples of character constants and the number of characters in a constant. The number of characters in a character constant is also called the *length* of the character constant.

Character Constant	Value	Length
'RENU'	RENU	4
'FORTRAN 77'	FORTRAN 77	10
'SHE CAN' 'T DO IT'	SHE CAN'T DO IT	15
'15 AUGUST'	15 AUGUST	9
''''	'	1
'$1 = RS. 10'	$1 = Rs. 10	8

Note that a blank (space) is a perfectly valid character. In the remaining chapter we write a blank as ƀ in its place to ensure clarity. Some of the invalid character constants are given below:

Invalid String Constant	Reason
RENU	Not delimited by apostrophes
' '	Null (zero length) string not allowed in FORTRAN
"A/B+C*D"	Quote marks cannot be used as delimiters
'SHEƀ CAN' TƀDOƀIT'	Single apostrophe in a character constant is not allowed.

A character constant will always represent the same information as a numeric constant does. A character constant may contain any character from the FORTRAN 77 character set which is composed of the 26 alphabetic letters (A . . . Z, a . . . z), the 10 numeric digits (0 . . . 9), a blank, and the following 12 symbols:

$$+ - * / = (\ ),\ .\ '\ \$:$$

Any string containing characters from this FORTRAN 77 character set can also be used to represent a *character variable*. Like FORTRAN variables (discussed in Chapter 3), character variables have names and represent character strings that may remain constant or may change. A character variable must always be declared in a nonexecutable specification statement whose form is:

CHARACTER [* len [,]] cvname [, cvname] . . .

where

cvname is one of the forms

v [*len]

a ([dl$_1$:]du$_1$[, [dl$_2$:] du$_2$] . . .) [*len]

v is a FORTRAN 77 variable name;

a is a FORTRAN 77 array name (the dimension declarators have been discussed in Chapter 6); and

len is the specified length (number of characters) of a character variable or character array element; len must be an unsigned positive integer constant.

Note that all quantities within square brackets are optional. Some examples of valid character variables are as follows:

Example (a)

The statement

CHARACTER*10 TITLE, NAME

declares the character variables TITLE and NAME of length 10 each. There is no significance to the first letter of a character variable and it need not necessarily be an alphabetic character.

Example (b)

The statements

CHARACTER*20 SENTEN
CHARACTER*5 WORD

declare variable SENTEN of length 20 and WORD of length 5. These variables can, however, be declared in one statement with the following form:

CHARACTER SENTEN*20, WORD*5

So lengths may be declared for all of the variables in a CHARACTER statement either by following the word CHARACTER with an asterisk and the number of characters or by following the name of a variable in a CHARACTER statement with an asterisk and the number of characters. If a CHARACTER-type statement contains no length information, the length of the character declared in it is one. For example, the statements

CHARACTER X, Y, A
CHARACTER*29 Z,W*10, U

declare that character variables X, Y and A are of length one each, the variables Z and U are of length 29 and the variable W is of length 10.

The elements of an array can also be of character type. For example, consider the following statement:

CHARACTER*10 NAME (0:99)
CHARACTER AREA (10,10)*5

The first statement declares a one-dimensional array NAME having 100 elements (0 to 99), each of length 10. The second type declaration statement says that array AREA is a two-dimensional character array having ten rows and ten columns, and each array element has five characters.

Before we close our discussion on character constants and variables, we must point out that there is a significant difference in the standard storage modes of character strings and numerical strings. A character string is left justified within the reserved storage space while a number is right justified. In the case of a character string, unused space is padded (filled out) with blank characters. For example, a character variable NAME has been declared as

CHARACTER*15 NAME

and that variable NAME is assigned the value as 'RENUʰKUMAR', then the storage scheme for NAME will be shown as:

1	2	3	4	5	6	7	8	9	10	11	12	13	14	15
R	E	N	U	ƀ	K	U	M	A	R	ƀ	ƀ	ƀ	ƀ	ƀ

In this example, we have simply assumed that the variable NAME is assigned a value and we did not show how this value was assigned. The assignment operation and many other operations that can be performed with character strings are now discussed in the following section.

8.4 OPERATIONS WITH CHARACTER STRINGS

We cannot use character strings in numerical computations, but we can perform basic operations with character strings. These are:

(1) Character Assignment
(2) Character Comparison
(3) Character Substrings
(4) Character Concatenation
(5) Character Library Functions

Each of these five operations involving character strings is discussed separately.

8.4.1 Character Assignment

Character values can be assigned to a character variable in much the same manner as one would assign a numeric value to a real or integer variable. Consider the following statements:

CHARACTER*15 NAME
NAME = 'RENU♭KUMAR'

The second statement assigns character string RENU♭KUMAR to the character variable NAME. A general form of character assignment statement is

cvname = ce

where

cvname is the name of a character string variable; and

ce is a character expression.

Both cvname and ce must be of type **CHARACTER**. They may, however, have different lengths. If the length of ce is shorter than the length of the variable cvname, blanks will be added to the right of the ce until the lengths are equal. For example, the statement

NAME = 'RENU♭KUMAR'

is equivalent to the statement

NAME = 'RENU♭KUMAR♭♭♭♭♭'

If the length of ce is greater than the length of the variable cvname, then the excess characters on the right of ce will be ignored. Thus, the statement

NAME = 'RENU♭KUMAR♭AGARWAL'

would store the first 15 characters RENU♭KUMAR♭AGAR in the variable NAME.

A character string variable can also be used to initiate another character variable as shown in the following program segment:

CHARACTER*7, TITLE, HEAD
TITLE = 'THE♭END'
HEAD = TITLE

Both variables, TITLE and HEAD, contain the character string THE♭END. Character strings may also be initiated with the DATA and PARAMETER statements. For example, the statements

CHARACTER*5 HEAD, TITLE(5)
PARAMETER (HEAD = 'BEGIN')

DATA TITLE / 'ARORA', 'KUMAR', 'RAY', 'PAI', 'NEHRU' /

store a character string BEGIN in the variable HEAD and the array TITLE stores five character constants ARORA, KUMAR, RAY♭♭, PAI♭♭, NEHRU in TITLE(1) . . . TITLE(5) respectively.

Examples

Here are some valid character assignment statements. The declaration statement

CHARACTER X*5, Y*10, Z*18, A

is assumed for all the examples.

Assignment Statement	Value of the left hand side variable
Y = 'TOGETHER'	TOGETHERɃɃ
X = Y	TOGET
Z = Y	TOGETHERɃɃɃɃɃɃɃɃɃɃ
A = 'YES'	Y
Y = A	YɃɃɃɃɃɃɃɃɃ

8.4.2 Character Comparison

For a variety of character manipulations, one needs to compare character strings quite frequently. An IF statement can be used to compare character strings. The comparison is quite analogous to the comparison of numeric data as discussed in Chapter 4. A general form of the logical expression contained within the IF statement is

$$ce_1 \ ro \ ce_2$$

where

ce$_1$ is character expression 1;
ro is relational operator; and
ce$_2$ is character expression 2.

The result of a character relational expression is again true or false. Character entities are compared based upon the collating sequence of the processor. A collating sequence lists characters from the lowest to the highest value. Partial collating sequences for two most popular codes ASCII and EBCDIC are given in Table 8.1.

Table 8.1: Partial Collating Sequences for Characters

```
-------------------------------------------------------
                            ASCII
-------------------------------------------------------
b " # $ % & ( ) * + , - . /
0 1 2 3 4 5 6 7 8 9
; = ? @
A B C D E F G H I J K L M N O P Q R S T U V W X Y Z
-------------------------------------------------------
                           EBCDIC
-------------------------------------------------------
b . ( + & $ * ) ; - / , % ? : # @ = "
A B C D E F G H I J K L M N O P Q R S T U V W X Y Z
0 1 2 3 4 5 6 7 8 9
-------------------------------------------------------
```

The FORTRAN 77 standard allows for collating sequences different from the ASCII and EBCDIC codes, but the following four conditions must hold:

(1) Capital letters are in order from A to Z; that is
$$'A' < 'B' < 'C' \ldots < 'Z'$$

(2) Digits are in order from 0 to 9, that is
$$'0' < '1' < '2' \ldots < '9'$$

(3) Capital letters and digits do not overlap; digits either precede letters, or letters precede digits. That is, no intermingling between capital letters and digits is allowed in a collating sequence.

(4) The blank character '⌴' is less than any letter or any other character in a collating sequence.

To evaluate a logical expression containing character data types, the user must first of all look at the length of the two character strings. If one string is shorter than the other, the shorter string is extended by adding blanks to the right so that the lengths of both strings are equal. A comparison is then made on a character by character basis, that is, the first character in each string is compared, then the second, and so on. Users must consult the manual for the collating sequence that is applicable to their computers. In this book, collating sequence is assumed to be the ASCII code.

Example (a)

Below are a few examples of character relational expression, their value and a short explanation:

Character Relational Expression	Value	Explanation
'X' .LT. 'Y'	TRUE	The letter X is less than the letter Y
'JOHN' .GT. 'JOHNSON'	FALSE	The fifth character ⌴ in string 'JOHN' is less than the fifth character 'S' of the string 'JOHNSON'
'176' .NE. '177'	TRUE	'6' is not equal to '7'
'$' LE. 'DOLLAR'	TRUE	'$' is less than D'
'FOUR' .LT. 'TWO'	TRUE	'F' is less than 'T'

Example (b)

Consider the following program segment:

```
        INTEGER OUTLUN
        PARAMETER (OUTLUN = 5)
        CHARACTER*10 A, B
        A = 'GOOD'
        B = 'BAD'
        IF (A.GT.B) THEN
            WRITE (OUTLUN, 100)
        ELSE
            WRITE (OUTLUN, 200)
        END IF
    100 FORMAT ('⌴GOOD⌴IS⌴GREATER⌴THAN⌴BAD')
    200 FORMAT ('⌴BAD⌴IS⌴GREATER⌴THAN⌴GOOD')
```

Since the character string 'GOOD' is greater than 'BAD', the IF condition is true and therefore the message

GOOD IS GREATER THAN BAD

appears on the CRT screen.

Users must note that if character strings contain letters only, their order is alphabetical. This ordering is called a *lexicographic ordering*.

8.4.3 Character Substrings

A substring of a character string is any string that represents a contiguous subset of the original string. For example, for the string

'FORTRANƀ77'

some of the substrings are:

'FOR', 'TRAN', '77', 'OR', 'AN', '7', 'Nƀ77'

You can select a substring from a character variable or character array element by specifying the name of the variable or array element, followed by two delimiter integer expressions in parentheses separated by a colon. A general form is

cvname ([e_1] : [e_2])

where

cvname is a character string variable or character array element;

e_1 is an integer expression indicating the leftmost character position of the substring; if e_1 is omitted, a value of one is assumed (that is, the first character of the substring is the first character in cvname); and

e_2 is an integer expression indicating the rightmost character position of the substring and if e_2 is omitted, a value of len (the length of the string) is assumed (that is, the rightmost character of the substring is the last character in cvname).

The values of e_1 and e_2 for a string must satisfy:

$$1 \leqslant e_1 \leqslant e_2 \leqslant len$$

The length of the substring is given by

$$e_2 - e_1 + 1$$

and if e_1 and e_2 are omitted, the length of the substring is equal to the length of the string.

Users must also note that e_1 and e_2 must be positive integers only.

Examples

Assume that the character variable TITLE stores the string

'UNITYƀINƀDIVERSITY'

then some of its substring references will be as follows:

Reference	Substring
TITLE (1:5)	'UNITY'
TITLE (6:6)	'ɓ'
TITLE (10:)	'DIVERSITY'
TITLE (20:)	Not valid, e_1 > length of the string
TITLE (:)	'UNITYɓINɓDIVERSITY'

8.4.4 Character Concatenation

Concatenation is the operation of combining (linking) together two or more character strings into one character string. This operation is analogous to the arithmetic operator + which adds two numeric values. The general form of concatenation is

CS1 / / CS2

where

CS1 and CS2 are two character operands (character constants, character variables or character array elements); and
/ / (double slash) is the concatenation operator.

Example (a)

The following operation

'TO' / / 'GET'

on two strings 'TO' and 'GET' produces the string

'TOGET'

and a further operation

'TOGET' / / 'HER'

produces the string

'TOGETHER'

Example (b)

We want to create a character variable called NAME, consisting of the following variables:

FIRST
MIDDLE
LAST

Using the following program segment:

```
CHARACTER NAME*30, FIRST*10, MIDDLE*10, LAST*10
    FIRST = 'JAGAN'
    MIDDLE = 'LAL'
    LAST = 'MAGISTRATE'
    NAME = FIRST // MIDDLE // LAST
```

the variable NAME will store the following string:

'JAGANⱠⱠⱠⱠⱠLALⱠⱠⱠⱠⱠⱠMAGISTRATE'

Users must note that although the variable FIRST is assigned 'JAGAN', it stores

'JAGANⱠⱠⱠⱠⱠ'

because ten spaces are reserved for this variable and the same is the case with other variables.

8.4.5 Character Library Functions

FORTRAN 77 provides for the following intrinsic functions associated with character data types:

Function Name	Argument Type	Function Type	Action by Function
CHAR (i)	Integer	Character*1	Returns an ith character in the collating sequence
ICHAR (c)	Character*1	Integer	Returns an integer equivalent to the character c in the collating sequence
INDEX (c_1, c_2)	Character	Integer	Returns the starting position of substring c_2 in string c_1
LEN (c)	Character	Integer	Returns the length of the string c
LGE (c_1, c_2)	Character	Logical	Returns True if $c_1 \geqslant c_2$, otherwise False
LGT (c_1, c_2)	Character	Logical	Returns True if $c_1 > c_2$, otherwise False
LLE (c_1, c_2)	Character	Logical	Returns True if $c_1 \leq c_2$, otherwise False
LCT (c_1, c_2)	Character	Logical	Returns True if $c_1 < c_2$, otherwise False

A brief explanation of each of the above intrinsic functions is given below.

8.4.5.1 *Char Function*

The CHAR function returns a single character value equivalent to the integer ASCII code value passed as its argument. The general form is:

        CHAR(i)

where

      i is an integer expression equivalent to an ASCII code.

For example, if i is 65 then the function returns 'A'. If i is 90, the function returns 'Z'.

8.4.5.2 *ICHAR Function*

The ICHAR function returns an integer ASCII code equivalent to the character expression passed as its argument. The general form is:

        ICHAR(c)

where

c is a character expression; if c is longer than one character, the ASCII code equivalent to the first character is returned and the remaining characters are ignored.

For example, if c is 'A' then the function returns 65 and if c is 'Z' the function returns 90.

The function ICHAR is inverse of the function CHAR. That is,

$$ICHAR (CHAR (i)) = i$$

or,

$$CHAR (ICHAR (c)) = c$$

8.4.5.3 *INDEX Function*

The INDEX function returns the starting position of a substring in a character string. It has the form:

$$INDEX (c_1, c_2)$$

where

c_1 is the character string; and

c_2 is the substring for which a match is desired in the string c_1.

For example, if c_1 = 'CHARICHARINDEX' and c_2 = 'INDEX', then the function returns a value of ten; if c_2 = 'RICH', then the function returns a value of four; and if c_2 = 'CHAR', then the function returns a value of one. Usere must note that the string c_1 contains two occurrences of string c_2, but it returns the leftmost (first) occurrence of the string. If the string c_2 is not contained inside the string c_1, the function returns a value of zero.

8.4.5.4 *LEN Function*

The LEN function returns an integer value that indicates the length of a character expression. The general form is:

$$LEN (c)$$

where

c is a character expression.

For example, if c = 'STRINGLENGTH', the function returns a value of 12; and if c = 'FORTRAN⊭ 77' the function returns a value of ten.

8.4.5.5 *Logical Functions (LGE, LGT, LLE and LLT)*

The remaining four functions, LGE, LGT, LLE and LLT, are used for comparing standard logical relationships of two character strings according to the ASCII collating sequence. They return a value which is either true or false. The comparison of two strings is made on a character basis as explained in Section 8.4.2. Some examples of these intrinsic functions are as follows:

(a) If c_1 = 'A' and c_2 = 'B' then functions LGE (c_1, c_2) and LGT (c_1, c_2) return false value while functions LLE (c_1, c_2) and LLT $(c_1.c_2)$ return true value.

(b) If c_1 = 'YES' and c_2 ='YES' then functions LGE (c_1,c_2)
and LLE (c_1,c_2) return true value while functions LGT (c_1,c_2)
and LLT (c_1,c_2) return false value.

These intrinsic functions are equivalent to the .GE. , . GT. , . LE. , .LT. relational operators as shown below:

Function Name	Equivalent Operation using relational operator
LGE (c_1,c_2)	$(c_1. \text{GE. } c_2)$
LGT (c_1,c_2)	$(c_1. \text{GT. } c_2)$
LLE (c_1,c_2)	$(c_1. \text{LE. } c_2)$
LLT (c_1,c_2)	$(c_1. \text{LT. } c_2)$

8.5 INPUT AND OUTPUT OF CHARACTER STRINGS

When a variable is declared to be a character string, computer sets up a storage block using the variable name. Until the string variable is assigned a value, the storage block will contain no characters. A string variable may be assigned a value using DATA, PARAMETER, assignment statement or READ statement. In this section we will discuss READ and corresponding WRITE statements for the character strings I/O.

When a character string is used in a list-directed READ statement, the corresponding input data must be enclosed in apostrophes (a character constant). If the input string is shorter than the associated input list variable, then the variable is padded on the right with blanks. If the character string is longer than the list variable, it is truncated. When a character string is used in a formatted READ statement, apostrophes are not needed, and the format specification Aw can be used. If w is less than the length of the character string, the rightmost positions in memory will be filled with blanks. If w is greater than the length of the character string, only the rightmost characters will be stored. If w is omitted, the length of the string will be used to determine the number of positions to be read.

To illustrate the list-directed input of character strings, consider the following program segment:

```
          CHARACTER*10 TITLE
          :
          READ (5,*) TITLE
```

and if we want to read FORTRAN77, then the input data must be either 'FORTRAN77' or 'FORTRAN77ъ'. If the input string to be read is COMPUTERъPROGRAM', then only 'COMPUTERъP' will be stored in TITLE because the length of TITLE is ten only. If the input string to be read is 'PASCAL', then 'PASCALъъъъ' will be stored in TITLE.

To illustrate the formatted input, assume that TITLE is a character string with length 10. If the input data is FORTRANъ77 and it is between columns

1 and 10, then the execution of the following program segment would yield the results as shown:

```
        CHARACTER*10 TITLE
        ⋮
        READ(5,10) TITLE
```

FORMAT	Contents of TITLE
10 FORMAT (A)	FORTRANƀ77
10 FORMAT (A10)	FORTRANƀ77
10 FORMAT (A15)	ANƀ77ƀƀƀƀƀ
10 FORMAT (A8)	FORTRANƀƀƀ
10 FORMAT (A12)	RTRANƀ77ƀƀ
10 FORMAT (A5)	FORTRƀƀƀƀƀ

8.5.1 OUTPUT OF CHARACTER STRINGS

When a character string is used in a list-directed output statement, the entire character string is printed without delimiting apostrophes. When a character string is used in a formatted output, Aw is used as the format field specification. If w is omitted, the entire string is printed. If w is greater than the length of the string, the extra positions will be filled with blanks on the left of the string. If w is less than the length of the character string, the first w positions of the character string will be written.

Example

Consider the following program segment:

```
        CHARACTER X*2, Y*5, Z*3, U*5, V*15
        X = 'Aƀ'
        Y = 'HAVEƀ'
        Z = 'DAY'
        U = 'NICEƀ'
        V = Y//X//U//Z
        WRITE (5,*) V
        WRITE (5,10) V
        WRITE (5,20) V
        WRITE (5,30) V
        WRITE (5,40) V
   10   FORMAT (' ',A)
   20   FORMAT (' ',A15)
   30   FORMAT (' ',A20)
   40   FORMAT (' ',A10)
        STOP
        END
```

The output would appear as follows:

```
HAVEƀAƀNICEƀDAY
HAVEƀAƀNICEƀDAY
HAVEƀAƀNICEƀDAY
ƀƀƀƀƀHAVEƀAƀNICEƀDAY
HAVEƀAƀNIC
```

8.6. APPLICATIONS OF CHARACTER STRINGS

In this section, we will describe a few examples that illustrate the manipulation of character strings. The first example gives many subroutines that show the basic manipulation of character strings. These subroutines have been tested on computer for their accuracy but we are not including input and output data for them. Readers may try these subroutines on their computers.

8.6.1 Subroutine COUNT

This subroutine counts the total number of alphabetic characters (A,B. . .Z) in a character string NAME (declared in the main program as CHARACTER*20) which is passed as one of the arguments of the subroutine. The other argument is the number of alphabetic characters, NUMBER.

```
      SUBROUTINE COUNT (NAME,NUMBER)
          CHARACTER*20 NAME, CHAR*1
          NUMBER = 0
          DO 10 I = 1, LEN (NAME)
              CHAR = NAME (I : I)
              IF (CHAR.GE 'A'. AND. CHAR. LE. 'Z') THEN
                  NUMBER = NUMBER+1
              END IF
   10     CONTINUE
          RETURN
          END
```

8.6.2 Subroutine INSERT

This subroutine inserts the contents of the substring NAMSUM (declared in the main program as CHARACTER*3) into the string NAME (declared in the main program as CHARACTER*50) at the specified character location LOC. For example, if NAME = 'THISƀIT' and NAMSUB = 'ISƀ' and LOC = 5, then after inserting the substring NAME = 'THISƀISƀIT'. If LOC = 60 (> length of the string), then an error message is written and the substring is not inserted.

```
      SUBROUTINE INSERT (NAME,NAMSUB,LOC)
          CHARACTER NAME*50, NAMSUB*3
```

```
            IF (LOC. GT. LEN (NAME). OR. LOC. LT 0) THEN
               WRITE (5,10)
    10         FORMAT ('AN ERROR IN INSERTING LOCATION')
               RETURN
            END IF
            IF (LOC. EQ.0) THEN
               NAME = NAMSUB//NAME
            ELSE
               NAME = NAME (: LOC)//NAMSUB//NAME (LOC+1 :)
            END IF
            RETURN
            END
```

8.6.3 Subroutine REMOVE

This subroutine removes the specified number of characters NUMBER starting at the character location LOC from a character string NAME (declared in the main program as CHARACTER*50). For example, if NAME = 'THISⱵISⱵIT' and NUMBER = 1, LOC = 5, then after removing NAME = 'THISⱵSⱵIT'. If NUMBER =5 and LOC = 0, then after removing NAME = 'ISⱵIT'. If 0> LOC ⩾ length of the string NAME, then an erroi message is written. If LOC < length but (LOC+NUMBER) ⩾ length of the string, then all the characters to the right of the character location LOC are removed. For example, if NUMBER = 10 and LOC = 5, then NAME = 'THISⱵ'.

```
            SUBROUTINE REMOVE (NAME, NUMBER, LOC)
            CHARACTER*50 NAME
            IF (LOC. LT. 0. OR. LOC. GE. LEN (NAME)) THEN
               WRITE (5,10)
    10         FORMAT ('AN ERROR IN REMOVING LOCATION')
               RETURN
            END IF
            IF (LOC. EQ.0) THEN
               IF (NUMBER. GE. LEN (NAME)) THEN
                  NAME = ' '
               ELSE
                  NAME = NAME (NUMBER+1:)
               END IF
            ELSE
               IF ((NUMBER+LOC). GE. LEN (NAME)) THEN
                  NAME = NAME (: LOC)
               ELSE
                  NAME (: LOC)//NAME (LOC+NUMBER+1:)
               END IF
            END IF
            RETURN
            END
```

8.6.4 Subroutine STN_CN

This subroutine returns a count (NUMBER) of the number of times the substring NUMBER*2 appears in the string NAME*50. For example,

if NAME = 'THIS␢IS␢IT' and NAMSUB = 'IS' then NUMBER = 2
if NAME = 'THIS␢IS␢IT' and NAMSUB = 'IT' then NUMBER = 1

```
          SUBROUTINE STN_CN (NAME, NAMSUB, NUMBER)
          CHARACTER NAME*50, NAMSUB*2, TEMP*50
          NUMBER = 0
          TEMP = NAME
          I = INDEX (TEMP, NAMSUB)
          DO WHILE (I. GT. 0)
               NUMBER = NUMBER+1
               CALL REMOVE (TEMP, (LEN (NAMSUB)+I−1),0)
               I = 0
               IF (LEN (TEMP). GT. 0) THEN
                    I = INDEX (TEMP, NAMSUB)
               END IF
          END DO
          RETURN
          END
```

Users must note that this subroutine calls another subroutine REMOVE described earlier. Variable TEMP is used so that the original string name is not destroyed. The INDEX function finds out the starting position of the first occurrence of the substring NAMSUB in the string TEMP and stores it in variable I. If a match for the substring is found out (that is, I > 0) in the string then the string TEMP is modified so that all the leftmost characters till the end of the first occurrence of the substring are removed. This process is repeated until a match for the substring is found in the string.

8.6.5 Subroutine FORM

This subroutine receives three character strings, FIRST, MIDDLE and LAST, each declared in the main program as CHARACTER*15. The subroutine returns a character string NAME*35 that contains the first name followed by one blank, the middle initial followed by a period and one blank, and finally the last name. For example, if FIRST = 'RENU', MIDDLE = 'KUMAR', LAST = 'AGARWAL', then the string name = 'RENU␢K. ␢AGARWAL'

```
          SUBROUTINE FORM (FIRST, MIDDLE. LAST, NAME)
          CHARACTER*15 FIRST, MIDDLE, LAST, NAME*15
              NAME = FIRST//'␢'//MIDDLE (1:1)//'.␢'//LAST
          RETURN
          END
```

8.7 ARGUMENTS OF TYPE CHARACTER IN A SUBROUTINE

When an actual argument and dummy argument are of type CHARAC-
TER, the length of the string must also be communicated. This can be done
explicitly by having the same length declaration in the calling program and
the subprogram. This approach is limiting in that the argument's length is
fixed. A more powerful approach is to have a variable length declaration. The
general form for a variable length declaration is

$$\text{CHARACTER *(*) } p_1, p_2, \ldots, p_n$$

where

(*) indicates that the dummy character arguments $p_1, p_2, \ldots, p_n$ are of
variable length. The length is determined automatically from the length of
the actual argument when a subprogram is called.

Example

Consider the following program segment:

Subroutine	Main program
SUBROUTINE VICTOR (FOOL)	CHARACTER FOOL1*5, FOOL2*20
CHARACTER *(*) FOOL	————
————	————
————	CALL VICTOR (FOOL1)
	————
	————
	CALL VICTOR (FOOL2)
	————
	————

Note that the variables FOOL1 and FOOL2 are declared in the main program having a length of 5 and 20 respectively. In the subroutine, the dummy
argument FOOL is declared to have a variable length. For the first call to
the subroutine, the length of the dummy variable FOOL in the subroutine
will be five. For the second call, a length of 20 will be assumed.

8.8 PROGRAMMING EXAMPLES

Example 8.1

In Section 6.5 of Chapter 6, we discussed the problem of processing students'
scores. In the problem, the students' identity was recorded by their numbers
and not by their names. In this example, we illustrate the use of character
arrays to store students' names. The program reads students' names and their
scores from a data file SCORE. DAT. It then determines the average marks
for each student. It also prints the information about the student who obtained the highest marks.

The input data file is of the form given below:

'AJAYþKUMAR'	90	80	60	95
'AMARþSINGH'	73	45	30	84
'BRIJþMOHAN'	50	71	75	73

The maximum number of characters in a student's name is assumed to be 20. The number of students in the class is not known in advance. However, it is known that the maximum number of students in the class is 100. The source program is given in Figure 8.1. The input data and the output results are shown in Figure 8.2.

```
****************************************************************************
*          THIS PROGRAM PROCESSES STUDENTS' SCORES                        *
****************************************************************************
*
          CHARACTER*20 NAME(100)
          REAL SCORE(100,4),AVG(100),MAXSCR
          INTEGER INLUN,OUTLUN
          PARAMETER (INLUN = 1,OUTLUN = 2)
*
          OPEN(UNIT=INLUN,FILE='EX8_1.DAT',STATUS='OLD')
          OPEN(UNIT=OUTLUN,FILE='EX8_1.OUT',STATUS='NEW')
* READ STUDENTS' NAMES AND THEIR SCORES
          N_STU=0
          DO 10 I=1,100
            READ(INLUN,*,END=20)NAME(I),(SCORE(I,J),J=1,4)
            N_STU=N_STU+1
10        CONTINUE
20        CONTINUE
* READ STUDENTS' NAMES AND THEIR SCORES
          WRITE(OUTLUN,100)(NAME(I),(SCORE(I,J),J=1,4),I=1,N_STU)
100       FORMAT(' ',A20,4F7.1)
* CALCULATE STUDENTS' SCORE AVERAGE
          DO 40 I=1,N_STU
            AVG(I)=0.0
            DO 30 J=1,4
              AVG(I)=AVG(I)+SCORE(I,J)
30          CONTINUE
            AVG(I)=AVG(I)/4.0
40        CONTINUE
* FIND OUT THE STUDENT WHOSE AVERAGE SCORE IS MAXIMUM
          MAXPOS=1
          MAXSCR=AVG(1)
          DO 50 I=2,N_STU
            IF(MAXSCR.LT.AVG(I))THEN
              MAXSCR=AVG(I)
              MAXPOS=I
            END IF
50        CONTINUE
          AVERAG=SUM/N_STU
* WRITE THE NAME OF THE STUDENT WHO HAS OBTAINED MAXIMUM AVERAGE SCORE
          WRITE(OUTLUN,200)NAME(MAXPOS),MAXSCR
200       FORMAT(' ',A20,'OBTAINED MAXIMUM AVERAGE MARKS = ',F10.2)
          CLOSE(UNIT=INLUN)
          CLOSE(UNIT=OUTLUN)
          STOP
          END
****************************************************************************
```

Figure 8.1: Program Listing of Example 8.1.

Input File Ex8_1.DAT

```
'AJAY KUMAR' 90 80 60 95
'AMAR SINGH' 73 45 30 84
'BRIJ MOHAN' 50 71 75 73
'DEEPAK' 99 89 54 68
'GANGA RAM' 40 30 20 10
'LAKSHMAN SINGH' 85 59 84 87
'NARESH CHANDRA' 91 78 45 56
'NIAMAT ALI' 65 100 46 44
'SUKESH KUMAR' 64 99 63 39
'SUNIL VAIDHYANATHAN' 45 100 74 94
```

```
                    Output File EX8_1.OUT

AJAY KUMAR              90.0     80.0     60.0     95.0
AMAR SINGH             73.0     45.0     30.0     84.0
BRIJ MOHAN             50.0     71.0     75.0     73.0
DEEPAK                 99.0     89.0     54.0     68.0
GANGA RAM              40.0     30.0     20.0     10.0
LAKSHMAN SINGH         85.0     59.0     84.0     87.0
NARESH CHANDRA         91.0     78.0     45.0     56.0
NIAMAT ALI             65.0    100.0     46.0     44.0
SUKESH KUMAR           64.0     99.0     63.0     39.0
SUNIL VAIDHYANATHAN    45.0    100.0     74.0     94.0
AJAY KUMAR             OBTAINED MAXIMUM AVERAGE MARKS =        81.25
```

Figure 8.2: Input Data and Output Results of Example 8.1.

Example 8.2

This example accepts a character string. The maximum length of the string is 300 characters. The program also accepts a right margin position. The position of the left margin is assumed to be one. The program writes the string within the specified margins without splitting words between lines. For example, the string

'YOU CAN FOOL SOME OF THE PEOPLE ALL OF THE TIME
AND ALL OF THE PEOPLE SOME OF THE TIME BUT NOT
ALL OF THE PEOPLE ALL OF THE TIME.'

is printed as follows with a right margin of 20:

YOU CAN FOOL SOME OF
THE PEOPLE ALL OF
THE TIME AND ALL OF
THE PEOPLE SOME OF
THE TIME BUT NOT ALL
OF THE PEOPLE ALL OF
THE TIME.

The program continues until a string 'ZZZZ' is entered. If the string 'ZZZZ' is entered, the program terminates. The source program is given in Figure 8.3. The input data and the output results are shown in Figure 8.4.

```
***********************************************************************
*          THIS PROGRAM ACCEPTS A STRING (MAXIMUM LENGTH 250 CHARACTERS)  *
*          AND A RIGHT MARGIN. IT THEN PRINTS THE STRING WITH THE         *
*          SPECIFIED MARGINS. THE LEFT MARGIN IS ASSUMED TO BE 1.         *
*          LIST OF VARIABLES:                                             *
*          NAME                      USAGE                                *
*          ----                      -----                                *
*          TEXT               STRING TO BE PRINTED WITHIN MARGINS         *
*          R_MARG             RIGHT MARGIN POSITION                       *
*          WIDTH              WIDTH OF LINE LESS 1                         *
*          FIRST              INDEX OF THE BEGINNING OF A LINE            *
*          LAST               INDEX OF THE END OF A LINE                  *
*          LENGTH             LENGTH OF THE STRING                        *
***********************************************************************
*
          CHARACTER*250 TEXT
          INTEGER INLUN,OUTLUN,R_MARG,FIRST,WIDTH
          PARAMETER (INLUN = 5,OUTLUN = 6)
*
* INPUT A STRING
          WRITE(OUTLUN,*),'PLEASE ENTER A STRING <= 250 CHARACTERS'
          READ(INLUN,*)TEXT
          DO WHILE (TEXT(1:1).NE.'ZZZZ')
            LENGTH=LEN(TEXT)
* INPUT A RIGHT MARGIN POSITION
            WRITE(OUTLUN,*),'PLEASE ENTER RIGHT MARGIN'
            READ(INLUN,*)R_MARG
            FIRST=1
            WIDTH=R_MARG-1
* WRITE THE TEXT WITHIN SPECIFIED MARGINS
            DO WHILE (FIRST.LE.LENGTH)
* WITHIN SPECIFIED MARGINS, FOR EACH LINE DETERMINE THE STARTING
* POSITION ( A NON-BLANK CHARACTER) IN THE STRING
              DO WHILE(TEXT(FIRST:FIRST).EQ.' ')
                FIRST=FIRST+1
              END DO
* FOR EACH LINE DETERMINE THE END POSITION IN THE STRING
              LAST=FIRST+WIDTH
              IF(LAST.GT.LENGTH)THEN
                LAST=LENGTH
              ELSE
                IF(TEXT(LAST+1:LAST+1).NE.' ')THEN
                  DO WHILE(TEXT(LAST:LAST).NE.' ')
                    LAST=LAST-1
                  END DO
                END IF
              END IF
* PRINT THE LINE
              WRITE(OUTLUN,*)TEXT(FIRST:LAST)
              FIRST=LAST+1
            END DO
* INPUT ANOTHER STRING
            WRITE(OUTLUN,*),'PLEASE ENTER A STRING <= 250 CHARACTERS'
            READ(INLUN,*)TEXT
          END DO
          STOP
          END
***********************************************************************
```

Figure 8.3: Program Listing of Example 8.2.

```
PLEASE ENTER A STRING <= 250 CHARACTERS
'A B C D E F G H I J K L M N O P Q R S T U V W X Y Z'
PLEASE ENTER RIGHT MARGIN
4
A B
C D
E F
G H
I J
K L
M N
O P
Q R
S T
U V
W X
Y Z

PLEASE ENTER A STRING <= 250 CHARACTERS
'YOU CAN FOOL SOME OF THE PEOPLE ALL OF THE TIME AND
ALL OF THE PEOPLE SOME OF THE TIME BUT NOT ALL OF THE
PEOPLE ALL OF THE TIME.'
PLEASE ENTER RIGHT MARGIN
20
YOU CAN FOOL SOME OF
THE PEOPLE ALL OF
THE TIME AND ALL OF
THE PEOPLE SOME OF
THE TIME BUT NOT ALL
OF THE PEOPLE ALL OF
THE TIME.

PLEASE ENTER A STRING <= 250 CHARACTERS
'ZZZZ'
```

Figure 8.4: Input Data and Output Results of Example 8.2.

8.9 SUMMARY

This chapter introduced you to input, output and manipulation of character strings' data types. Character data is also referred to as *alphanumeric data*, since it includes any character acceptable to computer system. An alphanumeric data item must never be used in numerical calculation. There are, however, a number of applications where alphanumeric data items are used. This is illustrated in Sections 8.6 and 8.8 of the chapter. This chapter has described the 1977 standard FORTRAN features available for the manipulation of the character strings.

With the conclusion of this chapter we come to the end of our discussion on most of the 1977 standard FORTRAN features available to a FORTRAN programmer. The next chapter describes some of the important application programs written in FORTRAN 77.

OBJECTIVE QUESTIONS

(1) Which of the following statements is not correct to declare
NAME and TITLE as character variable names of length 10?
   (a) CHARACTER*10 NAME, TITLE
   (b) CHARACTER NAME*10, TITLE*10
   (c) CHARACTER*10 NAME, TITLE*10
   (d) CHARACTER NAME, TITLE*10
   (e) CHARACTER*10 TITLE, NAME*10

(2) Which of the following statements is correct to declare a ten-element character array SCORE of length 5?
   (a) CHARACTER SCORE(10)
   (b) DIMENSION SCORE(10)
       CHARACTER*5 SCORE
   (c) INTEGER SCORE(10)
       CHARACTER*5 SCORE
   (d) DIMENSION SCORE(10)*5
   (e) CHARACTER STORE(5)*10

(3) Which of the following statements about character arrays is false?
   (a) Character arrays are declared by a character statement.
   (b) Alphanumerics and special symbols can all be stored in character arrays.
   (c) The number of elements to be stored in a character array must be specified in the CHARACTER statement.
   (d) FORTRAN 77 allows character arrays to be used.
   (e) Character arrays may be multi-dimensional arrays.

(4) Which of the following statements extract the substring UNIX, from the string THEᵇUNIXᵇSYSTEM contained in variable NAME?

   (a) NAME (4:8)
   (b) NAME (5:8)
   (c) NAME (5:)
   (d) NAME (:9)
   (e) NAME (4:9)

Study the following program segment and answer questions (5) and (6) :

$$A = \text{'FORTRAN}ᵇ\text{COBOL'}$$
$$B = A (4:)$$
$$C = \text{'PASCAL'}$$
$$D = B // C$$
$$I = \text{LEN}(D)$$
$$E = \text{'XYZ'} // D // A (:2)$$

(5) What is the correct value of I?
   (a) 16
   (b) 15
   (c) 17
   (d) 10
   (e) 6

(6) What is stored in variable E?
   (a) XYZDFO
   (b) XYZTRANᵇCOBOLA
   (c) XYZDA 2
   (d) XYZTRANᵇCOBOLPASCAL
   (e) XYZTRANᵇCOBOLPASCALFO

(7) What is the correct result if the string HINDUSTAN is printed using a format specification A5?
   (a) HINDUSTAN
   (b) HINDU
   (c) USTAN
   (d) ⊔HIND
   (e) HINDU⊔⊔⊔⊔

(8) Which of the following statements returns a TRUE value?
   (a) LLT ('X', 'Z')
   (b) LLE ('XXY', 'XXX')
   (c) LGE ('A⊔REST', 'A⊔RUST')
   (d) LGT ('A⊔B', 'AB')
   (e) LGE ('A', 'B')

DRILL EXERCISES

(1) Give the result of the last statement for each of the following program segments:
   (a) A = 'STRUCTURED⊔FORTRAN⊔ 77'
      L = LEN(A)
   (b) X = 'FIFTH'
      Y = 'COMPUTER'
      Z = 'GENERATION'
      D = 'THEMSELVES'
      E = D (: 3)
      F = E // X // Z // Y
   (c) CHARACTER*2, NAME, TITLE*6
      NAME = 'ABCD'
      TITLE = NAME
   (d) CHARACTER*4 NAME, TITLE*6, OK
      OK = 'O.K. SIR'
      NAME = 'MY'
      TITLE = OK // NAME
   (e) CHARACTER NAME*7, SUM*6, PLUS*2
      NAME = 'FORTRAN'
      NAME = NAME (: 6)
      NAME = NAME (1 : 7)
      NAME = NAME (: 7)
      PLUS = '0+'
      SUM = NAME // PLUS // '2 = 2'

(2) Find out the mistakes in the following program segments:
   (a) CHAR*10 NAME
      NAME = RAJIV GANDHI
      L = LENGTH (NAME)
      STOP
      END
   (b) CHARACTER*10 TITLE, 123
      TITLE = 'BHARAT⊔RATAN
      NAME = TITLE (: 20)
      TITLE = TITLE // XYZ
      STOP
      END

    (c) CHARACTER*5 ARRAY (5)
         ARRAY(1) = 123
         ARRAY(2) = 321
         ARRAY(3) = ARRAY (1)+ARRAY (2)
         ARRAY(6) = ARRAY (1) / / ARRAY (2)
         STOP
         END

(3) Assume the declaration
    CHARACTER NAME*20, TITLE*4
    What is printed by each of the following program segments?

    (a) NAME = 'I♭DON' 'T♭CARE'
         WRITE(5, *) NAME
         WRITE(5, *) NAME(4 : 6)

    (b) NAME = 'ABSTRACTION♭XYZ'
         WRITE(5,*) NAME / / 'ABC'
         WRITE(5, 100) NAME
    100 FORMAT (' ', A 10)

    (c) TITLE = 'WHO'
         NAME = 'CARES'
         NAME = TITLE / / NAME
         L = LEN(NAME)
         WRITE (5,*) L, NAME

(4) In Section 8.6 on applications, we have given many subroutines for string manipulations. Implement these subroutines on your computer and try them for various input data.

(5) Write a FORTRAN 77 program segment to count the number of vowels in the following string:
    'SILENCE!♭THE♭COURT♭IS♭IN♭SESSION'

(6) Write a FORTRAN 77 program segment that reads ten letters into an array and then prints them in reverse order.

(7) Write a FORTRAN 77 program segment to replace all occurrences of 'E' by 'Z' in the following string:
    'I♭WISH♭THESE♭CALCULATIONS♭HAD♭BEEN♭
                       EXECUTED♭BY♭STEAM'

(8) Write a FORTRAN 77 subroutine REPLIC which contains two arguments—a character variable, NAME, and a replication factor, N. The subroutine replicates the given string NAME N times and stores the new replicated string in the variable NAME. For example, if the variable NAME contains 'AH!' then after the execution of the subroutine call
    CALL REPLIC(NAME, 4)
the variable NAME should contain the following string:
    'AH!AH!AH!AH!'

PROGRAMMING EXERCISES

(1) Write a FORTRAN 77 program to count the number of occurrences of each of the articles 'A', 'AN' and 'THE', in a string.

(2) Write a FORTRAN 77 program to count the double-letter occurrences in a given string. For example, the number of double letter occurrences in the string 'OCCURRENCES' is two.

(3) A string is said to be a palindrome if it does not change when the order of characters in the string is reversed. For example,

BOB
MADAM
3 2 1 4 5 4 1 2 3

are palindromes. Write a FORTRAN 77 program to read a string and then determine whether it is a palindrome.

(4) Write a FORTRAN 77 program for converting ordinary Hindu-Arabic numerals into Roman numerals. Table 8.1 gives the correspondence between the two number systems.

Table 8.1

Roman Symbol	Hindu-Arabic Symbol
I	1
V	5
X	10
L	50
C	100
D	500
M	1,000

(5) For a set of three letters, the total number of permutations is 6 which is factorial three (3!). For example, if the letters are A, B, and C, the permutations are:

ABC, ACB, BAC, BCA, CAB, CBA

Similarly for four letters, the total number of permutations is 24 (= 4!) and so on. Write a FORTRAN 77 program segment that accepts four letters and prints out all 24 permutations of these letters.

(6) Cryptography is a science that involves the encoding and decoding of messages for the sake of security and/or secrecy. Once a message has been encoded (encrypted), it can no longer be read unless the code is known or can be figured out.

The simplest form of encryption uses a code in which the usual letters of the alphabet are switched around. For example, the letter D might be substituted for the letter A, R might be substituted for B, and so on. In this way, each letter in the original message gets replaced by a different one. The following table gives a complete substitution list:

```
A B C D E F G H I J K L M N O P Q R S T U V W X Y Z
| | | | | | | | | | | | | | | | | | | | | | | | | |
D R T L O W Q S X B N U I P A Z E C V F G H Y J M K
```

Using the above substitution code, the message

ATTACK♭TARGET♭TO♭YOUR♭RIGHT

is changed into the encoded message

DFFDTN♭FDCQOF♭FA♭MAGC♭CXQSF

Write two FORTRAN 77 programs, the first to accept a message and encode it using the above substitution scheme, and the second to accept the encoded message and print the decoded message. Try your programs on the following messages:

(i) I HAVE BUT ONE LIFE TO GIVE FOR MY COUNTRY
(ii) FREEDOM IS MY BIRTHRIGHT
(iii) OH GOD I HAVE GONE CRAZY
(iv) LET US GO TO DELHI
(v) GOD CREATED THE INTEGERS AND ALL THE REST IS THE WORK OF MAN

(7) Sometimes it is required to print 'banner headlines', in larger than normal characters; for example, 'FORTRAN' might be output as:

```
FFFFF     00000     RRR     TTTTT     RRR         A        N     N
F         0   0     R  R      T      ˙R  R       A A       NN    N
FFF       0   0     RRR       T        RRR      AAAAA      N N   N
F         0   0     RR        T        RR       A   A      N  N  N
F         0   0     R  R      T       R  R      A   A      N   NN
F         00000     R   R     T       R  R      A   A      N     N
```

Write a FORTRAN 77 program to write the above banner headline. You may have to use an array of type character declared as

CHARACTER*7 LETTER(8)

to create each letter. For example, the letter A may be printed as:

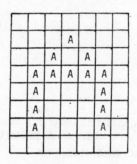

ANSWERS TO OBJECTIVE QUESTIONS

(1) d;   (2) b;   (3) c;   (4) b;   (5) a;
(6) e;   (7) b;   (8) a.

Chapter 9

Applications

9.1 INTRODUCTION

This chapter illustrates the use of the several programming tools we have developed in this book in a variety of scientific, engineering and business applications. An appropriate selection of programming techniques while writing a FORTRAN 77 program for a particular problem is important since a suitable selection not only enhances the clarity of a program, it also reduces the computational time required to run a program.

We have attempted to include a wide range of application areas that require a thorough understanding of the problem and the available programming tools. Readers are strongly advised to go through each exercise and then try to solve the problems given at the end of this chapter. The application areas for which FORTRAN 77 programs have been given are:

(1) Simultaneous solution of linear equations
(2) Numerical integration
(3) Sorting
(4) Searching
(5) Prime numbers
(6) Sparse matrices
(7) Computer matrimonial service.

A detailed conceptual discussion on advanced data structures is also included to give the user an idea of the various data structures that are extensively used in solving more advanced problems. This will be of special interest to those who are planning to major in computer science/engineering as well as those who are planning to learn other languages such as PASCAL, PL/1 and LISP, etc.

9.2 SIMULTANEOUS SOLUTION OF LINEAR EQUATIONS

Various methods are available for the solution of linear simultaneous equations, represented in a general form by $[A][X] = [B]$. We will discuss the following two methods:

1. Gauss elimination method.
2. Gauss-Seidel method.

9.2.1 Gauss Elimination Method

Gauss elimination is a systematic process of eliminating variables from the linear simultaneous equations. The method consists of two parts: *forward elimination* and *backward substitution*.

(a) Forward Elimination

(i) The entire first row of the coefficient matrix [A] is divided by the diagonal element, a_{11} (the pivot element). This generates the value of unity in the diagonal position.

(ii) The first unknown is eliminated from the second row by subtracting it from a multiple of the first row; the multiple being the first element of the second row.

(iii) In a similar fashion, the first variable is eliminated from the third and the following rows.

(iv) Steps (i), (ii) and (iii) are again carried out till all the diagonal elements become unity.

(b) Backward Substitution

(i) Solve the very last equation for the last unknown.

(ii) Using the value of this unknown, work backward, solving each equation in succession.

The accuracy of the Gauss elimination method can be improved by interchanging two rows so that the element with the largest absolute magnitude becomes the pivot element. A FORTRAN 77 program listing is given in Figure 9.1. Figure 9.2 gives the input data and the output results.

9.2.2 Gauss-Seidel Method

Gauss elimination method may involve rounding errors if the number of equations to be solved is quite large. In that case, the Gauss-Seidel method is more appropriate. The Gauss-Seidel method finds the solution to a set of equations by employing an iterative technique. Starting with an initial approximation, the solution is repeatedly refined until final result is within acceptable limits. The stopping criteria generally employed in this method is to check if the largest difference of any two successive values for any variable is within the tolerance limit. An added feature of this method is that the equations need not be linear. The application of this method is illustrated with the following example:

Example

Consider a set of two simultaneous equations

$$4x_1 - x_2 = 1 \tag{1}$$
$$x_1 + x_2 = 4 \tag{2}$$

```
****************************************************************************
*         PROGRAM TO SOLVE N LINEAR SIMULTANEOUS EQUATIONS BY GAUSS        *
*         ELIMINATION METHOD. THE FORM OF EQUATIONS IS:                    *
*                 [A] [X] = [B].                                           *
*         THE DIMENSION OF MATRIX [A] IS NxN.                              *
****************************************************************************
*
        INTEGER INLUN,OUTLUN,N
        COMMON/A01/INLUN,OUTLUN
        LOGICAL ERROR
        REAL A(100,100),B(100),X(100)
        INLUN = 1
        OUTLUN = 2
*
        OPEN(UNIT=INLUN,FILE='EX9_21.DAT',STATUS='OLD')
        OPEN(UNIT=OUTLUN,FILE='EX9_21.OUT',STATUS='NEW')
*
        CALL INPUT(A,B,N)
*
        IF(N.LT.2) THEN
                WRITE(OUTLUN,100)N
                STOP
        END IF
100     FORMAT(' # OF EQUATIONS IS LESS THAN ',I4)
*
        CALL GAUSSE(A,B,X,N,ERROR)
*
        IF(.NOT.ERROR) THEN
*
                CALL OUTPUT(A,B,X,N)
*
        END IF
        CLOSE(UNIT=INLUN)
        CLOSE(UNIT=OUTLUN)
        STOP
        END
*
        SUBROUTINE INPUT(A,B,N)
*
        INTEGER INLUN,OUTLUN,N
        COMMON/A01/ INLUN,OUTLUN
        REAL A(100,100),B(100),X(100)
*
        READ(INLUN,*)N
        READ(INLUN,*)((A(I,J),J=1,N),I=1,N)
        READ(INLUN,*)(B(I),I=1,N)
        RETURN
        END
*
        SUBROUTINE GAUSSE (A,B,X,N,ERROR)
*
        INTEGER INLUN,OUTLUN,N,MX_POS
        COMMON/A01/ INLUN,OUTLUN
        REAL A(100,100),B(100),X(100)
        REAL TEMP_A(100,100),TEMP_B(100),MAX,SUM
        LOGICAL ERROR
* INITIALIZE TWO ARRAYS TEMP_A & TEMP_B WHICH ARE SUBSEQUENTLY
* USED IN PLACE OF ORIGINAL ARRAYS A & B.
        ERROR=.TRUE.
```

(Figure 9.1—Contd.)

```
              DO 20 I = 1,N
                 DO 10 J = 1,N
                      TEMP_A(I,J) = A(I,J)
10               END DO
                 TEMP_B(I) = B(I)
20            END DO
* PIVOTAL ORDERING AND FORWARD ELIMINATION.
              DO 70 I = 1,N-1
* SELECTION OF PIVOT ELEMENT THAT HAS LARGEST ABSOLUTE MAGNITUDE.
              MAX = ABS(TEMP_A(I,I))
              MX_POS = I
              DO 30 J = I+1,N
                 IF(ABS(TEMP_A(J,I)).GT.MAX) THEN
                    MAX = ABS(TEMP_A(J,I))
                    MX_POS = J
                 END IF
30            END DO
* INTERCHANGING ROWS TO PUT LARGEST ELEMENT ON DIAGONAL.
              IF(MAX.NE.0.0) THEN
                 IF(MX_POS.NE.I) THEN
                    DO 40 J = 1,N
                       CALL SWAP (TEMP_A(MX_POS,J),TEMP_A(I,J))
40                  END DO
                    CALL SWAP (TEMP_B(I),TEMP_B(MX_POS))
                 END IF
* FORWARD ELIMINATION.
                 DO 60 J = I+1,N
                    RATIO = TEMP_A(J,I)/TEMP_A(I,I)
                    DO 50 K = I+1,N
                       TEMP_A(J,K) = TEMP_A(J,K)-RATIO*TEMP_A(I,K)
50                  END DO
                    TEMP_B(J) = TEMP_B(J)-RATIO*TEMP_B(I)
60               END DO
              END IF
70            END DO
* TEST FOR THE MATRIX [A] SINGULARITY.
              IF(TEMP_A(N,N).EQ.0.0) THEN
                 WRITE(OUTLUN,100)
100              FORMAT('ERROR -- MATRIX [A] IS SINGULAR')
                 RETURN
              END IF
* BACK SUBSTITUTION.
              X(N) = TEMP_B(N)/TEMP_A(N,N)
              I=N-1
              DO 90 I = N-1,1,-1
                 SUM = 0.0
                 DO 80 J = I+1,N
                    SUM = SUM+TEMP_A(I,J)*X(J)
80               END DO
                 X(I) = (TEMP_B(I)-SUM)/TEMP_A(I,I)
90            END DO
              ERROR = .FALSE.
              RETURN
              END
*
              SUBROUTINE SWAP (VAR_1,VAR_2)
*
              REAL VAR_1,VAR_2,TEMP
              TEMP = VAR_1
              VAR_1 = VAR_2
              VAR_2 = TEMP
              RETURN
              END
```

(Figure 9.1—Contd.)

```
*
         SUBROUTINE OUTPUT (A,B,X,N)
*
         INTEGER INLUN,OUTLUN,N
         COMMON/A01/ INLUN,OUTLUN
         REAL A(100,100),B(100),X(100)
         WRITE(OUTLUN,100)
100      FORMAT('0',T<N*3>,'MATRIX [A]',/,T<N*3>,10('⌣'),/)
         WRITE(OUTLUN,200)((A(I,J),J=1,N),I=1,N)
200      FORMAT('0',<N>F8.4)
         WRITE(OUTLUN,300)
300      FORMAT('0',T<N*3>,'VECTOR [B]',/,T<N*3>,10('-'),/)
         WRITE(OUTLUN,200)(B(I),I=1,N)
         WRITE(OUTLUN,400)
400      FORMAT('0',T<N*2>,'THE SOLUTION VECTOR [X] IS',/,T<N*2>,26('-'),
/)
         WRITE(OUTLUN,200)(X(I),I=1,N)
         RETURN
         END
************************************************************************
```

Figure 9.1: Program Listing of Example 9.2.1.

```
4
1.2    2.1  -1.1    4.0
-1.1   2.0   3.1    3.9
-2.1  -2.2   3.7   16.0
-1.0  -2.3   4.7   12.0
6.0    3.9  12.2    4.0
```

Figure 9.2.1: Input Data of Example 9.2.1.

MATRIX [A]

```
1.2000    2.1000  -1.1000    4.0000

-1.1000    2.0000   3.1000    3.9000

-2.1000  -2.2000   3.7000  16.0000

-1.0000  -2.3000   4.7000  12.0000
```

VECTOR [B]

```
6.0000    3.9000  12.2000    4.0000
```

THE SOLUTION VECTOR [X] IS

```
-2.1291    1.2679  -1.6112    1.0300
```

Figure 9.2.2: Output Results of Example 9.2.1.

x_1 and x_2 can be obtained from Equations (1) and (2) as

$$x_1 = \frac{1+x_2}{4} \tag{3}$$

$$x_2 = 4 - x_1 \tag{4}$$

The exact values of x_1 and x_2 are 1.0 and 3.0 respectively. Starting with the initial value of $x_2 = 0$, we find from (3) that

$$x_1 = 0.25$$

and then from Equation (4), using $x_1 = 0.25$, x_2 is obtained as 3.75. Again x_1 is calculated from Equation (3) after substituting $x_2 = 3.75$ and this process is continued till results are within the tolerance limit. The tolerance limit for this example is chosen as 0.0001. Table 9.1 gives the sequence of values for x_1 and x_2 and also the largest difference for two successive values. In ten iterations, the results obtained are within acceptable limits. The final values of x_1 and x_2 are 0.99989 and 3.000011, respectively.

Table 9.1 Gauss-Seidel Iteration for the Example 9.2.2

Iteration #	x_1	x_2	largest difference
1	—	0	3.75
2	0.25	3.75	0.9375
3	1.1875	2.8125	0.234375
4	0.953125	3.046875	0.058594
5	1.011719	2.988281	0.014649
6	0.99707	3.00293	0.003662
7	1.000732	2.999268	0.000915
8	0.999817	3.000183	0.000229
9	1.000046	2.999954	0.000057
10	0.999989	3.000011	

There are several potential problems with this method. The most notable problem is that the method may not converge at all. That is, successive values may drift farther and farther away from the correct solution. Readers may check this divergence by deriving expressions for x_1 and x_2 from Equations (2) and (1) respectively and starting with an initial estimate of x_1 as 0.0. This divergence may be avoided by interchanging rows to bring the largest element into the pivot position.

A FORTRAN 77 program implementation of the Gauss-Seidel method is given in Figure 9.3 and example runs are given in Figure 9.4. Three runs of results are given: starting with a tolerance value of 10^{-4} for the first run, the tolerance value is decreased to 10^{-5} and 10^{-6} for the second and third runs, respectively. The lower the tolerance, the higher will be the accuracy of the results. With a decrease in the tolerance limit, the number of iterations

```
***********************************************************************
*       PROGRAM TO SOLVE N LINEAR SIMULTANEOUS EQUATIONS BY GAUSS     *
*       SIEDEL METHOD. THE FORM OF EQUATIONS IS:                      *
*            [A] [X] = [B].                                           *
*       THE DIMENSION OF MATRIX [A] IS NxN.                           *
*                                                                     *
*       N_MXIT    = MAXIMUM NUMBER OF ITERATIONS FOR ONE RUN.         *
*       N_SET     = TOTAL NUMBER OF RUNS.                             *
***********************************************************************
*
        INTEGER INLUN,OUTLUN,N
        COMMON/A01/INLUN,OUTLUN,TOLRAN,N_MXIT
        COMMON/A02/N_SET
        LOGICAL ERROR
        REAL A(100,100),B(100),X(100)
        INLUN = 1
        OUTLUN = 2
*
        OPEN(UNIT=INLUN,FILE='EX9_22.DAT',STATUS='OLD')
        OPEN(UNIT=OUTLUN,FILE='EX9_22.OUT',STATUS='NEW')
*
        CALL INPUT(A,B,N)
*
        IF(N.LT.2) THEN
                WRITE(OUTLUN,100)N
                STOP
        END IF
100     FORMAT(' # OF EQUATIONS IS LESS THAN ',I4)
        TOLRAN = 0.0001
        N_MXIT = 50
        N_SET = 1
        DO 10 WHILE (N_SET.LE.3)
*
                CALL GAUSSS(A,B,X,N,ERROR)
*
                IF(ERROR) STOP
*
                CALL OUTPUT(A,B,X,N)
* DECREASE TOLERANCE AND INCREASE NUMBER OF ITERATIONS FOR THE NEXT RUN
                TOLRAN = TOLRAN * 0.1
                N_MXIT = N_MXIT * 2
                N_SET = N_SET + 1
10      END DO
        CLOSE(UNIT=INLUN)
        CLOSE(UNIT=OUTLUN)
        STOP
        END
*
        SUBROUTINE INPUT(A,B,N)
*
        INTEGER INLUN,OUTLUN,N
        COMMON/A01/INLUN,OUTLUN,TOLRAN,N_MXIT
        REAL A(100,100),B(100),X(100)
        READ(INLUN,*)N
        READ(INLUN,*)((A(I,J),J=1,N),I=1,N)
        READ(INLUN,*)(B(I),I=1,N)
        RETURN
        END
```

(Figure 9.3—Contd.)

```
          SUBROUTINE GAUSSS (A,B,X,N,ERROR)
*
          INTEGER INLUN,OUTLUN,N,MX_POS,N_MXIT,N_ITER
          COMMON/A01/INLUN,OUTLUN,TOLRAN,N_MXIT
          REAL A(100,100),B(100),X(100)
          REAL TEMP_A(100,100),TEMP_B(100),MAX,MX_DIF,SUM
          LOGICAL ERROR
* INITIALIZE TWO ARRAYS TEMP_A & TEMP_B WHICH ARE SUBSEQUENTLY
* USED IN PLACE OF ORIGINAL ARRAYS A & B.
          ERROR=.TRUE.
          DO 20 I = 1,N
            DO 10 J = 1,N
                  TEMP_A(I,J) = A(I,J)
10          END DO
            TEMP_B(I) = B(I)
20        END DO
* PIVOTAL ORDERING.
          DO 50 I = 1,N-1
* SELECTION OF PIVOT ELEMENT THAT HAS LARGEST ABSOLUTE MAGNITUDE.
          MAX = ABS(TEMP_A(I,I))
          MX_POS = I
          DO 30 J = I+1,N
            IF(ABS(TEMP_A(J,I)).GT.MAX) THEN
              MAX = ABS(TEMP_A(J,I))
              MX_POS = J
            END IF
30        END DO
* INTERCHANGING ROWS TO PUT LARGEST ELEMENT ON DIAGONAL.
          IF(MAX.NE.0.0) THEN
                IF(MX_POS.NE.I) THEN
                  DO 40 J = 1,N
                      CALL SWAP (TEMP_A(MX_POS,J),TEMP_A(I,J))
40                END DO
                  CALL SWAP (TEMP_B(I),TEMP_B(MX_POS))
                END IF
          END IF
50        END DO
* TEST FOR THE MATRIX [A] SINGULARITY.
          IF(TEMP_A(N,N).EQ.0.0) THEN
                WRITE(OUTLUN,100)
100             FORMAT('ERROR -- MATRIX [A] IS SINGULAR')
                RETURN
          END IF
* INITIALIZE SOLUTION VECTOR [X].
          DO 60 I = 1,N
            X(I)=0.0
60        END DO
          N_ITER = 1
* GAUSS SIEDEL ALGORITHM.
          DO 90 WHILE (N_ITER.LE.N_MXIT)
            MX_DIF = 0.0
            DO 80 I = 1,N
                  SUM = TEMP_B(I)
                  X_OLD = X(I)
                  DO 70 J = 1,N
                      IF(J.NE.I) THEN
                            SUM = SUM - TEMP_A(I,J)*X(J)
                      END IF
70                END DO
```

(Figure 9.3—Contd.)

```
* CALCULATION OF MAXIMUM DIFFERENCE.
               X(I) = SUM/TEMP_A(I,I)
               IF(ABS(X_OLD-X(I)).GT.MX_DIF) THEN
                   MX_DIF = ABS(X_OLD-X(I))
               END IF
80          END DO
* TEST FOR STOPPING CRITERION.
            IF(MX_DIF.LT.TOLRAN) THEN
                ERROR = .FALSE.
                RETURN
            END IF
            N_ITER = N_ITER+1
90       END DO
* NON-CONVERGENCE SITUATION.
         WRITE(OUTLUN,200)TOLRAN,N_MXIT
200      FORMAT(' SOLUTION DOES NOT CONVERGE FOR TOLRAN ',F9.7,
      1  ' IN',I7,' ITERATIONS',/)
         RETURN
         END
*
         SUBROUTINE SWAP (VAR_1,VAR_2)
*
         REAL VAR_1,VAR_2,TEMP
         TEMP = VAR_1
         VAR_1 = VAR_2
         VAR_2 = TEMP
         RETURN
         END
*
         SUBROUTINE OUTPUT (A,B,X,N)
*
         INTEGER INLUN,OUTLUN,N
         COMMON/A01/INLUN,OUTLUN,TOLRAN,N_MXIT
         COMMON/A02/N_SET
         REAL A(100,100),B(100),X(100)
         IF(N_SET.EQ.1) THEN
            WRITE(OUTLUN,100)
100         FORMAT('0',T<N*3>,'MATRIX [A]',/,T<N*3>,10('-'),/)
            WRITE(OUTLUN,200)((A(I,J),J=1,N),I=1,N)
200         FORMAT('0',<N>F8.4)
            WRITE(OUTLUN,300)
300         FORMAT('0',T<N*3>,'VECTOR [B]',/,T<N*3>,10('-'),/)
            WRITE(OUTLUN,200)(B(I),I=1,N)
            WRITE(OUTLUN,400)
400         FORMAT('0',T<N*3>,'THE SOLUTION VECTOR [X] IS',/,
      1     T<N*3>,26('-'),/,' TOLRAN',/)
         END IF
         WRITE(OUTLUN,500)(TOLRAN,(X(I),I=1,N))
500      FORMAT(' ',F9.7,5X,<N>F8.4,/)
         RETURN
         END
******************************************************************
+
```

Figure 9.3: Program Listing of Example 9.2.2.

```
7
4 1 0 0 1 0 0
1 4 1 0 0 1 0
0 1 4 1 0 0 1
0 0 1 4 1 0 0
1 0 0 1 4 1 0
0 1 0 0 1 4 1
0 0 1 0 0 1 4
8 4 8 9 5 6 10
```

Figure 9.4.1: Input Data of Example 9.2.2.

MATRIX [A]

4.0000	1.0000	0.0000	0.0000	1.0000	0.0000	0.0000
1.0000	4.0000	1.0000	0.0000	0.0000	1.0000	0.0000
0.0000	1.0000	4.0000	1.0000	0.0000	0.0000	1.0000
0.0000	0.0000	1.0000	4.0000	1.0000	0.0000	0.0000
1.0000	0.0000	0.0000	1.0000	4.0000	1.0000	0.0000
0.0000	1.0000	0.0000	0.0000	1.0000	4.0000	1.0000
0.0000	0.0000	1.0000	0.0000	0.0000	1.0000	4.0000

VECTOR [B]

8.0000	4.0000	8.0000	9.0000	5.0000	6.0000	10.0000

THE SOLUTION VECTOR [X] IS

TOLERANCE

0.0001000	2.0000	0.0000	1.0000	2.0000	0.0000	1.0000	2.0000
0.0000100	2.0000	0.0000	1.0000	2.0000	0.0000	1.0000	2.0000
0.0000010	2.0000	0.0000	1.0000	2.0000	0.0000	1.0000	2.0000

Figure 9.4.2: Output Results of Example 9.2.2.

may increase. Therefore, starting with 50 as the maximum number of iterations (N_MXIT), the number is doubled for each subsequent run.

9.3 NUMERICAL INTEGRATION

A numerical integration involves determination of the area underneath a curve between the limits. Consider a curve $y = f(x)$ as shown in Figure 9.5.

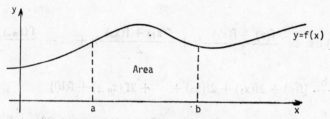

Figure 9.5: Area Under the Curve y = f(x)

The definite integral

$$\int_a^b f(x)\ dx$$

can be interpreted as the area of the region under the curve of the function y = f(x) and above the x-axis and between the lines x = a and x = b. If the function f(x) is too complex and the integration of the function is difficult to obtain, approximate numerical integration methods are used to calculate the area. Some of the commonly employed integration methods are:

1. Rectangle Rule.
2. Trapezoid Rule.
3. Simpson's Rule.
4. Romberg's Method.
5. Monte Carlo Method.

The first four methods are analytical techniques and are not very different from each other. The Monte Carlo method is a simulation technique; therefore a full discussion on Monte Carlo method is presented along with one of the analytical techniques—the Trapezoid Rule.

9.3.1 THE TRAPEZOID RULE

In this method, the region is divided into uniformly spaced sections. For each section, the function f(x) is approximated by a straight line. If a region is divided into n sections, then section width, h, is:

$$h = \frac{b-a}{n}$$

As illustrated in Figure 9.6, the total area of the region can be calculated by summing up the areas of all the sections as given below.

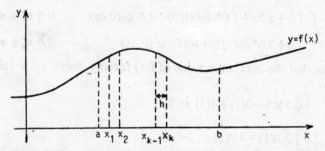

Figure 9.6: Calculation of Area Under Curve y=f(x) Using Trapezoid Rule.

$$\int_a^b f(x)\,dx \cong \frac{f(a)+f(x_1)}{2}h + \frac{f(x_1)+f(x_2)}{2}h + \cdots + \frac{f(x_{n-1})+f(b)}{2}h$$

$$= \frac{h}{2}\,[f(a)+2f(x_1)+2f(x_2)+\cdots+2f(x_{n-1})+f(b)]$$

$$= \frac{h}{2}\,[f(a)+f(b)+2f(a+h)+2f(a+2h)+\cdots+2f(a+(n-1)h)].$$

The accuracy of this method obviously depends on the value of n. The higher the value of n, the more accurate will be the result. A FORTRAN 77 program is given in Figure 9.7. The value of n (NSECTS) is increased in each iteration till the difference in two successive values of the area is within tolerance. A ceiling on the maximum number of sections (N_MAX) has been fixed as 50000. The output results for the function

$$f(x) = \begin{cases} 1.0+0.5x+3.0*\sin\,(x/10)+4.0\cos(0.4x) & 0.0 \leqslant x \leqslant 2.0 \\ 3.0+3.0*\sin(x/10)+4.0\cos(0.4x): & 2.0 \leqslant x \leqslant 4.0 \end{cases}$$

are shown in Figure 9.8.

9.3.2 THE MONTE CARLO METHOD

In this method, the region A is encompassed within a bigger region, B, whose area can be easily calculated (see Figure 9.9). Two random numbers using intrinsic function RAN corresponding to x and y coordinates of a point are generated. A check is made to determine whether the point is inside or outside the region A. For a fixed number of random points, say k (NPNTS), let us assume that n (NBPNTS) points are in region A.

The area of region A in terms of the known area of region B will be:

$$\text{Area of region A} = \frac{n}{k} * \text{Area of region B}$$

A FORTRAN 77 program for this method is given in Figure 9.10. The value of k should be high in order to get an accurate estimate of the area. However, higher values of k result in large computational time. In Figure 9.11, the output results for the function are given.

$$f(x) = \begin{cases} 1.0+3.5x+3.0*\sin(x/10)+4.0\cos(0.4x) & 0.0 \leqslant x \leqslant 2.0 \\ 3.0+3.0*\sin(x/10)+4.0\cos\,(0.4x) & 2.0 \leqslant x \leqslant 4.0 \end{cases}$$

It is obvious that the maximum value of f(x) for any value of x cannot be greater than

$$1+0.5\times4+3(1)+4(1) = 10$$

or

$$3.0+3.0(1)+4.0(1) \quad = 10.$$

```
******************************************************************
*                INTEGRATION USING THE TRAPEZOID RULE            *
******************************************************************
*
      INTEGER OUTLUN,NSECTS,N_MAX
      REAL LBOUND,UBOUND,XBOUND,YBOUND
      REAL H_WIDT,DIFF,AREA_O,AREA_N,BOUNDS,SUM
      PARAMETER (OUTLUN = 2)
*
      OPEN(UNIT=OUTLUN,FILE='EX9_31.OUT',STATUS='NEW')
* INITIALIZE.
      XBOUND = 0.0
      YBOUND = 4.0
      NSECTS = 2
      N_MAX = 50000
      H_WIDT = (YBOUND - XBOUND)/NSECTS
      DIFF = 0.0001
      AREA_O = 0.0
      LBOUND = CURVE(XBOUND)
      UBOUND = CURVE(A_UBOUND)
      BOUNDS = LBOUND + UBOUND
      WRITE(OUTLUN,100)
* CALCULATE THE AREA.
      DO 20 WHILE (NSECTS.LE.N_MAX)
         SUM = 0.0
         DO 10 I = 1,NSECTS - 1
            SUM = SUM + CURVE(XBOUND + I * H_WIDT)
10       END DO
         AREA_N = H_WIDT / 2.0 * (BOUNDS + 2.0 * SUM)
         WRITE(OUTLUN,200)AREA_N,AREA_O,H_WIDT,NSECTS
* CHECK SOLUTION TOLERANCE.
         IF(ABS((AREA_N - AREA_O)/AREA_N).LT.DIFF) THEN
            STOP
         ELSE
            AREA_O = AREA_N
            H_WIDT = H_WIDT / 2.0
            NSECTS = NSECTS * 2
         END IF
20    END DO
      WRITE(OUTLUN,300)N_MAX
100   FORMAT('0',T20,'AREA',T43,'SECTION WIDTH',T60,'SECTIONS',/
     1      ,T7,'CALULATED VALUE',T25,'PREVIOUS VALUE'/)
200   FORMAT(' ',T7,F12.7,T25,F12.7,T42,F12.7,T60,I7)
300   FORMAT(' AREA IS NOT CALCULATED TO DESIRE ACCURACY',/,
     1      ' ALTHOUGH NUMBER OF SECTIONS CONSIDERED IS:',I8)
      CLOSE(UNIT=OUTLUN)
      STOP
      END
*
      FUNCTION CURVE(X)
*
      IF (X.LT.2.0)THEN
         CURVE = 1.0 + 0.5*X + 3.0*SIN(X/10.0) + 4.0*COS(0.4*X)
      ELSE
         CURVE = 3.0 + 3.0*SIN(X/10.0) + 4.0*COS(0.4*X)
      END IF
      RETURN
      END
******************************************************************
```

Figure 9.7: Program Listing of Example 9.3.1.

AREA		SECTION WIDTH	SECTIONS
CALULATED VALUE	PREVIOUS VALUE		
22.7656708	0.0000000	2.0000000	2
22.2025700	22.7656708	1.0000000	4
21.8172073	22.2025700	0.5000000	8
21.5990200	21.8172073	0.2500000	16
21.4835777	21.5990200	0.1250000	32
21.4242706	21.4835777	0.0625000	64
21.3942184	21.4242706	0.0312500	128
21.3791046	21.3942184	0.0156250	256
21.3715057	21.3791046	0.0078125	512
21.3677101	21.3715057	0.0039063	1024
21.3658085	21.3677101	0.0019531	2048

Figure 9.8: Output Results of Example 9.3.1.

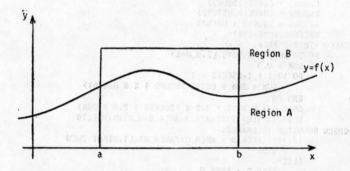

Figure 9.9: Calculation of Area Under Curve y=f(x) Using Monte
Carlo Method.

So the area of the known region B will be 40. The program is quite simple
to follow. The accuracy of this method depends largely on the number of random points used for determining the area. As pointed out earlier, the greater
the number of random points, the more accurate will be the result. The output
results show the area obtained by varying the number of random points. In
each run the number of random points is doubled from its previous value.
The maximum number of random points (N_MAX) has been chosen as
100000. Increasing the maximum number of random points to a higher value
(e.g. 10^7) will result in more CPU time. So a judicious decision about the
maximum number of points is quite important.

9.4 SORTING

The commonest business data-processing problem is sorting a list of items;
that is, arranging these items so that they are either in ascending sequence or
in descending sequence. The sorting operation is also important in many
scientific applications. Some of the most popular sorting techniques are: bubble sort, quick sort, merge sort, heap sort and radix sort. In the following example, we will describe the bubble sort techinque, which is one of the simplest.

```
*******************************************************************
*           INTEGRATION USING THE MONTO-CARLO METHOD              *
*******************************************************************
*
        INTEGER*4 I_RAN,J_RAN
        INTEGER OUTLUN,NPNTS,NBPNTS,N_MAX
        REAL WIDTH,HEIGHT,AREREC,AREA,X,Y
        PARAMETER (OUTLUN = 2)
*
        OPEN(UNIT=OUTLUN,FILE='EX9_32.OUT',STATUS='NEW')
* INITIALIZE.
        I_RAN = 99999999
        J_RAN = 999999999
        WIDTH = 4.0
        HEIGHT = 10.0
        AREREC = WIDTH*HEIGHT
        NPNTS = 1000
        N_MAX = 100000
* CALCULATE AREA BY GENERATING RANDOM POINTS.
        DO 20 WHILE (NPNTS.LE.N_MAX)
            NBPNTS = 0
            DO 10 I = 1,NPNTS
                X = WIDTH*RAN(I_RAN)
                Y = HEIGHT*RAN(J_RAN)
                IF(Y.LE.CURVE(X))THEN
                    NBPNTS = NBPNTS + 1
                END IF
10          END DO
            AREA = FLOAT(NBPNTS)/NPNTS*AREREC
            WRITE(OUTLUN,100)NPNTS,AREA
            NPNTS = NPNTS*2
20      END DO
100     FORMAT(' AREA BY MONTE CARLO METHOD USING',/,
     1  I10,' RANDOM TRIALS IS ',F14.8//)
        CLOSE(UNIT=OUTLUN)
        STOP
        END
*
        FUNCTION CURVE(X)
*
        IF (X.LT.2.0) THEN
            CURVE = 1.0 + 0.5*X + 3.0*SIN(X/10.0) + 4.0*COS(0.4*X)
        ELSE
            CURVE = 3.0 + 3.0*SIN(X/10.0) + 4.0*COS(0.4*X)
        END IF
        RETURN
        END
*******************************************************************
```

Figure 9.10: Program Listing of Example 9.3.2.

BUBBLE SORT

Suppose we have an array of n elements, Item [1], Item [2]...Item [n]. We scan the array, comparing Item[1] and Item[2] and interchanging them immediately if they are in the wrong order. Then Item [2] and Item [3] are compared and are interchanged if they are out of order. This process of comparing and interchanging continues throughout the array. This constitutes one complete pass through the array. There can be at most n−1 passes required.

After each pass through the array, a check is made to determine whether any interchanges occurred during that pass. If no interchanges took place,

```
AREA BY MONTE CARLO METHOD USING
   1000 RANDOM TRIALS IS    20.52000046


AREA BY MONTE CARLO METHOD USING
   2000 RANDOM TRIALS IS    21.65999985


AREA BY MONTE CARLO METHOD USING
   4000 RANDOM TRIALS IS    21.17000198


AREA BY MONTE CARLO METHOD USING
   8000 RANDOM TRIALS IS    21.37500000


AREA BY MONTE CARLO METHOD USING
  16000 RANDOM TRIALS IS    21.21500015


AREA BY MONTE CARLO METHOD USING
  32000 RANDOM TRIALS IS    21.42250061


AREA BY MONTE CARLO METHOD USING
  64000 RANDOM TRIALS IS    21.21375084
```

Figure 9.11: Output Results of Example 9.3.2.

then the array must be sorted and no further scanning of the array is required. Let us consider that the following elements in an array are to be sorted into an ascending order:

68 55 96 34 97

We first compare 68 and 55 and interchange them, giving

55 68 96 34 97

Now we compare 68 and 96 but no interchanging is needed as they are in order. Next 96 and 34 are compared and interchanged, giving

55 68 34 96 97

Finally, 96 and 97 are compared but not interchanged. This completes one pass through the array. Figure 9.12 shows other passes for this example.

j	Item [j]	Pass Number		
		1	2	3 (Sorted)
1	68	55	55	34
2	55	68	34	55
3	96	34	68	68
4	34	96	96	96
5	97	97	97	97

Figure 9.12: Passes of a Bubble Sort.

Note that the largest element in the array sinks to the bottom of the array and some of the smaller elements bubble up towards the top.

A FORTRAN 77 program listing of the bubble sort technique is given in Figure 9.13. The input data and the sorted output results are shown in Figure 9.14.

9.5 SEARCHING

Another equally important business data–processing problem is searching a set of data for a specified item. Two simple searching techniques are *linear search* and *binary search*. In a linear search, each data is scanned in a sequential manner until the desired item is found. Although this method is quite simple, it is not efficient for a large data set. A more efficient technique is the binary search, if the data to be searched have been previously sorted. A binary search for an item in a data set is like searching for a name in telephone directory. With the binary search method, we first examine the middle entry in the data set; if this is the desired item, the search is successful. In an array sorted in ascending order, if the middle entry is higher than the desired item, the first half of the array is examined and the procedure is repeated on the first half until the desired item is found. If the middle entry is lower than the desired item, the second half of the array is scanned. The procedure is repeated only on the secaned half of the array. Now using the middle entry of the second half array, the process continues until the desired item is found or the search interval becomes empty.

To illustrate, suppose that the data array to be searched is:

2, 75, 76, 99, 108, 1000, 9029, 10023 and 99999

and that we are looking for 99. We first examine the middle element, 108, in the fifth position. The middle position is the integer quotient (first + last) divided by 2. 108 is greater than 99, so we can disregard the second half of the array and scan the first half

2, 75, 76, 99

The middle number is 75 in the second position. Since 75 is less than 99 so we disregard the first half of the array and scan the second half:

76, 99

```
*************************************************************************
*  PROGRAM TO READ AN ARRAY OF COUNTRIES AND THEIR CAPITALS AND SORT *
*  THE COUNTRY ARRAY IN ASCENDING ORDER USING BUBBLE SORT.           *
*  THE RESULT DISPLAYS SORTED COUNTRIES AND THEIR CAPITALS.          *
*        N_CUNY       = TOTAL NUMBER OF COUNTRIES                     *
*        CUNTRY       = ARRAY CONTAINING THE NAME OF COUNTRIES        *
*        CAPTAL       = ARRAY CONTAINING THE NAME OF CAPITALS         *
*************************************************************************
*
        INTEGER INLUN,OUTLUN,N_CUNY
        CHARACTER*15 CUNTRY(50),CAPTAL(50)
        PARAMETER (INLUN = 1, OUTLUN = 2)
*
        OPEN(UNIT=INLUN,FILE='EX9_4.DAT',STATUS='OLD')
        OPEN(UNIT=OUTLUN,FILE='EX9_4.OUT',STATUS='NEW')
        READ(INLUN,*)N_CUNY
        READ(INLUN,100)(CUNTRY(I),CAPTAL(I),I=1,N_CUNY)
100     FORMAT(4A15)
        WRITE(OUTLUN,200)N_CUNY
200     FORMAT(T5,' TOTAL NUMBER OF COUNTRIES TO BE SORTED:',I5)
*
        CALL BUBSOR(N_CUNY,CUNTRY,CAPTAL)
*
        WRITE(OUTLUN,300)
300     FORMAT(/,T5' SORTED LIST OF COUNTRIES AND THEIR CAPITALS',
     1    //,T15,'COUNTRY',T30,'CAPITAL',//,T15,'-------',T30,'-------',/)
        WRITE(OUTLUN,400)(CUNTRY(I),CAPTAL(I),I=1,N_CUNY)
400     FORMAT(T15,2A15)
        CLOSE(UNIT=INLUN)
        CLOSE(UNIT=OUTLUN)
        STOP
        END
*
        SUBROUTINE BUBSOR(N_CUNY,CUNTRY,CAPTAL)
*
        CHARACTER*15 CUNTRY(50),CAPTAL(50)
        INTEGER LAST,N_CUNY
        LOGICAL DONE
*
        LAST = N_CUNY
        DO 20 I = 1,N_CUNY-1
                DONE = .TRUE.
* SCAN THE ARRAY COMPARING COSECUTIVE ITEMS.
                DO 10 J = 1,LAST-1
                        IF(CUNTRY(J).GT.CUNTRY(J+1)) THEN
                                CALL SWAP(CUNTRY(J),CUNTRY(J+1))
                                CALL SWAP(CAPTAL(J),CAPTAL(J+1))
                                DONE = .FALSE.
                        END IF
10              END DO
* IF INTERCHANGE OCCURED, SCAN AGAIN, BUT REDUCE THE SIZE OF THE
* UNSORTED ARRAY, OTHERWISE RETURN.
                IF(.NOT.DONE) THEN
                        LAST = LAST - 1
                ELSE
                        RETURN
                END IF
20      END DO
        RETURN
        END
```

(Figure 9.13—Contd.)

```
*
        SUBROUTINE SWAP(VAR_1,VAR_2)
*
        CHARACTER*15 VAR_1,VAR_2,TEMP
*
        TEMP = VAR_1
        VAR_1 = VAR_2
        VAR_2 = TEMP
        RETURN
        END
```
****

Figure 9.13: Program Listing of Example 9.4.

```
25
TURKEY          ANKARA          SYRIA           DAMASCUS
ISREAL          JERUSALAM       IRAQ            BAGHDAD
IRAN            TEHRAN          SAUDI_ARBIA     RIYADH
JORDAN          AMMAN           LEBANON         BEIRUT
AFGHANISTAN     KABUL           PAKISTAN        ISLAMABAD
INDIA           NEW_DELHI       NEPAL           KATHMANDU
BANGLADESH      DAKKA           SRI_LANKA       COLOMBO
CHINA           BEIJING         MONGOLIA        ULAAN_BAATAR
SOUTH_KOREA     SEOL            NORTH_KOREA     PYONGYANG
JAPAN           TOKYO           BURMA           RANGOON
THAILAND        BANGKOK         MALAYSIA        KUALA_LUMPUR
KAMPUCHIA       PHNOM_PENH      PHILIPPNES      MANILA
TAIWAN          TAI_PEI
```

Figure 9.14.1: Input Data of Example 9.4.

```
TOTAL NUMBER OF COUNTRIES TO BE SORTED:    25

SORTED LIST OF COUNTRIES AND THEIR CAPITALS

            COUNTRY         CAPITAL
            -------         -------

            AFGHANISTAN     KABUL
            BANGLADESH      DAKKA
            BURMA           RANGOON
            CHINA           BEIJING
            INDIA           NEW_DELHI
            IRAN            TEHRAN
            IRAQ            BAGHDAD
            ISREAL          JERUSALAM
            JAPAN           TOKYO
            JORDAN          AMMAN
            KAMPUCHIA       PHNOM_PENH
            LEBANON         BEIRUT
            MALAYSIA        KUALA_LUMPUR
            MONGOLIA        ULAAN_BAATAR
            NEPAL           KATHMANDU
            NORTH_KOREA     PYONGYANG
            PAKISTAN        ISLAMABAD
            PHILIPPNES      MANILA
            SAUDI_ARBIA     RIYADH
            SOUTH_KOREA     SEOL
            SRI_LANKA       COLOMBO
            SYRIA           DAMASCUS
            TAIWAN          TAI_PEI
            THAILAND        BANGKOK
            TURKEY          ANKARA
```

Figure 9.14.2: Output Results of Example 9.4.

The middle number is 76 in the first position. Since 76 is less than 99, we consider the second half of the array:

    99

Now the middle number is 99 and this is the desired item.

A FORTRAN 77 program listing of the binary search is shown in Figure 9.15. The input data and the output results are given in Figure 9.16.

```
****************************************************************
*  THIS PROGRAM READS IN AN ARRAY OF STATE NAMES IN AN ASCENDING    *
*  ORDER. IT THEN SEARCHES A STATE IN THE ARRAY USING BINARY SEARCH. *
*       N_STAT        = TOTAL NUMBER OF STATES IN THE ARRAY          *
*       STATE         = ARRAY CONTAINING NAME OF STATES              *
*       S_STAT        = STATE TO BE SEARCHED                         *
****************************************************************
*
        INTEGER INLUN,OUTLUN,MIDDLE,N_STAT
        CHARACTER*15 STATE(50),S_STAT
        LOGICAL SEARCH
        COMMON N_STAT,STATE,S_STAT,MIDDLE,SEARCH
        PARAMETER (INLUN = 1, OUTLUN = 2)
*
        OPEN(UNIT=INLUN,FILE='EX9_5.DAT',STATUS='OLD')
        OPEN(UNIT=OUTLUN,FILE='EX9_5.OUT',STATUS='NEW')
        READ(INLUN,*)N_STAT
        READ(INLUN,100)(STATE(I),I=1,N_STAT)
100     FORMAT(4A15)
        READ(INLUN,200) S_STAT
200     FORMAT(A15)
        WRITE(OUTLUN,300)N_STAT
300     FORMAT(' TOTAL NUMBER OF STATES TO BE SEARCHED:',I5)
        WRITE(OUTLUN,400)
400     FORMAT(/' STATES AMONG WHICH A SEARCH IS MADE ARE AS FOLLOWS :')
        WRITE(OUTLUN,500)(STATE(I),I=1,N_STAT)
500     FORMAT(4A18)
*
        CALL BINSRH
*
        IF (SEARCH) THEN
                WRITE(OUTLUN,600)S_STAT,MIDDLE
600             FORMAT(/' SUCCESSFUL SEARCH, ',A15,' IS IN POSITION',I
5)
        ELSE
                WRITE(OUTLUN,700)S_STAT
700             FORMAT(/' UNSUCCESSFUL SEARCH, ',A15,' IS NOT FOUND')
        END IF
        CLOSE(UNIT=INLUN)
        CLOSE(UNIT=OUTLUN)
        STOP
        END
*
        SUBROUTINE BINSRH
*
        INTEGER LOW,HIGH,MIDDLE,N_STAT
        CHARACTER*15 STATE(50),S_STAT
        LOGICAL SEARCH
        COMMON N_STAT,STATE,S_STAT,MIDDLE,SEARCH
* INITIALIZE.
        SEARCH = .FALSE.
        LOW = 1
        HIGH = N_STAT
* PERFORM BINARY SEARCH.
        DO 10 WHILE ((LOW.LE.HIGH).AND.(.NOT.SEARCH))
* OBTAIN INDEX OF MID POINT OF THE ARRAY.
        MIDDLE = (LOW + HIGH)/2
*COMPARE.
                IF(S_STAT.LT.STATE(MIDDLE)) THEN
                        HIGH = MIDDLE - 1
```

(Figure 9.15—Contd.)

```
          ELSE  IF(S_STAT.GT.STATE(MIDDLE)) THEN
                    LOW = MIDDLE + 1
                ELSE
                    SEARCH = .TRUE.
          END IF
    10    END DO
          RETURN
          END
   **********************************************************************
```

Figure 9.15: Program Listing of Example 9.5.

```
15
ANDHRA_PRADESH ASSAM            BIHAR           GUJARAT
HARAYANA       JAMMU_KASHMIR    KARANATAKA      KERALA
MADHYA_PRADESH MAHARASTRA       PUNJAB          RAJASTHAN
TAMIL_NADU     UTTAR_PRADESH    WEST_BENGAL
MADHYA_PRADESH
```

Figure 9.16.1: Input Data of Example 9.5.

```
TOTAL NUMBER OF STATES TO BE SEARCHED:    15

STATES AMONG WHICH A SEARCH IS MADE ARE AS FOLLOWS :
    ANDHRA_PRADESH   ASSAM            BIHAR           GUJARAT
    HARAYANA         JAMMU_KASHMIR    KARANATAKA      KERALA
    MADHYA_PRADESH   MAHARASTRA       PUNJAB          RAJASTHAN
    TAMIL_NADU       UTTAR_PRADESH    WEST_BENGAL

SUCCESSFUL SEARCH,   MADHYA_PRADESH   IS IN POSITION    9
```

Figure 9.16.2: Output Results of Example 9.5.

9.6 PRIME NUMBERS

A prime number is an integer greater than one whose only positive divisors are one and the integer itself. One method for finding all the prime numbers in the range of 1 through n is known as the *Sieve of Eratosthenes* named after the Greek mathematician who devised it. Consider an array of numbers from 2 through n. Two is the first prime number, but the multiples of 2 (4, 6, 8, 10, ...) are not, and so they are deleted from the array. The first number after 2 that is not deleted is 3, the next prime. We then delete all higher multiples of 3 (9, 15, . . .). The next number not deleted is 5, the next prime, and so we delete all higher multiples of 5 (25,35, . . .). We repeat this procedure until we reach the first number in the array that has not been deleated and whose square is greater than n. Then all the numbers that remain in the array will be the primes from 2 through n.

To illustrate this method, consider the problem of finding all primes in the range of 2 through 20. The array Sieve contains 19 elements (2,3,...,20). The higher multiples of the first prime number, 2, are deleted. One way of deleting these entries is to replace them by the next non-deleted entry, as shown in Figure 9.17. Now the array Sieve contains 10 entries.

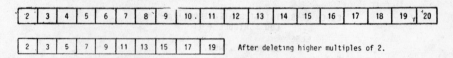

Figure 9.17: Generation of Prime Numbers.

In the next step, the higher multiples of the next prime number, 3, are deleted and now the array Sieve contains only 8 entries. The next prime number is 5, but the process is terminated here since prime number 5^2 is greater than 20. A simpler way of deleting entries in the array Sieve is to replace them by zero, thus keeping the size of the array constant. This is illustrated in Figure 9.18. Figure 9. 19 shows a FORTRAN 77 program listing of Eratosthenes's method. A sample output is also shown in Figure 9.20.

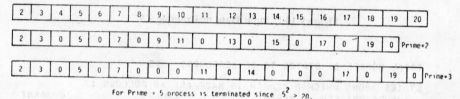

For Prime = 5 process is terminated since $5^2 > 20$.

Figure 9.18: Replacing Multiples of Prime Numbers by Zero.

9.7 SPARSE MATRICES

A detailed discussion on vectors and matrices has already been given in Chapter 6. In many scientific and engineering applications, one comes across very large matrices containing hundreds or even thousands of rows and columns. In many situations, these large matrices contain a preponderance of zero elements. These matrices are called *sparse matrices*. Representing these matrices in a conventional manner as discussed in Chapter 6 is a waste of storage, and moreover operations with these matrices are inefficient. A different kind of storage scheme is employed for representing sparse matrices. This representation does not store zero entries of a matrix.

Consider a sparse matrix [A]

$$[A] = \begin{bmatrix} 0 & 2 & 0 & 0 & 0 & 0 \\ 1 & 0 & 0 & 0 & 0 & 3 \\ 4 & 1 & 0 & 0 & 0 & 0 \\ 0 & 0 & 0 & 0 & 0 & 0 \\ 0 & 0 & 2 & 0 & 0 & 0 \\ 0 & 0 & 0 & 5 & 0 & 0 \end{bmatrix} \text{(6x6)}$$

```
**************************************************************************
* PROGRAM TO FIND ALL PRIME NUMBERS IN THE RANGE FROM 2 THROUGH N   *
* USING THE SIEVE METHOD OF ERATOSTHENIZE.                          *
*      PRIME   = ARRAY CONTAINING PRIME NUMBERS                     *
**************************************************************************
*
        INTEGER OUTLUN,PRIME(1000),N
        PARAMETER (OUTLUN = 2)
*
        OPEN(UNIT=OUTLUN,FILE='EX9_6.OUT',STATUS='NEW')
        TYPE*,' TO FIND PRIMES IN RANGE FROM 2 THROUGH N,'
        TYPE*,' TYPE IN THE VALUE OF N'
        ACCEPT*,N
* INITIALIZE.
        DO 10 I = 2,N
                PRIME(I) = I
10      END DO
*
        CALL ERATOS (PRIME,N)
*
        WRITE(OUTLUN,100)N
100     FORMAT('   PRIME NUMBERS < = ',I5,' ARE:')
        DO 20 I = 2,N
        IF(PRIME(I).NE.0)THEN
                WRITE(OUTLUN,200)PRIME(I)
        END IF
20      END DO
200     FORMAT(T7,I8)
        CLOSE(UNIT=OUTLUN)
        STOP
        END
*
        SUBROUTINE ERATOS (SIEVE,N)
*
        INTEGER SIEVE(1000),P_NUMS
* FIRST PRIME NUMBER.
        P_NUMS = 2
        DO 30 WHILE (((P_NUMS)**2).LE.N)
                J = P_NUMS + 1
* REPLACE MULTIPLES OF PRIME NUMBER BY ZERO.
                DO 10 I = J,N
                        IF(MOD(SIEVE(I),P_NUMS).EQ.0) SIEVE(I) = 0
10              END DO
* SEARCH FOR THE NEXT PRIME NUMBER.
                DO 20 WHILE (SIEVE(J).EQ.0)
                        J = J + 1
20              END DO
                P_NUMS = SIEVE(J)
30      END DO
        RETURN
        END
**************************************************************************
```

Figure 9.19: Program Listing of Example 9.6.

```
    TO FIND PRIMES IN RANGE FROM 2 THROUGH N,
    TYPE IN THE VALUE OF N
    100
    FORTRAN STOP
```

Figure 9.20.1: Interactive Mode Input Data of Example 9.6.

```
     PRIME NUMBERS < =   100 ARE:
                    2
                    3
                    5
                    7
                   11
                   13
                   17
                   19
                   23
                   29
                   31
                   37
                   41
                   43
                   47
                   53
                   59
                   61
                   67
                   71
                   73
                   79
                   83
                   89
                   97
                    .
```

Figure 9.20.2: Output Results of Example 9.6.

Of the 36 elements in this 6×6 matrix, only seven are non-zero. These are:

A[1,2] = 2, A[2,1] = 1, A[2,6] = 3, A[3,1] = 4, A[3,2] = 1
A[5,3] = 2, A[6,4] = 5.

One of the basic methods for storing such matrix is to store non-zero elements in a one-dimensional array and to identify each array element with row and column position, as shown in Figure 9.21.

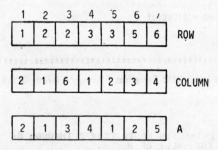

Figure 9.21: Sequential Representations of Sparse Matrices.

A more efficient representation is to further modify the ROW vector as shown in Figure 9.22. The ROW vector is changed so that its ith element indicates to the first of the column positions for the elements in row i of the matrix. Consider the third element of ROW vector whose value is 4: This indicates to the first column position corresponding to 3rd row. The fourth

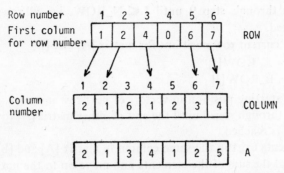

Figure 9.22: A More Efficient Sequential Representation of Sparse Matrices.

element of COLUMN vector is 1 and so A[3,1] = 4. The fourth element of ROW vector is zero, which indicates that the fourth row does not contain any non-zero elements. The value of the fifth element of ROW vector is 6. So the sixth element of COLUMN vector gives the first of the column position for the fifth row position, i.e. A[5,3] which is 2. But what about the fifth element of COLUMN vector? As indicated earlier, the third element of ROW vector indicates to the first of the column positions for the elements in the third row of the matrix [A], A[3,1] = 4. The next position of the COLUMN vector also corresponds to the third row of the matrix [A]. The fifth position of COLUMN vector is 2, so A[3,2] = 1. It should be noted that size of the ROW vector is 6 which is equal to the number of rows in matrix [A]. The size of each of the vectors COLUMN and A is 7 which is equal to the number of non-zero entries in matrix [A].

This efficient representation of the sparse matrix can be used for matrix operations such as addition, subtraction, multiplication, transpose and inverse etc. Using the representation described above, an algorithm for adding two matrices is discussed below.

ADDITION OF TWO MATRICES [A] AND [B]

Two given sparse matrices [A] and [B] are represented by vectors A and B with row and column position vectors A_ROW and A_COL, B_ROW AND B_COL, respectively. It is required to form matrix [C] = [A]+[B]. The number of rows in each matrix [A] and [B] is N_ROW. Each matrix contains A_ENTY AND B_ENTY non-zero elements, respectively. The number of non-zero elements in matrix [C] is C_ENTY. An algorithm for the addition of two matrices is given below. The variable I is used to index the rows of the matrices and J and K index the matrix elements in vectors A and B, respectively.

Algorithm

(1) [Initialization]

   I = 1

   C_ENTY = 0

(2) Repeat through step 9 until I ⩽ N_ROW, i.e. all rows have been processed.
(3) Obtain current row positions for matrix [A] and [B]

   J = A_ROW[I]
   K = B_ROW[I]

(4) Obtain starting position in vectors of next row in matrix [A] and [B]
(5) Repeat through step 7 until the end of either matrix [A] row or matrix [B] row is reached.
(6) If elements exist in the same column in matrix [A] and [B]
   then find the sum of the elements and move on to the next column in matrix [A] and [B]

else if matrix [A] column number is less than matrix [B]'s column number
   then move on to the next column in matrix [A]
   else move on to the next column in matrix [B].

(7) Add new element to matrix [C].
(8) If the end of matrix [A]'s row has not been reached,
   add remaining elements in row to matrix [C].
(9) If the end of matrix [B]'s row has not been reached,
   add remaining elements in row to matrix [C].

A FORTRAN 77 program listing is shown in Figure 9.23. The input data and the output results are shown in Figure 9.24.

9.8 COMPUTER MATRIMONIAL SERVICE

In India, the search for a suitable match for a bride is generally done by the bride's parents or her immediate family members. The chairperson of a computer firm has come up with a proposal which she claims to be better than the existing system of matching suitable partners. She asks every eligible bachelor in her city to fill out a form that contains a list of 100 factors. For each factor, she asks to give a rating with a number between 0 and 10. Zero represents 'NO' or 'Intense Dislike' for that factor, while ten represents 'YES' or 'Intense Like' for that factor. A rating of five means that the candidate does not really care for that factor. The chairperson keeps this entire record in her computer. If a person wishing to getting married approaches her, she asks her/him to fill out the same form and within seconds of the computer matching, she comes out with the name of the most suitable partner.

The method that she uses for matching is based on the *least-square method*. She compares each of the factor ratings of the applicant with all the candidates and then sums up the squares of the differences between the factor ratings of the applicant and each candidate. The candidate (or candidates) with the least sum of squares is considered the most suitable match.

As an example, consider the following input data:

```
           2  3
'AJAY'     M  1  9  3
'VINAY'    M  6  4  5
```

```
**********************************************************************
*   PROGRAM TO ADD TWO SPARSE MATRICES [A] AND [B]. EACH MATRIX IS   *
*   REPRESENTED BY VECTORS A_VECT & B_VECT WITH ROW AND COLUMN       *
*   POSITION INDICES A_ROW & A_COL, B_ROW & B_COL, RESPECTIVELY.     *
*   THE SUM MATRIX [C] IS ALSO REPRESENTED IN THE SAME MANNER AS [A] *
*   & [B] BY FORMING C_VECT,C_ROW & C_COL. THE NUMBER OF NON-ZERO    *
*   ENTERIES IN MATRICES [A],[B] & [C] IS A_ENTY,B_ENTY & C_ENTY.    *
*   THE NUMBER OF ROWS IN EACH MATRIX IS N_ROW.                      *
**********************************************************************
*
        INTEGER INLUN,OUTLUN,I,J,K,L
        INTEGER N_ROW,A_MAX,B_MAX,COLUMN
        INTEGER A_ENTY,A_ROW(100),A_COL(100)
        INTEGER B_ENTY,B_ROW(100),B_COL(100)
        INTEGER C_ENTY,C_ROW(100),C_COL(100)
        REAL A_VECT(100),B_VECT(100),C_VECT(100)
        COMMON N_STAT,STATE,S_STAT,MIDDLE,SEARCH
        PARAMETER (INLUN = 1, OUTLUN = 2)

        OPEN(UNIT=INLUN,FILE='EX9_7.DAT',STATUS='OLD')
        OPEN(UNIT=OUTLUN,FILE='EX9_7.OUT',STATUS='NEW')
* READ MATRICES [A] AND [B].
        READ(INLUN,*)N_ROW
        READ(INLUN,*)A_ENTY
        READ(INLUN,100)(A_ROW(I),I=1,N_ROW)
        READ(INLUN,100)(A_COL(I),I=1,A_ENTY)
        READ(INLUN,200)(A_VECT(I),I=1,A_ENTY)
        READ(INLUN,*)B_ENTY
        READ(INLUN,100)(B_ROW(I),I=1,N_ROW)
        READ(INLUN,100)(B_COL(I),I=1,B_ENTY)
        READ(INLUN,200)(B_VECT(I),I=1,B_ENTY)
100     FORMAT(10I3)
200     FORMAT(10F7.2)
* INITIALIZE (STEP 1).
        I = 1
        C_ENTY = 0
* PROCESS EACH ROW (STEP 2).
        DO 60 WHILE (I.LE.N_ROW)
* OBTAIN ROW INDICES FOR MATRICES [A] AND [B] (STEP 3).
          J = A_ROW(I)
          K = B_ROW(I)
* OBTAIN STARTING POSITION (STEP 4).
          C_ROW(I) = C_ENTY + 1
          A_MAX = 0
          B_MAX = 0
          IF (I.LT.N_ROW) THEN
              L = I + 1
              DO 10 WHILE ((A_MAX.EQ.0).AND.(L.LE.N_ROW))
                    IF(A_ROW(L).NE.0) A_MAX = A_ROW(L)
                    L = L + 1
10            END DO
              L = I + 1
              DO 20 WHILE ((B_MAX.EQ.0).AND.(L.LE.N_ROW))
                    IF(B_ROW(L).NE.0) B_MAX = B_ROW(L)
                    L = L + 1
20            END DO
          END IF
          IF(A_MAX.EQ.0) A_MAX = A_ENTY + 1
          IF(B_MAX.EQ.0) B_MAX = B_ENTY + 1
```

(Figure 9.23—Contd.)

```
* SCAN COLUMN OF THIS ROW (STEP 5).
        DO 30 WHILE ((J.NE.0).AND.(K.NE.0))
* ELEMENTS IN THE SAME COLUMN (STEP 6).
            IF(A_COL(J).EQ.B_COL(K)) THEN
                SUM = A_VECT(J) + B_VECT(K)
                COLUMN = A_COL(J)
                J = J + 1
                K = K + 1
            ELSE
                IF(A_COL(J).LT.B_COL(K)) THEN
                    SUM = A_VECT(J)
                    COLUMN = A_COL(J)
                    J = J + 1
                ELSE
                    SUM = B_VECT(K)
                    COLUMN = B_COL(K)
                    K = K + 1
                END IF
            END IF
* ADD NEW ELEMENTS TO MATRIX [C] (STEP 7).
            IF (SUM.NE.0) THEN
                C_ENTY = C_ENTY + 1
                C_VECT(C_ENTY) = SUM
                C_COL(C_ENTY) = COLUMN
            END IF
* END OF EITHER MATRICES' ROW (STEP 8).
            IF (J.EQ.A_MAX) THEN
                J = 0
            END IF
            IF (K.EQ.B_MAX) THEN
                K = 0
            END IF
30          END DO
* ADD REMAINING ELEMENTS OF A ROW (STEP 9).
        IF((J.EQ.0).AND.(K.NE.0)) THEN
            DO 40 WHILE (K.LT.B_MAX)
                C_ENTY = C_ENTY + 1
                C_VECT(C_ENTY) = B_VECT(K)
                C_COL(C_ENTY) = B_COL(K)
                K = K + 1
40          END DO
        END IF
        IF((J.NE.0).AND.(K.EQ.0)) THEN
            DO 50 WHILE (J.LT.A_MAX)
                C_ENTY = C_ENTY + 1
                C_VECT(C_ENTY) = A_VECT(J)
                C_COL(C_ENTY) = A_COL(J)
                J = J + 1
50          END DO
        END IF
* ADJUST MATRIX [C] INDEX AND INCREASE ROW INDEX.
        IF(C_ENTY.LT.C_ROW(I)) THEN
            C_ROW(I) = 0
        END IF
        I = I + 1
60  END DO
```

(Figure 9.23—Contd.)

```
* PRINT OUTPUT RESULTS.
      WRITE(OUTLUN,300)N_ROW
300   FORMAT(' TOTAL NUMBER OF ROWS : ',I5/)
      WRITE(OUTLUN,400)A_ENTY
400   FORMAT(/,T12,' MATRIX A DETAILS ARE:',//,' TOTAL NUMBER OF
     1 NON-ZERO ENTERIES IS :',I6,/,' THE ROW VECTOR IS :')
      WRITE(OUTLUN,100)(A_ROW(I),I=1,N_ROW)
      WRITE(OUTLUN,500)
500   FORMAT(/' THE COLUMN VECTOR IS :')
      WRITE(OUTLUN,100)(A_COL(I),I=1,A_ENTY)
      WRITE(OUTLUN,600)
600   FORMAT(/' THE VECTOR IS :')
      WRITE(OUTLUN,200)(A_VECT(I),I=1,A_ENTY)
      WRITE(OUTLUN,700)B_ENTY
700   FORMAT(/,T12,' MATRIX B DETAILS ARE:',//,' TOTAL NUMBER OF
     1 NON-ZERO ENTERIES IS :',I6,/,' THE ROW VECTOR IS :')
      WRITE(OUTLUN,100)(B_ROW(I),I=1,N_ROW)
      WRITE(OUTLUN,500)
      WRITE(OUTLUN,100)(B_COL(I),I=1,B_ENTY)
      WRITE(OUTLUN,600)
      WRITE(OUTLUN,200)(B_VECT(I),I=1,B_ENTY)
      WRITE(OUTLUN,800)C_ENTY
800   FORMAT(/,T12,' MATRIX C DETAILS ARE:',//,' TOTAL NUMBER OF
     1 NON-ZERO ENTERIES IS :',I6,/,' THE ROW VECTOR IS :')
      WRITE(OUTLUN,100)(C_ROW(I),I=1,N_ROW)
      WRITE(OUTLUN,500)
      WRITE(OUTLUN,100)(C_COL(I),I=1,C_ENTY)
      WRITE(OUTLUN,600)
      WRITE(OUTLUN,200)(C_VECT(I),I=1,C_ENTY)
      CLOSE(UNIT=INLUN)
      CLOSE(UNIT=OUTLUN)
      STOP
      END
**********************************************************************
```

Figure 9.23: Program Listing of Example 9.7.

```
6
10
  1   3   7   8   0   9
  3   5   1   4   5   7   1   3   4   7
  6.00    9.00    2.00    7.00    8.00    4.00   10.00   12.00    3.00    5.00
8
  0   1   5   6   7   0
  1   2   6   8   5   2   4   7
  9.00    2.00   17.00    8.00    1.00   29.00    3.00   64.00
```

Figure 9.24.1: Input Data of Example 9.7.

The first line of the input data gives the number of candidates and the number of factors considered. The following lines of input data give the details about each candidate and his/her rating. Each line contains the name of the candidate, the sex (M for male, F for female) and the ratings of each of the factors in a chronological order. A female applicant approaches the chairperson with the following input data:

'RITA'   F   2   3   9

For this applicant, the sum of the squares of the differences between factor ratings for each candidate is as given below:

Candidate	Sum of the squares
AJAY	$(2-1)^2+(3-9)^2+(9-3)^2 = 73$
VINAY	$(2-6)^2+(3-4)^2+(9-5)^2 = 33$

So for RITA, VINAY is a better match.

```
TOTAL NUMBER OF ROWS :      6


           MATRIX A DETAILS ARE:
TOTAL NUMBER OF       NON-ZERO ENTERIES IS :     10
THE ROW VECTOR IS :
  1   3   7   8   0   9

THE COLUMN VECTOR IS :
  3   5   1   4   5   7   1   3   4   7

THE VECTOR IS :
  6.00    9.00    2.00   7.00    8.00    4.00   10.00   12.00   3.00   5.00

           MATRIX B DETAILS ARE:

TOTAL NUMBER OF       NON-ZERO ENTERIES IS :      8
THE ROW VECTOR IS :
  0   1   5   6   7   0

THE COLUMN VECTOR IS :
  1   2   6   8   5   2   4   7

THE VECTOR IS :
  9.00    2.00   17.00   8.00    1.00   29.00    3.00   64.00

           MATRIX C DETAILS ARE:

TOTAL NUMBER OF       NON-ZERO ENTERIES IS :     17
THE ROW VECTOR IS :
  1   3  10  12  14  16

THE COLUMN VECTOR IS :
  3   5   1   2   4   5   6   7   8   1
  5   2   3   4   7   4   7

THE VECTOR IS :
  6.00    9.00   11.00   2.00    7.00    8.00   17.00    4.00   8.00   10.00
  1.00   29.00   12.00   3.00   64.00    3.00    5.00
```

Figure 9.24.2: Output Results of Example 9.7.

A FORTRAN 77 program written by the chairperson is given in Figure 9.25. A sample of input and output results is given in Figure 9.26.

9.9 MORE ON DATA STRUCTURES

The previous chapters have dealt with simple data types such as INTEGER, REAL and LOGICAL. Such data types contain single *indivisible* data values that are not combinations of two or more of the other (simple) data types. We have also come across compound data types such as COMPLEX, which is composed of two separate REAL values. Compound data types are called *data structures*. An array is another example of a data structure. FORTRAN explicitly provides three data structures: arrays, strings and type COMPLEX. These data structures are linear and that is why they are called *linear data structures*. There are other linear data structures such as *stacks*, *queues* and *link lists*, which are not explicitly supported by FORTRAN. *Non-linear data structures* such as trees, forests and graphs also exist but these are not provided by FORTRAN.

```
*********************************************************************
*   PROGRAM TO SEARCH FOR A MOST SUITABLE MATRIMONIAL PARTNER FOR AN  *
*   APPLICANT FROM A LIST OF CANDIDATES.                              *
*      N_CAND    = TOTAL NUMBER OF CANDIDATES                         *
*      N_FACT    = TOTAL NUMBER OF FACTORS                            *
*      N_BEST    = TOTAL NUMBER OF SUITABLE PARTNERS                  *
*      APLCAN    = NAME OF THE APPLICANT                              *
*      CANDS     = ARRAY CONTAINING NAME OF ALL CANDIDATES            *
*      AP_RAT    = ARRAY CONTAING FACTOR RATINGS OF THE APPLICANT     *
*      CN_RAT    = ARRAY CONTAING FACTOR RATINGS OF EACH CANDIDATE    *
*      AP_SEX    = SEX OF THE APPLICANT (M = MALE, F = FEMALE)        *
*      CN_SEX    = ARRAY CONTAINING THE SEX OF ALL CANDIDATES         *
*      CN_BEST   = ARRAY CONTAINING NAMES OF SUITABLE PARTENERS       *
*********************************************************************
*
        INTEGER INLUN,N_CAND,N_FACT,N_BEST
        INTEGER CN_RAT(100,50),AP_RAT(50),CN_BEST(100)
        CHARACTER AP_SEX,CN_SEX(100)
        CHARACTER*12 CANDS(100),APLCAN
        COMMON/A01/ CN_RAT,AP_RAT
        COMMON/A02/ CN_SEX,AP_SEX
        COMMON/A03/ CN_BEST,N_BEST
        COMMON/A04/N_CAND,N_FACT
        PARAMETER (INLUN = 1)
*
        OPEN(UNIT=INLUN,FILE='EX9_8.DAT',STATUS='OLD')
        READ(INLUN,*)N_CAND,N_FACT
        READ(INLUN,100)(CANDS(I),CN_SEX(I),(CN_RAT(I,J),
      1 J=1,N_FACT),I=1,N_CAND)
100     FORMAT(A12,A1,<N_FACT>I4)
        PRINT*,' ENTER THE APPLICANT NAME,'
        PRINT*,' IF YOU WANT TO STOP TYPE IN ZZZZ'
        READ(5,*)APLCAN
        DO 10 WHILE (APLCAN.NE.'ZZZZ')
        PRINT*,' TYPE IN THE APPLICANT SEX'
        READ(5,*)AP_SEX
        PRINT*,' TYPE IN THE APPLICANT RATING OF THE FACTORS'
        READ(5,*)(AP_RAT(I),I=1,N_FACT)
*
        CALL SELECT
*
        PRINT 200
200     FORMAT(/,T5,' *** THE OUTPUT IS AS FOLLOWS ***',/)
        PRINT*,' APPLICANT NAME IS:'
        PRINT 300,APLCAN
        PRINT*,' THE BEST MATRIMONIAL MATCH(S) IS:'
        PRINT 300,(CANDS(CN_BEST(I)),I=1,N_BEST)
300     FORMAT(T10,A12,/)
        PRINT*,' ENTER THE APPLICANT NAME,
        PRINT*,' IF YOU WANT TO STOP TYPE IN ZZZZ'
        READ(5,*)APLCAN
10      END DO
        CLOSE(UNIT=INLUN)
        STOP
        END
*
        SUBROUTINE SELECT
*
        INTEGER N_CAND,N_FACT,N_BEST
        INTEGER CN_RAT(100,50),AP_RAT(50),CN_BEST(100)
        CHARACTER AP_SEX,CN_SEX(100)
        CHARACTER*12 CANDS(100),APLCAN
```

(*Figure 9.25—Contd.*)

```
            COMMON/A01/ CN_RAT,AP_RAT
            COMMON/A02/ CN_SEX,AP_SEX
            COMMON/A03/ CN_BEST,N_BEST
            COMMON/A04/N_CAND,N_FACT
            REAL STATSQ(100),MIN
* COMPUTE THE DIFFERENCE OF CANDS' AND APLCAN'S SUM OF SQUARES
* FACTOR RATINGS.
            DO 20 I = 1,N_CAND
                STATSQ(I)=0.0
                IF(AP_SEX.NE.CN_SEX(I)) THEN
                    DO 10 J = 1,N_FACT
                        STATSQ(I) = STATSQ(I) + (CN_RAT(I,J) -
     1                  AP_RAT(I))**2
10                  END DO
                END IF
20          END DO
* DETERMINE THE MINIMUM DIFFERENCE OF SUM OF SQUARES.
            I = 1
            DO WHILE(AP_SEX.EQ.CN_SEX(I))
                I = I + 1
            END DO
            MIN = STATSQ(I)
            DO 30 J = I,N_CAND
                IF((AP_SEX.NE.CN_SEX(J)).AND.(STATSQ(J).LT.MIN)) THEN
                    MIN = STATSQ(J)
                END IF
30          END DO
* SELECT THOSE CANDIDATE(S) HAVING MINIMUM DIFFERENCE IN SUM OF SQUARES.
            N_BEST = 0
            DO 40 I =1,N_CAND
                IF((AP_SEX.NE.CN_SEX(I)).AND.(STATSQ(I).EQ.MIN)) THEN
                    N_BEST = N_BEST + 1
                    CN_BEST(N_BEST) = I
                    PRINT*,CANDS(I)
                END IF
40          END DO
            RETURN
            END
```
****

Figure 9.25: Program Listing of Example 9.8.

All the data structuring facilities provided explicitly in FORTRAN involve homogeneous data structures, i.e., compound data types whose constituent parts are all of the same simple data type. Data structures, however, need not be homogeneous; that is, all the constituent parts need not be of the same data type. Many important data structures such as stacks, queues, trees, graphs and lists are constructed of parts with different data types. A *record* is a rather general data structure, having many parts or fields of arbitrary data types. Records are extremely important data structures in all large systems and data processing applications of computing. Files, which are essentially arrays of records have already been discussed at length in Chapter 5. We now proceed to brief description of some of the more complex data structures.

An array is an ordered set which consists of a fixed number of elements. You cannot delete or insert an element into an array; at best, elements can be changed to a unique value which represents an element to be ignored. This is illustrated in Example 9.6 of Eratosthenes's method of generating prime numbers, where elements to be deleted were set to zero. However, if

```
30 10
VINAY         M    9    6    1    0   10    3    5    3    3    4
DEEPAK        M    8    5    2   10    0    3    4    9    5    5
RITA          F    4    6    3    8    1    3    7    3    6    9
ANJU          F    7    0   10    3    6    5    4    9    2    0
NARESH        M    3    1    8    0   10    9    1    6    8    4
SARIKA        F    5    2   10    3    4    9    7    5    8    9
POONAM        F    6    3    1    3    7    3    9    0    0    7
GANGA_RAM     M    0   10    3    5    4    9    2    0   10   10
SUKESH        M    1    8   10    9    1    6    4   10    0    6
ANIL          M    1    0    1    5    3    4    7    2   10    9
PRAVIN        M    2   10    4    9    7    5    8    9    1    1
PAWAN         M    3    1    3    7    3    9    0    7    9    4
MADHU_BALA    F   10    3    5    4    2    0   10   10    0    3
ARPANA        F    8   10    9    1    4   10    0    6    8    5
RASHMI        F    6    1    0   10    3    5    3    3    4    9
GEETA         F    5    2   10    0    4    9    5    5    7    7
RAJENDRA      M    6    3    8    1    3    7    3    6    9   10
REKHA         F    0   10    6    5    9    2   10   10   10   10
PRIYA         F    6    1    0   10    3    5    3    3    4    9
VIKAS         M    0    0    8    0   10    9    0    0    1    4
ASHOK         M    5    3    4    7    2   10    9    9    9    0
PREM_NATH     M   10    4    9    5    8    9    1    6    8    5
LAVIN         M    3    7    3    9    7    9    4    9    5    7
LAVIKA        F   10    3    5    4    2    0   10   10    0    3
PRIYANKA      F    0   10    6    5    9    2   10   10   10   10
GAGAN         M    0    0    8    0   10    9    0    0    1    4
NALINI        F    6    1    0    1    3    5    3    4    7    2
ANU           F    8   10    9    1    4   10    0    6    8    5
GAURI         F    5    2   10    0    4    9    5    5    7    7
RAHUL.        M.   6    3    8    1    3    7    3    6    9   10
```

Figure 9.26.1: Input Data of Example 9.8.

the number of elements can be changed at the time of execution by either inserting or deleting elements, then such a data structure is defined as a *dynamic data structure*.

A dynamic data structure consists of dynamic variables. A dynamic variable is a variable that is created and disposed of during execution of a program. Conversely, a static variable can be neither created nor destroyed during execution of a program, although the value of the variable may change during execution. A variable is a symbolic address of a memory location. Once a variable in a program is declared, a static relationship between the variable name and a memory location is established and this relationship exists throughout the execution of the program. To illustrate the difference between a static and a dynamic data structure, consider that we need to store three numbers, 10, 20 and 30, in a program. One way of storing these numbers is to use a one-dimensional array [A] as shown below:

```
Memory
Location     100    101    102
          ┌───────┬───────┬───────┐
          │  10   │  20   │  30   │   [A]
          └───────┴───────┴───────┘
```

```
TYPE IN THE APPLICANT NAME, IF YOU WANT TO STOP TYPE IN ZZZZ
'NITA'
TYPE IN THE APPLICANT SEX
'F'
TYPE IN THE APPLICANT RATING OF THE FACTORS
10 10 10 10 10 10 10 10 10 10


      *** THE OUTPUT IS AS FOLLOWS ***

APPLICANT NAME IS:
      NITA

THE BEST MATRIMONIAL MATCH(S) IS:
      VIKAS

      GAGAN

TYPE IN THE APPLICANT NAME, IF YOU WANT TO STOP TYPE IN ZZZZ
'ANKIT'
TYPE IN THE APPLICANT SEX
'M'
TYPE IN THE APPLICANT RATING OF THE FACTORS
1 2 3 4 5 6 7 8 9 10


      *** THE OUTPUT IS AS FOLLOWS ***

APPLICANT NAME IS:
      ANKIT

THE BEST MATRIMONIAL MATCH(S) IS:
      RITA

TYPE IN THE APPLICANT NAME, IF YOU WANT TO STOP TYPE IN ZZZZ
'VINITA'
TYPE IN THE APPLICANT SEX
'F'
TYPE IN THE APPLICANT RATING OF THE FACTORS
1 4 5 6 7 2 5 9 0 10


      *** THE OUTPUT IS AS FOLLOWS ***

APPLICANT NAME IS:
      VINITA

THE BEST MATRIMONIAL MATCH(S) IS:
      DEEPAK

TYPE IN THE APPLICANT NAME, IF YOU WANT TO STOP TYPE IN ZZZZ
'ZZZZ'
FORTRAN STOP
```

Figure 9.26.2: Output Results of Example 9.8.

where $A[1] = 10$, $A[2] = 20$, and $A[3] = 30$. Some memory space is allocated to store these numbers. Variable $A[1]$ is associated with memory location 100, variable $A[2]$ with memory location 101, and so on .... In such a case, if we know the memory location of $A[1]$, we can easily calculate the memory location of $A[3]$ since the memory space allocated to array [A] is one continuous block. The allocation of the memory is done by declaring dimension of array [A]. If we declare the dimension of array [A] as five; i.e.

DIMENSION A[5]

then five memory locations are allocated to array [A] as shown below:

100   101   102   103   104

[A]

The memory allocation af array [A] is fixed and it cannot be changed during execution of a program. In the above example, two memory locations remain unused throughout the program execution. In such a situation, a dynamic memory allocation is superior, i.e. when we do not know in advance how much memory will be required by a program. Dynamic allocation and de-allocation of the memory can be done by using pointers. A pointer is an address or reference to a data structure and it is sometimes called a *link*. In FORTRAN, a pointer is of INTEGER type. Therefore, as imple dynamic data structure, also called *node*, consists of two parts as shown below:

Arbitrary type   Type INTEGER

| INFO | LINK |

Node

The two parts are INFO and LINK. The parts of a dynamic data structure are normally called *fields*. Field INFO can be any data type, integer, real, logical or string, etc. One of the simplest dynamic structures for storing the three numbers, 10, 20 and 30, is a *linked list*.

A linked list involves a set of nodes. The INFO fields contain the information while the LINK fields are used to link the nodes together in any desired sequence. A linked list representation of array [A] values may be displayed as follows:

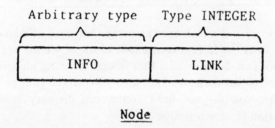

100 INFO	LINK		101 INFO	LINK		102 INFO	LINK
10	101		20	102		30	

The INFO field contains the value while LINK field contains the memory location of the next array element. A better pictorial representation of this linked list is obtained by using arrows as shown below:

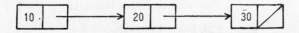

The arrow points its logical successor and $\boxed{/}$ indicates a *null pointer*, i.e. the end of the list. The LINK fields may be used to establish any desired logical order for these nodes and one does not have to worry about the physical order. In an array, however, the physical order of its elements is quite important. This will be clearer when we consider the following example, which also illustrates the superiority of dynamic allocation over static allocation.

Assume that you and your friend share a computer whose memory size is only 10 units. The storage requirement for one variable is one memory unit. You are running a program X which uses an array that needs three memory units and your friend is running program Y which uses an array that needs five memory units. The memory allocation is shown below when both the programs are running. After you have run your program X, you want to

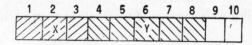

run another program Z which uses an array that needs 4 memory units. The memory space does not have a continuous block of 4 units available, so your program cannot run. Now assume that instead of using an array in program Z, you use a linked list data structure then you can run your program because using linked list you do not need continuous memory space. A possible memory allocation is shown below:

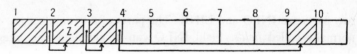

Now without going into complicated programming details, we will describe some of the dynamic data structures.

9.9.1 Linked List

A linked list consists of an ordered set of elements which may vary in number. A simple way to represent a linked list is to expand each node to contain a link to its successive node as displayed in Figure 9.27.

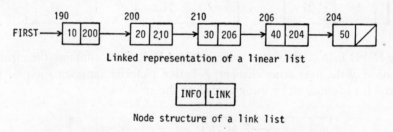

Linked representation of a linear list

Node structure of a link list

Figure 9.27: Linear List Representation.

The variable FIRST contains an address which gives the memory location of the first node of the list. Two commonly performed operations on linked lists are:

(i) Insertion; and (ii) Deletion.

(i) Insertion

In the above list we want to insert a new node (Figure 9.28) between third and fourth nodes. The new node's address is contained in the variable

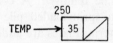

Figure 9.28: Structure of a Node to be Inserted.

TEMP. The insertion is quite straightforward, only links of node 3 and the new node are modified as shown in Figure 9.29.

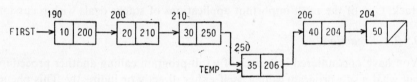

Figure 9.29: Linear List After Node is Inserted.

(ii) Deletion

The deletion of a node is also performed in a straightforward manner. The deletion of second node from the original link list is shown in Figure 9.30. The Link of node 1 is modified.

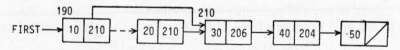

Figure 9.30: Linear List After a Node is Deleted.

9.9.2 Stack

We have seen in the section on linked list, delete and insert operations can be performed at any position in the list. An important sub-class of lists allows these operations to occur at one end. A linear linked list belonging to this subclass is called a stack. A stack is a list in which elements may be inserted or deteled at only one end of the list, called the top of the stack. So the top element of a stack is the most accessible element while the bottom element of a stack is the least accessible element.

An example of a stack, phenomenon can be simulated by putting 50 paisa coins in a pipe closed at one end. The diameter of the pipe is equal to the diameter of the coin. The coin that is inserted first will be the bottom coin and the last inserted coin will be the top coin. Now if you want to take out the bottom coin, you must take out all the other coins. Such a discipline is known as LIFO, Last-In-First-Out, because the last item added to the stack will be the first to be removed. A common example of a stack is a springloaded pile of plates or trays used in a cafeteria. Plates are added

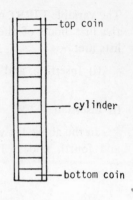

to the pile by pushing them onto the top of the pile. When a plate is removed from the top of the pile, the spring causes the next plate to pop out. In stacks, PUSH- and POP operations are equivalent to insert and delete operations in a list. The only difference is that in a stack, only the first element can be deleted (POP) and an element can be inserted (PUSH) at the top of the stack. One of the most important applications of stacks deals with recursion.

9.9.2.1 *Recursion*

You have encountered instances of a sub-program calling another procedure, but what a sub-program calling itself-either directly or indirectly. This phenomenon is called a recursion. FORTRAN does not explicitly allow recursion, but by using stacks, recursion can be achieved. Recursion is most useful when the quantity being defined or the problem being solved is described recursively. For example, a function definition is said to be recursive if it satisfies two conditions:

(i) A *base* condition in which one or more values of the function are given.

(ii) An *inductive step* in which additional values of the function are defined in terms of previously defined values.

As an example, consider a factorial function. Factorial n (n!) is defined as:

$$n! = n \times (n-1) \times (n-2) \times \ldots \times 3 \times 2 \times 1$$

Similarly,

$$(n-1)! = (n-1) \times (n-2) \times \ldots \times 3 \times 2 \times 1$$
$$\vdots$$
$$0! = 1$$

Now n! can be defined as:

$$n! = \begin{cases} 1 & \text{if } n = 0 \quad \text{(base condition)} \\ n \times (n-1)! & \text{if } n > 0 \quad \text{(inductive step)} \end{cases}$$

9.9.3 Queues

In stack, we came to know about the LIFO (Last-In-First-Out) discipline. Another important discipline is FIFO (First-In-First-Out) or FCFS (First-Come-First-Serve) which is represented by another important subclass of lists, frequently referred to as a queue. We experience queues in our daily life, at railway stations, at supermarkets, at cinema ticket windows, etc. A queue is a list in which elements may be deleted at only one end of the list, called the front or head of the queue, and inserted only at the other end, called the back or rear of the queue, as shown in Figure 9.31.

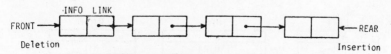

Figure 9.31: Representation of a Queue.

Some of the application areas where queues can be used include simulation and data management facilities in most operating systems.

9.9.4 Trees

Data structures such as stacks and queues have only one link field and belong to the linear list class. There are other data structures which have more than one link field. The most important data structure in this category is a tree, which has at least two link fields. A binary tree has two link fields, LEFT and RIGHT, and the INFO field, as shown in Figure 9.32. Both the link fields may be used for interconnecting various nodes in a tree. Tree structures are therefore quite complex as compared to the linear linked list structures which have only one link for interconnection. In FORTRAN, binary trees can most conveniently be represented by using single-dimensional arrays. A binary tree and its representation in FORTRAN are shown in Figure 9.33 and Figure 9.34, respectively.

Note that the tree is structured so that the INFO value of a name on the left side is less (i.e. earlier in alphabetical order) than the INFO value of its parent while the INFO value of the name on the right side is greater than its parent, e.g. the left child of node 7 'NEHRU' is node 2 'INDIRA' while its right child is node 3, 'PARSAD'. Such a tree is called a *lexically ordered binary tree*. ROOT is the address of the head (root) node. Starting with the

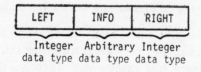

Figure 9.32: The Node Structure of Binary Tree.

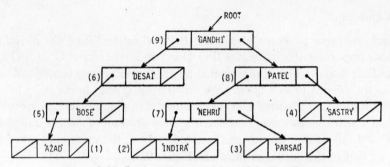

Figure 9.33: Logical Representation of the Tree Structure.

	LEFT		INFO		RIGHT
1	NIL		'AZAD'		NIL
2	NIL		'INDIRA'		NIL
3	NIL		'PARSAD'		NIL
4	NIL		'SASTRY'		NIL
5	1		'BOSE'		NIL
6	5		'DESAI'		NIL
7	2		'NEHRU'		3
8	7		'PATEL'		4
9	6		'GANDHI'		8

ROOT
9

Figure 9.34: FORTRAN Representation of the Tree Structure.

root node ('GANDHI') in a tree, there is only one path of links that leads
to any particular node of the tree; i.e. each node of a tree has exactly one
link leading into it. In other words, the parent node of a child node in a tree
is uniquely defined. However, the creation of a lexically ordered tree from a
set of data is not unique. For example, another logical representation of the
tree structure shown in Figure 9.33 could be as shown in Figure 9.35.

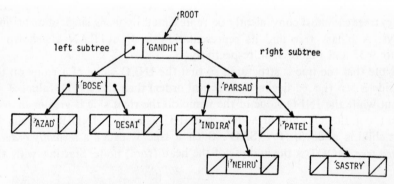

Figure 9.35: Another Logical Representation of the Tree Shown in Figure 9.33.

We will now briefly describe one simple operation for binary trees that is
used in many applications. The operation is traversing the tree; that is, visiting each node in the binary tree exactly once. There are three basic steps in
traversing a binary tree:

1. Visit a node (N).
2. Traverse the left subtree (L).
3. Traverse the right subtree (R).

A left subtree at a node is a tree whose root is the left link, and similarly, a right subtree at a node is a tree whose root is the right link. Left and right subtrees of root node 'GANDHI' are shown in Figure 9.35. The left subtree of node 'BOSE' contains only one node, 'AZAD'; while the left subtree of node 'PARSAD' contains two nodes, 'INDIRA' and 'NEHRU'.

The three steps involved in traversing a binary tree can be performed in any order. There are six different orders:

(1) NLR   i.e. visit a node, then traverse left subtree and then traverse right subtree

(1) LNR

(3) LRN

(4) NRL

(5) RNL

(6) RLN

We can reduce this ordering list to the first three orders if we agree to always traverse the left subtree before the right subtree. The traversals that result from these three orders are identified by special names:

NLR: Preorder Traversal

LNR: Inorder Traversal

LRN: Postorder Traversal

For the tree shown in Figure 9.33, the three types of traversal visit the nodes in the following sequence:

(i) Preorder: GANDHI, DESAI, BOSE, AZAD, PATEL, NEHRU, INDIRA, PARSAD, SASTRY

(ii) Inorder: AZAD, BOSE, DESAI, GANDHI, INDIRA, NEHRU, PARSAD, PATEL, SASTRY

(iii) Postorder: AZAD, BOSE, DESAI, INDIRA, PARSAD, NEHRU, SASTRY, PATEL, GANDHI

The postorder traversal is obtained as follows: we begin at the root 'GANDHI' but before we write it, we must traverse its left and right subtrees. The left and right subtrees are shown in Figure 9.36:

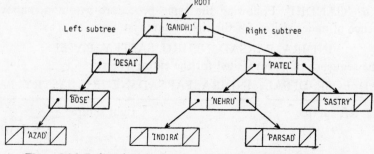

Figure 9.36: Left and Right Subtrees of the Tree Shown in Figure 9.33.

The left subtree has root 'DESAI' but before writing it, we must traverse its left and right subtrees. The subtrees of 'DESAI' are shown in Figure 9.37.

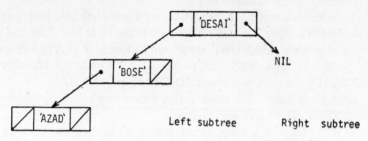

Figure 9.37: Left and Right Subtrees of "DESAI".

The left subtree has root 'BOSE' but again we must traverse its left and right subtrees before writing it. These subtrees are shown in Figure 9.38.

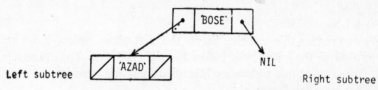

Figure 9.38: Left and Right Subtrees of "BOSE".

Again, the left subtree has root 'AZAD' and we must traverse its left and right subtrees before writing it. The left and right subtrees of 'AZAD' are nil (EMPTY), so we may now write 'AZAD'. After traversing the left subtree of 'BOSE' we must now traverse right subtree which is empty as shown in Figure 9.38. So we may now write the node. The sequence of nodes visited thus far is:

AZAD, BOSE.

After visiting the left subtree of 'DESAI', we must traverse its right subtree which is empty. So we now write the node. The sequence of nodes visited is:

AZAD, BOSE, DESAI

After visiting the left subtree of 'GANDHI', we must now visit the right subtree of 'GANDHI'. Following the same procedure as outlined above, the sequence of nodes visited for the right subtree is:

INDIRA, PARSAD, NEHRU, SASTRY, PATEL

So the sequence of nodes visited for the entire tree is:

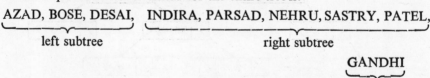

The reader can try the preorder and inorder traversals in similar manner. You should note that inorder traversal of a lexically ordered binary tree gives the node INFO in a sorted manner (in this case, alphabetical order). This can be checked by performing an inorder traversal on the tree as shown in Figure 9.35. The other two traversals visit nodes in a different manner as shown below:

Inorder: AZAD, BOSE, DESAI, GANDHI, INDIRA, NEHRU, PARSAD, PATEL, SASTRY

Preorder: GANDHI, BOSE, AZAD, DESAI, PARSAD, INDIRA, NEHRU, PATEL, SASTRY

Postorder: AZAD, DESAI, BOSE, NEHRU INDIRA, SASTRY, PATEL, PARSAD, GANDHI

There are many other important operations that can be performed on a binary tree. These operations include: insertion of a node, deletion of a node, search of a node and threading of a tree, etc. The applications of these trees are found in the manipulation of arithmetic expressions, construction and maintenance of symbol trees and in syntax analysis where a tree is used to display the structure of a sentence in a language.

As noted earlier, the programming details of various operations involving data structures discussed above are not included. The intention of this section was to introduce basic concepts and basic operations relating to some important data structures. If the user is interested in writing programs for the operations discussed earlier or for any other operations, the following text books may be consulted:

(1) *Structured FORTRAN WATFIV-S Programming* by Jean-Paul Tremblay and Richard B. Bunt, McGraw-Hill, Inc., 1980.

(2) *FORTRAN for Humans* by Rich Didday and Rex Page, 4th edition, West Publishing Company, U.S.A., 1984.

9.10 SUMMARY

This chapter has been exclusively devoted to the use of the fundamental statements and techniques of the FORTRAN language to a variety of problems—scientific, engineering and business. These statements and techniques have been introduced and explained in earlier chapters. We have, however, included a brief conceptual discussion on advanced data structures. The user should be aware that there is much more to learn and that this introductory discussion on data structures has only opened a door to dynamic data structures and their applications.

We are fully convinced that a programming language is like any other language such as Hindi, English, Spanish, French, German, etc. A person tends to forget a language if he/she does not use it. The same is true of any programming language. The user should, therefore, try to write his/her own programs for various problems. We have attempted to include general problems from different desciplines and these should help a user write more complex programs in his/her own discipline. Users are strongly advised to go through programming exercises of this chapter and try to solve them. Many of the programming exercises are quite popular and useful. We have given a full discussion on each problem so that a reader can easily understand the problem. These problems have been arranged in the order of their complexity and difficulty.

DRILL EXERCISES

(1) Run FORTRAN programs given in Examples 9.2.1 and 9.2.2 for the following set of equations:

(a)
$$\begin{bmatrix} 1.2 & 2.1 & 1.1 & 4.0 \\ -1.1 & 2.0 & 3.1 & 3.9 \\ -2.1 & -2.2 & 3.7 & 16.0 \\ -1.0 & -2.3 & 4.7 & 12.0 \end{bmatrix} \begin{bmatrix} a \\ b \\ c \\ d \end{bmatrix} = \begin{bmatrix} 6.0 \\ 3.9 \\ 12.2 \\ 4.0 \end{bmatrix}$$

(b)
$$\begin{bmatrix} 1 & 1 & 1 & 1 & 1 \\ 1 & 2 & 3 & 4 & 5 \\ 1 & 3 & 6 & 10 & 15 \\ 1 & 4 & 10 & 20 & 35 \\ 1 & 5 & 15 & 35 & 70 \end{bmatrix} \begin{bmatrix} u \\ v \\ w \\ x \\ y \end{bmatrix} = \begin{bmatrix} 1 \\ 0 \\ 0 \\ 0 \\ 0 \end{bmatrix}$$

(c)
$$x_1 + (1/2) x_2 + (1/3) x_3 + (1/4) x_4 = 1$$
$$(1/2) x_1 + (1/3) x_2 + (1/4) x_3 + (1/5) x_4 = 0$$
$$(1/3) x_1 + (1/4) x_2 + (1/5) x_3 + (1/6) x_4 = 0$$
$$(1/4) x_1 + (1/5) x_2 + (1/6) x_3 + (1/7) x_4 = 0$$

(2) Determine the area under the curve $y = f(x)$ using the FORTRAN programs given in Examples 9.3.1 and 9.3.2.

(a)

i	0	1	2	3	4	5	6
x_i	0.0	0.1	0.2	0.3	0.4	0.5	0.6
$y = f(x_i)$	1.0	0.905	0.819	0.741	0.670	0.607	0.549

(b) $y = \sqrt{1 - \frac{1}{4} \sin^2 x}$ $0 \leq x \leq \pi/2$

(c) $y = 1/(\sin^2 x + \frac{1}{4}\cos^2 x)$ $0 \leq x \leq \pi/2$

(3) Prepare an input data file that contains the name of your 25 colleagues. Using the FORTRAN program given in Example 9.4, sort them in alphabetical order.

(4) Scanning a map of Africa from north to south, prepare a list of all countries in this continent. Using the FORTRAN program given in Exercise 9.4, sort them in alphabetical order. Then use binary search program given in Example 9.5 to search the following countries:

> Libya
> Tanzania
> Uganda
> Namibia

(5) Run the FORTRAN program given in Example 9.6 to generate prime numbers less than 200. You should modify the program slightly so that you can print four numbers in one line as shown below:

$$
\begin{array}{cccc}
2 & 3 & 5 & 7 \\
11 & 13 & 17 & 19 \\
\cdot & \cdot & \cdot & \\
\cdot & \cdot & \cdot &
\end{array}
$$

(6) Add two sparse matrices [A] and [B] using the FORTRAN program given in Example 9.7 for the following cases:

(a)

$$
[A] = \begin{bmatrix}
1 & 0 & 0 & 2 & 4 \\
3 & 0 & 0 & 0 & 0 \\
0 & 0 & 0 & 0 & 0 \\
4 & 5 & 0 & 0 & 9 \\
0 & 0 & 0 & 0 & 0 \\
1 & 9 & 30 & 0 & 0
\end{bmatrix}
\qquad
[B] = \begin{bmatrix}
0 & 0 & 0 & 0 & 0 & 0 \\
0 & 0 & 0 & 0 & 0 & 0 \\
1 & 1 & 1 & 1 & 1 & 1 \\
0 & 0 & 0 & 0 & 0 & 0 \\
0 & 0 & 0 & 0 & 0 & 0 \\
0 & 0 & 0 & 0 & 0 & 0
\end{bmatrix}
$$

(b)

$$
[A] = \begin{bmatrix}
2 & 3 & 4 & 0 & 0 & 0 & 0 \\
1 & 0 & 0 & 0 & 0 & 0 & 0 \\
3 & 0 & 0 & 0 & 0 & 4 & 0 \\
4 & 0 & 0 & 2 & 0 & 5 & 0 \\
0 & 0 & 0 & 0 & 0 & 0 & 0 \\
0 & 40 & 0 & 0 & 0 & 0 & 0 \\
0 & 0 & 30 & 0 & 0 & 0 & 0 \\
0 & -2 & 0 & -1 & 0 & 0 & 1 \\
0 & 0 & 0 & -2 & 0 & 0 & 0 \\
0 & 0 & 0 & -3 & 0 & 0 & 0 \\
0 & 0 & 4 & 0 & 0 & -1 & 0 \\
0 & 0 & 0 & 0 & 0 & 0 & 0
\end{bmatrix}
\qquad
[B] = \begin{bmatrix}
-2 & -3 & -4 & 0 & 0 & 0 & 0 \\
-1 & 0 & 0 & 0 & -1 & 0 & 0 \\
0 & 0 & 0 & 0 & 0 & 0 & 0 \\
0 & 0 & 3 & 0 & 0 & 0 & 4 \\
0 & 0 & 4 & 0 & 0 & 0 & -2 \\
2 & 0 & -1 & 0 & 5 & 0 & 0 \\
0 & 0 & 0 & 0 & 0 & 6 & 0 \\
-1 & 0 & 0 & 0 & 0 & 0 & 7 \\
0 & 8 & 0 & 0 & 0 & 0 & 0 \\
-11 & 0 & 0 & 5 & 0 & 0 & 0 \\
0 & 0 & 0 & 0 & 0 & 0 & 0 \\
0 & -2 & 0 & 0 & -4 & 0 & 0
\end{bmatrix}
$$

(7) If you want to know who comes closest to you in your group, list all the relevant factors that you think are important in you. Distribute the list among your group members and ask them to give suitable rating. You can choose your own rating scale if you wish. Prepare the necessary input data file and run the FORTRAN program given in Example 9.8 to determine who is the closest to you.

(8) Figure 9.39 shows a linked list representation of a stack. Perform the following operations on the stack and display the stack after each operation is completed

Figure 9.39: Linked List Representation of a Stack.

(a) PUSH a node whose info field is **'PURPLE'**.

(b) POP an element. What is its info field?

(c) POP an element. What is its info field?

(9) Figure 9.40 shows a linked list representation of a queue. Perform the following operations on the queue and display the queue after each operation is completed.

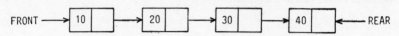

Figure 9.40: Linked List Representation of a Queue.

(a) Delete an element. What is its info field?

(b) Insert a node whose info field is 5.

(c) Delete an element. What is its info field?

(10) An ordered linear linked list is shown in Figure 9.41. Show graphically how would you perform the following operations on the list. You should preserve the ordering in the list.

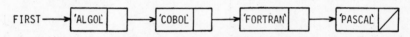

Figure 9.41: An Ordered Linked List.

(a) Insert a node whose info field is **'APL'**.

(b) Delete node whose info field is **'PASCAL'**.

(c) Insert a node whose info field is **'C'**.

(d) Insert a node whose info field is **'SIMULA'**.

(e) Delete node whose info field is **'COBOL'**.

(11) A logical representation of two trees is shown in Figures 9.42 and 9.43. Traverse each tree in preorder, inorder and postorder.

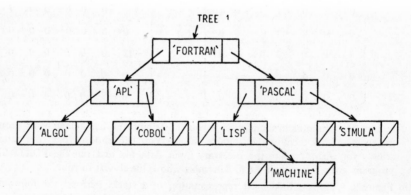

Figure 9.42: Logical Representation of Tree #1.

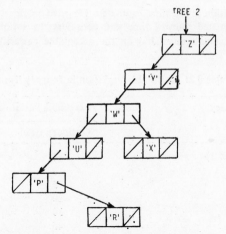

Figure 9.43: Logical Representation of Tree ⧣ 2.

PROGRAMMING EXERCISES

(1) Estimated Entry Search

In Example 9.5, we discussed the binary search algorithm to perform a search operation on a sorted array. The algorithm is very stable and it is well suited to searching for keys (entries) in a given range as well as searching for one unique key. There are, however, more efficient searching algorithms than the binary search and one such method is *interpolation search* or *estimated entry search* algorithm. It is one of the most natural ways to search a sorted array which contains numerical keys. It differs from binary search in calculating (estimating) the value of variable MIDDLE. In a binary search, MIDDLE is calculated as the mid-position in the array but the interpolation search algorithm makes a guess (or interpolation) of where the desired key is apt to be in the array, basing its guess on the value of the key being sought and the values of the LOW and HIGH keys in the array. Using the same variable names as in the program, an estimation of MIDDLE can be made by the following formula

$$\text{MIDDLE} = \left[\frac{(\text{S\_STAT}-\text{STATE (LOW)})}{\text{STATE (HIGH)}-\text{STATE (LOW)}} *(\text{HIGH}-\text{LOW}) \right] + \text{LOW}.$$

Modify the FORTRAN program to implement the interpolation search algorithm. You must then come up with an array of suitable numerical keys for which: (i) the interpolation search performs better than binary search (ii) the interpolation search does not perform better than binary search.

(2) Fibonacci Numbers

The Fibonacci number sequence is used in memory-storage management. The sequence of Fibonacci numbers begins with the integers

1, 1, 2, 3, 5, 8, 13, 21, 34, . . .

where each number after the first two is the sum of the two preceding numbers. Write a FORTRAN program to calculate all the Fibonacci numbers smaller than 1000. Print all the prime numbers contained in this sequence.

(3) Indian Railways

The Chairman of Indian Railways wants to determine whether or not their current estimates of journey times are accurate. Keeping in view various limitations, he allows a variation in the time estimates. He then compares an actual journey time with an estimated journey time and considers the estimate to be too large, acceptable or too small, depending on the acceptable variation in times given in Table 9.2.

Table 9.2: Acceptable Variation in Journey Time

Estimated journey time in hours	Acceptable variation in minutes	
	Ordinary train	Express train
0 – 1 (< 1)	4	2
(⩾ 1) 1 – 4	10	4
4 – 9	15	6
9 – 10	20	10
10 – 15	30	15
15 – 20	45	20
20 – 23	60	25
23 – 30	90	40

For example, if an estimated journey time is 22 hours for an ordinary train, then the acceptable variation is 60 minutes. Thus the estimated time is too large if the actual journey time is less than 21 hours, or the estimated time is too small if the actual time is greater than 23 hours; otherwise the estimate is acceptable. Write a FORTRAN program that reads an estimated time, an actual time and the type of train (EXPRESS or ORDINARY) and then calculates and prints whether the estimated time is too large, small or acceptable. The program should also calculate the amount of the overestimate or underestimate.

(4) *Smart Worm Problem*

In the May 1975 issue of *Scientific American*, an amusing problem about a worm who crawls on a rope is described:

A worm is sitting on the left end of a rubber rope. The length of the rope is 1 meter and the worm can crawl at the rate of 10 cms/second. After every second the rope is uniformly stretched an extra meter in length. Write a FORTRAN program that *computes* and *plots* the progress of the worm at different times. Print out its distance travelled at time t = 1, 100, 500, 1000, 2000 and 5000 seconds. Can you guess if the worm will ever reach the right end of the rope?

To help the users, a brief description of one of the solution methods is given below:

Let $x(t)$ be the distance crawled by the worm at any time t. At $t = 0$, $x(t) = 0$. At $t = 1$, the worm will crawl 10 cms. The rope is stretched uniformly by an extra meter length at $t = 1$. Now the rope is 2 meters long and the worm would be actually at 20 cms from the left end. During the next second, the worm crawls another 10 cms, to be at 30 cms (3/20 of the way down the rope). The rope is then uniformly stretched an extra meter. So the worm would be at 45 cms ($30 + \frac{3}{20} \times 100$). A mathematical relationship can be given a follows:

$$x(t+1) = \left[(x(t) + \text{distance crawled by the worm in one unit of time})* \right.$$

$$\left. \frac{\text{Rope length at the beginning of } (t + 2)\text{th instant}}{\text{Rope length at the beginning of } (t + 1)\text{th instant}} \right]$$

or

$$x(t+1) = \left[\begin{array}{c} (x(t) + \text{distance crawled by the worm in one unit of time})^* \\[4pt] \frac{(t+2)}{(t+1)} \end{array} \right]$$

(5) *Newton's Method*

A very simple method of solving non-linear equations is Newton's method. Consider a general function

$$f(x) = 0$$

Starting with an initial approximation x_1, an updated value of x_1 in the next iteration is obtained as follows:

$$x_{i+1} = x_i - \frac{f(x_i)}{f'(x_i)} \quad \text{where } f'(x_i) \text{ is derivative value of the function } f(x)$$

at $x = x_1$. The stopping criterion is same as in the Gauss-Seidel method, i.e.

$$\left[\text{abs}(x_{i+1} - x_i)/\text{abs}(x_{i+1}) \right] \le \text{tolerance.}$$

Write a FORTRAN program to implement Newton's method and then apply it to calculate the degree of dissociation, x, of hydrogen sulfide (H_2S) gas using the expression

$$(1 - Pk^2) x^3 - 3x + 2 = 0$$

where P is the total pressure and k is the equilibrium constant. Use $k = 0.608$ and $P = 1.0$. Use 0.5 as the initial estimate of x.

(6) *Curve-fitting Using Least Squares Method*

It is often useful to find the equation of a curve that best fits a given set of points (x, y). One way of finding such a curve is curve-fitting by the least squares approximation. In Figure 9.44, P and Q are two of a given set of points and $y = f(x)$ is a possible curve that fits best. P' and Q' are points on the curve having the same x-coordinates as the points P and Q. $f(x)$ is chosen so that the sum of the squares of all the lengths PP' and QQ' is a minimum. Curve $y = f(x)$ can be approximated by a quadratic curve $y = ax^2 + bx + c$.

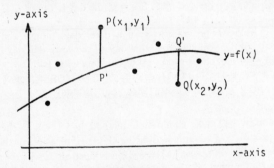

Figure 9.44

The corresponding equations for fitting a quadratic curve $y = ax^2 + bx + c$ to a set of N points (x, y) are:

$$a\Sigma x^4 + b\Sigma x^3 + c\Sigma x^2 = \Sigma x^2 y$$
$$a\Sigma x^3 + b\Sigma x^2 + c\Sigma x = \Sigma xy$$
$$a\Sigma x^2 + b\Sigma x + cN = \Sigma y$$

Write a FORTRAN program to calculate a, b and c for the input data given in Table 9.3.

Table 9.3 Input Data for Curve-Fitting

X	Y
1.0	6.20
2.0	11.50
3.0	13.40
4.0	26.00
5.0	28.65
6.0	28.50
7.0	40.75
8.0	35.00
9.0	45.00

(7) *Zeller's Formula*

A formula for computing the day of the week on which a given date fell or will fall was developed by Zeller. Suppose that we let i, j, k and l be integers defined as follows:

i = the month of the year, with March = 1, April = 2 . . . January = 11 and February = 12.

j = the day of the month.

k = the year of the century.

l = the century.

For example, for August 20, 1930, i = 6, j = 20, k = 30, l = 19; for January 10, 1985, i = 11, j = 10, k = 84 (note!), l = 19. Now calculate the following integer quantities:

a = the integer quotient $(13i-1)/5$

b = the integer quotient $k/4$

c = the integer quotient $l/4$

d = $a+b+c+j+k-2l$

e = remainder of d divided by 7. If e = 0, the day is Sunday, if e = 1 the day is Monday and so on . . .

Write a FORTRAN program to read a date, day, month and year (e.g. 31, January, 1985) and then calculate on what day of the week that day fell or will fall. Determine on what day of the each of the following dates fell:

15, AUGUST, 1947; 26, JANUARY, 1950; 2, OCTOBER, 1869;

7, JUNE 1958; 3, DECEMBER, 1961; Your Birthday.

(8) *The Gauss-Jordan Method*

A variation of the Gauss elimination method is known as the Gauss-Jordan method. It has a distinct advantage over the Gauss elimination method in that the inverse of the coefficient matrix [A] is readily obtained along with the solution vector. In the Gauss-Jordan method, the elements of the major diagonal (pivotal elements) are converted to unity, as they are in the Gauss elimination method. In Gauss elimination method, elements below the diagonal are converted to zeros, while in the Gauss-Jordan method elements both above and below the diagonal are converted to zeros. This avoids the need of backward substitution and the coefficient matrix is converted to a unit matrix. Write a FORTRAN program using the Gauss-Jordan method to solve the following linear simultaneous equations.

$$
\begin{bmatrix} 1 & 2 & 3 & 4 \\ 2 & 3 & 4 & 5 \\ 3 & 4 & 5 & 6 \\ 4 & 5 & 6 & 7 \end{bmatrix}
\begin{bmatrix} x_1 \\ x_2 \\ x_3 \\ x_4 \end{bmatrix}
=
\begin{bmatrix} 5 \\ 6 \\ 7 \\ 8 \end{bmatrix}
$$

(9) *Quick Sort or Partition-Exchange Sort*

An efficient method of sorting large arrays is *quick sort* or *partition-exchange sort*. In the bubble sort, two consecutive elements are compared while quick sort begins by comparing the elements at the opposite ends of the array.

An array to be sorted is successively partitioned into two smaller parts. The elements are rearranged so that all the elements on one side are smaller than all those on the other. The two new parts are then divided into two subparts and the process is repeated. Partitioning continues until there are many parts containing one element each, at which point the array is sorted.

As an example of this approach to sorting, consider the following array [K]:

1	2	3	4	5	6	7	8	9	10
40	20	70	10	60	50	90	30	100	80

Let us see how we can place 40 in its final position. We use index variables I and J with initial values of 2 and 10, respectively. The two keys 40 and K [I] are compared and, if K [I] < 40, then it means an exchange is required so I is incremented by 1 and this process is repeated till K [I] < 40. Note that the elements are not interchanged yet. When K [I] ≥ 40, the process is started from the other end, comparing K [J] and 40. If K [J] > 40, it means an exchange is required, so J is decremented by 1, and this process is repeated until K [J] > 40. At this point, elements K [I] and K [J] are interchanged. For the above example, I = 4 and J = 8 when K [I] = 70 and K [J] = 30 are interchanged. The entire process is then repeated with J fixed and I being incremented once again, when I ≥ J, the desired element (i.e. 40) is placed in its final postion by interchanging elements 40 and K [J]. At this stage, J = 4 so 40 and 10 are interchanged.

The sequence of exchanges for placing 40 in its final position is given in Table 9.4. The elements being compared are encircled. The values of I and J and the action resulting from each step are also given.

Table 9.4 Sequence of Exchanges for Quick Sort Method

1	2	3	4	5	6	7	8	9	10	I	J	Action
(40)	(20)	70	10	60	50	90	30	100	80	2	10	Incr. I
(40)	20	(70)	10	60	50	90	30	100	80	3	10	Compare with K[J]
(40)	20	70	10	60	50	90	30	100	(80)	3	10	Decr. J
(40)	20	70	10	60	50	90	30	(100)	80	3	9	Decr. J
(40)	20	70	10	60	50	90	(30)	100	80	3	8	Interchange 70 & 30 & repeat process again. Incr. I
(40)	20	30	(10)	60	50	90	70	100	80	4	8	Incr. I
(40)	20	30	10	(60)	50	90	70	100	80	5	8	Decr. J
(40)	20	30	10	60	50	(90)	70	100	80	5	7	Decr. J
(40)	20	30	10	60	(50)	90	70	100	80	5	6	Decr. J
(40)	20	30	10	(60)	50	90	70	100	80	5	5	Decr. J
(40)	20	30	(10)	60	50	90	70	100	80	5	4	Interchange 40 & 30 because I>J
10	20	30	40	60	50	90	70	100	80			

The original array has been partitioned into two sub-arrays, one containing 10, 20 and 30, and the other containing 60, 50, 90, 70, 100 and 80. The same process is applied to each of these sub arrays until the array is completely sorted.

Write a FORTRAN program to implement the quick sort algorithm and compare its performance (CPU time) with the bubble sort for different data sets.

(10) *Bank Accounting System*

The Central Bank of India hires you as a consultant to produce a monthly report for the savings account which should contain the following information:
(1) The total number of accounts.
(2) A list in alphabetic order of the names of all account holders, and the balance in each account.
(3) The interest paid at the end of the month to each account holder.
(4) A list in alphabetic order of the number of overdrawn accounts.
(5) A list in alphabetic order of those accounts whose monthly balance exceeds Rs 1000.
(6) A list of account holders and monthly balance. The list is ordered on the basis of their balance, i.e. the person who has maximam balance is the first person in the list and the person with the minimum balance is the last person.

The interest rate is 5% per annum paid on the minimum monthly balance. Try your program for the following input data:

Total number of accounts on Jan. 1, 1986 are as shown below:

Name	Balance
JANKI DAS	Rs 1000
LAKHAN PAL	Rs 2000
MUMTAZ KHAN	Rs 5000
KARORI MAL	Rs 10000
SHANTI DEVI	Rs 500

The following transactions took place in January 1986:
(1) Mumtaz Khan deposited Rs 8000 on January 6. He then closed his account on January 29.
(2) Janki Das withdrew Rs 200 on January 15, and again withdrew Rs 500 on January 16.
(3) Raunaq Ali opened an account on January 1 with a balance of Rs 50000.
(4) Lakhan Pal deposited Rs 5000 on January 1 and then withdrew Rs 500 on January 25.
(5) Karori Mal deposited Rs 2000 on January 14, 1986. He withdrew Rs 1500 on January 28.
(6) Ajay Kumar opened an account on January 29 with a balance of Rs 5.

Prepare your monthly report for January, 1986. Display your results in an appropriate manner which can be easily understood by the bank manager.

(11) *Palindrome Numbers*

A palindrome number is one that reads the same from left to right and right to left—such as 12321, 9834389, etc. There is a very ingenious algorithm to generate a palindrome number starting with any positive integer. The procedure is as follows:
(1) Start with any positive integer.
(2) Obtain another integer number by reversing the digits of the starting integer.
(3) Add two numbers together.
(4) Repeat the whole procedure again with the sum as the starting value, till you get a palindrome number. For example, start with the integer 87. The procedure yields 4884, a palindrome number, in four steps as shown below:

$$\frac{78}{165} \qquad \text{1 step}$$

$$\frac{561}{726} \qquad \text{2 steps}$$

$$\frac{627}{1353} \qquad \text{3 steps}$$

$$\frac{3531}{4884} \qquad \text{4 steps}$$

The number of steps after which one gets a palindrome is dependent on the starting integer. If your starting integer was 89, you would get a palindrome number (8813200023188) after 24 steps. And, of course, you may get a palindrome for a starting integer after too many steps. The number 196 does not yield a palindrome even after 8225 steps. It has, however, been observed that this procedure will yield a palindrome for most of the starting integers within 24 steps.

Write a FORTRAN program that computes palindromes by the above procedure. Try your program for starting values ranging from 50 to 100. Count the number of steps required to reach a palindrome. If a palindrome is not reached after 24 steps, terminate the procedure and print out this information. If a palindrome is reached, print out its value and the number of steps required, You should take care in storing large numbers since the computer cannot handle very large numbers. One way of storing large numbers is to store them in a vector. Dimension two vectors I(20) and J(20). Using the example shown above Vector I will assume 20 values as 00000000000000000087, thus $I(1) = 7$ and $I(2) = 8$ and $I(3) = I(4)$ = ... $I(20) = 0$. The vector J will read as 00000000000000000078, $J(1) = 8$ and $J(2)$ = 7. The sum of these two vectors 00000000000000000165 will be stored in vector I. Again vector J is obtained. The process is continued. You must check at each step if the number is a palindrome or not. This can be easily done by comparing non-zero digits of vector I. For n non-zero digits, check if $I(1) = I(n)$, $I(2) = I(n-1)$ and so on. ... .

(12) *Relatively Prime Numbers*

Using the program given in Example 9.6 to generate prime numbers, write a program to test if two randomly picked positive integers are relatively prime, i.e. if they do not have any factors in common. Test your program for 500 pairs of integers, chosen at random. The largest integer should not be greater than 400. So you need to generate prime numbers up to 400 only. Using these prime numbers, test if a randomly chosen pair having values between 0 and 400 is relatively prime or not. It is established that the probability that two randomly chosen integers are relatively prime is precisely $6/\pi^2$. Run your program to check how closely you can verify this fact. Keeping 500 as the number of the test pairs, if you decrease the limit of the largest integer (i.e. consider integer pairs, say, up to 200 only), do you get a probability value closer to $6/\pi^2$?

(13) *The Tower of Hanoi*

A one person game that is quite old and popular is the Tower of Hanoi problem. The game consists of three vertical pegs and a collection of circular disks, all of different radii with a hole in the centre of each through which a peg can pass (see Figure 9.45). The disks are initially placed on one peg with the largest disk at the bottom, and the disks get progressively smaller as you move up the peg.

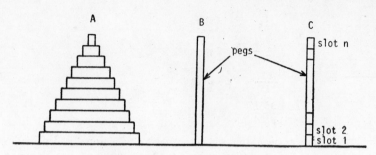

Figure 9.45: The Tower of Hanoi.

The problem is to move the disks from peg A to peg C according to the following rules:

(1) When a disk is moved, it must be placed on one of the three pegs.

(2) Only one disk may by moved at a time, and it must be the top disk on one of the pegs.

(3) A larger disk may never be placed on top of a smaller one.

Legend has it that the priests in the Temple of Bramah were given a puzzle consisting of a gold platform with three large diamond needles. One of the needles held 64 golden disks. The world was to end when they had successfully finished moving the disks to another needle, following the rules given above. This task would take an enormous number of moves. If the priests moved 1 disk per second, it would take them slightly more than 18,446,000,000,000,000,000 seconds to complete the task. Can you verify this fact by writing a FORTRAN program to solve this problem? You might want to use an array to handle the problem. Let there be n disks. Partition each peg into n slots with the 1st slot at the bottom and nth slot at the top as shown for peg C in Figure 9.45. Define an array A (i, j) by:

$$A (i, j) = \begin{cases} k, \text{ if disk (k) is in slot (j) of peg (i)} \\ 0, \text{ if no disk is in slot (j) of peg (i)} \end{cases}$$

When the game begins, $A(1, j) = j$ for $1 \leq j \leq n$ and $A(2,j)$ and $A(3, j) = 0$ for $1 \leq j \leq n$. The game will terminate when $A(i, j) = j$ for one $(i > 1)$ and $A (i, j) = 0$ otherwise. Do not run your program for 64 disks because it may take too much of CPU time. Try for $n = 5$ and $n = 10$.

(14) *Sequential Representation of Sparse Matrices*

The FORTRAN program given in Example 9.7 reads sparse matrices that use a more efficient sequential representation shown in Figure 9.22. Modify the program so that you can read sparse matrices by the sequential representation given in Figure 9.21.

(15) *Transpose of a Sparse Matrix*

Write a FORTRAN program that will form the transpose of a sparse matrix. The transpose of a matrix is obtained by interchanging the corresponding rows and column entries i.e. entry a_{ij} is interchanged with the entry a_{ji}. The sparse matrix is represented in the sequential manner given in Figure 9.21 (Example 9.7).

(16) *Multiplication of Two Sparse Matrices*

Write a FORTRAN program to multiply two sparse matrices $[A]_{m \times n}$ and $[B]_{n \times k}$ represented in the sequential manner shown in Figure 9.22 (Example 9.7).

(17) *Matrix Representation of Graphs*

A directed graph or digraph consists of a set of vertices (nodes) and a set of directed arcs (edges) joining vertices, as shown in Figure 9.46. The graph contains five nodes and seven edges. A directed graph having n nodes can be represented by

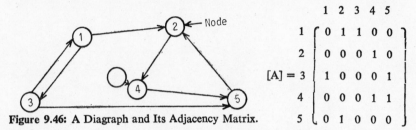

$$[A] = \begin{array}{c} \\ 1 \\ 2 \\ 3 \\ 4 \\ 5 \end{array} \begin{array}{ccccc} 1 & 2 & 3 & 4 & 5 \\ \left[\begin{array}{ccccc} 0 & 1 & 1 & 0 & 0 \\ 0 & 0 & 0 & 1 & 0 \\ 1 & 0 & 0 & 0 & 1 \\ 0 & 0 & 0 & 1 & 1 \\ 0 & 1 & 0 & 0 & 0 \end{array}\right] \end{array}$$

Figure 9.46: A Diagraph and Its Adjacency Matrix.

$n \times n$ matrix [A] whose elements a_{ij} are given by

$$a_{ij} = \begin{cases} 1 \text{ , if node i is joined to node j, direction from i to j} \\ 0 \text{ , otherwise} \end{cases}$$

Matrix [A] is called the *adjacency matrix* of the graph. The adjacency matrix for the above graph is also shown in Figure 9.46. Now let us consider the powers of an adjacency matrix [A]. The ith row and jth column element of $[A^k]$ gives the number of ways the node j can be reached from node i following k edges. For the above graph $[A^2]$ is given in Figure 9.47. For example, $a_{32} = 2$, the number of different ways node 3 can be reached from node 2 following exactly 2 edges (Paths $3 \to 1 \to 2$ and $3 \to 5 \to 2$). The diagonal elements represent the number of cycles. Write a FORTRAN program to read the number of nodes and entries a_{ij} in a directed graph. Using sparse matrix representation for the adjacency matrix, find the number

$$[A^2] = \begin{array}{c} \\ 1 \\ 2 \\ 3 \\ 4 \\ 5 \end{array} \begin{array}{ccccc} 1 & 2 & 3 & 4 & 5 \\ \left[\begin{array}{ccccc} 1 & 0 & 0 & 1 & 1 \\ 0 & 0 & 0 & 1 & 1 \\ 0 & 2 & 1 & 0 & 0 \\ 0 & 1 & 0 & 1 & 1 \\ 0 & 0 & 0 & 1 & 0 \end{array}\right] \end{array}$$

Figure 9.47: Square of Adjacency Matrix [A].

of ways in which each node can be reached from every other node by other nodes by following k edges. Try your program for k = 1, 2, 3, 4 and 5.

Ordering of Fortran Statements in a Program Unit

The statements in any FORTRAN program unit must conform to the order given below:

1. a. Main Program:- PROGRAM statement (if required by system).

   b. Subprogram:- FUNCTION, SUBROUTINE, or BLOCKDATA statement.

2. IMPLICIT statement.

3. Type statements:
   INTEGER
   REAL
   COMPLEX
   DOUBLE PRECISION
   LOGICAL
   CHARACTER

4. Other specification statements:
   DIMENSION
   EQUIVALENCE
   COMMON
   EXTERNAL

5. DATA statement.

6. Statement Function statements.

7. Executable statements: (In any order)
   Arithmetic IF
   Assignment statements
   BACKSPACE
   Block IF
   CALL
   CLOSE

    CONTINUE
    DO
    ELSE
    ELSE IF
    END IF
    ENDFILE
    GO TO
    IF THEN
    Logical IF
    OPEN
    PRINT
    READ
    RETURN
    REWIND
    STOP
    WRITE

8. END statement.

It must, however, be noted:

1) Comment statements can appear anywhere in a program unit before the END statement.

2) FORMAT statement can also appear anywhere in a program unit after the PROGRAM, FUNCTION, SUBROUTINE, or BLOCK-DATA statement and before the END statement.

Fortran Intrinsic Functions

In this appendix the following abbreviations are used:

I = Integer
R = Real
D = Double precision
C = Complex
Ch = Character
L = Logical

The arguments of the functions in Table B-1 are denoted by the following symbols:

J, K integer type
X, Y real type
DX, DY double precision type
C complex
Ch1, Ch2 character type
L logical type

Table B-1 Numeric functions

Function name	Number of arguments	Type of arguments	Type of function	Verbal description
INT(X)	1	R	I	Converts argument to an integer value.
IFIX(X)	1	R	I	
IDINT(DX)	1	D	I	
FLOAT(J)	1	I	R	
REAL(J)	1	I	R	Converts argument to a real value.
SNGL(DX)	1	D	R	
DBLE(J)	1	I	D	Converts argument to a double precision value.
DBLE(X)	1	R	D	
CMPLX(X, Y)	1 or 2	R	C	Converts arguments to a complex value (if one argument, imaginary part is assumed to be zero).
CMPLX(DX, DY)	1 or 2	D	C	
AINT(X)	1	R	R	Drops the fractional part of the argument.
DINT(DX)	1	D	D	
ABS(X)	1	R	R	Gives the absolute value of the argument. If $z = a + bi$, $CABS(z) = \sqrt{a^2 + b^2}$.
IABS(J)	1	I	I	
DBS(DX)	1	D	D	
CABS(C)	1	C	R	
NINT(X)	1	R	I	Rounds argument to the nearest integer.
IDNINT (DX)	1	D	I	
ANINT(X)	1	R	R	
DNINT(DX)	1	D	D	
MOD(J, K)	2	I	I	Gives the remainder when the first argument is divided by the second.
AMOD(X, Y)	2	R	R	
DMOD(DX, DY)	2	D	D	
MAX0(J, K,...)	2 or more	I	I	Gives the largest of all the arguments.
AMAX0(J, K,...)	2 or more	I	R	
AMAX1(X, Y,...)	2 or more	R	R	
MAX1 (X,Y,...)	2 or more	R	I	
DMAX1 (DX, DY,...)	2 or more	D	D	

Function	No. of arguments	Type of argument	Type of function	Description
MIN0(J, K,...)	2 or more	I	I	Gives the smallest of all the arguments.
AMIN0(J, K,...)	2 or more	I	R	
AMIN1(X, Y,...)	2 or more	R	R	
MIN1(X, Y,...)	2 or more	R	I	
DMIN1(DX, DY,...)	2 or more	D	D	
SQRT(X)	1	R	R	Gives the square root of the argument. Argument must be ≥ 0.
DSQRT(DX)	1	D	D	
CSQRT(C)	1	C	C	
REAL(C)	1	C	R	Gives real part of the complex argument.
AIMAG(C)	1	C	R	Gives the imaginary part of the complex argument.
CONJG(C)	1	C	C	Gives complex conjugate of the argument.
SIN(X)	1	R	R	Calculates the sine of the argument. (Argument in radian measure.)
DSIN(DX)	1	D	D	
CSIN(C)	1	C	C	
COS(X)	1	R	R	Calculates the cosine of the argument. (Arguments in radian measure.)
DCOS(DX)	1	D	D	
CCOS(C)	1	C	C	
TAN(X)	1	R	R	Calculates the tangent of the argument. (Argument in radian measure.)
DTAN(DX)	1	D	D	
ASIN(X)	1	R	R	Calculates the arcsine of the argument x. $|x| \leq 1$ and $-\pi/2 \leq \text{(D)ASIN}(x) \leq \pi/2$.
DASIN(DX)	1	D	D	
ACOS(X)	1	R	R	Calculates the arccosine of the argument x. $|x| \leq 1$ and $0 \leq \text{(D)ACOS}(x) \leq \pi$
DACOS(DX)	1	D	D	
ATAN(X)	1	R	R	Calculates the arctangent of the argument x. $-\pi/2 < \text{(D)ATAN}(x) < \pi/2$.
DATAN(DX)	1	D	D	
EXP(X)	1	R	R	Calculates the exponential e^x of the argument x, where $e = 2.71828 \ldots$ is the base of the natural logarithms.
DEXP(DX)	1	D	D	
CEXP(C)	1	C	C	
ALOG(X)	1	R	R	Calculates the natural logarithm $\ln(x)$ of the argument x. x must be > 0.
DLOG(DX)	1	D	D	
CLOG(C)	1	C	C	
ALOG10(X)	1	R	R	Calculates the common logarithm $\log_{10}(x)$ of the argument x. x must be > 0.
DLOG10(DX)	1	D	D	

Table B-2 Character functions

Function name	Number of arguments	Type of arguments	Type of function	Verbal description
ICHAR (Ch1)	1	Ch	I	ICHAR(c) is the numeric code of the character c.
CHAR(J)	1	I	Ch	CHAR(i) is the character that corresponds to the numeric code i.
LGE(Ch1, Ch2)	2	Ch	L	Gives a value true if the first argument does not precede the second in alphabetical order; otherwise false.
LGT(Ch1, Ch2)	2	Ch	L	Gives a value true if the first argument follows the second in alphabetical order; otherwise false.
LLE(Ch1, Ch2)	2	Ch	L	Gives a value true if the first argument does not follow the second in alphabetical order; otherwise false.
LLT(Ch1, Ch2)	2	Ch	L	Gives a value true if the first argument precedes the second in alphabetical order; otherwise false.
LEN(Ch1)	1	Ch	I	Gives the length of a character expression.
INDEX (Ch1, Ch2)	2	Ch	I	Gives the location of substring Ch2 within string Ch1.

ASCII Character Code Table

The ASCII (American Standard Code for Information Interchange) computer coding scheme is a 7-bit code used by many computers. The following table is given to show the ASCII character, the terminal key used to obtain this character, the equivalent forms in binary, decimal (dec), and hexadecimal (hex), and the definition of use for the 128 characters in the ASCII code.

ASCII	Terminal	– – –EQUIVALENT FORMS– – –			
Char	Key	Binary	Dec	Hex	Definition of Use
NULL	CTRL/@	0 000 000	0	0	Filler
SOH	CTRL/A	0 000 001	1	1	Start of Heading; Home Position
STX	CTRL/B	0 000 010	2	2	Start of Text
ETX	CTRL/C	0 000 011	3	3	End of Text
EOT	CTRL/D	0 000 100	4	4	End of Transmission
ENQ	CTRL/E	0 000 101	5	5	Enquiry
ACK	CTRL/F	0 000 110	6	6	Acknowledge
BELL	CTRL/G	0 000 111	7	7	Bell
BS	CTRL/H	0 001 000	8	8	Backspace; ←— arrow
HT	CTRL/I	0 001 001	9	9	Horizontal Tabulation
LF	CTRL/J	0 001 010	10	A	Line Feed; ↓ arrow
VT	CTRL/K	0 001 011	11	B	Vertical Tabulation; ↑ arrow
FF	CTRL/L	0 001 100	12	C	Form Feed; Clear Screen
CR	CTRL/M	0 001 101	13	D	Carriage Return
SO	CTRL/N	0 001 110	14	E	Shift Out
SI	CTRL/O	0 001 111	15	F	Shift In
DLE	CTRL/P	0 010 000	16	10	Data Link Escape
DC1	CTRL/Q	0 010 001	17	11	Device Control 1
DC2	CTRL/R	0 010 010	18	12	Device Control 2
DC3	CTRL/S	0 010 011	19	13	Device Control 3
DC4	CTRL/T	0 010 100	20	14	Device Control 4
NAK	CTRL/U	0 010 101	21	15	Negative Acknowledge
SYNC	CTRL/V	0 010 110	22	16	Synchronous Idle

Char	Key	Binary	Dec	Hex	Definition of Use
ETB	CTRL/W	0 010 111	23	17	End of Transmission Block
CAN	CTRL/X	0 011 000	24	18	Cancel
EM	CTRL/Y	0 011 001	25	19	End of Medium
SUB	CTRL/Z	0 011 010	26	1A	Substitute
ESC	CTRL/[	0 011 011	27	1B	Escape
FS	CTRL/\	0 011 100	28	1C	File Separator
GS	CTRL/]	0 011 101	29	1D	Group Separator
RS	CTRL/^	0 011 110	30	1E	Record Separator
US	CTRL/_	0 011 111	31	1F	Unit Separator
space	space	0 100 000	32	20	Space; blank
!	!	0 100 001	33	21	Exclamation Mark
"	"	0 100 010	34	22	Double quote
#	#	0 100 011	35	23	Number Symbol
$	$	0 100 100	36	24	Dollar Symbol
%	%	0 100 101	37	25	Percent Symbol
&	&	0 100 110	38	26	Ampersand
'	'	0 100 111	39	27	Single Quote; Apostrophe
(	(	0 101 000	40	28	Left Parenthesis
)	)	0 101 001	41	29	Right Parenthesis
*	*	0 101 010	42	2A	Asterisk
+	+	0 101 100	43	2B	Plus Symbol
,	,	0 101 011	44	2C	Comma
−	−	0 101 101	45	2D	Minus Symbol; Hyphen
.	.	0 101 110	46	2E	Period; Decimal Point
/	/	0 101 111	47	2F	Divide Symbol; Slash; Virgule
0	0	0 110 000	48	30	Digit Zero
1	1	0 110 001	49	31	Digit One
2	2	0 110 010	50	32	Digit Two
3	3	0 110 011	51	33	Digit Three
4	4	0 110 100	52	34	Digit Four
5	5	0 110 101	53	35	Digit Five
6	6	0 110 110	54	36	Digit Six
7	7	0 110 111	55	37	Digit Seven
8	8	0 111 000	56	38	Digit Eight
9	9	0 111 001	57	39	Digit Nine
:	:	0 111 010	58	3A	Colon
;	;	0 111 011	59	3B	Semicolon
<	<	0 111 100	60	3C	Less Than Symbol; Left Caret
=	=	0 111 101	61	3D	Equal Symbol
>	>	0 111 110	62	3E	Greater Than Symbol; Right Caret
?	?	0 111 111	63	3F	Question Mark
@	@	1 000 000	64	40	At Sign
A	A	1 000 001	65	41	Upper Case Letter A
B	B	1 000 010	66	42	Upper Case Letter B
C	C	1 000 011	67	43	Upper Case Letter C
D	D	1 000 100	68	44	Upper Case Letter D
E	E	1 000 101	69	45	Upper Case Letter E
F	F	1 000 110	70	46	Upper Case Letter F
G	G	1 000 111	71	47	Upper Case Letter G

Char	Key	Binary	Dec	Hex	Definition of Use
H	H	1 001 000	72	48	Upper Case Letter H
I	I	1 001 001	73	49	Upper Case Letter I
J	J	1 001 010	74	4A	Upper Case Letter J
K	K	1 001 011	75	4B	Upper Case Letter K
L	L	1 001 100	76	4C	Upper Case Letter L
M	M	1 001 101	77	4D	Upper Case Letter M
N	N	1 001 110	78	4E	Upper Case Letter N
O	O	1 001 111	79	4F	Upper Case Letter O
P	P	1 010 000	80	50	Upper Case Letter P
Q	Q	1 010 001	81	51	Upper Case Letter Q
R	R	1 010 010	82	52	Upper Case Letter R
S	S	1 010 011	83	53	Upper Case Letter S
T	T	1 010 100	84	54	Upper Case Letter T
U	U	1 010 101	85	55	Upper Case Letter U
V	V	1 010 110	86	56	Upper Case Letter V
W	W	1 010 111	87	57	Upper Case Letter W
X	X	1 011 000	88	58	Upper Case Letter X
Y	Y	1 011 001	89	59	Upper Case Letter Y
Z	Z	1 011 010	90	5A	Upper Case Letter Z
[	[	1 011 011	91	5B	Left Bracket
\	\	1 011 100	92	5C	Back Slash; Back Slant
]	]	1 011 101	93	5D	Right Bracket
^	^	1 011 110	94	5E	Circumflex; ASCII up arrow (↑)
—	—	0 011 111	95	5F	Underscore
`	`	1 100 000	96	60	Back Quote; Grave Accent
a	a	1 100 001	97	61	Lower Case Letter a
b	b	0 100 010	98	62	Lower Case Letter b
c	c	1 100 011	99	63	Lower Case Letter c
d	d	1 100 100	100	64	Lower Case Letter d
e	e	1 100 101	101	65	Lower Case Letter e
f	f	1 100 110	102	66	Lower Case Letter f
g	g	1 100 111	103	67	Lower Case Letter g
h	h	1 101 000	104	68	Lower Case Letter h
i	i	1 101 001	105	69	Lower Case Letter i
j	j	1 101 010	106	6A	Lower Case Letter j
k	k	1 101 011	107	6B	Lower Case Letter k
l	l	1 101 100	108	6C	Lower Case Letter l
m	m	1 101 101	109	6D	Lower Case Letter m
n	n	1 101 110	110	6E	Lower Case Letter n
o	o	1 101 111	111	6F	Lower Case Letter o
p	p	1 110 000	112	70	Lower Case Letter p
q	q	1 110 001	113	71	Lower Case Letter q
r	r	1 110 010	114	72	Lower Case Letter r
s	s	1 110 011	115	73	Lower Case Letter s
t	t	1 110 100	116	74	Lower Case Letter t
u	u	1 110 101	117	75	Lower Case Letter u
v	v	1 110 110	118	76	Lower Case Letter v
w	w	1 110 111	119	77	Lower Case Letter w
x	x	1 111 000	120	78	Lower Case Letter x

Char	Key	Binary	Dec	Hex	Definition of Use
y	y	1 111 001	121	79	Lower Case Letter y
z	z	1 111 010	122	7A	Lower Case Letter z
{	{	1 111 011	123	7B	Left Brace
|	|	1 111 100	124	7C	Vertical Bar
}	}	1 111 101	125	7D	Right Brace
~	~	1 111 110	126	7E	Tilde
DEL	DEL	1 111 111	127	7F	Delete; Rubout

EBCDIC Character Code Table

The EBCDIC (Extended Binary Coded Decimal Interchange Code) computer coding scheme is an 8-bit code used by many computers. The following table is given to show the EBCDIC character, the internal binary representation, the equivalent forms in hexadecimal (hex) and decimal (dec), and the definition of use for available characters in the EBCDIC code.

EBCDIC		--EQUIVALENT FORMS--		
Char	Hex	Binary	Dec	Definition of Use
space	40	0010 0000	64	Space; blank
¢ or [	4A	0100 1010	74	Cents Symbol on IBM; Left Bracket on Burroughs
.	4B	0100 1011	75	Period; Decimal Point
<	4C	0100 1100	76	Less Than Symbol; Left Caret
(	4D	0100 1101	77	Left Parenthesis
+	4E	0100 1110	78	Plus Symbol
!	4F	0100 1111	79	Exclamation Mark
&	50	0101 0000	80	Ampersand
! or]	5A	0101 1010	90	Exclamation Mark on IBM; Right Bracket on Burroughs
$	5B	0101 1011	91	Dollar Symbol
*	5C	0101 1100	92	Asterisk
)	5D	0101 1101	93	Right Parenthesis
;	5E	0101 1110	94	Semicolon
¬	5F	0101 1111	95	Logical Not Symbol
−	60	0110 0000	96	Minus Symbol; Hyphen
/	61	0110 0001	97	Divide Symbol; Slash
,	6B	0110 1011	107	Comma
%	6C	0110 1100	108	Percent Symbol
—	6D	0110 1101	109	Underscore
>	6E	0110 1110	110	Greater Than Symbol; Right Caret
?	6F	0110 1111	111	Question Mark
:	7A	0111 1010	122	Colon
#	7B	0111 1011	123	Number Symbol

Char	Hex	Binary	Dec	Definition of Use
@	7C	0111 1100	124	At Sign
'	7D	0111 1101	125	Single Quote; Apostrophe
=	7E	0111 1110	126	Equal Symbol
"	7F	0111 1111	127	Double Quote
a	81	1000 0001	129	Lower Case Letter a
b	82	1000 0010	130	Lower Case Letter b
c	83	1000 0011	131	Lower Case Letter c
d	84	1000 0100	132	Lower Case Letter d
e	85	1000 0101	133	Lower Case Letter e
f	86	1000 0110	134	Lower Case Letter f
g	87	1000 0111	135	Lower Case Letter g
h	88	1000 1000	136	Lower Case Letter h
i	89	1000 1001	137	Lower Case Letter i
j	91	1001 0001	145	Lower Case Letter j
k	92	1001 0010	146	Lower Case Letter k
l	93	1001 0011	147	Lower Case Letter l
m	94	1001 0100	148	Lower Case Letter m
n	95	1001 0101	149	Lower Case Letter n
o	96	1001 0110	150	Lower Case Letter o
p	97	1001 0111	151	Lower Case Letter p
q	98	1001 1000	152	Lower Case Letter q
r	99	1001 1001	153	Lower Case Letter r
~	A1	1010 0001	161	Tilde
s	A2	1010 0010	162	Lower Case Letter s
t	A3	1010 0011	163	Lower Case Letter t
u	A4	1010 0100	164	Lower Case Letter u
v	A5	1010 0101	165	Lower Case Letter v
w	A6	1010 0110	166	Lower Case Letter w
x	A7	1010 0111	167	Lower Case Letter x
y	A8	1010 1000	168	Lower Case Letter y
z	A9	1010 1001	169	Lower Case Letter z
A	C1	1100 0001	193	Upper Case Letter A
B	C2	1100 0010	194	Upper Case Letter B
C	C3	1100 0011	195	Upper Case Letter C
D	C4	1100 0100	196	Upper Case Letter D
E	C5	1100 0101	197	Upper Case Letter E
F	C6	1100 0110	198	Upper Case Letter F
G	C7	1100 0111	199	Upper Case Letter G
H	C8	1100 1000	200	Upper Case Letter H
I	C9	1100 1001	201	Upper Case Letter I
J	D1	1101 0001	209	Upper Case Letter J
K	D2	1101 0010	210	Upper Case Letter K
L	D3	1101 0011	211	Upper Case Letter L
M	D4	1101 0100	212	Upper Case Letter M
N	D5	1101 0101	213	Upper Case Letter N
O	D6	1101 0110	214	Upper Case Letter O
P	D7	1101 0111	215	Upper Case Letter P
Q	D8	1101 1000	216	Upper Case Letter Q
R	D9	1101 1001	217	Upper Case Letter R
\	E0	1110 0000	224	Black Slash; Back Slant

Char	Hex	Binary	Dec	Definition of Use
S	E2	1110 0010	226	Upper Case Letter S
T	E3	1110 0011	227	Upper Case Letter T
U	E4	1110 0100	228	Upper Case Letter U
V	E5	1110 0101	229	Upper Case Letter V
W	E6	1110 0110	230	Upper Case Letter W
X	E7	1110 0111	231	Upper Case Letter X
Y	E8	1110 1000	232	Upper Case Letter Y
Z	E9	1110 1001	233	Upper Case Letter Z
0	F0	1111 0000	240	Digit Zero
1	F1	1111 0001	241	Digit One
2	F2	1111 0010	242	Digit Two
3	F3	1111 0011	243	Digit Three
4	F4	1111 0100	244	Digit Four
5	F5	1111 0101	245	Digit Five
6	F6	1111 0110	246	Digit Six
7	F7	1111 0111	247	Digit Seven
8	F8	1111 1000	248	Digit Eight
9	F9	1111 1001	249	Digit Nine

Appendix E

New Features Available with FORTRAN 77 and may not be Available with FORTRAN 66

Section Number	Features	Chapter Number
1	List-directed input/output	3
2	Block IF (IF. . . THEN. . . ELSE. . . ENDIF)	4
3	READ fs, list and PRINT fs, list	3
4	Apostrophe edit descriptor	5
5	T edit descriptor	5
6	END for end of data and ERR for data error	5
7	Expression in output list	5
8	Use of any integer arithmetic expression for subscript (limited to $i \pm k$, $k * i$, and $k * i \pm k$ in 1966 FORTRAN)	6
9	DO loop index can be integer or real variable (instead of only integer variables)	4
10	DO loop parameters may be negative, real variable, or integer or real expression (instead of only an integer or integer variable)	4
11	If DO loop termination parameter value is greater than initial value, loop will not be executed (undefined previously)	4
12	Comma in DO statement after statement number allowed but optional, e.g. DOS [,] V = e_1, e_2, e_3	4
13	Comma optional before control variable in computed GOTO, e.g. GOTO (s_1, s_2) [,] i	4
14	Any integer expression allowed as index for computed GOTO	4
15	OPEN and CLOSE statements UNIT = and FMT = control specifiers	5
16	Additional intrinsic functions—ACOS, ANINT, ASIN, CHAR, COSH, DACOS, DASIN, DCOSH, DDIM, DNINT, DPROD, DSINH, DTAN, DTANH, ICHAR, IDNINT, INDEX, LEN, LOG, LOGI0, NINT, SINH	3, Appendix A
17	IMPLICIT declaration	3
18	CHARACTER DATA type	8

Section Number	Features	Chapter Number
19	Concatenation operator	8
20	Lexical relationship functions—LGE, LGT, LLE, and LLT	8
21	Additional format edit specifications BN, BZ, Ew, dEe, Iw, m, Gw, dEe, TRc, TLc, S, SP, SS, and:	5
22	FORMAT in input/output statement	5
23	PARAMETER statement	3
24	Upper and lower bounds for dimensions	6
25	Exclusive OR (EQV and NEQV)	4
26	SAVE statement	7
27	Alternate entry and alternate return points for subroutines	7
28	Variable dimensions	6
29	INTRINSIC statement	3

A Few Features that may not be Supported by Some of the FORTRAN 77 Compilers

In the book we have discussed all features available with an ANSI standard FORTRAN 77. There are, however, many versions of FORTRAN 77 that may not support all features. The following list gives a description of these features.

Section Number	Features that may not be available	Chapter Number
1	List-directed input and output PARAMETER statement DOUBLE PRECISION and COMPLEX types, expressions and intrinsic functions	3
2	DO variable as a real variable DO parameters as integer or real expressions Implied DO loops in a DATA statement Real variables allowed in Implied DO loop as index expression	4
3	OPEN (except for use with ACCESS = DIRECT and RECL = record length) READ f, list and PRINT f, list ERR specifier Expressions in output list Formatted direct-access records FORMAT edit descriptors—Iw.m, Dw.d, Gw.d, Gw.dEe, Ew.dEe, Tn, TLn, TRn, S, SP and SS UNIT = and FMT = Control specifiers Use of character variables or array elements as format specification	5
4	More than three subscripts (full FORTRAN allows seven subscripts) Lower bounds for array declarator	6

Section Number	Features that may not be available	Chapter Number
5	Array element reference or function reference in subscript	7
	SAVE statement without a list, ENTRY statement	
	Alternate return from subroutine	
	BLOCK DATA subprogram	
6	LEN, CHAR and INDEX functions	8
	Unequal length for character variables	
	Asterisk length specifier for character functions	
	Character functions	
	Substring	
	Concatenation operator	

Differences between WATFOR/WATFIV and Standard FORTRAN 77

WATFOR is a more restricted version of FORTRAN than WATFIV. The differences between WATFOR, WATFIV and Standard FORTRAN 77 are given below:

1. No asterisk (*) is required in list-directed input and output written in WATIV.

2. WATFIV allows multiple assignment statements on one statement line. This is not allowed in FORTRAN 77.

3. The Block IF construct is not available in WATFIV.

4. WATFOR does not allow list-directed I/O statements of the form READ [UNIT=] lun, *, ERR=s1, END=s2) list and WRITE ([UNIT =]lun, *) list. This is allowed in WATFIV.

5. The WATFIV statements DUMPLIST and ON ERROR GOTO are not allowed in FORTRAN 77.

6. WATFIV or WATFOR do not allow the use of real index variable in a DO loop and real or integer expressions as DO parameters.

7. The NAMELIST statement is allowed in WATFIV only.

8. FORTRAN 77 does not allow ending a DO loop on a transfer of control statement.

9. WATFIV and WATFOR allow variables in both unlabeled and named (labeled) COMMON to be initialized by DATA statements. In FORTRAN 77 only labelled COMMON can be initialized by DATA statements and only with a BLOCK DATA subprogram.

Subject Index

RE